Constitutional Courts

A Comparative Study

JCLStudies in Comparative Law

Editors
Professor William E. Butler
Professor Michael Palmer

A series dedicated to classic works in the field of comparative law, commonly with a modern introduction, contemporary monographs, and collected essays by leading and rising scholars:

No. 1: Constitutional Courts: Comparative Studies. Edited by Andrew Harding and Peter Leyland (2009)

No. 2: Building the Civilisation of Arbitration. Edited by Thomas Caronneau (2010)

No. 2: The Boundaries of Unity: Mixed Legal Systems in Action. Edited by Esin Orücü (2010)

JCL Studies in Comparative Law

Constitutional Courts

A Comparative Study

Edited by

Andrew Harding and Peter Leyland

Wildy, Simmonds & Hill Publishing

Constitutional Courts: A Comparative Study

British Library Cataloguing-in-Publication Data:
A catalogue record for this book is available from The British
Library

ISBN 9780854900633

First published in 2009 by
Wildy, Simmonds & Hill Publishing
58 Carey Street, London WC2A 2JB
England

Printed and bound in Great Britain by
CPI Antony Rowe, Chippenham, Wiltshire

Constitutional Courts:
A Comparative Study

Contents

Preface

CONSTITUTIONAL COURTS: A COMPARATIVE STUDY

This collection provides a selective global snapshot of constitutional courts. In recent years there has been a proliferation of courts exercising constitutional jurisdiction. The trend has not been confined to new democracies in Europe but, as will be apparent from a glance at the contents, has extended to nations in Africa, Asia and South America, with different contexts and trajectories as measured by the adoption of the norms of liberal democracy.

Constitutional courts have become a key element of constitutional design for obvious practical reasons. In addition to upholding values of legality and constitutionalism a constitutional court might be conceived as a device to counter-balance the otherwise potentially overwhelming capacity of the elected majority to achieve domination at the expense of any opposition. James Madison famously observed that: "The accumulation of all powers, legislative, executive, and judiciary, in the same hands ... may justly be pronounced the very definition of tyranny". Equally, in a long-established constitution this form of relatively independent justice offers the prospect of defending provisions intended to protect human rights and minority rights.

To be sure, there are critics who would dispute the claim that, in itself, any form of legal constitutionalism will safeguard human rights or act as an effective check on the government of the day. This study does not seek to investigate the wider theoretical framework. We have not discussed the viability of a tradition of liberal constitutionalism. Rather, these studies proceed on the basis that at a practical level constitutions in democracies or aspiring democracies have had to reconcile the legitimacy of the power resting in the hands of the elected majority with the formation of constitutional mechanisms fashioned to express and check that power. The point is that in many developing nations negotiating a hazardous path to democracy the constitutional court has come to be regarded as a vital guardian of the constitution.

In assembling these essays there was an obvious reason for starting with such archetypical European examples as Austria, Germany and France while at the same time covering the recent creation of such courts in Central and Eastern Europe following the collapse of communist-party regimes. We are aware that certain interesting examples have been omitted, but the task of selection was to some extent dictated to us by space and by the availability of scholars with the appropriate interest and expertise. Although there are numerous references to the United States in this book, we have not included an essay dedicated to consider the United States constitutional paradigm. It has undoubtedly been influential as the first truly modern constitution embodying separation of powers and it introduced a Supreme Court which could interpret the constitution. Following the decision in *Marbury v Maddison* (1 Cranch) 137 (1803), this Court has acted as the final arbiter of constitutionality with respect to the acts of both the legislature and the executive and, in so doing, it confirmed the superiority of constitutional law over ordinary law.

The absence of the United States Supreme Court can be justified on the grounds that, not withstanding its pivotal constitutional function, that Supreme Court is not a specialist constitutional court in the sense set out in our introductory essay. As a general high court it lacks the exclusive authority to directly intervene in constitutional matters. This collection mainly features courts which are related to two contrasting centralised models. The first and most widely diffused is based on the idea developed by Han Kelsen of a dedicated constitutional court being the only body empowered to deal with alleged infringements of the constitution. The second is based upon the *Conseil Constitutionnel* which had a special role advising on constitutitonal questions (although the French *Conseil Constitutionnel* has also not long ago been empowered to review the constitutionality of legislation). Nevertheless cross currents of global influence are indentified in regard to design and in relation the jurisprudence that is practiced in these courts. Further, constitutional courts often perform a crucial role as the main agency for the peaceful resolution of conflict between the main constitutional actors. In any constitutional context the evaluation of their effectiveness can be likened to the medical examination of a patient in order to provide a diagnosis of his or her condition.

We were unable to find a clear logic for the arrangement of these essays. For the convenience of readers we have opted to present them in alphabetical order under the continental headings of Europe, Africa, Asia and South America.

We hope that analyses in this book will be a useful resource for scholars, students and practitioners who share with us a special interest in the study of comparative public law but are frequently held back by limitations in up-to-date publications of a genuinely comparative nature.

This book would not have been possible without the assistance of others. In particular the editors would like to extend their sincere thanks to Brian Hill at Wildys, Michael Palmer, William E. Butler, Nick Foster, Tania Groppi, Justin Frosini, Jorg Fedtke, Alex Fischer, Ben Berger, Sonia Lamine, Joana Thackeray. Also special thanks go to Fraser Milner

Casgrain of Vancouver (who funded a summer fellowship facilitating Joana's excellent preparatory work towards this volume and the essay on Thailand and Indonesia).

Andrew Harding
Peter Leyland

1st September 2009

Constitutional Courts: Forms, Functions and Practice in Comparative Perspective

ANDREW HARDING, PETER LEYLAND, AND TANIA GROPPI *

INTRODUCTION

The purpose of this volume[1] is to examine comparatively specialist constitutional courts that have been set up in many countries across the world, particularly in the last two decades. Following this editorial essay are 14 studies which deal with the experience of a particular country or in some cases a group of countries in geographical proximity. This is a task which has not been previously undertaken in an English language publication, so far as we are aware, except for excellent studies of constitutional courts in Europe by Wojciech Sadurski,[2] and East Asia by Tom Ginsburg,[3] both of whom have contributed to this book.[4] Rather than striving for

* Professor of Asia-Pacific Law, University of Victoria, Canada; Professor of Public Law, London Metropolitan University, UK; Professor of Public Law, University of Siena, Italy, respectively.

[1] The editors wish to express their sincere thanks to the *Journal of Comparative Law*, and in particular to the present and former Editors for their encouragement and facilitation of this book; and to Justin Frosini for his unstinting help and advice and Joana Thackeray for her assistance.

[2] Sadurski, W (2002) *Constitutional Justice East and West: Democratic Legitimacy and Constitutional Courts in Post-Communist Europe in a Comparative Perspective*, Kluwer; and (2005) *Rights Before Courts: a Study of Constitutional Courts in Post-Communist States of Eastern and Central Europe*, Springer.

[3] Ginsburg, T (2003) *Judicial Review in New Democracies: Constitutional Courts in Asian Cases*, Cambridge UP; see also Ramos, F (2006), 'The Establishment of Constitutional Courts: A Study of 128 Democratic Constitutions', *Review of Law & Economics*: Vol. 2: Iss.1, Article 6, available at: http://www.bepress.com/rle/vol2/iss1/art6.

[4] Let us not overlook Arne Mavcic's compendious and very helpful work: Mavcic, A (2001), *The Constitutional Review* Bookworld Publications.

comprehensive coverage in a descriptive sense the contributions seek to provide selectively an evaluation of the pivotal characteristics of these courts. The articles in this book are structured to ensure that the reader can at least obtain an overview of the major part of global experience of these courts and sample some of the most instructive cases. The country-studies are all comparative, although to various extents and in various respects. Some compare across a particular region such West Africa or Central and Eastern Europe, while others concentrate on one country's experience only; but in all cases the contributors indicate awareness of general issues and experiences beyond their particular country or region, as well as relevant theoretical considerations. In the interests of inclusiveness some contributions have covered a large number of cases and therefore sacrificed detail and complete consistency in coverage in favour of making a meaningful contribution to the global picture we attempt to present. West European states, which in general have a far longer experience of constitutional courts than other regions to which the concept has diffused, often following West European patterns (for example the French pattern in West African states and the German in East Asia), have been privileged here over non-West European states; but our intention is that the experience of non-West European states should be canvassed as fully as is possible within the constraints of this book.

By examining the historical and contemporary experience of constitutional courts it is our hope that this book will contribute to an understanding of the problems and dynamics involved in setting up and operating constitutional courts; assist in formulating useful terminology to describe different models of court or sub-models for issues such as the appointment system for constitutional court judges or the relationship with 'ordinary courts'; inform those who seek to design or reform constitutional courts as to the possibilities and the dangers that are involved; and lead to some assessment of the overall success of the global diffusion of constitutional courts in this era of democratization. In short our purposes fall squarely within the ideals and objectives of the 'new comparative law' as conceived and promoted by the JCL.

In their contribution to this volume Frosini and Pegoraro have encapsulated the comparatist's dilemma in a way which speaks to our collective endeavour as clearly as it does to their work on Latin America:

> In many respects the object of this research poses a challenge that comparatists are typically faced with: on one hand, the need to avoid oversimplified classifications as these would not meet the aim of providing a precise picture of the legal institutions that are the object of study, on the other, the necessity of also avoiding

classifications that are too detailed as these would risk thwarting the very aim of classifying, i.e. to group together on the basis of similarities taking into account the differences the components of a certain group might bear to one another.

Clearly a balance has to be struck here between providing enough factual information and analytical insight to the various examples, and formulating general ideas and classifications that do sufficient justice to the complexity of the examples.

WHAT IS A CONSTITUTIONAL COURT?

Outlining this exercise immediately raises the question how we define a constitutional court. A 'constitutional court' as defined here does not mean merely a court acting in constitutional mode by interpreting a constitution or determining a constitutional issue, but a *specialist* court having *only* 'constitutional' jurisdiction. Here the judicial system is divided into two, each part coming under the authority of a different court, typically the 'constitutional court' or the 'supreme court', the latter being finally responsible for all matters of judicial determination not falling within the jurisdiction of the constitutional court. It has also been analyzed by Cappelletti[5] as a 'centralized' as opposed to 'decentralized' system, or even 'European' as opposed 'American' system,[6] of judicial review. In this analysis only one court, as opposed to any court of law, is empowered to interpret the constitution, reflecting that fact that according to general understanding (although Frosini and Pegoraro cast doubt on this, indicating that Venezuela may have been the first country, in 1858, to adopt a centralized system[7]) the constitutional court as conceived in the contemporary world was created initially in Austria under the influence of Hans Kelsen and then in several continental European systems, whereas many states are also influenced by the US system and the constitutional role of the US Supreme Court.

The essential feature of the constitutional court-based system of judicial review, whatever name one attaches to the institution as such,[8] and however the meaning of 'constitutional' may differ from one state to another, is that

---

[5] See Cappelletti M (1968) *Il controllo giudiziario di costituzionalità delle leggi nel diritto comparato* Giuffré; and (1971) *Judicial Review in the Contemporary World*, The Bobbs-Merill Company.

[6] Mavcic, supra note 4, at 22ff.

[7] They concede however that this did not develop into a prototype as the Austrian court did.

[8] E.g. 'constitutional tribunal', 'constitutional chamber', etc.

only one court, the constitutional court, has authority to adjudicate questions of constitutional interpretation or to review legislation, and this court is separate from the ordinary judicial system, forming, either by deliberate design or as a practical result, a fourth branch of government. Several of our contributors[9] have also identified a third, 'hybrid' model, in which division of powers between the constitutional court and the 'ordinary' or 'civil' courts is not entirely clear-cut, because in various respects the task of constitutional adjudication is, in practice, divided between the two types of court so that the latter do exercise constitutional jurisdiction over some areas. Italy provides one such case. Groppi, while avoiding use of the term 'hybrid', finds that over time the ordinary courts have played an expanded constitutional role. This has arisen, for example, in determining when a constitutional issue arising in a civil or criminal case should go forward to the constitutional court. Moreover it sometimes results in the ordinary courts paying little heed to Constitutional Court judgments, substituting their own view of the matter in hand.

It is also clear that many of the countries that have a constitutional court also have a civilian legal system based on that of France or Germany, which offer two strikingly different models of constitutional review,[10] and no doubt the apparent compatibility of a constitutional court and a civilian legal system, as opposed to a common-law system (in which constitutional courts, with the possible exception of the South African,[11] have not generally featured) has been a factor in favour of the creation of a constitutional court in some countries.[12] It is of course an interesting avenue of inquiry to discover the genealogy of such courts, as this genealogy may have important consequences both on the design and on the jurisprudence of the court.[13]

The reasons that usually motivate constitution-makers in creating a constitutional court are dealt with in more detail below: in general they are,

---

[9] An examination of the various contributions to this book will reveal the large extent of variation in configuration.

[10] Ponthoreau and Hourquebie; Miller and Kommers this book. However, recent amendments to the French Constitution discussed by Ponthoreau and Hourquebie, have narrowed considerably the gap between these two models. One obvious difference that remains is the inclusion of administrative jurisdiction (i.e., to review the validity of administrative acts against the Constitution) in the case of Germany.

[11] Klug, this book. However, South Africa has a civilian as well as a common law tradition.

[12] Tushnet, M (2002-3) 'Alternative Forms of Judicial Review' 101 *Michigan Law Review* 2781. Some civil law countries such as Argentina, Japan and the Philippines, have adopted the 'American' model of review by the Supreme Court despite having a legal system based on civilian principles.

[13] As with the South Korean court which shows German influence: Ginsburg, this issue; and the Scandinavian countries.

first, to ensure adherence to a new constitution and its protection against legislative majorities; second, to ensure unity and finality in interpretation, avoiding the possibility of different courts adopting different interpretations of the constitution; third, to provide a visible symbol of constitutional progress; and fourth, to ensure that judicial deferentialism, which may have characterized previous regimes of judicial review, does not undermine the constitution.[14]

One of the many paradoxes about constitutional courts is that, while their creation is usually the result of a perception that they have succeeded in other jurisdictions, their activity, as is endorsed without exception by the contributions to this book, is in fact peculiarly subject to the political tensions of the jurisdiction in which they are introduced, and the same applies to the design principles involved. Indeed tension between law and politics is an underlying theme of all the contributions to this book. The experience of the interplay of these two factors of politics and legal transplantation, to judge by the findings of these contributions, is however quite varied. The creation of a constitutional court[15] may be the result of an axial moment such as the catastrophic defeat of a regime, as occurred with the fall of fascism in Germany, Italy and Spain;[16] or political revolution as with the fall of communism in the formerly Soviet Union-dominated states of Central and Eastern Europe;[17] or the fall of apartheid in South Africa.[18] In East Asia and West Africa, by contrast, it has generally resulted from a gradual rather than revolutionary emergence of constitutional government, in place of authoritarian or military government.[19] In the interesting case of Egypt, as Lombardi in this book discusses, an authoritarian regime created a constitutional court for its own reasons of political economy, only to find the court, at least initially, taking an activist stance and finding a constituency among reformers and Islamists. As Ferreres indicates, in such kinds of situation a constitutional court may be 'fragile'; this does not mean, however, that it is more likely to be deferential in its approach compared to 'ordinary' courts. On the contrary, he argues, fragility will more likely lead to judicial activism as a means of asserting the relevance and legitimacy of the court.[20] Such activism may compound the complexity of its legitimation

[14] See further, Ferreres Comella, V (2004), 'The Consequences of Centralizing Constitutional Review in a Special Court: Some Thoughts on Judicial Activism', 82 *Texas Law Review* 1705.
[15] Or, for that matter, its resuscitation from a condition of comparative irrelevance, as in the case of the Council of Grand Justices in Taiwan, for which see Ginsburg, this book.
[16] Miller and Kommers, Groppi, Ferreres, this book.
[17] Sadurski and Lach, this book.
[18] Klug, this book.
[19] Kante; Ginsburg; Harding and Leyland, this book.
[20] Ferreres, supra note 14.

and in turn render the court even more fragile. These observations point towards an approach that would examine the constitutional court as a political actor and assess the success or otherwise of the constitutional court as a major contemporary legal innovation.

This editorial essay next attempts to schematise the types and areas of analysis of constitutional courts in the light of the country-based and regional studies. It is intended to summarise this experience but also to provide an analytical framework for assessing it. We look at the functions of constitutional courts, the reasons for creating them, the methods of constructing them, the modes of accessing their jurisdiction, and the significance of their performance. It is not our purpose, it should be stressed, to compare 'constitutional courts' with 'supreme courts' exercising constitutional powers. That would be an important and interesting task for others to undertake; our hope is that this book, apart from intrinsic interest and illumination of the phenomenon of constitutional courts, will render that comparison much easier than it might otherwise have been.

WHAT CONSTITUTIONAL COURTS DO

The constitutional courts discussed in this book reveal several typical or possible adjudicatory or other functions of a constitutional court, so that 'constitutional jurisdiction' may cover a number of different and diverse aspects of judicial activity. It may concern any combination of the forms of adjudication or decision listed below, which we can organise in the following way:

   (a) *Constitution-drafting jurisdiction* (controlling the constitution
         itself):
       adjudicating issues arising in the constitution-making process
       reviewing the constitutionality of constitutional amendments

   (b) *Judicial review of legislative acts* (controlling the legislature):
       reviewing the constitutionality of laws in advance of legislation
          (*ante factum*)
       reviewing the constitutionality of laws after legislation (*ex post
          facto*)
       reviewing the constitutionality of decisions by the legislature
       initiating or requiring legislation

(c) Jurisdiction over officials and agencies (controlling the executive):
  reviewing the constitutionality of executive actions and
    decisions[21]
  hearing impeachment proceedings against holders of public
    office
  consideration of criminal or civil cases in respect of official
    corruption
  consideration of qualifications of individuals to hold or
    continue to hold public office
  adjudication of appointment of office-holders under the
    constitution
  adjudication of disputes as to the competence of organs of state
  adjudication of disputes between organs of state

(d) Jurisdiction over political parties and elections (controlling elections):
  adjudication of the dissolution or merger of political parties
    and control over constitutionality of their actions
  examining the legality of elections and election results at any
    level
  hearing electoral petitions

No constitutional court considered here exercises all of these functions, but reviewing the constitutionality of laws appears to be regarded as the central or most typical of constitutional court functions; in practice it may not be, depending on the patterns of disputes arising and being settled. Ginsburg identifies a category of 'ancillary' functions,[22] thereby suggesting that some constitutional court functions are important and essential and others merely optional or incidental. Frosini and Pegoraro speak of 'plurifunctional' courts.[23]

It is not clear, however, how we can assess the importance or centrality of particular functions either generally or in particular instances, or indeed why we should regard judicial review of legislation as especially significant. Still less can we discern clearly any archetypal or essential functions of constitutional courts. In some systems judicial review of legislation appears to be rather insignificant in practice, being only occasionally invoked and rarely successful, whereas in others scrutiny of elections or dissolution of political parties or ascertainment of jurisdiction of regional governments appears particularly important. In addition the practical

---

[21] These are however often scrutinized by administrative courts.
[22] This book.
[23] This book.

focus of constitutional courts seems to change somewhat over time; here an important issue is whether the court has any control over its own case list: in other words, does the court have discretion to refuse to hear cases or delay hearing them, and if so on what grounds, or is it obliged to hear any properly presented petition? If the latter, then clearly it is probably litigants and the actual configuration of national politics that will determine in practice what the court does. At the same time a constitutional court can just by its decisions, and also by the kind of subtle messages it sends to the communities of lawyers, politicians and officials, encourage or discourage certain categories of litigation. Indeed, one of the most interesting aspects of constitutional courts is to discern what functions take on pre-eminence, how these change over time, and why and with what consequences for the court's legitimacy or perceived success. To indicate just a few examples, the Spanish Constitutional Court has in recent years focused heavily on adjudication of disputes regarding devolution of powers to regional entities; the West African and Indonesian Constitutional Courts have been inundated with electoral disputes; while several courts have had to consider challenges arising out of privatisation programs, an issue which hardly featured in the imaginations of those who set them up. The South African Constitutional Court and to some extent the Russian Constitutional Courts on the other hand have increasingly focused on human rights issues.[24]

Another very significant issue in setting up a constitutional court is to decide whether it should have jurisdiction to examine the constitutionality of executive acts and decisions. There are several different solutions here, but clearly the determination of the issue will depend on whether there is already a system of judicial review of executive acts; if there is a system of administrative courts, this jurisdiction may be reserved to those courts, leaving a somewhat awkward situation where the administrative court's interpretation of the constitution and the limits of judicial review may compete with that of the constitutional court, and leaving the latter with the narrow task of reviewing legislation only, which may or may not include delegated legislation. The lack of jurisdiction over delegated legislation may be a serious limitation on the powers of a constitutional court, and may even leave open the possibility of the executive power avoiding the court's decisions by the extensive use of delegated legislation.[25]

Our conclusion here is that the functions of constitutional courts need careful analysis. The formal statement of constitutional jurisdiction may tell us very little about the real functions of the court in practice or the

---

[24] Klug, Henderson, this book.
[25] Harding and Leyland, this book; Bell, J (2004), 'Reflections on Continental European Supreme Courts' 24 *Legal Studies* 157.

importance, relatively, of the various ostensible reasons for setting it up – these two sets of facts may indeed be in a state of mutual tension. Similarly, the statistical breakdown of cases may be deceptive in making an overall assessment, because the really significant cases may be actually few in number and may be differently dispersed subject-wise than the totality of the court's caseload. The analysis of caseloads and their significance will in turn impact on our assessment of the court's success.[26]

This analysis, moreover, says nothing about how such matters reach the constitutional court. Here again we can list different modes of access to the constitutional court (this aspect is discussed further below).

Official reference:
Here the constitutional court hears a case referred directly by a named official or agency such as the speaker, the ombudsman, the president, the corruption commission, or the election commission.
Legislative reference:
Here a member or stated number of members of the legislature, or of either house thereof, bring a petition to the court.
Judicial reference:
Here a court refers an issue of constitutional interpretation to the constitutional court, and is usually bound by its opinion on that issue when the matter is referred back to the court.
Individual petition:
Here an individual juristic person brings an issue directly before the constitutional court. This may include a civil society organization bringing a case as public interest litigation.

Clearly one the most important justifications for constitutional courts is to provide finality of interpretation among both courts and legislative and executive agencies, a factor which is particularly pressing in federal states. The need for uniform interpretation of the law means that in federal systems there should be no conflicting judgments in the same matter in different state jurisdictions. This is also important where there is a clear division between central and regional government. For example in both Spain and Italy the respective court exercises a constitutional role in determining the respective competences of central and regional government. Legal and constitutional reforms which have modified the status of regional and

---

[26] Variations in the availability and consistency of statistics make wide-ranging, like-for-like comparisons particularly difficult in this context. In addition there are differences in procedure, for example with regard to the filtering of cases, which complicate the issue even further.

devolved government impact directly on the court's role. The proportion of cases involving this issue in Italy notably rose from 2% to 24% between 2002 and 2006. By comparison in Germany where there is a Federal Constitutional Court 'Constitutional disputes between a Land (state) and the Bund (federation) ordinarily arise out of conflicts involving a state's administration of federal law or the federal government's supervision of state administration' (here the *Bundesrat* provides parliamentary representation for state interests).[27] In Austria however there has been conflict between the Constitutional Court and the federal constitutional legislature, even to the extent of triggering the referendum requirement on the basis that a 'total revision' of the Constitution had been attempted by the legislature. The South African Constitutional Court (even though South Africa is not technically a federal state) has exercised a power allocation function between National and Provincial government and it has held that Constitutional Principles 'contemplated that the national government would have powers that transcend provincial boundaries and competences', further that 'legitimate provincial autonomy does not mean that the provinces can ignore [the constitutional] framework or demand to be insulated from the exercise of such power'.[28]

Another factor which affects the trajectory of constitutional courts is that they are subject to supra-national influences. They have to reconcile the laws of the constitution with obligations originating beyond the constitution. Sadurski and Lach[29] deal with this issue in relation to the EU. 'The constitutional courts have become European courts, which not merely apply European law but also, as the guardians of the respective national constitutions, have been vested with the role of telling the constitutional story of European legal integration.' In this connection it is interesting to observe in some cases (Turkey, for example) a tension between national and international decisions (in this case decisions under the ECHR) and difficulties in ascertaining the correct hierarchy of legal norms (France, for example). In a similar vein, and reverting to the issue of genealogy, there is no doubt that constitutional court decisions themselves have effects going beyond national borders, litigators taking notice, particularly in the field of human rights, of the manner in which foreign constitutional (and supreme) courts have dealt with particular issues.

---

[27]   Miller and Kommers, this book.
[28]   Klug, this book.
[29]   This book.

RAISONS D'ETRE: RATIONALES FOR THE INTRODUCTION OF CONSTITUTIONAL JURISDICTION

The reasons leading to the adoption of a constitutional court must be analyzed separately from the more general reasons leading a legal system towards the establishment of a system of judicial review, and also from those militating in favour of the adoption of a centralized system. These reasons, which are linked to the needs to guarantee the supremacy of the constitution and provide legal certainty, do not necessarily imply the presence of a specialist constitutional court. Legal certainty is a source of concern in civil law countries, which do not have a system of binding precedent such as exists in common law countries, which, as is noted above, have rarely seen the need for a constitutional court. It may indeed be better protected if a single court is in charge of checking ordinary laws against constitutional norms, instead of that power being conferred on all courts; but such a solution does not necessarily require assigning this task to a specialist constitutional court. Indeed, it can be noted that the supremacy of the constitution is *also* fully guaranteed by the United States' decentralized system of judicial review, and conflicting interpretations are ultimately here prevented by a combination of the appeal system and the doctrine of precedent.[30] The introduction of a constitutional court satisfies both of these demands in their entirety, but, at the same time, offers a *quid pluris*. It is indeed this latter feature that needs to be considered in order to fully understand the raisons d'être of the institution, which represents: a) a new power of the state; b) placed outside the judicial branch; c) whose members are selected through procedures differing from those adopted for ordinary judges; which is also d) expressly foreseen and regulated by the constitution.

The origin of the modern system of constitutional justice, in the Austrian experience, can be seen as a mark of distrust towards the judicial branch: in achieving the purpose of protecting the supremacy of the constitution, there is clearly an intention to avoid the development of American-style judicial review of legislation, moving away from European experience of supreme courts during the 19th century.[31]

This perspective can be fully understood only by taking into account the European legal cultural context in the first half of the 20th century. At that time, constitutional interpretation was considered to be an activity closely

---

[30] Tushnet, M (2008) *The Constitution of the United States: A Contextual Analysis*, Hart Publishing, 135ff.

[31] For example, Norway, Greece, Portugal; and later Germany at the time of the Weimar Republic.

related to the legislative process and therefore not to be performed by the judicial branch; the idea of 'the judge makes the law' was completely absent in that context. According to this perspective, the principle of separation of powers embodied in Kelsen's work required the creation of an *ad hoc* institution, a body provided, due to its composition, with a higher political sensitivity than the ordinary judiciary, to review the constitutionality of legislation, even to the extent of acting as a 'negative legislator'. This is significantly evident with regard to the 1920 Austrian Constitution, which, while establishing the Constitutional Court, explicitly forbade ordinary judges from exercising any judicial control of the constitutionality of legislation.[32] In this way, the establishment of the Constitutional Court was seen as an exception to the general principle according to which judges were prevented from setting aside laws contrary to the Constitution.[33]

In the ensuing 'waves' of constitutional justice,[34] and in particular under the influence of international human rights law, this raison d'être has been reappraised. Distrust of the judicial branch has decreased to such an extent, even in civil law countries, that we are now witnessing to a higher degree the introduction of elements of decentralization, even into systems of judicial review traditionally considered as centralized. Hence the emergence of 'hybrid' systems (as discussed above).

Nowadays, the raison d'être for the establishment of constitutional courts appears to be different and should be linked to processes of democratization.[35] Indeed, a comparative analysis shows that, since the years after the Second World War, the establishment of a constitutional court has invariably gone hand in hand with a transition to democracy: when a legal system adopts a democratic constitution, a constitutional court is usually introduced into the system. It is not, however, an unavoidable choice, since, in facing these events, some countries prefer to preserve their own distinct tradition or to make a completely different choice: consider, for example, some countries in Latin America[36] which, even in their process of transition to democracy, preferred to keep a decentralized system of judicial review or choose to establish a specialized division (*Sala constitucional*) within the Supreme Court. Consider also the peculiar case of Japan, which eventually

---

[32] Constitution of Austria 1920, Article 89; Gamper and Palermo, this book.

[33] See, for example, also the Constitution of the Netherlands, Article 120: 'The Constitutionality of Acts of Parliament and Treaties shall not be Reviewed by the Courts', Kortmann, CAJM and Bovend'Eert, PPT (2000) *Dutch Constitutional Law*, Kluwer, 189.

[34] The words of Louis Favoreau, that speak of four waves of constitutional justice, since the Austrian 1920 Constitution: Favoreau, L (1996) *Les cours constitutionnelles*, 3 ed, PUF, at 4.

[35] Kante; Ginsburg; Henderson; Sadurski and Lach; Frosini and Pegoraro; Harding and Leyland; this book.

[36] Frosini and Pegoraro, this book.

chose a decentralized system also as a consequence of the pervasive influence exerted by the United States model.[37] By way of contrast Turkey is an example where the complexion of the court changed with phases of constitution-making: the emphasis on protecting the rights of citizens under the 1961 Constitution was re-conceived in 1982 as an instrument to protect the fundamental values and interests of the establishment. The concept of 'core of rights' was dropped from the latter Constitution.[38] Greece, finally, decided to adopt a centralized system, in its Supreme Court.[39]

In the past few decades there have been cases where a system of judicial review has been introduced, either through case law or by express provision in the constitution, in states that were already democratic: so far, however, this has more often happened with regard to decentralized rather than centralized systems of judicial review.[40]

In the new democratic constitutions, starting with the Italian and German Constitutions drafted in the aftermath of the Second World War, moving to the Spanish and Portuguese ones of the 1970s and eventually to the more recent waves of democratization that occurred during the 1990s in Central and Eastern Europe, East Asia and Africa,[41] the choice in favor of constitutional courts is clear. The choice here appears to be motivated, as shown by some of the essays in this book, by three main reasons.

First, there was distrust towards ordinary judges: not as judges per se, but as part of the previous authoritarian regime or as having in the past displayed timidity when faced with constitutional issues. As Ferreres has underlined with regard to the Spanish experience, ordinary judges that had been appointed under the previous dictatorial regime were not replaced when democracy arrived:

> Given this historical circumstance, it made no sense to grant them the power to check the validity of the laws enacted by the new democratic Parliament. The constitutional framers preferred to

---

[37] Kawagishi, N (2007), 'The Birth of judicial Review in Japan', 5:2 *International Journal of Constitutional Law* 308.

[38] See Örücü in this book.

[39] The court is called 'the Supreme Special Court'; see Mavcic, supra note 4, at 20. Currently there is a debate in Greece about proposals to set up a separate constitutional court.

[40] Judicial review of legislation was established through case law in Israel (1995), and through constitutional change in Ireland (1937), Sweden (1974), and Finland (1999). The introduction of a constitutional court in an already democratic state characterizes Belgium (1983) and Luxembourg (1996).

[41] See, e.g., in this book, Henderson; Kante; Lach and Sadurski; Ginsburg; Harding and Leyland; Frosini and Pegoraro.

ascribe the task of legislative review to a separate body, whose members would be selected by the political branches.[42]

Secondly, influence was exerted by the circulation of models and by comparative legal study. This is particularly evident in the Central and Eastern European countries, where the influence of the German and Austrian models has been very strong, due to reasons related not only to the geographic and cultural proximity but also to the role played by the Council of Europe and its experts, to an extent that allows the statement that 'the establishing of constitutional review was a clear case of institutional borrowing'.[43]

Thirdly, there is the symbolic value taken on by constitutional courts. Indeed, they have become such a clear symbol of a legal system's democratic character that it has been stated that 'the very existence of these courts obviously served as a 'trade mark', or as a proof, of the democratic character of the respective country'.[44]

On the other hand, even if the raisons d'être for the establishment of constitutional courts are now clear, there is no reason to assume that these same raisons d'être motivate its continuance or its direction, especially with regard to new democracies; it is worth asking if those same raisons d'être are still evident in consolidated democracies. Some signs such as, for example, the tendency to increase the degree of involvement of ordinary judges in the defence of the constitution, even in the presence of an established constitutional court, could weigh in favor of the conclusion that raisons d'être can indeed change.[45] However, some indications exist which might lead to the opposite conclusion: first, the intensity of debates arising from the opportunity to create a constitutional court, creating high expectations; and second, the actual performance of constitutional courts, which is generally considered in rather positive terms by some of the contributions here, and which may lead to the perhaps surprising conclusion that in some or even many cases the constitutional court actually does what it was intended to do.

These reflections, while no longer characterized by the distrust of the judicial branch which used to connote Kelsen's perspective, usually identify two fundamental raisons d'être for the setting up of constitutional courts. First there is their higher degree of sensitivity in dealing with 'political matters', compared to that of ordinary judges (achieved mainly through the special selection processes employed and the highly-qualified profiles

---

[42] Ferreres, this book.
[43] Sadurski and Lach, this book.
[44] Solyom, cited by Sadurski and Lach.
[45] Groppi, this book.

of the members),[46] which could eventually contribute to make the so called 'democratic objection' less compelling. Secondly there is the degree of visibility and authoritativeness they enjoy due to their constitutional status, which allows them to engage in a relationship with the political power on equal terms, and makes for easier dialogue with public opinion.

SET UP AND SELECTION OF JUDGES

No matter how they are conceived constitutional courts are not neutral or completely independent. Debates about whether to set up a constitutional court invariably also modulate into debates about the prospective composition of such a court. It is clear that no appointment process can overcome the fact that: 'Judges [...] have their own personal and political views which they take on to the bench with them and help shape their decisions; the law is not a value-free process'.[47] In analysing individual judicial contributions to the highest appellate court in the UK Professor Griffith emphasizes that:

> Every judge has to develop his own view of the judicial function and of the way that function relates to Parliament and Executive. In this sense every judge has to develop his own political philosophy. He must develop his own jurisprudence, that is to say his view of the nature of law itself, what he sees as its bases and purposes.[48]

Judicial independence as it applies to these courts is therefore a relative concept that can be understood in a variety of ways. Nevertheless, for the court to have authority it must be perceived as being, if not totally independent, at least heavily insulated in crucial respects from political and governmental processes.

The comparative sample which is represented by this collection reveals variations on some basic selection procedures and allows us to make some general observations upon their relative strengths.[49] Many of these systems are designed to avoid fatally undermining any notion of separation of powers by conferring an unqualified power of appointment on a single person or constitutional body. The separation of powers[50] arises as an

---

[46] See below.

[47] Stevens, R (2004), 'Reform in Haste and Repent at Leisure' 24 *Legal Studies* 27.

[48] Griffith, J (1993), *Judicial Politics since 1920: A Chronicle*, Blackwell, 1993, 103.

[49] Ginsburg, T (2003) *Judicial Review in New Democracies: Constitutional Courts in Asian Cases*, Cambridge University Press, provides a useful table at pp.50-4.

[50] The basic doctrine of separation of powers is in a sense extended with the Kelsenian constitutional court model which views a constitutional court as a fourth branch of the state.

issue when it comes to the appointment process in several other ways. In terms of formal status it means that, once appointed, judges should have security of tenure for a given term or until retirement protecting them from dismissal or non-renewal of office for passing down unpopular judgments.[51] Moreover, institutional design may, in part, be a response to supra-national obligations. The constitutional courts of many European nations as signatories to the European Convention on Human Rights must give the appearance of independence from outside pressures.[52] The challenge is to find an approach to selection which is transparent and which introduces an element of democratic accountability by allowing elected representatives to have some input into the process, but at the same time minimises or eliminates naked partisanship which would impact on the ideological leanings of the court. Of course, what distinguishes judging at the level of constitutional jurisdiction is that an appeal to a superior court, which is the usual form of judicial accountability, is not available (except at the supra-national level such as to the ECHR or the European Court of Justice). The appointment process for the majority of constitutional courts conforms largely to one of the following models.

Approaches to Selection

(1) One of the most widely adopted approaches divides the task of appointment between the executive and legislative organs of the state. This is broadly similar to the system in the United States and predictably occurs in constitutional systems where American influence is also most evident. Typically, the process involves nomination by the president but appointment only follows after there has been approval from the national assembly.[53] Prior to a confirmation by ballot democratic scrutiny is often provided by confirmation hearings which allow potential candidates to be examined as to both their personal suitability and their ideological stance. As in the United States these hearings are prone to become highly politicized, especially if the political persuasion of the president differs from that of the governing party in the legislature.

---

[51] Le Sueur, A (2004), 'Developing Methods for Judicial Accountability in the UK' 24 *Legal Studies*, 75.
[52] ECHR, Article 6.
[53] For example, this method is employed in Taiwan and some Latin American countries.

(2) In contrast, the legislature may be solely responsible for making the final appointment.[54] Once again such an approach introduces a central element of democratic involvement and scrutiny, but the problem here is preventing the dominant party within the legislature from always prevailing. Obviously a simple majority would result in only the nominees of the ruling party being appointed, and in order to prevent this from happening nominations will often require approval by a 'supermajority', for example two thirds. To achieve this threshold a process of negotiation and eventual compromise between government and opposition is required after suitable candidates have been nominated.

(3) Another alternative which preserves a democratic element is to divide the power of appointment between state actors.[55] This is where the appointment process allows constitutional bodies with distinct functions and different claims to legitimacy (e.g. the president, each house of the national assembly,[56] senior judges) to nominate a specified quota of the court's membership. A danger here might be to produce a divided panel which is likely to be sympathetic to the institutional interest that selected them. On the other hand, court members selected as representatives of the judicial branch might take professional pride in taking a strictly legalistic interpretation of their role in applying the law of the constitution and thereby acting as a counterweight to more political influences on the court. This model has the great merit of tending to avoid controversy over selecting the method of appointment and over the individual appointments. It can thereby forestall the possibility of one branch of the state dominating constitutional court appointments.

(4) In many systems a commission or specially dedicated selection committee makes an important contribution to the selection

---

[54] In Germany each house nominates an equal number of members of the Court. This method is also employed widely in Latin America.

[55] Italy may be cited as a paradigmatic case with three members nominated respectively by the President, Parliament and the Supreme Court. Other examples include: Chile, Columbia, the Dominican Republic, Ecuador, Guatemala, Indonesia, Mongolia, Paraguay, and South Korea.

[56] Under the Turkish Constitution there is a combination of institutions but the legislature is excluded from the process.

process before the candidates are finally endorsed.[57] For example, under the South African Constitution the President is required to act in harness with the Judicial Services Commission (JSC) in first appointing the Chief Justice and Deputy-Chief Justice, but then the JSC also provides nominees for the other appointments to the court.[58] To limit the politicisation of the process the President, after exercising a duty to consult, cannot simply reject nominees without submitting reasons, and any such rejection requires the JSC and not the President to submit a supplemental list of names. Another innovation which greatly enhances the transparency of the South African process is for the JSC to hold public interviews for the potential nominees. An obvious problem with placing heavy reliance on commissions is the decision as to who should be qualified to sit on the commission and what method of selection might be adopted to prevent the commission from becoming a forum for elected politicians. One approach has been to professionalise the membership by reserving a majority of places to serving judges and members of the legal profession. For example, there is some evidence to suggest that the level of judicial independence will be higher in higher Councils of the Judiciary where judges hold the majority of seats and are directly elected by their peers.[59]

Who should Serve as Constitutional Court Judges?

The selection process for constitutional courts is not simply about ensuring an appropriate degree of judicial independence from the wider political game; it also reflects a view as to the best type of candidates to act as constitutional court judges and how they should be equipped for the task. In a formal sense the founding instrument (constitution, organic law or founding statute) will nearly always set out requirements for candidates relating to their nationality, age, qualifications, experience, record, and so forth. The availability of a sufficiently qualified cohort of candidates may be problematic. For West African courts improved training and reinforcement of the teaching of constitutional law may need to become a more prominent

---

[57] The Constitution of the Kingdom of Thailand 2007, Article 206, requires the formation of a Judicial Selection Committee for the Constitutional Court; in Spain the same function is performed by the General Council for the Judiciary.
[58] South African Constitution, section 174.
[59] Guarnieri, C (2004) 'Appointment and Career of Judges in Continental Europe', 24 *Legal Studies* 176.

feature of the curriculum for judges of these courts to be able to better meet future challenges.[60] It has been explained that 'The normative task is to select an appointment mechanism that will maximise the chance that the judge will interpret the text in accordance with the intention of the constitution writers'.[61] On the other hand, it is not self-evidently the case that all the constitutional court judges need to be legally trained. It can be maintained that too much of a premium is placed on this type of technical judicial experience. The tasks confronting a constitutional court will often be different from those that are faced by ordinary courts. While cases are presented in legal terms the court may find itself presiding over disputes with profound political, social/ ethical and economic implications. Indeed, some courts, as has been the case in Thailand since 1997 require the composition to include a proportion of political or social scientists as well as lawyers; interestingly in this example, the latest version of an appointment system under the 2007 Constitution allows the selection committee to actually veto senatorial refusal to approve candidates, on the assumption that the Senate is more vulnerable to capture than the selection committee, which now includes senior judges, the leader of the opposition, and the president of one of the major independent 'watchdog' agencies.[62]

An equally important issue relating to the selection process concerns the issue of what social groups might be represented on the constitutional bench. In other words, judges selected from a homogeneous professional group of predominantly male lawyers might be technically equipped, but they might also be perceived as being out of touch with the lives of ordinary people or as representing a particular ethnic minority, age group, or gender. One commentator stresses that: 'Where greater diversity has been achieved in courts in other jurisdictions this has almost always been the consequence of an explicit political commitment to diversity'.[63]

GATEWAYS TO CONSTITUTIONAL COURTS

In a practical sense related to the effectiveness of operation the importance of access has been stressed by influential commentators:

---

[60] Kante, this book.
[61] Ginsburg, supra note 49, at 42.
[62] Harding and Leyland, this book.
[63] Malleson, K (2004), 'Selecting Judges in the Era of Devolution and Human Rights' in Le Sueur, A, *Building the UK'S New Supreme Court: National and Comparative Perspectives*, Oxford University Press, 306.

Access to the court is perhaps the most important ingredient in judicial power, because a party seeking to utilize judicial review as political insurance will only be able to do so if it can bring a case to court. Setting up a designated constitutional court, accessible only to a narrow set of organs, has the effect of limiting the insurance function of the constitutional court ... Open access decentralizes the monitoring function widely and makes it more likely that politicians will be challenged in court should they fail to abide by constitutional limitation.[64]

However, the means of access to a constitutional court will mainly be determined by the kind of model of constitutional justice which has been selected. Many authors note the influence of Kelsenian abstract review across the wide range of constitutional courts which feature in these studies. Under such a regime the court plays a fundamental role as special body representing a public interest in seeing that the law, at national and sub-national level, is in conformity with constitutional norms. The path to the constitutional court to determine the issue of legality is frequently confined to government and law makers. For example, in the case of the German Federal Constitutional Court the issue can be referred for resolution by the Federal government, the Land government or by a third of Bundestag members. There are many variations granting a right of referral to PM, prosecutor general, ombudsman, president of the high council of local authorities (Mali), president of the high broadcasting authority (Benin), or varying proportions of member of the legislature.[65]

By way of contrast the US model of judicial review established under the *Marbury v Madison* principle does not provide a right of direct referral on constitutional questions. Rather, it depends upon ordinary litigation through the courts. The Supreme Court, as the highest appellate court, is the final adjudicator over constitutional matters, for example as in *Bush v Gore*, with other constitutional organs regarding the court's decisions as binding. In continental systems (related to the Kelsenian model) the ordinary courts may also play a significant role as part of what is termed 'concrete' review which is initiated by a court referring a matter before it for constitutional adjudication. For example, Spain has a constitutional question procedure triggered by the courts, while in Italy judges also perform a screening function by submitting questions for determination indicating 'the

---

[64]   See Ginsburg, supra note 49, at 36-7.
[65]   It is worth noting that the French Constitutional Council differs from other constitutional courts as it can only be called upon to examine the constitutional conformity of legislation before the bill is passed.

relevance and plausibility of the question, the law challenged, and the constitutional provision that it allegedly violates.'[66]

Beyond the partly technical and structural questions relating to the validity of legislation and the relative powers of constitutional bodies, the constitutional court or council is often charged with overseeing the protection of rights under the constitution. The design dilemma in formulating rules of access for the court comes down to finding a procedure which encourages potentially valid claims even if litigants lack the means to pursue them, but at the same time allows the court sufficient discretion to filter out unworthy cases. Citizens are granted a right to petition the constitutional court or council if they consider that their rights guaranteed under the constitution have been violated but this right is qualified by further conditions. For example, the rules require that all other available remedies must first be exhausted. Another method of screening is for the court to have a prehearing stage[67] to prevent it becoming inundated by cases and to ensure timely justice for claims falling within the jurisdiction. Equally, there have been a variety of approaches to extending access. There are a number of systems which allow the ombudsman, other state official or even in some cases NGO's, to champion a case on behalf of potential litigants.

Finally, where the constitutional court or council has authority to determine the validity of elections the right to refer disputed matters and results may be given to candidates or the case may routed through special electoral judge or an electoral oversight body for investigation before the court finally decides the issue.

THE PERFORMANCE OF CONSTITUTIONAL COURTS

In this section we do not attempt to assess the actual performance of constitutional courts (instead we allow the various contributions to tell their own stories), but rather to discuss some of the considerations involved in such complex assessments.

Interpretation

An obvious common starting point to making a comparative evaluation of constitutional courts would be to look at their approach to the interpretation of the constitutional text.

---

[66] Groppi, this book.
[67] The German system of preliminary examining 'chambers' is one approach to performing the task of screening frivolous constitutional complaints. See Kommers and Miller in this book.

> Legalism in constitutional law has been associated with various tendencies, including literalism, formalism, positivism and originalism ... positivism might be defined as a conception of a constitution as a set of discrete written provisions, whose authority derives from their having been formally adopted or enacted.[68]

Undoubtedly the reasoning process adopted by the court, as is indicated in some of the contributions to this book, such as that of Harding and Leyland, is of prime importance to the establishment and maintenance of legitimacy. A court which is unable to demonstrate the logic and cogency of its interpretation of the constitution is likely to be seen, and may indeed in fact be, arbitrary and even politically biased in its decisions. The contributors to this book, already considerably overburdened with editor's instructions covering almost every other issue, were not asked to report on the very complex issues of judicial reasoning and interpretation.[69] Undoubtedly, however, as the quotation from Goldsworthy above indicates, this is a field for fruitful comparison of methods, procedures, and principles which should form the basis for a different type of inquiry on another occasion, and one which should encompass decentralized as well as centralised systems. On this issue we will therefore be brief.

The approach to interpretation is to some extent conditioned by the style of judicial reasoning associated with the tradition in question. For example, the Russian court's style of judgment with its 'past reasoning part' and the possibility of separate judicial opinions is, despite its discursive nature is 'similar to the structure of the decisions of the courts in common law countries'.[70] A decision by the court which is characterised as a precedent is binding upon the entire court system; its legal force is even higher than that of a law; it has both retroactive and prospective effect; and is subject to publication. The court also follows its own previous reasoning, particularly although not exclusively in relation to interpretation of the Constitution. The example indicates that even in a civil law system, where judgments tend towards formality and the absence of any but very basic reasoning, the need for a more transparent reasoning process which explains and contextualises the interpretation adopted in the legal-technical sense, may well be highly advisable.

---

[68] Goldsworthy, J (2006) *Interpreting Constitutions: A Comparative Study*, Oxford University Press, 322.

[69] However Groppi has indicated in her article the importance of the highly technical issues of interpretation that have arisen in Italy.

[70] Henderson, this book. See also the comments by Harding and Leyland, this book, contrasting Thailand and Indonesia.

Under its new Constitution from 1996 the South African Constitutional Court has relied less on the specifics of the Constitutional Principles and instead emphasized the fundamental elements of constitutionalism contained within the text. These have included: 'founding values which include human dignity, the achievement of equality, the recognition and advancement of human rights and freedoms, the supremacy of the Constitution and the rule of law'.[71]

The combined efficacy of interpretative modes and expected reasoning processes must, we feel, be crucial issues for any constitutional court attempting to ensure its own legitimacy.

Effectiveness

Although the contributors were asked to report on the general performance of the constitutional courts and how this has been perceived, given the large and disparate sample of cases covered in this book and the difficulty of laying down uniform and sufficiently stringent criteria (itself a highly complex task which would require further research) we cannot do more than attempt some impressionistic observations which might lead us towards an approach rather than a conclusion.

By what criteria are we to judge the effectiveness of these courts? Clearly the provision of statistics showing the proportion of cases in which a measure or decision was struck down or an official disqualified provides no real guidance as to effectiveness, since the efficacy of a decision has to be judged against the case presented. A high 'strike rate' might in some sense indicate a degree of independence or activism, but whether this would indicate that the court made correct decisions or decisions that appeared acceptable is again a difficult matter to judge. In any event, efficacy has to be judged against original intentions, and even here we are unsure whether to take ostensible raisons d'être or *realpolitik*-type reasons: if a constitutional court was set up to protect a party or policy that might or did lose political power[72] and in fact did so, this might logically be counted an effective court.

A more promising approach might be to assume that the ostensible purpose is to deter constitutional actors from abusing their position or abusing individual human rights. If we find that in fact they were so deterred because of the prospect of a robust response from the court, we could perhaps conclude there is success. But even here, how are we to

---

[71] Klug, this book.
[72] Cf. Ginsburg, supra note 49.

judge the motivation or not of the actors and what standards are we to apply if not those laid down by the court itself?

Pure statistical data is in the main informative only in terms of such things as the throughput of cases and the distribution of cases between different jurisdictional heads, itself of interest quite apart from the issue of assessment of performance. Beyond that, we can perhaps judge only by reference to the perceptions of those who hold a stake in the constitutional arrangements in question.

Constitutional courts are of course terribly exposed in this area of discussion in that they are always it seems open to being accused of either being 'subservient', 'timid', or 'failing to fulfil their remit', or of being overly 'jurocratic', 'ambitious', 'politically insensitive', and 'going beyond their remit': there seems to be no very obvious way of being a 'good' constitutional court other than to walk this tightrope with both good sense and strong nerves.

We suggest that the best way of assessing these courts is to look at them from the aspect of constitutionalism, by adopting a two-stage process which considers i) whether the court's interventions are consistent with the norms set out in the constitution, and whether these norms themselves are consistent with principles of 'good governance' as we understand this term in international law and development discourse; and ii) whether the court's pronouncements are then actually embedded in practice, that is, whether they are followed. In this sense the effectiveness of a court may lie, not merely in an evaluation of its performance on the basis of a kind of constitutional morality, but in an evaluation of its total effect on constitutional practice in light of widely supported principles of good governance and given the powers and resources at its disposal. In this sense comment on the effectiveness of a court may not simply be a comment on its actual performance: a court may (to take an extreme example) consistently make 'good' decisions which are equally consistently ignored except in the plaudits of scholars, and of course part of effectiveness must be whether the court's decisions are technically as well as practically capable of being enforced.

Equally, in assessing the worth of decisions, we should take into account the political and economic situation in the country and whether the court has done its best in a possibly difficult situation in which these social realities may even impact on the court's own practical resources.[73] Apart from that one can of course look at 'efficiency' (not the same as 'effectiveness') by examining whether the court manages to deliver

---

[73] Kante, this book.

reasonably speedy judgment in most of the cases coming before it, and whether in doing so it conforms with the procedural rules laid down for exercising its jurisdiction.

There are of course signal examples of state organs quarrelling with, failing to observe, or using devious techniques to avoid, constitutional court decisions. Russia provides examples of the President having to be persuaded of the need to obey the Constitutional Court. Even in Austria (the 'heartland' of constitutional jurisdiction) the Governor of the Land Carinthia declined to conform to several judgments requiring him to accept bilingual (German and Slovenian) place-name signs in a number of Carinthian municipalities, a problem dismissed in Austria as 'political'.[74] In Indonesia the government has attempted (to some applause, it might be added) to avoid Constitutional Court decisions on privatisation by passing subsidiary legislation which cannot be adjudicated upon by the Constitutional Court.[75]

Finally, it is not surprising that a number of contributions refer to the age and development or progress of the constitutional court as a relevant factor to consider.[76] There is a sense in which constitutions and the courts may seem to mature like a fine claret (part of Sadurski and Lach's title is 'between adolescence and maturity'). The introduction of a constitutional court has often been linked to wider constitutional developments, as is discussed above. The German Federal Constitutional Court is regarded as the ultimate symbol of constitutional continuity after a record of 50 years of activity. A number of authors seem to suggest that there is teleological development towards something, where others seem rather to see the court as cresting the waves of constitutional and political change. The idea of evolution implies (we suggest wrongly) that there is a given end or ideal which can be sought, presumably the aspiration to some kind of model of a 'democratic' or 'constitutionalist' court. We would advocate an approach which adverts not to an abstract notion of perfection but rather the solution or mitigation of certain types of problems which we see arising, and suggests the introduction and application of rules which, if applied in certain ways, can help to avoid obvious pitfalls. For example, it is relatively easy to see ways in which power allocation functions might be resolved, or certain types of abuses prevented. Political questions and ethical questions are not in the main resolved by courts, and to this extent there must always be limits to the propriety of constitutional jurisdiction.

---

[74] Gamper and Palermo, this book.
[75] Harding and Leyland, this book.
[76] e.g., Kante, Groppi, this book.

Legitimacy

Finally, we can address more directly the issue of legitimacy which has informed the discussion so far.

The extent of the influence exerted by constitutional courts on the political process inevitably raises the vexed question of their legitimacy. As Sadurski and Lach[77] note: 'After all, the courts are regarded as promoters and protectors of democratic values, and are not the most democratic institutions themselves, if the democratic nature of an institution is measured by its electoral mandate and direct accountability towards the electors'. The problem arises most obviously in respect to challenges to legislation which has been passed by a democratically elected parliament.

> It is understandable why most judges and jurists wish to ground an objective practice of judicial interpretation that obviates judicial value-choices and that does not tread on the democratic toes of legislative or executive decision-making. However, it is misplaced ambition and doomed to failure. As judicial review is anti-majoritarian and, therefore, presumptively undemocratic, no theory can reconcile judicial review with majority rule.[78]

It might be argued however that some sort of legitimacy is conferred on a constitutional court by the way it gained its authority in the first place, for example, if the court was introduced as part of a new constitution or as an amendment to an existing constitution which was endorsed by a referendum. It could be argued that the court has a claim to legitimacy equal to any of the institutions laid down by the constitution. The fact is that constitutional courts have been increasingly if not unreservedly accepted in most countries because of a limited trust in political institutions and because of the quality and wisdom of their decisions.

CONCLUSION

The contributors to this special collection have each provided valuable insights into the particular constitutional and legal cultures under consideration, but even more significantly, taken together, we believe that these essays create a useful addition to comparative law scholarship. In writing this introduction we have concentrated on discussing some of the

---

[77] This book.
[78] Hutchinson, A (2004) 'Judges and Politics: an Essay from Canada' 24 *Legal Studies* 275, at 283

crucial issues which have arisen in relation to the conception, formation and operation of constitutional courts. However, we have not had the space to address wider debates. Professor Van Caenegem, analysing the trend towards the adoption of constitutions based on the notion of *Rechtstaat*, notes that it first requires acceptance of the idea that the rulers have to operate under the law and also according to law, further, that the law itself has respect for the rules of justice. A corollary is that: 'Only the judges can in conscience and complete freedom reprimand the government and even force it to obey the law and redress injustice'.[79] The establishment of a constitutional court of some kind, as the wealth of examples represented in these essays demonstrates, provides evidence of what has become widespread reliance on constitutional adjudication, almost invariably conceived as part of the constitutional framework to act as a counterweight to the abuse of power by other organs of the state. The limitations of constitutional adjudication are equally recognised. For example, Loughlin states that 'what we often fail to appreciate, especially when theorizing about constitutions is that despite their textuality, constitutions are replete with gaps, silences, and abeyances.'[80] From this standpoint, it is a myth to claim that the answer to political issues can be found in *any* body of law. Of course the debate on the potential efficacy of these courts will continue. Finally, we believe that the extent of any conclusions we can draw is conditioned by the dynamic nature of the subject matter. Most of these courts are of recent and many of very recent origin. In consequence, the assessment of the project of diffusion of this particular constitutional device will always be provisional. Nonetheless, we hope that the reader will be inspired by this book to pursue this fruitful line of inquiry further.

---

[79] Van Caenegem, R (1995) *An Historical Introduction to Western Constitutional Law*, Cambridge University Press,15-16.
[80] Loughlin, M (2003), *The Idea of Public Law*, Oxford University Press, 50.

EUROPE

The Constitutional Court of Austria: Modern Profiles of an Archetype of Constitutional Review

ANNA GAMPER AND FRANCESCO PALERMO *

INTRODUCTION

The Austrian Constitutional Court (*Verfassungsgerichtshof*) is one of the two main historic prototypes of institutionalised constitutional review worldwide.[1] A large number of states, not only in Europe, adopted the same rationale of constitutional jurisdiction concentrated in a single and centralized court that, inter alia, is vested with the power to review and strike down laws as well as administrative acts.

---

*   Univ.-Prof. Dr. Anna Gamper, University of Innsbruck, Institut für öffentliches Recht, Staats- und Verwaltungslehre and Prof. Dr. Francesco Palermo, European Academy Bolzano/ Bozen, Institute for Studies on Federalism and Regionalism.
[1]   The second being the so called 'diffused' judicial review, stemming from the US prototype. See Cappelletti, M (1971) *Judicial Review in the Contemporary World* Bobbs-Merrill at 32; Öhlinger, T (1998) 'Constitutional Review. The Austrian Experience as seen from a Comparative Perspective' (53) *Zeitschrift für Öffentliches Recht* 421; Paulson, S (2003) 'Constitutional Review in the United States and Austria: Notes on the Beginnings', *Ratio Juris* 223; Korinek, K (1981) 'Die Verfassungsgerichtsbarkeit im Gefüge der Staatsfunktionen' (39) *Veröffentlichungen der Vereinigung der Deutschen Staatsrechtslehrer* 8 at 9; von Brünneck, A (1992) *Verfassungsgerichtsbarkeit in den westlichen Demokratien* Nomos at 29; Häberle, P (2004) 'Die Verfassungsgerichtsbarkeit auf der heutigen Entwicklungsstufe des Verfassungsstaates' *Europäische Grundrechte-Zeitschrift* 117 at 118; Häberle, P (2005) 'Funktion und Bedeutung der Verfassungsgerichte in vergleichender Perspektive' *Europäische Grundrechte-Zeitschrift* 685; Häberle, P (2008) *Europäische Verfassungslehre* (5th ed) Nomos at 462 f; Wieser, B (2005) *Vergleichendes Verfassungsrecht* Springer at 124 ff.

This article will analyse the peculiar characteristics that make the Austrian Constitutional Court and its model of adjudication so remarkable and relevant for comparative purposes. After a brief historical outline and the presentation of the basic features and legal foundations of the present system of constitutional adjudication (part II), the article focuses in detail on the organization and functions of the Court, illustrating the procedural instruments for access, the resulting type of scrutiny and the effects of the decisions (part III). Part IV deals with the admissibility of cases, with particular regard to individual appeals to the Court, which is a crucial point to be looked at when it comes to constitutional adjudication: whatever the functions of a constitutional court are, only a wide understanding of admissibility will allow them to be exercised properly in the interest of the citizens.

Subsequently, the constitutional rules regulating the relations between the Court and other judicial and quasi-judicial bodies (part V) will be described. This is particularly interesting in a system, where a triad of "supreme courts" is responsible for a plethora of different legal fields and cases, let alone the fact that Austria is subject to the jurisdiction of the European Court of Human Rights and the European Court of Justice. Not only the relations to other courts need some reflection in this paper, but also the relations between the Austrian Constitutional Court and other state organs (part VI). In particular, the Court's relations to the constitutional law-maker have not always been smooth, posing the question of ultimate democratic legitimacy and of *quis custodiet ipsos custodes*, but in certain cases there have been tensions also with other bodies. To conclude (part VII), a short evaluation of the role of the Constitutional Court in the Austrian legal arena and in a broader comparative perspective will be provided.

THE AUSTRIAN MODEL OF CONSTITUTIONAL ADJUDICATION

The Austro-Hungarian *Reichsgericht*, the forerunner model of the republican Constitutional Court, was established in 1867[2]. Its most relevant contribution to the development of judicial review was the power to adjudicate cases

---

[2] RGBl 1867/143. See Jellinek, G (1885) *Ein Verfassungsgericht für Österreich* Hölder. An overview of the historic development is given by Öhlinger, T (2002) 'Die Entstehung und Entfaltung des österreichischen Modells der Verfassungsgerichtsbarkeit' in Funk, BC, Holzinger, G, Klecatsky, HR, Korinek, K, Mantl, W and Pernthaler, P (eds) (2002) *Der Rechtsstaat vor neuen Herausforderungen - Festschrift für Ludwig Adamovich zum 70. Geburtstag* Verlag Österreich 581 ff; Paulson, 'Review' supra at 1; Schmitz, G (2003) 'The Constitutional Court of the Republic of Austria 1918-1920', *Ratio Juris* 240; Öhlinger, T (2003) 'The Genesis of the Austrian Model of Constitutional Review of Legislation', *Ratio Juris* 206.

where a person had been violated in his or her constitutionally guaranteed political rights, although this did not yet extend to a scrutiny of legislative acts. Subsequent to the end of the Austro-Hungarian monarchy, the Constitutional Court was established by the new Federal Constitutional Act (*Bundes-Verfassungsgesetz*, henceforth *B-VG*) of 1920. After having been abolished during the period of Austro-fascism (1934-1938) and Nazi occupation (1938-1945), the Constitutional Court was re-established after the end of World War II and resumed its former functions.[3]

Since then, a number of constitutional amendments have been added to establish the Court's present position, which was facilitated by the very flexible character of the Austrian Federal Constitution.

The prototypical nature of the Austro-Hungarian *Reichsgericht* as a model of constitutional review derived from its being the only court especially vested with the power to deal with violations of constitutionally guaranteed rights. This is also what makes the republican Constitutional Court the true successor of the *Reichsgericht* and, with particular regard to its power to review and strike down laws, the counter-model to the US model of constitutional review. Hans Kelsen[4], being one of the founding fathers of the Austrian Federal Constitution, particularly emphasized the necessity of having an independent constitutional court which would much more be able to fulfil the function of a 'protector of the constitution' than the head of state, which was Carl Schmitt's[5] argument with regard to the Weimarian-*Reichspräsident*.

Three main features characterize the Austrian model of constitutional adjudication:

1. Centralized and exclusive adjudication: the Austrian Constitutional Court is a centralized and exclusive body, which means on the one hand that only one constitutional court exists (no decentralized constitutional courts are established in the Austrian *Länder*) and on the other hand that it is not up to the ordinary courts nor to any other state authority to decide on constitutional issues.

---

[3] See Ermacora, F (1956) *Der Verfassungsgerichtshof* Styria; Öhlinger 'Entstehung' supra at 2.
[4] See Kelsen, H (1931) *Wer soll der Hüter der Verfassung sein?* Walther Rothschild; Kelsen, H (1929) 'Wesen und Entwicklung der Staatsgerichtsbarkeit' (5) *Veröffentlichungen der Vereinigung der Deutschen Staatsrechtslehrer* 30. Kelsen's influence on the shaping of the Austrian Federal Constitution is discussed by Öhlinger, T (2008) 'Hans Kelsen – Vater der österreichischen Bundesverfassung?' in Kohl, G, Neschwara, C and Simon, T (eds) (2008) *Festschrift für Wilhelm Brauneder zum 65. Geburtstag – Rechtsgeschichte mit internationaler Perspektive* Manz 407.
[5] Schmitt, C (1931) *Der Hüter der Verfassung* J.C.B. Mohr.

2.   Abstract and concrete review: the Austrian Constitutional Court has the power to review laws and regulations both on an abstract and on a concrete basis. Therefore, the Court's competence to decide a case does not depend on a person's actual violation of rights in a concrete procedure or on any concrete case, but it can be invoked also by certain "abstract" appeals.[6]

3.   Striking down laws and declaration of unconstitutionality: the Austrian Constitutional Court strikes down laws (and other legal provisions) if they are unconstitutional. If the law was amended or repealed during the Constitutional Court's procedure (e.g. because Parliament wanted to anticipate the Court's decision), the Court declares that the former law *was* unconstitutional. The Court's power thus extends to a "negative kind of law-making" and is not limited to just non-application of unconstitutional laws in a concrete case.

Due to these three main characteristics, the Constitutional Court enjoys a strong and unique position among other Austrian courts.[7] In fact, it holds a 'monopoly' in interpreting and in adjudicating constitutional law. Following Austria's accession to the European Convention on Human Rights and Fundamental Freedoms (1958) and, much later, to the European Union (1995), however, the Constitutional Court has had to deal with (and, in fact, to accept) the jurisdiction of other courts that are frequently regarded as some sort of European 'constitutional super-courts'. In contrast to other national constitutional courts, the Austrian Constitutional Court has had no apparent difficulty in developing an ongoing dialogue with the supranational European courts.[8]

---

[6] See below 38.

[7] See below 46f.

[8] The Austrian Verfassungsgerichtshof was the first Constitutional Court to refer a case to the European Court of Justice in 2000 (see VfSlg 15.450/2001, and later VfSlg 17.065/2003; 17.075/2003). Moreover, the constitutional rank of the European Convention on Human Rights in Austria requires the dialogue with the European Court of Human Rights. See Schäffer, H (2005) 'Österreich und die Europäische Union – Erfahrungen und Leistungen des österreichischen Verfassungsgerichtshofes' (60) *Zeitschrift für Öffentliches Recht* 345 at 374; Schäffer, H (2007) 'Die Grundrechte im Spannungsverhältnis von nationaler und europäischer Perspektive' (62) *Zeitschrift für Öffentliches Recht* 1 at 4; Chojnacka, Z (2004) 'Zur Kooperation von EuGH und nationalem Verfassungsgericht' (59) *Zeitschrift für Öffentliches Recht* 415 at 429; Novak, R (2002) 'Der Verfassungsgerichtshof im Dialog mit dem Europäischen Gerichtshof' in Funk, BC, Holzinger, G, Klecatsky, HR, Korinek, K, Mantl, W and Pernthaler, P (eds) (2002) *Der Rechtsstaat vor neuen Herausforderungen – Festschrift für Ludwig Adamovich zum 70. Geburtstag* Verlag Österreich 539 ff.

ORGANISATION AND FUNCTIONS OF THE CONSTITUTIONAL COURT

Legal Basis

In Austria, as a civil law country, all basic legal provisions with regard to the Constitutional Court are entrenched in the B-VG as the main source of the fragmented Austrian Federal Constitution. When it comes to the organisational structure and functions of the Court, therefore, it is mainly the text of the Constitution that has to be looked at and elaborated. The 6th part of the B-VG is titled "Constitutional and Administrative Guarantees" and it sets up the bodies responsible for administrative and constitutional review. These are the Independent Administrative Senates of the *Länder*[9], the Asylum Court[10], the Administrative Court and, finally, the Constitutional Court (art. 137-148). Art. 148 B-VG refers to an ordinary federal law that determines the Court's organisation and procedure in detail[11] and to the Constitutional Court's Rules of Procedure that have to be issued by the Court itself. Only in a few cases reference is made to the Constitutional Court in other parts of the B-VG.[12]

The Organisation of the Constitutional Court

Art. 148 para 1 B-VG stipulates that the Constitutional Court consists of the President, the Vice-President, 12 justices and 6 substitute justices, who replace the judges if they are temporarily prevented from attending a session. All must have completed the study of law and must have worked for at least ten years in a legal profession, for which an academic law degree is a requisite. Although no minimum age is fixed, legal training and professional expertise are thus a precondition for becoming a constitutional judge. In practice, the justices usually are university professors, judges, barristers, public notaries or senior civil servants working for the public administration. According to art. 148 para 4 B-VG, it would be incompatible for a member of the Federal or a *Land* Government, of the National Council (first chamber of the Federal Parliament), of the Federal Council (second chamber of the Federal Parliament) or of another general representative

---

[9]   These quasi-judicial bodies in the *Länder*, responsible for decisions on several kinds of administrative appeal, were established in 1988 (BGBl 1988/685) in conformity with art. 6 ECHR ('tribunal'); see below 46.
[10]   See below 46.
[11]   Verfassungsgerichtshofgesetz 1953 (BGBl 1953/85 as lastly amended by BGBl I 2008/4).
[12]   See, e.g., art. 89, 119a, 126a, 148e and 148f B-VG.

body or of the European Parliament, for employees or functionaries of political parties to be at the same time a constitutional judge.[13]

All justices, including the President and Vice-President, are appointed by the Austrian head of state who is himself elected by general suffrage. The head of state, however, is bound to consider proposals made either by the Federal Government or by the two chambers of the Federal Parliament (the National Council and the Federal Council). Whereas the Federal Government is entitled to propose the President, the Vice-President, six justices and three substitute justices, the National Council proposes three justices and two substitute justices and the Federal Council three justices and one substitute, following a principle of rotation. Three justices and two substitutes must have their permanent residence outside Vienna: this provision, together with the Federal Council's right to propose some judges, seeks to serve *Länder* interests, although in practice its impact is very limited.

This procedure of selecting justices is the main reason why, despite the aforementioned rule of incompatibility, some political influence is inevitable:[14] Irrespective of the professional qualifications that all justices must possess, it is clear that justices are selected and appointed due to political preferences of the governing parties. Although the justices must not be employees or functionaries of political parties themselves, they usually have a reputation for being politically oriented, even though this is seldom openly visible when it comes to the judgments. Nonetheless, justices normally are very keen to behave strictly neutrally. This is due to a number of factors, but particularly to the constitutional rules on their independence. The justices cannot be bound by any instructions nor can they be removed from office or transferred. Moreover, individual independence is strengthened by the fact that they usually either decide in plenary or, if it is a case of minor importance, in chambers of four senior justices (so-called Permanent Rapporteurs), together with the President and Vice-President. Unlike other countries, where constitutional judges are either appointed for lifetime or conversely only for a pre-determined period of time, the Austrian justices may remain in office until the end of the year when they reach the age of 70 (art. 147 para 6 B-VG). A justice can be removed against his or her will before that date only by a decision taken by the Constitutional Court itself.

---

[13] Even more rigorous incompatibility provisions apply in case of the President and Vice-President of the Constitutional Court.

[14] The original intention of the Federal Constitution's Founders was quite different, though: See Kelsen 'Wesen' supra at 4 at 56 f and 85.

Unlike the ordinary courts, the Constitutional Court does not sit permanently, but it meets four times a year (three week sessions in March, June, October and December). Although decisions are usually only taken during the sessions, much work is done in the meantime as well, for example with regard to minor procedural steps, necessary research work and the exemplification of judgments. Special sessions have recently become necessary in order to deal with an increasing number of appeals against decisions taken by the new Asylum Court.

The judges are supported by professional and administrative staff consisting of approximately 80 persons. The President is supported by the President's Office that is split into different departments. All Permanent Rapporteurs have a number of qualified lawyers who mainly work as recording clerks and supervise the exemplification of judgments. There is also an information office in charge with the publication of the judgments electronically and in print version.[15]

The Functions of the Constitutional Court

General Features

The Constitutional Court performs a large number of different functions. The amount of its activities puts it above the average of what constitutional courts' work normally consists of.[16] There seems to be just one very typical function that is missing, namely the competence to render expertise, particularly legally binding pre-legislative opinions. With one small exception,[17] the Constitutional Court is limited to post-legislative scrutiny. This may be unsatisfactory since pre-legislative scrutiny, as exercised by a Court,[18] could prevent unconstitutional laws from the beginning and save the inconveniences and problems arising from post-legislative appeals – the more so as unconstitutional laws remain in force if nobody undertakes an appeal. On the other hand, however, it is also inherent in the Austrian separation of powers that courts, including the Constitutional Court, neither form part of the democratic legislature nor take part in

---

[15] Downloadable from www.vfgh.gv.at and www.ris.bka.gv.at. For statistical information see below 50.
[16] See the comparison drawn by Wieser 'Verfassungsrecht' supra at 1 at 133 ff; cf. also the contributions to special issue 3 of 2005 (60) *Zeitschrift für Öffentliches Recht* and Häberle 'Funktion' supra at 1.
[17] See art. 138 para 2 B-VG and below 43.
[18] The Austrian Federal President authenticates the constitutional enactment of federal laws by his signature according to art. 47 para. 1 B-VG, but this does not make up for the lacking system of *ex-ante* judicial scrutiny.

the legislative process. All of the Constitutional Court's functions are enumerated exhaustively in art. 137-145 B-VG and put into further detail by the Constitutional Court Act.

Scrutiny of Laws

According to art. 140 B-VG,[19] the Constitutional Court is responsible for the (post-legislative) scrutiny of federal and regional (*Land*) legislation. This power also comprises the scrutiny of federal and *Land* constitutional laws. The Court reviews the conformity of ordinary federal laws with the Federal Constitution, and of ordinary *Land* laws with the Federal and the *Land* Constitution (not however with ordinary federal laws, because ordinary federal laws and ordinary *Land* laws are basically of equal rank). *Land* constitutional law is struck down if it is in breach of the Federal Constitution. A federal constitutional law may also be struck down if it is in serious breach of one of the (explicitly or implicitly entrenched) basic principles of the Federal Constitution (democracy, republicanism, federalism, rule of law, separation of powers, human rights), which would, according to both doctrine and constitutional jurisprudence, constitute what is enigmatically called a 'total revision of the Federal Constitution' (art. 44 para 3 B-VG) and thus require an additional referendum.[20]

Post-legislative scrutiny may take place on an abstract or concrete basis. On an abstract basis – that is, without being adversely or at all concretely affected – the Federal Government or (if this is provided by the respective *Land* Constitution) one third of the members of a *Land* Parliament may challenge a *Land* law before the Court, whereas a *Land* Government, one third of the members of the National Council or one third of the members of the Federal Council may challenge a federal law.

On a concrete basis, all (ordinary) courts of second instance, the Independent Administrative Senates, the Supreme Court, the Administrative Court, the Asylum Court and the Federal Procurement Agency may lodge an appeal against all kinds of laws that they have to

---

[19] Cf. in detail Rohregger, M (2003) 'Art. 140 B-VG' in Korinek K and Holoubek M (eds) (2003) *Österreichisches Bundesverfassungsrecht* Springer; Schäffer, H (2006) 'Art. 140 B-VG' in Rill, HP and Schäffer, H (eds) (2006) *Bundesverfassungsrecht* Verlag Österreich; Öhlinger, T and Hiesel, M (2001) *Verfahren vor den Gerichtshöfen des öffentlichen Rechts* (2nd ed) Manz at 140; Walter, R, Mayer, H and Kucsko-Stadlmayer, G (2007) *Grundriss des österreichischen Bundesverfassungsrechts* (10th ed) Manz at 531 ff.

[20] Cf., as a leading case, VfSlg 2455/1952 and Gamper, A (2007) 'Die Rolle der Bauprinzipien in der Judikatur des österreichischen Verfassungsgerichtshofes' (55) *Jahrbuch des Öffentlichen Rechts der Gegenwart* 537. Only once, the Constitutional Court decided to strike down a federal constitutional provision (VfSlg 16.327/2001). The question what a 'serious breach' of the Federal Constitution precisely means is certainly difficult to resolve.

apply in a certain (concrete) procedure. In addition to that, a single person (physical or legal) may lodge an individual appeal if the law directly and currently violates this person in his or her rights without the possibility to get a judgment or an administrative ruling that could be challenged via the regular remedies (subsidiarity of individual appeals).

Finally, the Constitutional Court itself may start a reviewing procedure *ex officio* if the Court deals with a law in another procedure and doubts its constitutionality. As a consequence, the Court strikes down the law or that part of it which is unconstitutional or, if it is not in force anymore, declares it to have been unconstitutional.

Scrutiny of Regulations

Under Article 139 B-VG[21] the Constitutional Court reviews and strikes down general regulations (Verordnungen) issued by a federal, *Land* or municipal authority if they are in breach of (ordinary or constitutional) laws, again either on an abstract or concrete basis.

On a concrete basis, the aforementioned authorities (including for this purpose *all* courts) and individual persons may lodge an appeal as in the case of concrete review of laws under art. 140 B-VG. The Federal Government and the Federal or a *Land* Ombudsman may challenge a *Law* regulation *in abstracto*, whereas a *Land* Government and the Federal Ombudsman may do so with regard to a challenge of a federal regulation. The municipalities may challenge a supervisory regulation passed by a federal or *Land* authority that is responsible for the supervision of municipalities.[22] Again, the Court strikes down the regulation or that part of it which is illegal or, if it is not in force anymore, declares it to have been illegal.

Scrutiny of Administrative Rulings

According to art. 144 B-VG,[23] the Constitutional Court reviews complaints against individual administrative rulings (including those issued by the Independent Administrative Senates). All administrative remedies must

---

[21]   Cf. in detail Aichlreiter, JW (2003) 'Art. 139 B-VG' in Rill, HP and Schäffer, H (eds) (2003) *Bundesverfassungsrecht* Verlag Österreich; Öhlinger and Hiesel 'Verfahren' supra at 19 at 70; Walter, Mayer and Kucsko-Stadlmayer 'Grundriss' supra at 19 at 516 ff.

[22]   See also art. 119a B-VG.

[23]   Cf. in detail Kneihs, B and Rohregger, M (2005) 'Art. 144 B-VG' in Korinek K and Holoubek M (eds) (2005) *Österreichisches Bundesverfassungsrecht* Springer; Potacs, M and Hattenberger, D (2001) 'Art. 144 B-VG' in Rill, HP and Schäffer, H (eds) (2001) *Bundesverfassungsrecht* Verlag Österreich; Öhlinger and Hiesel 'Verfahren' supra at 19 at 257; Walter, Mayer and Kucsko-Stadlmayer 'Grundriss' supra at 19 at 553 ff.

have been exhausted, and the person that lodges the complaint must allege to have suffered a violation of a constitutionally guaranteed right (fundamental right) or of any subjective right through the application of an illegal general norm. If the Constitutional Court follows this allegation, it strikes down the administrative ruling, and the administrative authority that was responsible for it will have to issue another ruling in conformity with the Court's views. This separate sector of 'special administrative jurisdiction' by the Constitutional Court – whilst it is normally the Administrative Court that is responsible for reviewing and striking down administrative decisions – plays an eminent role in the Constitutional Court's work, not only quantitatively, but also substantively.[24] Since 1 July 2008, moreover, when the provisions on the new Asylum Court came into force, the Constitutional Court has also been responsible for the scrutiny of decisions taken by the Asylum Court according to art. 144a B-VG,[25] if the person that lodges the complaint alleges a violation of a constitutionally guaranteed right or of any subjective right through the application of an illegal general norm by the Asylum Court. Although this provision has only been in force for a short time, the Constitutional Court already complains of being overwhelmed with cases, since the Administrative Court can only decide on the Asylum Court's decisions in exceptional cases (Art 132a B-VG).

Scrutiny of Republished Laws

According to art. 139a B-VG,[26] the Constitutional Court reviews and eventually strikes down laws or international treaties that have been republished formally (whilst the content remains unchanged: e.g. rearrangement of article numbers, slight linguistic changes etc) on application of an ordinary court, an Independent Administrative Senate, the Federal Procurement Agency, an individual person directly and currently violated by the republication or *ex officio* (concrete review). The Court may also review and strike down republished *Land* laws on application of the Federal Government and the republication of federal laws on application of a *Land* government (abstract review).

---

[24] For statistical data, see below 50.
[25] BGBl I 2008/2.
[26] Cf. in detail Öhlinger and Hiesel 'Verfahren' supra at 15 at 138; Walter, Mayer and Kucsko-Stadlmayer 'Grundriss' supra at 19 at 527 ff.

Scrutiny of State Treaties and Violations of Public International Law

According to art. 140a B-VG,[27] the Constitutional Court determines whether an international treaty is in breach of constitutional or ordinary laws, which means that state treaties are scrutinized on their compatibility with domestic law, irrespective of their international validity. This provision, however, has not been applied in practice so far. In addition, art. 145 B-VG[28] empowers the Court to ascertain violations of public international law by the Austrian authorities, on the basis of a specific federal law. Since such an empowerment law has never been passed, the Court has not yet exercised this particular function.

Scrutiny of Elections

According to art. 141 B-VG,[29] the Constitutional Court may be addressed to control the legality of elections, including the election of the Federal President, the National Council, the Austrian members of the European Parliament, *Land* Parliaments, *Land* Governments and Municipal Bodies as well as the elections of representative assemblies of the professional associations. It also decides on the loss of mandate of a delegate to one of these assemblies. As a consequence, the Court may either declare the loss of mandate or the illegality of the election procedure, if there was sufficient evidence for the illegality and if the illegality was relevant to determine the outcome of the election. As a result, the election procedure, or part of it, will have to be repeated. Further to that, ordinary legislation authorizes the Court to review the legality of plebiscites, such as referenda, people's initiatives and popular consultation (art. 141 para 3 B-VG).[30]

---

[27] Cf. in detail Öhlinger, T (2005) 'Art. 140a B-VG' in Korinek K and Holoubek M (eds) (2005) *Österreichisches Bundesverfassungsrecht* Springer; Öhlinger and Hiesel 'Verfahren' supra at 19 at 240; Walter, Mayer and Kucsko-Stadlmayer 'Grundriss' supra at 19 at 542 ff.

[28] Cf. in detail Zellenberg, U (1999) 'Art. 145 B-VG' in Korinek K and Holoubek M (eds) (1999) *Österreichisches Bundesverfassungsrecht* Springer; Öhlinger and Hiesel 'Verfahren' supra at 19 at 298.

[29] Cf. in detail Strejcek, G (2002) 'Art. 141 B-VG' in Korinek K and Holoubek M (eds) (2002) *Österreichisches Bundesverfassungsrecht* Springer; Öhlinger and Hiesel 'Verfahren' supra at 19 at 242; Walter, Mayer and Kucsko-Stadlmayer 'Grundriss' supra at 19 at 544 ff.

[30] For a survey of the Court's case-law on elections cf. Strejcek, G and Urban, D (eds) (2008) *Der Verfassungsgerichtshof als Wahlgericht* Verlag Österreich.

Decision on Accusations against Supreme Federal or Land Bodies or Functionaries

According to art. 142 B-VG,[31] the Constitutional Court decides on accusations against the Federal President, the Members of the Federal or a *Land* Government, the Austrian representative to the Council of Ministers of the EU and other functionaries in case of illegal (regarding the Federal President only unconstitutional) actions committed culpably by these persons when acting in their official capacity. The prosecuting parties differ: it is a classical parliamentary power to prosecute supreme executive bodies in case of their illegal actions, so that it is the Federal Assembly's (i.e. the assembly composed by both chambers of the Federal Parliament) power to accuse the Federal President, the National Council's power to accuse members of the Federal Government and the *Land* Parliaments' power to accuse members of the *Land* Governments. Specific provisions apply with regard to the accusation against other bodies mentioned in art. 142 B-VG; for example, the Federal Government may accuse the *Land* Governor of illegal actions when acting on behalf of the Federal Government ('indirect federal administration').[32]

Decision on Subsidiary Pecuniary Claims

Art. 137 B-VG[33] provides that pecuniary claims that can neither be settled in proceedings before the ordinary courts nor by an administrative ruling are decided by the Constitutional Court, if these claims are made against the Federation, the *Länder*, the municipalities or municipal associations. This means that the Constitutional Court may decide only as a subsidiary umpire, if no other authority is responsible.

Decision on Competence Disputes

Under art. 138 para 1 B-VG,[34] the Constitutional Court decides competence disputes between courts and administrative authorities, between courts

---

[31] Cf. in detail Öhlinger and Hiesel 'Verfahren' supra at 19 at 252; Walter, Mayer and Kucsko-Stadlmayer 'Grundriss' supra at 19 at 550 ff.

[32] Art. 102 B-VG.

[33] Cf. in detail Zellenberg, U (2005) 'Art. 137 B-VG' in Korinek K and Holoubek M (eds) (2005) *Österreichisches Bundesverfassungsrecht* Springer; Öhlinger and Hiesel 'Verfahren' supra at 19 at 37; Walter, Mayer and Kucsko-Stadlmayer 'Grundriss' supra at 19 at 506 ff.

[34] Cf. in detail Zellenberg, U (2002) 'Art. 138/1 B-VG' in Korinek K and Holoubek M (eds) (2002) *Österreichisches Bundesverfassungsrecht* Springer; Zellenberg, U (2001) 'Art. 138/2 B-VG' in Korinek K and Holoubek M (eds) (2001) *Österreichisches Bundesverfassungsrecht* Springer; Öhlinger and Hiesel 'Verfahren' supra at 19 at 61; Walter, Mayer and Kucsko-Stadlmayer 'Grundriss' supra at 19 at 508 ff.

themselves, between the *Länder* and between the Federation and a *Land*. Such a competence dispute may also lead to an individual person's complaint to have been violated in the constitutionally guaranteed right to a lawful judge.[35]

Apart from these concrete cases of conflict, where the Court decides which of the conflicting authorities has jurisdiction over a specific matter, the Constitutional Court may also be appealed by the Federal Government or by a *Land* Government in order to determine whether a draft law or regulation is in conformity with the distribution of powers between the federal and the *Land* level (art. 138 para 2 B-VG). This is the Court's only power of pre-legislative review, whereas normally its jurisdiction is restricted to provisions that are already in force or even those that have ceased to be in force. Within the framework of this exceptional type of review, the Constitutional Court's scrutiny is limited to determine whether or not the draft is in conformity with the distribution of powers provided by the Federal Constitution and it cannot extend to other aspects of constitutionality (e.g. whether the draft violates fundamental rights). The Court's statement on the division of powers in such a specific case is called 'authentic interpretation' and is to be considered as if it were passed as a constitutional law. The Court considers itself bound by this kind of precedent, which means that if the Court will be later called to hold whether a law (that was submitted to the Court as a draft) violates the distribution of powers, it would revert to its previous authentic statement on the draft of the law.

Decision on the Validity of Constitutional Agreements

According to art. 138a B-VG,[36] the Constitutional Court also decides on the validity of constitutional agreements concluded under art. 15a B-VG ('treaties' between the Federation and the *Länder* or between the *Länder* among each other) as well as whether all obligations that emerge from these agreements are met. The Court has no power, however, to impose any sanction on the Federation or a *Land* if it finds that the obligations have not been met.

---

[35] Art. 83 para 2 B-VG.
[36] Cf. in detail Thienel, R (2000) 'Art. 138a B-VG' in Korinek K and Holoubek M (eds) (2000) *Österreichisches Bundesverfassungsrecht* Springer; Öhlinger and Hiesel 'Verfahren' supra at 19 at 69; Walter, Mayer and Kucsko-Stadlmayer 'Grundriss' supra at 19 at 515 f.

ADMISSION OF CASES

It follows from the multiplicity of functions exercised by the Constitutional Court that a large number of bodies and individuals are entitled to access the Court. In particular, the coexistence of abstract and concrete review allows plenty of gateways to invoke the Court's jurisdiction. On the other hand, however, not every state authority and not everybody is admitted to the Court. Where concrete review is concerned, only (superior) courts and tribunals under Art 6 ECHR are admitted in most cases, whereas administrative authorities are denied access, unless they are supreme executive bodies, such as a *Land* Government or the Federal Government. Parliaments also may lodge an appeal in certain cases, which is either due to the classical parliamentary power of controlling the supreme executive bodies or due to an opposition-friendly scheme that allows the parliamentary minority (at least one third of the members) to challenge a law that was passed by the parliamentary majority.

In principle, both the Federation and the *Länder* have the same possibilities to challenge the respective legislation before the Court, as the Federal Constitution clearly establishes the Constitutional Court as a neutral umpire between the central state and the constituent units.

Where individual persons are concerned, there are two possible ways to be admitted to the Constitutional Court: The main gateway is via art. 144 B-VG, i.e. a complaint against an administrative decision that violates a person in his or her fundamental rights or in any other subjective right by means of the application of an illegal general norm (*Bescheidbeschwerde*). This procedural way is not as easy as it looks, though. The complainant must previously have exhausted all administrative channels, i.e. tried all remedies granted by administrative law so that in practice it is only the ruling of the last (supreme) administrative instance that may be made an object of the Court's review. Furthermore, the individual complaint can be lodged only within 6 weeks upon delivery of the (last) administrative ruling. The complaint must follow a formal pattern prescribed by the Constitutional Court Act[37] and be written or at least be signed by a barrister. It is not unusual that a decision takes nearly a year, and if the complainant does not succeed he or she will be condemned to pay 2,620 Euro which are the basic costs arising from legal counsel, application fee and taxes.

The only other way open to individuals is the so-called 'individual appeal' (*Individualantrag*) via art. 139 or 140 B-VG. If the person states that his or her rights are violated directly and currently by an unconstitutional

---

[37]   Cf. § 82 Verfassungsgerichtshofgesetz 1953.

law or by an illegal regulation, the appeal will be admissible. There must, however, be no chance of obtaining another legal remedy, which is the case if neither a judgment nor an administrative ruling were delivered in that case. What is more important, is that it is not sufficient for an individual to affirm that such a decision is lacking, but the person is expected to have sought for such a decision. Only in subsidiary cases, where it would be 'unbearable' for a person to seek for another authority's decision (for example, if the person would have to commit a crime in order to 'provoke' a decision or would have to pay large sums of money [for example for planning materials, expert opinions, etc.] in the course of an administrative procedure, but not just because it would be 'inconvenient' or 'inefficient'), he or she will be allowed to lodge an 'individual appeal' and thus directly challenge the law or regulation before the Constitutional Court.[38] It is no surprise, therefore, that individual appeals are rare – and cases where the Court admits such appeals even rarer.

Compared to other systems, the Austrian model lacks an important gateway to constitutional review. It is not normally possible to challenge a court's judgement before the Constitutional Court even if the judgment violates a fundamental right. Since 1992, a specific kind of appeal ('*Grundrechtsbeschwerde*') may be lodged at the Supreme Court (*Oberster Gerichtshof*), if an ordinary court's decision interferes with the right of personal liberty.[39] Neither with regard to personal liberty nor with regard to other fundamental rights that might be violated by an ordinary court, including the Supreme Court, does the Constitutional Court have any jurisdiction.

This question has been discussed for some time, however, and the constitutional reform draft of 2007[40] indeed proposed a change: if an ordinary court does not challenge a law or regulation before the Constitutional Court (as it ought to do under the present system if doubting the constitutionality of a norm that it applies), a concerned party may do so, provided that a violation of constitutionally guaranteed rights is at stake and that the case is pending before an ordinary court of last instance. Whilst this proposal was not enacted, however, a new art. 144a was inserted into the B-VG[41] according to which the Constitutional Court may indeed scrutinize decisions of the new Asylum Court (since 1 July

---

[38] Cf., with examples, most recently, Walter, Mayer and Kucsko-Stadlmayer 'Grundriss' supra at 19 at 519 f.

[39] BGBl 1992/864.

[40] See *Entwurf eines Bundesverfassungsgesetzes, mit dem das Bundes-Verfassungsgesetz geändert und ein Erstes Bundesverfassungsrechtsbereinigungsgesetz erlassen wird* (issued 23 July 2007 by the Federal Chancellery, www.austria.gv.at).

[41] BGBl I 2008/2.

2008) analogously to art. 144 B-VG, i.e. if constitutionally guaranteed rights were violated or if any subjective rights were violated by the application of an illegal general norm. Although the Asylum Court is not an ordinary court, it is remarkable that the Constitutional Court may thus for the first time scrutinize decisions taken by a court.

THE CONSTITUTIONAL COURT'S RELATIONSHIP WITH OTHER JUDICIAL BODIES

As yet no administrative courts exist in Austria, apart from the new Asylum Court (*Asylgerichtshof*) and the Administrative Court (*Verwaltungsgerichtshof*) in Vienna, which latter, together with the Supreme Court and the Constitutional Court, forms the triad of 'Austrian supreme courts'. Other judicial bodies are the ordinary courts (including the Supreme Court at the top of the ordinary court hierarchy) and the independent tribunals under art. 6 ECHR.

The Constitutional Court had some difficulty accepting the broad interpretation of 'judicial bodies' given by the Strasbourg Court under art. 6 ECHR. On several occasions, the European Court of Human Rights stated that the traditional Austrian dualism of ordinary courts and administrative bodies was not sufficient in a number of cases where an independent tribunal should have decided instead of an instruction-bound administrative authority. The Constitutional Court held that an extensive construction of art. 6 ECHR – that was not predictable when Austria ratified the ECHR – *could* amount to a total revision of the Austrian Federal Constitution (by modifying the prevailing organisation of state authorities) and would therefore possibly have required a referendum.[42] The Court did not, however, go as far as to acknowledge that such a total revision had indeed taken place. As a consequence, a federal constitutional amendment[43] (without referendum, though) was passed, establishing the Independent Administrative Senates which are tribunals under art. 6 ECHR. Other tribunals have since been established as well. Moreover, art. 133 no. 4 B-VG provides for the creation of collegial bodies with at least one judge amongst their members. Again, the Constitutional Court had problems in accepting an unlimited introduction of such collegial boards that cannot be bound by any instructions of the supreme administrative bodies,[44] and it is at least doubtful how the Court will handle the recent

---

[42] VfSlg 11.500/1987.
[43] BGBl 1988/685.
[44] VfSlg 11.500/1987; 15.427/1999; 15.886/2000; 16.048/2000; 16.189/2001; Grabenwarter C (1999) 'Art. 133 B-VG' in Korinek K and Holoubek M (eds) (1999) *Österreichisches*

constitutional amendment[45] according to which ordinary law may establish a wide range of administrative authorities that cannot be bound by instructions. All these independent bodies that would replace the present administrative structures would also have an impact on the principle of democracy where the supreme administrative bodies (government as a whole and its individual members) are entitled to give instructions to the lower administrative bodies, being, however, themselves supervised by various instruments of parliamentary control. The enhanced introduction of independent bodies would affect the rigid separation of powers and democratically legitimized system of administration as designed by the constitutional framers and would have a major impact on the very structure of state organization.

The relationship between the three 'Supreme Austrian Courts' raises no particular problems, since the Federal Constitution precisely determines the different functions of each court.[46] There is just one sector of constitutional adjudication that seems to entangle both the Constitutional and Administrative Court's functions. It is normally for the Administrative Court to decide on the illegality of administrative rulings after the exhaustion of all channels of intra-administrative control. Any person who feels his or her rights have been violated, as *guaranteed by ordinary laws* (e.g. neighbour rights), may lodge an appeal before the Administrative Court under art. 131 para 1 no. 1 B-VG. An appeal to the Constitutional Court is the correct remedy, however, if the person feels a *constitutionally guaranteed* right has been violated even though the violation was caused by an administrative ruling (art. 144 para 1 B-VG). In this case, the Constitutional Court serves also as a judicial body with regard to administrative rulings.

THE CONSTITUTIONAL COURT'S RELATIONSHIP WITH OTHER STATE ORGANS

The Federal Constitution provides a separation of powers between the legislative, administrative and judicial power. In principle, therefore, the Constitutional Court's relationship with other state organs does not create particular problems, due to the clear division of functions among the various bodies and the powers they exercise. In practice, however, tensions

---

Bundesverfassungsrecht Springer.

[45] BGBl I 2008/2.

[46] Another species of administrative court was introduced in 2008: The Asylum Court is no supreme judicial body, though, since its decisions can be challenged before the Constitutional Court and, in certain fundamental cases, before the Administrative Court. For further detail, see the articles in the special issue of the *Journal für Rechtspolitik* (2008).

may arise from time to time, putting into question the very role of the Court as the guarantor of the rule of law.

One arena of potential conflicts concerns the relationship between the Constitutional Court and the federal constitutional legislature, and especially so in times when the Federal Government commands a two-third majority in the National Council, which is required for federal constitutional amendments (art. 44 para 1 B-VG). Such a majority means that constitutional amendments may be passed easily by the Parliament, and this was done particularly in the end-1980s, 1990s and between 2007 and 2008, when strong coalition-governments were in power. As a consequence, Parliament adopted a number of constitutional laws and provisions even when they violated fundamental rights (for example, the principle of equality, the right of gainful acquisition, etc.). Sometimes, federal constitutional legislation was even adopted with a clear intention of violating fundamental rights, if this was deemed necessary for political reasons. In addition to these cases of *ex-ante* abuse of constitutional law, there were even cases when, after the Constitutional Court had struck down an ordinary law on account of a violation of fundamental rights, Parliament enacted exactly the same law as an *ex-post* constitutional law, clearly in order to immunise it against being struck down a second time. This incited the Constitutional Court to affirm that repeated avoidance of the Court's jurisdiction by enacting (substantively) unconstitutional laws as (formally) constitutional laws could amount to a total revision and be struck down by the Court on account of the missing referendum required for a total revision.[47]

The Court has never put its threat into practice yet (which may also be due to the fact that there has been no governmental two-third majority in the National Council in recent years, except for the brief period of 2007-2008[48]), but this option was fervently discussed among scholars.[49] The central question was whether the Constitutional Court should be regarded

---

[47] VfSlg 11.756/1988; 11.757/1988; 11.758/1988; 11.829/1988; 11.916/1988; 11.918/1988; 11.927/1988; 11.972/1989; 15.373/1998; 15.887/2000; 15.938/2000; 16.327/2001.

[48] During this period cf., e.g., the *Pflege-Verfassungsgesetz* (BGBl I 2008/43).

[49] See, e.g., Rill, HP and Schäffer, H (2001) 'Art. 44 B-VG' in Rill, HP and Schäffer, H (eds) (2001) *Bundesverfassungsrecht* Verlag Österreich; Hiesel, M (1995) *Verfassungsgesetzgeber und Verfassungsgerichtshof* Manz; Barfuß, W (1997) Grenzen der Verfassungsänderung: Baugesetze – Grundrechte – Neukodifikation, *13. ÖJT I/1*; Pernthaler, P (1998) *Der Verfassungskern* Manz at 70 ff; Gamper, A (2000) *Die verfassungsrechtliche Grundordnung als Rechtsproblem* Verlag Österreich at 39 ff; Janko, A (2004) *Gesamtänderung der Bundesverfassung* Verlag Österreich at 313; Gamper 'Rolle' supra at 20 at 537; Wiederin, E (2006) 'Gesamtänderung, Totalrevision und Verfassunggebung' in Akyürek, M, Baumgartner, G, Jahnel, D, Lienbacher, G and Stolzlechner, H (eds) (2006) *Staat und Recht in europäischer Perspektive – Festschrift Heinz Schäffer* Manz 961.

as the ultimate protector of the Federal Constitution or whether Parliament should have the last word since it represents the sovereign people.

In one of the most spectacular cases of recent years,[50] the Constitutional Court *obiter* remarked that it did not now have to answer the question whether a "suspension" of the Federal Constitution could be legitimate, even after a referendum according to Art 44 para 3 B-VG took place. Without excluding the possibility of sanctioning illegitimate violations of the constitution (that could not even be legitimized by a referendum and would therefore go beyond a 'total revision of the Federal Constitution' as mentioned in Art 44 para 3 B-VG), the Court has nevertheless given no clear signal in either direction.

On a more political level, the last Presidents of the Constitutional Court were not reluctant to publicly criticise governmental policies where these policies, according to their opinion, massively infringed fundamental rights.[51] Such presidential appeals are regularly published via the media and have recently concerned issues such as data protection or refugee and asylum questions. Despite the political character of these appeals, they succeed in triggering off a discussion on the value of rights protection which seems of paramount importance at a time where liberty is at stake for the purposes of enhanced security.

Another recent example which led to political tensions arising from the Court's case-law concerns the behaviour of the late Governor of the *Land* Carinthia (*Jörg Haider*, who died in 2008) who doggedly declined to conform to several judgments that would have required him to accept bilingual (German and Slovenian) place-name signs in a number of Carinthian municipalities. The Constitutional Court interpreted art. 7 of the Vienna State Treaty to the effect that "mixed" municipalities with at least 10 % Slovene population are entitled to bilingual signs.[52] The Governor opposed these signs for years with the Court in the meantime pronouncing the same verdict in a couple of further cases.[53] The topic became a troublesome and embarrassing matter on the political agenda of a number of supreme bodies, including the Federal Parliament, the Federal President and the Federal Government, since in principle the Federal Constitution would

---

[50] VfSlg 16.327/2001.
[51] See, e.g., the speech delivered by the present President of the Constitutional Court, *Gerhart Holzinger*, on the occasion of the *Verfassungstag 2008* (1 October 2008), who severely criticized the new constitutional provisions on the Asylum Court.
[52] VfSlg 16.404/2001.
[53] See VfSlg 17.723/2005; 17.733/2005; 17.895/2006; 18.024/2006; 18.025/2006; 18.044/2006; VfGH 12 Dec 2007, V 8/07; 18 June 2008, V 310-311/08, 329-331/08.

allow for several legal solutions, but none of them was apparently possible for political reasons.[54]

In spite of the aforementioned problems, the Court's judgments are in general accepted and enforced, and if they are criticised politically this is mostly done with caution. The Court's adjudication is perhaps rather more centralist than federalist,[55] but this is also due to the rather centralistic concept of the Austrian Federal Constitution and to the extremely fragmented division of powers which in practice has a centripetal effect.[56]

CONCLUDING REMARKS

The Austrian Constitutional Court deals with between 2000 and 3000 (in 2007: 2565) cases a year. Nevertheless, the average time for passing a judgment is limited to nine months, which means that the Court is a rather efficient institution. Most of the decisions, with an increasing number from year to year,[57] relate to administrative rulings (art. 144 B-VG; in 2007, 2205 such cases were disposed of, while 1170 cases were pending at the end of the year), followed by the scrutiny of laws (art. 140 B-VG; in 2007, 233 such cases were disposed of, while 101 cases were pending at the end of the year), and general regulations (art. 139 B-VG; in 2007, 99 such cases were disposed of, while 50 cases were pending at the end of the year).[58] Apart from the quantity of decisions, however, an evaluation of the Constitutional Court's adjudication must not neglect the functional and qualitative aspect of the Court's work: there is no doubt that the B-VG has established a fully-fledged constitutional court that exercises a wide range of functions – wider perhaps than in many other countries discussed in this

---

[54] Cf. in detail also Adamovich, L (2006) 'Verfassungsrecht und Minderheitenschutz' in Amt der Kärntner Landesregierung (ed) (2006) *Die Ortstafelfrage aus Expertensicht* Verlag Land Kärnten 9 ff; Jabloner, C (2006) 'Am Rande des Rechtsstaats' *Zeitschrift für Verwaltung* 429; see also Walter, Mayer and Kucsko-Stadlmayer 'Grundriss' supra at 19 at 564 f.
[55] For example, there is just one case (VfGH 8 March 2007, V 17/06) where the Constitutional Court applied the „principle of mutual consideration", which requires both the federal government and the *Länder* to consider the aims of each other's legislation, in favor of the *Länder*, whilst in all other cases the federal government benefited from the application of the principle.
[56] With varying views: Ermacora, F (1976) *Österreichischer Föderalismus* Braumüller at 122 f; Pernthaler, P (2004) *Österreichisches Bundesstaatsrecht* Verlag Österreich at 332 ff; Schäffer, H (1998) 'Die Kompetenzverteilung im Bundesstaat' in Schambeck, H (ed) (1998) *Bundesstaat und Bundesrat in Österreich* Verlag Österreich 65 at 75; Öhlinger, T (2007) *Verfassungsrecht* (7th ed) Facultas WUV at 138.
[57] The number is likely to increase even more strongly, given the situation that many appeals against the Asylum Court's decisions are lodged at the Constitutional Court many of them even without having an obvious chance to succeed.
[58] See http://www.vfgh.gv.at/cms/vfgh-site/attachments/8/0/9/CH0011/CMS1207730706100/taetigkeitsbericht _2007.pdf.

book, although a general power of pre-legislative control is lacking as well as the power to scrutinize decisions of the ordinary courts. As to individual appeals, the Austrian system of constitutional adjudication provides for a comparatively limited access to the Court, although more gateways have been provided since 1920 when the B-VG was adopted.

The quality of the Court's legal reasoning is, even though not perfect, on the whole satisfactory and sometimes the arguments follow an almost scholarly approach – not surprisingly, since many justices are constitutional law professors which also alleviates the effects of 'political' appointment of justices that is based on proposals of the Federal Government, the National Council and the Federal Council respectively. Nevertheless, legal commentators are always prone to discuss individual decisions critically. In some cases, especially relating to human rights, the Court tends to adopt a proactive and extensive interpretation and in fact approaches what is called an 'open development of law'. Improved underpinning of decisions through more extensive legal reasoning would also be required in some of the Court's *obiter dicta*.

In the final analysis we would argue that viewed from the standpoint of the courts' compliance with its functions, including both the general traceability of decisions and the large through put of cases, there must be a clearly positive evaluation of the courts role. Moreover, one particularly commendable feature is the open-mindedness with which the Court ventured into the judicial dialogue with the European Courts in Strasbourg and Luxemburg.[59] Being the first constitutional court that asked the European Court of Justice for a preliminary ruling, it paved a way that was subsequently followed by several other national constitutional courts. Such an open-minded approach could give the Austrian Constitutional Court a new model function with regard to the next era in European constitutionalism, similar to the pivotal role played in the early stages of judicial review.

---

[59]   Schäffer 'Österreich' supra at 8 at 371.

Constitutional Courts of Central and Eastern Europe: Between Adolescence and Maturity

KASIA LACH* AND WOJCIECH SADURSKI**

Almost 20 years after the establishment of constitutional courts in Central and Eastern Europe (CEE), the time is ripe for assessing CEE constitutional adjudication and reflecting upon its continued relevance. The article attempts to achieve two goals. Firstly, it provides a comparative overview of the constitutional adjudication in seven Central Eastern European countries: the Czech Republic, Hungary, Poland, Slovakia, Slovenia, Bulgaria and Romania. All these countries have experienced a regime change in the late 1980s and the early 1990s and all of them have transformed their economic and legal systems pursuant to the EU accession negotiations. Secondly, the article goes beyond the comparative paradigm and asks the question about the current relevance of constitutional adjudication. If the constitutional courts were established in order to facilitate transition from an authoritarian regime to democracy what is their current role in the seemingly stable setting of a region which is well anchored in European structures?

It is claimed that constitutional courts are as much needed now as they have ever been. In the domestic sphere they are of utmost importance in the face of the recent political instability or "backsliding" of the region. In the external, European setting, with the accession to the European Union the constitutional courts have become European courts, which through their interpretation of the Constitution participate in the process of shaping the

* At the time of writing, a doctoral candidate at the University of Melbourne, and Research Assistant at the European University Institute, Florence.
** Professor in the Department of Law, European University Institute, Florence, and in the Faculty of Law, University of Sydney.

course and setting the pace of European legal integration. And yet, those who argue for the ongoing relevance and importance of the Courts do not supersede the need to address, especially, by the Courts themselves, the fundamental challenges to their political legitimacy in a system based on the centrality of democratically elected and electorally responsive institutions.

INTRODUCTION, OR ARE THE HEY-DAYS OVER?

The collapse of the communist regimes in Central Eastern Europe brought about the need to establish new constitutional foundations for the emerging democracies, and constitution makers faced many questions concerning constitutional design. Some answers proved to be more problematic, others more obvious. The issue of constitutional review definitely fell into the latter category and soon constitutional courts became a permanent and uncontroversial element of the political and legal landscape of Central Eastern Europe. In fact, the dominant slogan of the period of designing the institutions and constitutions right after the fall of Communism was 'No experiments!', and the associated slogan of the 'Return to normalcy' assumed, perhaps largely in a question-begging way, that a 'normal' democratic system incorporates a concentrated, centralised and abstract judicial review best exemplified by German, Italian, Spanish and other (but not all) continental European constitutional courts.

The first years post-1989 have shown that the constitutional courts not merely *were* there; they also proved to be effective in their interventions in the choices and actions of political branches of government, in particular, the executive and the legislature. While overseeing elections and referendums, deciding upon the issues concerning the existence of political parties, or adjudicating on competence conflicts between state institutions have been important aspects of the courts' activity, the competence to review enacted legislative acts proved to be the most crucial of them all. The courts[1] decided on constitutionality of statutes concerning matters ranging from economic[2]

---

[1] Note that any reference to 'courts' in the text refers to constitutional courts, unless otherwise specified.

[2] For example, the Hungarian Constitutional Court struck down important aspects of a number of laws which were meant to constitute a package of austerity measures introduced by the Government in 1995; see Decision 43/1995 of 30 June 1995 on social security benefits, reprinted in Sólyom, L and Brunner, G (2000) *Constitutional Judiciary in a New Democracy: The Hungarian Constitutional Court* University Michigan Press at 214-28.

and social policy[3] to past injustices,[4] communist political crimes[5] or public morality.[6]

The extent of the influence exerted by the constitutional courts inevitably raises the vexed question of their legitimacy.[7] After all, the courts are regarded as promoters and protectors of democratic values, and are not the most democratic institutions themselves, if the democratic nature of an institution is measured by its electoral mandate and direct accountability towards the electors. The legitimacy of the constitutional courts is derivative; the constitutional court judges are appointed by a directly elected parliament, the president or, in some cases, both. Accountability (at least, as measured by revocability from office) is even less pronounced: the terms of office of constitutional judges are usually much longer than those of the members of parliament or presidents. Further, the visibility of individual judges' actions to the general public is much lower. Consequently, constitutional courts' authority to have a final say over the legislative choices of parliamentary majorities might cast some doubts about the very concept of constitutional review.

In the initial period of the courts' functioning a convenient explanation of the legitimacy conundrum was the claim that there existed a transitional character to the legal and political environment in which the courts operated. As the argument went, in the period of dramatic transformation from an authoritarian to a democratic system, ordinary intuitions concerning the role of adjudication might need to be modified.[8] This conviction,

---

[3] For example, the Polish Constitutional Tribunal ruled on 17 July 1996 that a 1995 law suspending the indexation of pensions in the fourth quarter of 1996 was unconstitutional; see Decision K. 8/96 in *Orzecznictwo Trybunału Konstytucyjnego, Rok 1996* [*Case Law of the Constitutional Tribunal, Year 1996*] (1998) vol. 2, C.H. Beck, at 46-65.

[4] For more on the matter see for example: Halmai, G and Scheppele KL (1997) 'Living Well Is the Best Revenge: The Hungarian Approach to Judging the Past' in Mc Adams, AJ (ed) *Transitional Justice and the Rule of Law in New Democracies* University of Notre Dame Press, 155 at 177-8; Teitel, R (1994) 'Post-Communist Constitutionalism: A Transitional Perspective' (26) *Columbia Human Rights Law Review* 167 at 180-2.

[5] For example, in a Decision 11/1992 of 5 March 1992 the Hungarian Constitutional Court struck down *An Act Concerning the Right to Prosecute Serious Criminal Offences committed between 21 December 1944 and 2 May 1990 that Had Not Been Prosecuted for Political Reasons of 4 November 1991*. In Sólyom and Bruner above n. 3, at 214-228.

[6] For example, Decision of the Polish Constitutional Tribunal of 28 May 1997, no. K. 26/96 reprinted in (1999) (6) *East European Case Reporter of Constitutional Law* , 38-129.

[7] Sadurski, W (2002) 'Legitimacy and Reasons of Constitutional Review after Communism' in Sadurski, W (ed) *Constitutional Justice, East and West. Democratic Legitimacy and Constitutional Courts in Post-Communist Europe in a Comparative Perspective* Kluwer Law International 163-187.

[8] Teitel, R (1997) 'Transitional Jurisprudence: The Role of Law in Political Transformation' (196) *Yale Law Journal* 2009 at 2034.

although not universally accepted by all commentators,[9] certainly had some explanatory value as to the sudden rise and success of constitutional adjudication combined with a relative absence of critical reflection about legitimacy of this institutional system.

Yet, almost 20 years after the rapid emergence and consolidation of constitutional review in Central Eastern Europe, there is growing ambivalence towards the role played by the constitutional courts. While the critical voices are not as strong as those heard in the US,[10] some degree of constructive scepticism urging a critical evaluation of the role of constitutional courts is nevertheless present.[11]

One argument that might be advanced against the activism of the constitutional courts is that the transformation period is over. The countries of CEE are integrated within European structures be it the European Union or the Council of Europe and in the times of stability and economic prosperity the courts ought not to enjoy as extensive a mandate as they did during the transformation period. In other words, this line of argumentation is premised on the assumption that democracy in the region is robust enough to do without excessively powerful constitutional courts.

Yet, this claim holds only as long as one accepts the story of a completed and successful transformation. Recent political developments in the region cast doubt on the seemingly good condition of democracy in Central Eastern Europe. There is a growing conviction that things in the region have not been going as smoothly as many have thought. Some authors talk about the 'backsliding' of the CEE countries. The relapse has taken place since the accession of these states to the European Union in 2004 and 2007[12] and it is explained in terms of the post-transitional and post-accession backlash against a liberal-democratic policy consensus of the post-1989-period.[13] The enthusiasm generated by the events of 1989 and the accession negotiations brought about a tacit agreement among political parties and various social

---

[9] For example see Holmes, S (1993) 'Back to the Drawing Board' 2 *East European Constitutional Review* no. 1, 21-5; Sajó, A (1995) 'Reading the Invisible Constitution: Judicial Review in Hungary' (15) *Oxford Journal of Legal Studies* 253-67; Sadurski, W (2002) 'Constitutional Justice, East and West: Introduction' in Sadurski, W (ed) *Constitutional Justice, East and West. Democratic Legitimacy and Constitutional Courts in Post-Communist Europe in a Comparative Perspective* Kluwer Law International 1 at 14.

[10] See for example: Tushnet, M (1999) *Taking the Constitution Away from the Courts*, Princeton University Press, 1999; Sunstein, S (1999) *One Case at a Time: Judicial Minimalism of the Supreme Court* Harvard University Press

[11] Sadurski, above n 9, 1-18.

[12] Mungiu-Pippidi, M (2007) 'EU Accession is No "End of History"' (18) *Journal of Democracy*, 8 at 14; Rupnik, J (2007) 'From Democracy Fatigue to Populist Backlash' (18) *Journal of Democracy* 18 at 18.

[13] Rupnik, ibid at 20; Krastev, I (2007) 'The Strange Death of the Liberal Consensus' (18) *Journal of Democracy* 57 at 60.

groups – every significant political player in these countries was on best behaviour in order not to hamper the CCE countries prospects of joining the EU. However, almost immediately after the goal was achieved the earlier discipline has disappeared and tensions have erupted with a great force. The rise of populist parties, violent street demonstrations, radicalisation of both sides of the political spectrum, serious conflicts between branches of the government, the growing gap between the elites and 'the people', all these features exemplify a 'backsliding' of the region.[14]

The backlash against the elements of the post-1989 consensus also concerns the issue of institutional design and certain institutions, the existence of which has been taken for granted. This tendency affects, among others, the constitutional courts.[15] On the one hand, the very nature of the constitutional court as seemingly politically neutral institution is put under question; there is a growing understanding that courts' pronouncements might seriously impact upon policy choices. On the other hand, in situations where the constitutional courts are called upon to adjudicate on controversial aspects of day-to-day politics, they are under increasing pressure to decide according to preferences of the governing parliamentary majority; an unfavourable decision might result in a legislative attempt to curtail the role of courts. The recent decision of the Polish Constitutional Tribunal in the *Lustration Case* (discussed below, in the text corresponding to footnotes 101-102) illustrates this problem well. Thus, although criticism towards too great a role accorded to constitutional courts might be well founded in stable settings, constitutional courts seem to be indispensable guarantors of democratic values and, more broadly, constitutionally enshrined principles while the new CEE democracies face some populist or authoritarian tendencies.

Further, the accession of the CCE countries to the European Union has created a totally new sphere of the courts' activity. The constitutional courts have become European courts, which not merely apply European law but also, as the guardians of the respective national constitutions, have been vested with the role of telling the constitutional story of European legal integration. The supranational account is well known; it has been created and reiterated by the European Court of Justice. It amounts to the conceptualisation of the relationship between the Community law and national laws based on the unconditional primacy of the Community legal order. The Courts in the region readily assumed the new role. By vigorously putting forward their own interpretation of the relationship between the

---

[14] Ibid.
[15] Rupnik includes in this category also the central banks the boards supervising public media. Rupnik, above n 13, at 19.

two legal systems they engaged in the process of shaping the course and setting the pace of European legal integration.

The article will outline these developments. First, we will discuss the circumstances surrounding the establishment of constitutional courts in the region, and in particular, the reasons behind setting up the system of constitutional justice. Then, we will briefly describe the dominant model of constitutional adjudication and departures from it, addressing issues such as the scope of constitutional courts' jurisdiction, the type of exercised control (*ex ante* or *ex post*), the accessibility to judicial review, and the procedures of the selection of constitutional judges. Next, we are going to identify the main patterns of the relationship between constitutional courts and other branches of the government for the reason that, as we believe, constitutional court's success or failure depend as much on legal design as on the political culture in which a court operates. Finally, we will analyse how Central and Eastern European constitutional courts have responded to the new legal environment resulting from the accession of their respective countries to the European Union and, especially, how the courts have approached their new role as European courts.

The limited scope of analysis forced us to make a careful selection of cases. Speaking of Central Eastern European constitutional courts we refer to the courts of seven CEE countries, as mentioned at the beginning of this article. These courts share many common futures. They operate in similar legal and political environment: all of these countries experienced regime change in the late 1980s and the early 1990s, embarked on economic and legal transformation and, eventually, all of them acceded to the European Union. Also, all of these constitutional courts are similar in terms of their institutional design. Yet, as the following analysis will show, the experiences of individual constitutional courts differ considerably.

THE REASONS FOR HAVING OR SETTING UP A CONSTITUTIONAL COURT

The modern constitutional review in Central Eastern Europe dates back to the regime transformation of the late 1980s and the early 1990s.[16] The only two countries where a constitutional body was in place before the velvet revolution were Yugoslavia, since 1963, and Poland, since 1985. Other states of the region introduced constitutional review only after

[16] There is also a brief episode of pre-World War Two constitutional review in the region but it has not played any role even in the justificatory myths created for the purpose of reinforcing the legitimacy of these courts.

57

1989, beginning with Hungary[17] that was followed by Czechoslovakia,[18] Bulgaria,[19] Romania[20] and Slovenia.[21]

As much as the sequence of establishing constitutional courts is unproblematic, the answer to the question why the courts were set up in the first place proves to be more challenging. Recalling the constitutional discourse in the first years after Communism it is striking that a constitutional court was such an obvious institutional element of the newly designed democratic systems that the need to set it up was neither seriously debated nor questioned. Sólyom remarks: 'the very existence of these courts obviously served as a 'trade mark', or as a proof, of the democratic character of the respective country'.[22] Equally under-theorised was the choice of the specific model of constitutional review. Consequently, when discussing the beginnings of the constitutional justice in the region one should be careful not to take arguments that justify ex-post the creation and continuous existence of the present model for arguments that explain its emergence.

The establishing of constitutional review was a clear case of institutional borrowing. The CEE courts followed the European model of constitutional review as initially proposed by Kelsen, first embodied in the Austrian *Verfassungsgerichtshof*, and currently best exemplified by German *Bundesverfassungsgericht*. Yet, one might legitimately ask why the countries opted for the European model of centralised and abstract review as opposed to the US-style of concrete review? Surely, the geographic proximity might have inclined the political elites to look up to Germany

---

[17] The Constitution Amendment was introduced on 23 October 1989 and the Court started to operate on 1 January 1990. Halmai, G (2002) 'The Hungarian Approach to Constitutional Review: The End of Activism? The First Decade of the Hungarian Constitutional Court' in Sadurski, W (ed) *Constitutional Justice, East and West. Democratic Legitimacy and Constitutional Courts in Post-Communist Europe in a Comparative Perspective* Kluwer Law International 189 at 191.

[18] A statute providing for a Federal Constitutional Court was enacted on 1 April 1991 but it was not until January 1992 when the Court started to work. Přibáň, J (2002) 'Judicial Power vs. Democratic Representation: The Culture of Constitutionalism and Human Rights in the Czech Legal System' in Sadurski, W (ed) *Constitutional Justice, East and West. Democratic Legitimacy and Constitutional Courts in Post-Communist Europe in a Comparative Perspective* Kluwer Law International 372 at 374.

[19] A Constitutional Court Act was passed on 16 August 1991 and the Constitutional Court was constituted on October 3, 1991. Available at: < http://www.constcourt.bg/ks_eng_frame. htm> visited on 13 June 2007

[20] This Constitutional Court of Romania was established in June 1992. Available at: <http:// www.ccr.ro/default.aspx?lang=EN>

[21] The Constitution of the Republic of Slovenia was adopted on 23 December 1991. <http:// www.concourt.sk/A/a_index.htm>

[22] Sólyom L (2003) 'The Role of Constitutional Courts in the Transition to Democracy: With Special Reference to Hungary' (18) *International Sociology* 133 at134.

or Italy rather than the US, but the allure of everything American-made and the strong presence of American constitutional experts at the time of deciding constitutional design, renders the explanation based on simple geographic determinism less than convincing. The literature on the subject offers a number of explanations as to why constitutional courts have been set up and why the European/continental type of constitutional review has been adopted by the CEE countries. Let us consider them briefly.

The most often repeated explanations views the emergence of constitutional courts as a direct consequence of the fact that a country has just emerged from the period of the authoritarian rule. Constitutional courts of CEE are portrayed as the third generation of post-authoritarian constitutional courts, which necessarily had to follow the path taken previously by the first (Germany and Italy) and the second (Spain and Portugal) wave of constitutional justice.[23] Consequently, arguments that might explain the emergency and the model of constitutional review adopted in Western and Southern Europe are extrapolated into CEE constitutional settings. As one such claim goes, constitutional courts were to remedy the fact that authoritarian regimes left compromised judiciaries that could not take on the task of guarding constitutional values of the newly created democratic order. This claim, whilst having a grain of truth, cannot be regarded as the most accurate description of the post-Communist reality of CEE. It would be neither just to describe the ordinary judges as obedient servants of the communist authorities, nor would it be correct to portray the constitutional courts as exclusively consisting of individuals untainted by associations with the former regime.

More convincing is the aspect of the comparison between Western and Southern on one hand, and the CEE constitutional courts on the other that points to the element of the institutional novelty that the constitutional courts brought. Even if this observation needs to be immediately qualified by mentioning the Polish and ex-Yugoslavian courts, the claim that new constitutional forums created a symbolic break from past political arrangements cannot be rejected.[24]

Another explanation advanced in the constitutional literature is the process of European integration. It is claimed that the countries of CEE wanted to meet democratic criteria for the accession to the European Community, by adopting a 'European' model of judicial review, which granted constitutional courts a strong position vis-à-vis the legislative power.[25] The claim is however unfounded; there is no evidence of such

---

[23] Ibid.
[24] Teitel, above n 8, at 2032.
[25] Ackerman, B (1997) 'The Rise of World Constitutionalism' (83) *Virginia Law Review* 771

demands voiced on the part of the European Community/European Union. Further, even a more diluted assertion that the prospect of applying for the membership in the European Union might have induced the constitution makers to set up constitutional courts[26] seems to be highly improbable and this is so at least for two reasons. Firstly, although after the fall of Communism the mantra of the return to Europe was often repeated, the actual accession to the European Communities was still beyond the wildest dreams of the political elites from the region. Most of the constitutional courts were set up at the beginning of the 1990s, that is, well before serious talks about a possible membership begun. Further, the idea that prospective members have to meet certain democratic standards was first put forward only during the 1993 Copenhagen European Council.[27] Consequently, although the link between the establishment of constitutional review and the prospective membership in the EU seems to be quite plausible from the perspective of 2008, it is nothing more than an educated (and wrong) guess, if considered in the light of the early 1990s.

Incidentally, when it comes to a question concerning the external encouragement for setting up a constitutional court coming from European institutions it is more plausible that the idea was supported by the Council of Europe. Laszlo Sólyom writes that the Council 'had been aware of the impact of constitutional courts on democratic development, and clearly encouraged their establishment'.[28] As he claims, during the accession negotiations 'the existence of a constitutional court has been a particularly important point and the Council scrutinized the conditions of constitutional review'.[29]

Another reason for establishing constitutional courts often advanced by constitutional scholars is the belief that constitutional courts were regarded as necessary to counterbalance majoritarian institutions, in particular, parliaments. However, whereas the subsequent functioning of the constitutional courts in the region clearly indicates that the courts have been often effectively fulfilling this role, it was hardly the main concern at the time of the constitutional courts' creation. During the communist

---

at 776.

[26] Procházka, R (2002) *Mission Accomplished. On Founding Constitutional Adjudication in Central Europe* Central European University Press 17-20.

[27] 'Membership requires that the candidate country has achieved stability of institutions guaranteeing democracy, the rule of law, human rights and respect for and protection of minorities, the existence of a functioning market economy as well as the capacity to cope with competitive pressure and market forces
within the Union'. *Presidency Conclusions,* Copenhagen European Council - 21-22 June 1993, available at: <http://ue.eu.int/ueDocs/cms_Data/docs/pressdata/en/ec/72921.pdf>

[28] Sólyom, above n 22, at 134.

[29] Id at 153.

period the real holder of the power was the Communist Party and not the parliament. After the fall of communism, a dominant vision of democracy was an unadulterated majoritarian conception. It is not very likely that drafters of the constitutions necessary thought in counter-majoritarian terms.

The counter-majoritarian argument should not be equated with the limited faith in the will of politicians to protect constitutional values. Limited trust in political institutions was certainly one of the main reasons for establishing constitutional courts.[30] In the context of a very weak political and constitutional culture, there was a general distrust in the virtues of the 'new-old' political class. People were as suspicious of the former communist apparatchiks who remained in power, as they doubted the skills of the communist oppositionists or the motives of the emerging political elites.[31]

MODEL OF CONSTITUTIONAL REVIEW

The type and scope of competences of a constitutional court result from the historical context and political settings in which the court operates. Yet, even if there are some divergences among the CEE constitutional courts, it is possible to define a common Central Eastern European model of constitutional adjudication. Constitutional review is "concentrated" or "centralised", which means that it is conducted by a specialised court or tribunal[32] composed of judges appointed for a limited period of time by the political branches of the government. The courts typically exercise abstract, *ex post* and final review of the constitutionality of statutes and other infra-constitutional acts. Further, constitutional review in the CEE countries might be characterised by a broad range of actors authorised to commence the proceeding and, in particular, by a special role accorded to individuals through the constitutional complaint procedure. Unavoidably while comparing seven countries one will encounter some specific features that depart from the general model. In this section, these variations will be briefly discussed.

The constitutional courts enjoy the right to carry out an abstract judicial review, that is, they can adjudicate on the constitutionality of a legislative act without a need for a specific case or a controversy to arise. The abstract norm control is a predominant way of exercising constitutional justice.

---

[30] Sadurski, above n 7, at 186.
[31] Ibid.
[32] The only exception is Estonia where constitutional review is carried out by a special chamber of the Supreme Court, known as the Chamber of Constitutional Control.

The courts also have the power to exercise concrete review, namely, if an ordinary court while deciding a case is faced with a doubt concerning constitutionality of a norm that it is going to apply, the court is obliged to stay the proceedings and to submit a question to the constitutional court. Further, in some countries concrete norm control might be curtailed by a limitation upon subjects that are authorised to bring the question before the constitutional court. For example, in Bulgaria concrete review can be initiated only by the Supreme Court of Cassation, or the Supreme Administrative Court.[33]

As already noted, the dominant model of constitutional review in the region is the *ex post* control, that is, a control of constitutionality of enacted legal acts. Some constitutions also provide for a limited *ex ante* review – a form of control that might be instigated after a given act has been passed by the Parliament but before it has been promulgated.[34] Additionally, in Hungary and Poland, the President of the Republic, before signing the legislative act in question, can ask the Court to conduct an *ex ante* review. Further, the Courts typically also have jurisdiction to review statutes providing for ratification of international treaties.[35]

Another aspect of constitutional adjudication design that varies from country to country is the identification of actors who can commence the proceedings before the constitutional court. Abstract review is typically initiated by the president,[36] the government or prime minister.[37] Many constitutions grant the power to instigate the proceedings to groups of parliamentarians which are defined either as a certain minimal number of deputies or as a fraction of their total number. Also, in some countries abstract review can be initiated by the Prosecutor General,[38] the Ombudsman,[39] a Supreme Court,[40] or central audit institutions.[41] Finally, there are various other bodies that might be vested with the power of initiative, for example, local governments[42] or trade unions.[43]

---

[33] Article 150 (2) of the *Constitution of the Republic of Bulgaria.*
[34] For example, in Romania.
[35] For example in Bulgaria, Hungary, Poland, Slovenia, and Romania.
[36] The exception is Romania where the President can only initiate preventative control of statutes.
[37] The exception is the Czech Republic where the government can initiate review of only sub-statutory laws.
[38] For example, Bulgaria, Poland and Slovakia.
[39] For example, in Poland,
[40] For example, in Bulgaria and Poland.
[41] In Poland.
[42] In Slovenia.
[43] In Slovenia

A very important characteristic of the CEE constitutional adjudication is the availability of constitutional complaint proceedings. Of the countries discussed here, only Romanian and Bulgarian constitutions do not provide citizens with the possibility of challenging legislative acts. Yet, even in these two countries, there may be some other, although limited, ways open to citizens to attempt to initiate judicial proceedings before the constitutional court.[44] There is a clear correlation between the existence of an activist and powerful constitutional court and the availability of a direct complaint procedure.[45]

In some countries it has been possible for courts to act *sua sponte* - on its own motion.[46] The Hungarian Constitutional Court is the leading example of the court possessing such a power.[47] The Court has had delivered a number of important decisions pursuant to self-initiated procedures, in particular, these concerning unconstitutionality of legislative omissions.[48] An important aspect of the delineation of courts' jurisdiction closely related to the *sua sponte* initiative is whether the court is bound by the limits of the petition submitted before it. In some countries, for example in Poland,[49] the Constitutional Tribunal is prohibited from going beyond the original submission. In others, courts are not limited by the scope of the petition; they might be forbidden to regard themselves to be bound by the petition[50] or, more often, the law remains silent on the issue and the courts through their interpretative practice decide to what extent they are limited by the original submission.

Another important aspect of the CEE courts' jurisdiction is their ability to declare unconstitutionality of legislative omission. This competence is particularly problematic since it allows the courts to intrude into the legislative domain. Indeed, an authoritative identification of the matters where the parliaments should enact laws is dangerously close to courts

---

[44] 'In Bulgaria, when the ordinary courts are confronted with the argument that a particular provision is unconstitutional, they may refer the issue to the Supreme court of Cassation, which, in turn may stay the proceedings and file a petition to the Constitutional Court.

[45] Sadurski, W (2005) *Rights Before Courts. A Study of Constitutional Courts in Postcommunist States of Central and Eastern Europe* Springer at 8.

[46] Ibid.

[47] The other example from amongst the discussed here case studies is Poland – such possibility was provided for in the 1985 Statute of the Constitutional Tribunal. However, the new 1997 statute on the Tribunal extinguished this procedure and, additionally, by the virtue of Article 66 established that the Tribunal is bound by the limits of a submitted to it petition.

[48] For example a 1992 decision in which the Court established that the Parliament failed its constitutional duty to enact a law regulating the broadcast media. Yet, with time the recourse to this way of initiating the proceedings become less frequent. Sadurski, above n 45, at 9.

[49] Article 66 of The Constitutional Tribunal Act of 1 August 1997. Available at: <http://www.trybunal.gov.pl/eng/index.htm>

[50] For example in Slovenia. Article 30 of the Constitutional Court Act.

acting as legislators. Again, while the Hungarian Constitutional Court is the best example here, this power has been also effectively claimed by the Polish Constitutional Tribunal[51] and by the Bulgarian Constitutional Court.[52]

Further, some of the constitutional courts from CEE have the power to provide a binding interpretation of their respective constitutions[53] independently from any examination of the constitutionality of legislative acts. Such a role has been often viewed as a logical consequence of the courts' function as guardians of the constitution. For instance, it was often resorted to by the executive branch of government in Hungary. In the case of Hungary, on one hand such practices were caused by the less than perfect constitution[54] the interpretation of which was often highly problematic. On the other hand, the executive used the Court's competence in order to clarify specific regulatory concepts before a draft law was introduced.[55] Since such practices effectively blurred the line between interpretation and *ex ante* control, the Hungarian Court strived to restrict the use of abstract interpretation by declaring that there must be an actual dispute calling for an interpretation of the Constitution. In spite of its attempts, the Hungarian Court has delivered a number of important judgements pursuant to the proceedings of that type.[56] It should be added that the judges of constitutional courts tend to be divided on the power to provide a binding abstract interpretation of the Constitution or/and of statutes outside any specific proceedings of judicial review. Some of

---

[51]   The Tribunal stated that if a given matter has been regulated by statute, a claim of unconstitutionality 'may apply both to what the legislators did in a given statute and to what they failed to do even though, in accordance with the Constitution, they should have regulated'. Decision K 37/97 of 6 May 1998, (1999) *Orzecznictwo Trybunału Konstytucyjnego, Rok 1998* [*Case Law of the Constitutional Tribunal, Year 1998*] C.H. Beck 167 at 172.

[52]   The Bulgarian Constitutional Court on a number of occasions declared 'the lack of law' to be unconstitutional. For example, in 1995 when the budget law adopted by the (post-Communist) BSP-dominated parliament did not allocate any moneys for the Supreme Judicial Council, dominated then by the rival (liberal) UDF party, the Court declared this omission unconstitutional and, as a result, the Parliament duly amended the budget law. For more see Schwartz, H (2000) *The Struggle for Constitutional Justice in Post-Communist Europe* University of Chicago Press, at 176-7.

[53]   In Bulgaria, Hungary, Slovakia. In Poland until the introduction of 1997 Constitution the Constitutional Tribunal had authority to pronounce binding interpretation of statutes.

[54]   During the Round Table negotiations the decision was reached to substantially amend the existing constitution instead of introducing a totally new act. Halmai, above n 17, at 189-190.

[55]   Brunner, G 'Structure and Proceedings of the Hungarian Constitutional Judiciary' in Sólyom, L and Brunner, G (2000) *Constitutional Judiciary in a New Democracy: The Hungarian Constitutional Court* University Michigan Press at 80.

[56]   For example, in 1995 the Court pronounced that the Constitution cannot be amended by a referendum. Decision 5/1995 (V.10) AB hat. , discussed in (1995) 'Constitutional Watch', *East European Constitutional Review* at 10-11.

the judges, in private conversations with us, took a negative position on this competence.[57] Its exercise, as they claimed, has a capacity to produce unnecessary and destructive tensions with other courts, in particular, with the supreme courts, which typically refuse to see the constitutional court as the 'super-court' of the legal system.

Finally, like their Western counterparts, the constitutional courts from CEE perform a number of other functions that do not add to their specificity, but should be mentioned for the sake of completeness of the current overview. Thus, the courts have the power to decide on jurisdictional disputes between the highest institutions of the state as well as between local and central authorities.[58] Next, some of the courts rule on constitutional liability of the senior state officials, in particular the president.[59] Further, the constitutional courts are vested with the authority to outlaw a political party on the basis of inconsistency of party's aims and/or activity with the fundamental act.[60] Also, some of the courts carry out specific functions concerning the control of the validity of presidential elections and national referenda.[61]

The decisions on the unconstitutionality of statutes in CEE countries are final; the only way to reverse the verdict is to pass a constitutional amendment. Until 2003 in Romania,[62] judgments of the Constitutional Court resulting from abstract review and conducted prior to promulgation of a legislative act could be overridden by a two-thirds majority of both chambers of the Parliament.[63] A similar possibility existed in Poland, but it was extinguished by the 1997 Constitution to a great applause by virtually all members of the legal community and the majority of legal scholars.[64]

---

[57] For example in Poland.

[58] Sadurski, above n 45, at 13.

[59] Ibid.

[60] Ibid.

[61] Ibid.

[62] The Law for the revision of the Constitution, adopted by Parliament on 18th September 2003, and approved by the 18th–19th October referendum.

[63] Currently Article 147 paragraph 2 provides: 'In cases related to laws declared unconstitutional before their promulgation, Parliament must reconsider those provisions concerned in order to bring such into line with the decision rendered by the Constitutional Court'.

[64] Article 190 section 1 of the Constitution provides: 'Judgments of the Constitutional Tribunal shall be of universally binding application and shall be final'. Transitional provisions for the Constitution of 1997 within the 2 years period kept in force the possibility for the Sejm to reject the Tribunal's judgments on the non-conformity of a statute, but only according to statutes preceding the constitution and ones passed in the abstract procedure of norm review. Available at <http://www.trybunal.gov.pl/eng/index.htm>

SELECTION PROCEDURE AND TERM OF OFFICE OF JUDGES

The procedure of selecting and appointing judges of the constitutional courts is an important element determining the character, functioning and public perception of the constitutional courts. The number of the judges varies from 9 in Slovenia and Bulgaria to 15 in Czech Republic and Poland. Judges are appointed for a limited tenure. In most of the CEE countries the term of office is 9 years with the exceptions of the Czech Republic (10 years) and Slovakia (12 years) and, in general, judges cannot be re-elected.[65] Typically, constitutional judges are recruited from among legal scholars, in particular, constitutional law professors, or senior members of the 'ordinary' judiciary.[66] Whether those courts are highly politicised or not is a matter of an ongoing cvontroversy, and those who believe in the relative lack of politicisation of constitutional courts in the region trace it to fears that politicians on the bench could undermine courts' operation and credibility in the young and unstable democracies of CEE. The experience of the Constitutional Court of Romania provides such a warning.[67]

There is no universal procedure for the selection and appointment of judges in Central Eastern Europe. In principle, it is possible to distinguish three different models. First, the power of appointment might be divided between a few bodies that act independently from each other – the so-called 'split' appointment system. For example, in Romania the Chamber of Deputies, the Senate and the President appoint one justice every three years.[68] The second type might be described as 'collaborative' for the reason that it requires cooperation between two branches of the government: president and the legislative. This procedure is applied in the Czech Republic, Slovakia and Slovenia. The third model vests the power of appointment exclusively with parliament that decides either by qualified majority (Hungary), or by simple majority (Poland). In practice it has

---

[65] The Czech Republic is an exemption here. However, the possibility of re-electing a constitutional judge is considered as an error made during writing the constitution. For more see Sadurski, above n 45, at 14-5.

[66] The notable exception here is Romania. There are also individual cases in other countries. For instance, in Poland a politician has been recently elected to the Constitutional Court who, though having legal education, has been neither a legal scholar nor a judge before.

[67] In 2005 a political crisis was caused by the Court, which consisting mostly of former socialist politicians, took the side of the socialist party Kühn, Z and Kysela, J (2006) 'Nomination of Constitutional Justices in Post-Communist Countries: Trial, Error, Conflict in the Czech Republic' *European Constitutional Law Review* 183 at 204-5.

[68] A similar procedure is followed in Bulgaria where the Constitutional Court is composed of twelve members one third of which are elected by the National Assembly, one third by the President and one third are elected during a joint session of the justices of the Supreme Court of Cassation and the Supreme Administrative Court. Available at: <http://www.constcourt. bg/ks_eng_frame.htm>

been demonstrated that each of these models has its pitfalls, and their success largely depends on the political culture of the country. The divided powers of appointment might, although do not have to, result in political nominations and in a fragmented court. The experience of the Romanian Constitution offers an example, when in 2005 a political crisis was caused by the Court staffed mostly by former socialist politicians who took the side of the Socialist Party.[69]

On the other hand, the cooperative procedure resulted in a standstill in the Czech Republic where, between 2003 and 2005, the President and the Senate could not achieve accord on the new appointments. The nominees presented to the Parliament by President Klaus were repetitively rejected. As a result, between summer 2003 and autumn 2004, the Court was not able to decide on the constitutionality of laws. Initially, the controversy was caused by the fact that the candidates were formal politicians. The second divisive issue concerned the question whether it was advisable to reappoint constitutional judges who had been already serving on the bench. In reality, the main cause of the conflict was the difficult relationship between the President, formerly a party leader, and the Senate controlled by the rival parties.

The parliamentary model based on a simple majority requirement undoubtedly ensures speedy appointments. It might also result in high professional standards of appointees, as it was by and large until recently the case of Poland.[70] Yet, this is at the price of politicisation of the process. As the practice of the selection of constitutional judges in Poland has demonstrated nominations are typically controlled by the parliamentary majority of the day; the opposition does not play any meaningful and constructive role.[71] In effect, political configurations of the lower house are reflected in the appointments to the Tribunal.[72] This is not to say that constitutional judges necessarily decide in accordance with preferences of the party that nominated and selected him or her. However, if pursuant to subsequent elections a change in composition of the Parliament occurs, the argument of the 'political pedigree' of the specific judges might be used in order to undermine the neutrality of Tribunal's pronouncements.

A common feature of the appointment processes is their insufficient transparency and publicity. The general public is neither informed about

---

[69] Kühn and Kysela, above n 67.
[70] Garlicki, L (2002) 'The Experience of the Polish Constitutional Court' in Sadurski, W (ed) *Constitutional Justice, East and West. Democratic Legitimacy and Constitutional Courts in Post-Communist Europe in a Comparative Perspective* Kluwer Law International 264 at 269.
[71] Of course, the opposition has the power to nominate the candidates to judicial post but the chances of them being elected are not very high.
[72] Garlicki, above n 70, at 268.

the nominations, nor is it particularly concerned about them. In part, this might be due to a lack of understanding of the role of the constitutional courts. They are often perceived as yet another 'ordinary' court; hence there is not the expectation that the appointment procedure should be publicly debated. However, this practice seems to undergo a change due to some highly controversial cases that bring the courts and their members to the centre of public attention as well as due to the increasingly proactive role assumed by the media and non-governmental organisations.[73]

THE RELATIONSHIP WITH OTHER BRANCHES OF GOVERNMENT

As much as it is possible to talk about one model of constitutional justice in CEE—the underlying rules and principles are similar and there is rather little local variation—the relationships between the CEE constitutional courts and other branches of government diverge to a great extent. Yet, since the scope of the current analysis does not allow for a detailed examination of each country, being aware of all dangers that generalisations typically involve, we will describe only some recurrent characteristics of the relationship between the CEE constitutional courts and other branches of government.

The starting point of the analysis has to be the nature of the constitutional courts. Irrespectively of whether one describes the constitutional courts as judicial bodies of a special type, or the quasi-legislative institutions, the political dimension of the courts' activity is obvious. Firstly, there is an unavoidable connection with the political sphere since the courts are often being asked to decide on matters that have great impact on the politics of the day. Secondly, and more controversially, the fact that politicians, either exclusively or predominantly, as is the case in the 'divided' systems of appointment, elect judges might cast doubts on political neutrality of the latter. It also might be used as a convenient argument against an unfavourable ruling by the politicians who lost their courtroom battles. In other words, there is a certain conundrum inscribed in the very concept and design of constitutional review. Consequently, the constitutional courts in the region have had to face various challenges resulting form their dual, legal-political nature while carving out for themselves a place on the political scene. These processes have taken different forms in individual countries. They have been influenced by a number of factors, some of

---

[73] For instance, in Poland: the initiative of the main daily – *Gazeta Wyborcza* and the Batory Foundation.

which could be described as country-specific, others as universal to the CEE region.

Firstly, the very design of a constitutional court has a great impact upon the relationship between the court and other branches of the government. In Romania the availability of the *ex ante* control of the laws resulted in a specific perception of the role of the Constitutional Court by the politicians. Parliamentary groups of senators or deputies were the subjects that most often initiated preventative control.[74] The proposals of legislative acts were brought before the Court not so much in order to control their constitutionality as to secure interests of political parties.[75] In effect, the Court was cast in the role of the arbiter of political disputes of the day and exposed to political pressures.[76] Also, the fact that Court's decisions did not enjoy an unconditionally binding force and could be overturned by a majority of two-thirds of both chambers of the Parliament had created a particular situation. The rulings of the Court have been regarded as yet another, perhaps more authoritative, opinion on the law debated by the Parliament, but not as the ultimate legal decision about a contested issue. Yet, despite these institutional factors, the Romanian Constitutional Court has managed to gain the respect and acceptance of political actors.[77]

Another factor that might determine the relationship between a constitutional court, on the one hand, and the parliament and the government, on the other, is the constitutional text. Depending on the level of precision of the provisions and their ideological coherence, that is, the extent to which they promote conflicting values that the court will have to balance while adjudicating, the position of the individual courts vis-à-vis other branches of government will differ. For example, the Hungarian Constitution marked by its Round Table origin had given the Court a considerable scope for manoeuvre. This is also true for other countries from the region.[78]

---

[74] Since the establishment of the Court until 31 May 2007, 91 out of 111 *ex ante* proceedings have been initiated by Deputies or Senators. *Constitutional Court Activity chart.*
[75] Weber, R (2002) 'The Romanian Constitutional Court: In Search of its Own Identity' in Sadurski, W (ed) *Constitutional Justice, East and West. Democratic Legitimacy and Constitutional Courts in Post-Communist Europe in a Comparative Perspective* Kulwer Law International 283 at 291.
[76] Weber writes: 'MP's perception that the Constitutional Court should serve their interest was better noted in those instances when the speakers of the Chambers or individual MPs asked for the Court's opinion on issues related to the interpretation of the Constitution without any connection to a particular law, in a procedure which was not within the competence of the Court'. Id at 293.
[77] Ibid.
[78] Cerar, M (2002) 'Slovenia's Constitutional Court within the Separation of Power' in Sadurski, W (ed) *Constitutional Justice, East and West. Democratic Legitimacy and Constitutional Courts in Post-Communist Europe in a Comparative Perspective* Kulwer Law International 214

Further, the relationship between the Court and other branches of government might be influenced by the attitude of the ruling party towards other independent sources of state authority. This was the case of Bulgaria. The Bulgarian Socialist Party (BSP), the successor of the Communist Party, in its attempts to minimise the departures from the previous political regime, was particularly determined to subordinate the Constitutional Court.[79] The conflict escalated between 1995 and 1996. Interestingly, the BSP-dominated Government and Parliament did not launch an open attack. Instead, they resorted to more cunning practices of intimidating the Court by, for example, attempting to move its premises to a new location without obtaining the Court's approval.[80] The Court responded by declaring, pursuant to a petition submitted by the President of the Republic, the governmental decree unconstitutional.[81] The Court withstood this pressure while deciding politically controversial cases. In 1996, in the situation of absolute domination of the political scene by the Socialist Party, the Court was asked to pronounce on the provision of the Constitution concerning the eligibility requirements for the office of the President of the Republic.[82] It interpreted the constitutional norms in a way which effectively brought about the exclusion from the presidential race of the already nominated candidate of the Socialists. The Foreign Minister Georgi Pirinski could not stand for the office for the reason that he had not obtained Bulgarian citizenship by birth, as the Constitution required.[83] Despite the difficult beginnings and the initial struggle to establish its authority vis-à-vis other branches of government, the Bulgarian Constitutional Court has eventually accustomed the politicians to its presence and involvement in state affairs.[84]

Yet, perhaps most important for the CEE constitutional courts' relationship with other branches of the government has been the political landscape in which the courts operate. Generally speaking, the greater the tensions between the political forces are, the greater is the possibility that sooner or later the adversaries will turn to the constitutional court to contest policy choices of political opponents. The consequence of the court's involvement in politically coloured disputes, even if they have

---

at 240-2.

[79] Schwartz, above n 52. at164

[80] Ganev, VI (2002) 'The Rise of Constitutional Adjudication in Bulgaria' in Sadurski, W (ed) *Constitutional Justice, East and West. Democratic Legitimacy and Constitutional Courts in Post-Communist Europe in a Comparative Perspective* Kulwer Law International 247 at 252.

[81] Ibid.

[82] Decision 12/96, Ibid at 255.

[83] Ibid at 256.

[84] Ganev writes: 'Only days after NATO and Russia requested access to Bulgarian air space, the government asked the Court to specify the conditions under which such access may be granted'. Ibid at 259.

been already translated into the language of legislative acts, is the threat of compromising the court's neutrality and, consequently, its public credibility. In some, extreme situations where a constitutional court's adjudication leads to decisions unfavourable to a ruling party, the danger is even greater – there might be attempts to actually or formally limit the court's independence.

The situation of the Constitutional Court of the Slovak Republic well illustrates such a scenario. In the late 1990s, the Court was caught in the struggle for power within the executive, that is, between Prime Minister Vladimir Mečiar and President Michal Kováč.[85] Kováč, although also a former Communist and a member of Mečiar's party, once elected the President proved to be, unlike Mečiar, a committed democrat. This resulted in recurring clashes between the two centres of the executive power. [86] Many of these conflicts ended up before the Constitutional Court and, more often than not, the Court found for the President. Only between 1994 and 1998, it ruled 16 times against the Mečiar government. Unsurprisingly, the government responded with fierce criticism of the Court[87] and attempts to undermine its prestige.[88]

The cases of the Bulgarian and Slovak Constitutional Courts might suggest that very young democracies, with constitutional and political culture 'in the making', are more prone to experience power struggles between the constitutional courts and the executive and/or the legislative branches of the government. After all, both Courts have overcome the initial difficulties and now are firmly established and esteemed institutions in their respective countries. Such an optimistic conclusion would be, however, premature. As developments in the Czech Republic at the beginning of the 2000s and recent controversies in Poland have shown, constitutional justice, even if firmly entrenched in the constitutional systems of the CEE countries, is likely to be called into question each time when undemocratic or authoritarian tendencies resurface.

The predicament of the Czech Constitutional Court resulted from a rivalry within the executive branch, as well as a peculiar understanding

---

[85] Schwartz, above n 52, at 201.
[86] Ibid.
[87] Mečiar described the Court as 'a sick element of Slovakia's political scene'. Malová, D (2002) 'The Role and Experience of the Slovakian Constitutional Court' in Sadurski, W (ed) *Constitutional Justice, East and West. Democratic Legitimacy and Constitutional Courts in Post-Communist Europe in a Comparative Perspective* Kulwer Law International 349 at 355.
[88] Perhaps one of the most curious attempts was Mečiar's decision to take away the car and bodyguard provided by the Government from the Chairman of the Court. The decision was soon cancelled but this incident well illustrates the difficult relationship between the Government and the Constitutional Court. Ibid.

of the role of the Court exhibited by the leading politicians. This is not to say that the first ten years of the Court's activity were uncontroversial,[89] yet the situation became particularly complicated in 2003 when the Parliament elected Václav Klaus to the post of the President.[90] Klaus, a former Prime Minister and a leader of one of the major political parties, was notorious for his mistrust of lawyers and fierce criticism of the Constitutional Court for its alleged activism.[91] Since the term of office of 9 judges expired in July 2003, and the President was the one to put forward new candidacies to the Senate, Klaus got an opportunity to shape the destiny of the so-disliked institution. Another dimension of the appointment process was the obvious hostility between the President and the Senate. The majority of the members of the upper house of the Parliament could hardly be regarded as enthusiasts of the new President. Consequently, Klaus' disrespect for the traditional selection procedures coupled with Senate's reluctance towards most of the Presidential nominees, led to a paralysis of the Constitutional Court. For over a year the Court could not pronounce on the constitutionality of law due to the insufficient number of justices on the bench.[92] The nomination saga finally concluded in December 2005, when the elections to the Senate gave the majority to the President's party.[93]

Yet, the controversies surrounding the Constitutional Court did not end with selection of the judges. The most recent episode in the battle between the Court and the President was caused by Klaus's dismissal of the President of the Supreme Court - Iva Brozova. The Constitutional Court's decision that found the dismissal unconstitutional[94] triggered a fierce response from Klaus. The President described it as 'an example of judicial corporativism' [sic] and a 'threat to democracy'.[95] He even went as far as saying that it could have a negative impact on the situation of the Czech judiciary.[96]

The troubles of the Polish Constitutional Tribunal started after 2005 parliamentary and presidential elections.[97] The new government led by the

---

[89] Přibáň, above n 18.
[90] On 7 March 2003.
[91] Kühn and Kysela, above n 67, at 195.
[92] Between summer 2003 and autumn 2004. Id at 198.
[93] Id at 205.
[94] Pl. ÚS 18/06; 'Brozova remains Supreme Court chairwoman-Constitutional Court' *CeskéNoviny* (12.09.2006) Available at: <http://www.ceskenoviny.cz/news/index_view. php?id=209019>
[95] Klaus considers Constitutional Court ruling on Brozova erroneous. Available at: <http:// www.ceskenoviny.cz/news/index_view.php?id=209019>
[96] Ibid.
[97] Of course, some earlier rulings of the Tribunal such as these concerning a tax amnesty or the National Healthcare Fund created some controversies and were criticised by politicians but the scale of the attack after 2005 has been unprecedented in the history of the Tribunal.

Law and Justice Party perceived the Tribunal as an institutional barrier to reform the Polish state – to finish with the Third Republic controlled by "the network" and to create a new Fourth Republic based on law, justice and solidarity. Consequently, not only the judgments of the Tribunal have come under attacks but also the institution itself.[98] The Tribunal was criticised for its allegedly arbitrary ways of rendering the decisions, which Prime Minister Jarosław Kaczynski described as 'legal circus-tricks'.[99] No less challenged were the moral and professional standards of Tribunal's members – the 'disgusting, opportunistic cowards'.[100] The proceedings and the decision concerning constitutionality of the so-called 'lustration' law proved to be the culmination of the hostilities.[101]

The Statute, as the pillar of the Law and Justice's de-communisation policy, was of a great symbolic importance for the government. The opposition and various human rights groups were alerted not only by the controversial purpose of the Act but also by the employed legal means. Thus, the Tribunal found itself under enormous political pressure and not lesser strong public scrutiny as the proceedings were televised and widely commented by the press. Eventually, after protracted and controversial hearings, the Tribunal invalidated a large number of the provisions on the basis of unconstitutionality, which for all practical purposes rendered the entire Act void.[102]

The decision provoked outrage in the ranks of the Law and Justice party and it led to submitting to the Parliament of a draft proposing amendments (eventually aborted) to the statute on the Constitutional Tribunal. The ruling party sought to curtail the powers of the Tribunal by introducing a number of seemingly minor organisational and procedural changes. The party proposed that the President of the Republic of Poland would appoint the President and Vice-President of the Tribunal for a period of three years[103] instead of the whole office term, that is, 9 years. Also, the order of adjudication of cases would be determined by the order of their

---

[98] Some of the controversial decisions concerned invalidation of the amendment of a law on the Broadcasting Council, which enabled the new government to appoint its own protégé as the chairperson of the council; the provision on the law on public assembly according to which local authorities (including Lech Kaczynski, when he was still President of Warsaw) could refuse permission for gay parades to take place; and the law on the reduction of the bar association's control over access to the legal profession.

[99] A statement of Prime Minister Jarosław Kaczyński made before an expected announcement of an unfavourable ruling by the Constitutional Tribunal. *Overview of the State of Democracy in Poland*, Report No. 1/2007 Experience for the Future at 14-15.

[100] Ibid.

[101] The screening of officials suspected of improprieties under the old regime.

[102] Decision K 2/07.

[103] Article 15, paragraph 1 of the submitted draft.

submission.[104] Finally, the so-called Full Chamber was to be enlarged from 9 to 11 judges and all cases would be adjudicated by the Full Chamber.[105] Such changes, if implemented, would prevent the effective operation of the institution and make it more dependent on the executive branch, in particular, on the President.[106]

CONSTITUTIONAL COURTS AND THE EUROPEAN UNION

Apart from being set up as protectors of the rule of law and fundamental rights, the constitutional courts of Central and Eastern Europe have been also vested or, depending on the adopted view, claimed for themselves a particular role in the supranational settings. The membership of the CEE countries in the European Union resulted in a profound change of their respective legal landscapes. From the perspective of constitutional law and constitutional courts, one of the most pertinent questions has been that of the relationship between the national and European legal orders. Although the European Court of Justice (ECJ) offered its interpretation that accorded absolute primacy to Community law,[107] the issue remained controversial since most of the constitutional courts from the 'old' EU Member States have not unconditionally accepted the view of the ECJ.[108] Instead, they have provided their own, constitution-based accounts of the integration story that might be summarised as recognition of the validity of Community law on the basis of it being derived from the national constitutions.[109]

Upon accession to the European Union, the CEE constitutional courts have encountered questions that previously were dealt with by their Western counterparts. Is the accession constitutional? What are the limits of European integration? In the case of a conflict of norms shall a constitutional or a Community law norm prevail? Of course, it would be a mistake to view the constitutional courts as national Don Quichotes facing, imagined or real, supranational windmills. The courts operate from within their respective legal systems. Even if the often imprecise 'European

---

[104] Article 37, paragraph 1. Ibid.

[105] Article 25. Ibid.

[106] Among others such opinions voiced, former President of the Tribunal Professor Marek Safjan, Siedlecka, E., 'Osłabić Trybunał' ('To weaken the Tribunal'), *Gazeta Wyborcza*, 29 June 2007.

[107] ECJ, Case 11/70, *Internationale Handelsgesellschaft* [1970] ECR 1125, at 1134.

[108] *Solange I*, Solange II, Maastricht decisions of the German Federal Constitutional Court, *Granital* and *Frontini* judgments of the Italian Constitutional Court, or the *Maastricht* decision of the Danish Supreme Court. Craig, P and de Búrca, G (2007) *EU Law. Cases and Materials* Oxford University Press.

[109] De Witte, B, 'Direct Effect, Supremacy and the Nature of the Legal Order, in Craig, P and de Búrca, G (eds), *The Evolution of EU Law* Oxford University Press 1999 at 177.

clauses' have given them some room for manoeuvre, the Constitutions stressing the principles of sovereignty[110] and supremacy of the national constitution effectively predetermine the approaches that the constitutional courts might assume. Further, the above mentioned jurisprudence of the "old" constitutional courts provided some inspiration as how to tackle the challenges posed by European law.[111]

Yet, the picture of the CEE constitutional courts simply expanding on the constitutional texts or travelling down the road determined earlier by the constitutional courts of the 'old' Member States would be an unjust oversimplification. Providing a constitutional perspective on the process of European legal integration was neither a mere interpretative exercise nor a straightforward imitation of the Western scenarios. However pompous it might seem, the courts' involvement in European affairs has also required a certain amount of self-confidence; it necessitated a conscious decision to stand up as an equal among other well-established and powerful European constitutional courts and to take responsibility for the course of the European project. And as such, the CEE Courts' involvement in shaping European legal sphere must be regarded as a sign of maturity of constitutional justice in Central Eastern Europe as well as a proof of its continuous relevance.

The Hungarian Constitutional Court delivered the first post-accession 'European' decision. In the *Surplus Act Judgment*, the Court found a national law implementing EU regulations on surplus sugar stocks[112] retroactive and, thus, contrary to the Constitution.[113] The decision might be characterised as very cautious; the Hungarian Constitutional Court seemed to test the new European ground. Although the provisions of the Surplus Act, as passed by the Hungarian Parliament, were almost identical to the provisions of the

---

[110] Sadurski W (2003) *Constitutionalization of the EU and the Sovereignty Concerns of the New Accession States: The Role of the Charter of Rights* EUI Working Paper Law No. 2003/11; Albi, A (2005) *EU Enlargement and the Constitutions of Central and Eastern Europe* Cambridge University Press 2005.

[111] Sadurski, W (2008) 'Solange, chapter 3: Constitutional Courts in Central Europe – Democracy – European Union' *European Law Journal*, forthcoming.

[112] European Commission Regulation (EC) 1972/2003 of 10 November 2003 on transitional measures to be adopted in respect of trade in agricultural products on account of the accession of the Czech Republic, Estonia, Cyprus, Latvia, Lithuania, Hungary, Malta, Poland, Slovenia and Slovakia, [2003] OJ L 293, as amended by Regulation (EC) 230/2004 of 11 February 2004, [2004] OJ L 39 and Regulation (EC) 735/2004 of 20 April 2004, [2004] OJ L 114; also Regulation (EC) 60/2004 of 14 January 2004 laying down transitional measures in the sugar sector by reason of the accession of the Czech Republic, Estonia, Cyprus, Latvia, Lithuania, Hungary, Malta, Poland, Slovenia and Slovakia, [2004] OJ L 9.

[113] Decision 17/2004 (V. 25.) AB. The Community regulations also led to proceedings before other constitutional courts in the region.

Commission's Regulations,[114] the Court chose to approach the legal issues in question as being solely confined to the application of domestic law. It seems that being aware of the obvious Community law dimension of the case, the Court wanted to avoid an impression that it disregards obligations resulting from Hungary's membership in the European Union. At the same time, the Court was determined to send a signal that constitutional law did not lose its relevance upon accession. In the view of the Hungarian Constitutional Court, the principle of legal certainty was such a strong component of the democratic State that it prevailed over Hungary's obligations resulting from European Union membership. In other words, depending on the response from the European institutions, constitutional principles as expressed in the Hungarian Constitution were either a limit to or a factor influencing the process of European legal integration.

The EC Sugar Regulations also left a bitter-sweet aftertaste in the Czech Republic. The Czech Constitutional Court dealing with the provisions of a governmental regulation[115] giving effect to the Community measures took the opportunity to express its views on direct applicability and supremacy of Community law.[116] Although the Community principles were accepted to a large extent, the acceptance was not unconditional. The Court reserved for itself the authority to have a say in situations where Community norms might be in conflict with the requisites and foundations of the democratic State.[117]

A year later, in 2005, the Polish Constitutional Tribunal delivered two important judgments that made it into leading textbooks on EU law.[118] The Polish Tribunal proved to be outspoken on the issue of the relationship between national and European law. In the *European Arrest Warrant* decision[119] the Tribunal annulled national law implementing EU framework decision on European Arrest Warrant[120] due to its non-conformity with Article 55 of the Constitution that, at that time, prohibited the extradition

---

[114] Sajó, A (2004) 'Learning Co-operative Constitutionalism the Hard Way: the Hungarian Constitutional Court Shying Away from EU Supremacy', (2) *Zeitschrift für Staats- und Europawissenschaften* 352 at 360-1.
[115] Governmental Regulation "Laying Down certain Conditions for the Implementation'.
[116] Decision Pl. ÚS 50/04 the Czech Constitutional Court.
[117] Article 9 para 2 and 3 of the Czech Constitution.
[118] Chalmers, D *et all* (2006) *European Union Law* Cambridge University Press; Craig and de Burca, above n 108.
[119] Judgment of 27 April 2005 in Case P 1/05. An English summary available at: <www.trybunal.gov.pl/eng/summaries/documents/P_1_05_GB.pdf>.
[120] Council Framework Decision 2002/584/JHA of 13 June 2002 on the European arrest warrant
and the surrender procedures between Member States, OJ [2002] L 190/1.

of Polish citizens.[121] Some two weeks later, the Tribunal handed down the *Accession Treaty* decision, in which it found the accession to the European Union constitutional but it also took an opportunity to state that the Constitution is the supreme law of the land and its norms should prevail in an event of a conflict with Community law norms.[122]

Despite what at first glance might seem a hostile approach to the European Union, the Constitutional Tribunal went to great lengths to answer legal questions in a way that simultaneously would be faithful to its role as the guardian of the Constitution and respectful for the obligations stemming from the EU membership. In the *European Arrest Warrant* judgment, although the Court stressed that '[t]he obligation to interpret domestic law in a manner sympathetic to EU law has its limits'[123] and annulled the provisions implementing the framework decision, it also decided to delay the loss of binding force of the provision for the longest period possible,[124] thereby leaving the legislator sufficient time to act.[125] It is also important to stress that the framework decision was an act issued under the so-called third pillar, that is, the Police and Judicial Cooperation in Criminal Matters, which neither entails direct effect nor supremacy of European law. The *Accession Treaty* decision can also be interpreted as an attempt to achieve the twofold purpose. Indeed, while it stressed the supremacy of the Polish Constitution, its effects were EU friendly since the Court unambiguously stated that the accession to the European Union was in accordance with the Constitution.

Pursuant to the accession of the CEE countries to the European Union, their constitutional courts have become European courts. Although their 'European' jurisprudence met with various receptions - some saw it as a lack of understanding of the rules of European co-operative constitutionalism,[126] others as a sign of adherence to the outdated concept of 'unconditional national constitutional sovereignty',[127]- it seems that a more nuanced assessment should be advanced. The constitutional courts passed the test of constructive involvement in European legal integration.

[121] Paragraph 1 of Article 55 stated: 'The extradition of a Polish citizen shall be forbidden'.
[122] Judgment of 11 May 2005 in Case K 18/04. An English summary available at: <www.trybunal.gov.pl/eng/summaries/documents/K_18_04_GB.pdf>.
[123] Ibid, point 8.
[124] The provision will lose its validity 18 months following the publication of the judgment in the Journal of Laws (4 May 2005).
[125] The Tribunal also urged the legislator to take an appropriate action since its absence would not only 'amount to an infringement of the constitutional obligation of Poland to observe binding international law but could also lead to serious consequences on the basis of European Union law' Point 17.
[126] Sajó, above n 114, at 351.
[127] Chalmers, D et all (2006) *European Union Law* Cambridge University Press at 198 and 201.

Whereas the extent of their activity varied, in general, they did not shy away from taking on their responsibility as European courts. Perhaps they did not always respond in the way a Euro-enthusiast would wish them to, but their activity has not posed any danger to the integration process, rather it stimulated European debates. It should not be surprising that given their origin, role and unavoidable institutional bias, the courts stressed the supremacy of their respective constitutions, but it is worth stressing that while doing so they were mindful of the obligations resulting for the EU membership.

A corollary of the CEE courts' assertion of a right to establish and enforce criteria of democracy, rule of law and human rights protection, which would inform the relationship between the European and national constitutional orders, was an increased importance of the Courts in the international sphere. Such a power would further increase their position vis-à-vis the political branches in their respective countries by delineating those aspects of the supremacy of European law which they deemed unacceptable, or by dictating the need to introduce constitutional amendments if certain effects of supremacy of Community law were to be accepted.[128]

CONCLUSIONS

Almost 20 years of constitutional courts in Central and Eastern Europe brought about a consolidation of their position. They are powerful institutional actors and it is rather difficult to imagine the political and legal CEE landscape without their presence. Further, the constitutional courts seem to have risen to the challenge posed by the membership in the European Union; not giving up their function of guardians of national constitutions, they have actively engaged in the building of the European legal space. In short, one may say that being at 18, the third generation of European constitutional courts has reached, or is about to reach, the legal age of maturity and, while younger and less experienced, the constitutional courts of CEE can be confidently ushered into the European constitutional salons.

And yet, this story of successful and undisturbed rise of constitutional justice in Central and Eastern Europe has to be slightly spoiled. Constitutional courts should not be taken for granted. Their role must be always critically evaluated and this is so at least for two related reasons. Firstly, whereas the legitimacy conundrum makes and will always make the institution of constitutional adjudication questionable, this in-built fault

---

[128] Sadurski, above n 111.

line can be as much the source of constitutional courts' weakness as of their strength. It all depends on the constitutional courts' self-understanding and constitutional practice. In the long run, doing less and in a more restrained manner might prove more effective than an excessive pro-activity. Such restrained presence on the political scene might effectively counterbalance the political pedigree of the courts as well as help to build trust in their institutional impartiality and in the neutrality of their judicial pronouncements. This, in turn, might make the constitutional courts less vulnerable when political disputes sweep across the political scene and eventually reach the constitutional court. The recent undemocratic developments in CEE described as 'backsliding' of the region, clearly demonstrate how fragile the position of constitutional courts is even in seemingly well functioning CEE democracies.

From this point of view, that is from the point of view of the actual practice of CEE constitutional courts' case law, their 'score card' is overall positive but it is not unconditionally and unquestionably *only* positive, from the point of view of fundamental democratic values. There was no room in this article even for a sketch of this case law, and in any event, it would not be possible to do it with regard of seven courts of CEE discussed here. One of the co-authors of this article has offered recently a book-length analysis of this case law,[129] and the conclusion is that it is a mixed bag of undoubtedly courageous and democracy-strengthening decisions as well as of decisions which seem like a set-back to these values. Ultimately, what matters for the public opinion of their countries – which is the ultimate judge of their success – is the 'outcome legitimacy': legitimacy based on the actual consequences of the constitutional maintenance conducted by the courts. And here, while the 'score card' contains more 'pluses' than 'minuses', we do not subscribe to those accounts of the constitutional courts in the region which are unqualifiedly apologetic.[130]

One popular line, especially in the so-called 'transitologist' literature on post-communist developments, of 'immunizing' CEE courts from the criticism is to emphasize their 'exceptionalism'. Since the context within which they are called upon to operate is special, it is sometimes suggested that our usual intuitions about the proper role of judicial review in a democracy must be suspended, or at least qualified, and constitutional courts in the region must be looked at with less concern for possible non-democratic consequences of their *de facto* legislative role. We do not subscribe to this argumentative strategy. For one thing, the constitutional

---

[129] Sadurski, above n 45.
[130] See, for example, Schwartz , above n 52.

courts themselves resist, whenever they have an occasion, appeals to special factors of the transition period: their perception is that they operate in a 'normal' democratic context, and this self-perception should be taken at face value. Second, we fear that 'exceptionalism' may become a self-fulfilling diagnosis: if no 'normal' democratic criteria and templates are applied to the assessment of post-communist regimes, the non-democratic elements will persist without the challenges and objections they deserve. Third, in many respects, post-communist systems of CEE *are* already consolidated democracies, and various pathologies and aberrations which they experience (such as the recent populist backlash, mentioned before) have its opposite numbers (sometimes, coming in nastier and more dangerous versions) on the other side of the East-West divide in Europe.

So, what is the future of constitutional justice in Central Eastern Europe? As the famous quip goes it is very difficult to make an accurate prediction, especially when it concerns the future. It seems that the constitutional courts will remain important institutional players in Central and Eastern Europe. There will be times of great deference to the constitutional courts but, perhaps, even more often there will be situations when a more realistic approach towards the courts will be displayed by political actors and general public alike. Namely, constitutional courts will continue to be important guarantors of democracy, the rule of law and constitutional values in both national and supranational settings, but they will be not, and rightly, outside the reach of critical evaluation and, at times, criticism.

The French *Conseil Constitutionnel*: An Evolving Form of Constitutional Justice

MARIE-CLAIRE PONTHOREAU* AND FABRICE
HOURQUEBIE**

The recent constitutional reforms in France have made very important modifications to the Constitution of 1958. Although the *Conseil Constitutionnel* ('CC') has been a much contested institution for a long time these recent constitutional changes[1] have confirmed both its usefulness and its legitimacy. The aim of this article is to help understand the nature of French constitutional review in light of this constitutional amendment, and, in particular, why the specific nature of the court has been preserved even if the reform has also had the effect of reducing the difference between the French model of constitutional review and that of other European models.[2] The question is all the more topical today, as after 50 years of debates, and further to the recent constitutional amendment, the citizen has acquired the power to refer matters to the CC, but in an indirect way via the mechanisms of certified questions. This is not novel in terms of the procedures applying to other European constitutional courts but in terms of constitutional review *'à la française'* it can be regarded as revolutionary, confirming a trend towards legal centralism.

* Professor of Constitutional Law and Comparative Law, University of Bordeaux (France)
** Professor of Public Law, University of Toulouse (France)
1 L. n° 2008-724, 23 July 2008 in *Journal Officiel* 24 July 2008, p.11890.
2 However the main characteristic of the European model is its diversity. See Rubio Llorente F, (1996) 'Tendances actuelles de la juridiction constitutionnelle en Europe', *Annuaire international de justice constitutionnelle*, XII, 11.

THE ORIGINS OF THE *CONSEIL CONSTITUTIONNEL*

French constitutional review is quite unique. In order to explain the main characteristics, it is necessary to go back to its origins. Although very remote from French legal tradition, the CC is solidly rooted in the French political system. Two elements deserve to be underlined.[3] The first feature highlights an important difference between the French system and other European legal systems.

The lack of an explicit constitutional charter of fundamental rights

A constitutional charter of fundamental rights is a familiar feature of other post- World War Two constitutions. On the other hand, the French Constitution is without an explicit constitutional charter. This is due to a series of political circumstances which do not concern the issue of constitutional review.

The first draft Constitution of 1946, adopted by the National Assembly – where the three major parties were the Communists, Socialists and Christian-Democrats – contained a catalogue of rights similar to the Italian Constitution of 1947. But this draft Constitution was rejected by a negative referendum in May 1946. A new amended version was adopted during the summer on the basis of a consensus amongst the three major parties. The charter of rights included in the first version could have been adopted with small amendments, but for an unresolved battle about freedom of education. In the French context 'free schools' means catholic education, and the tradition of the political left has been very much opposed to religious education since the beginning of the 20th century, as the Church was seen as a major opponent of revolution and democracy. As no agreement was possible on this major and very sensitive issue, the Assembly decided to adopt only a Preamble, recognising a number of new rights on a declarative mode in addition to the old Declaration of 1789. The Preamble also referred to 'the fundamental principles recognised by the Republic's laws' (*principes fondamentaux reconnus par les lois de la République*), an ambiguous sentence which obviously was referring mainly to the Freedom of the Press Act of 1884 and the Freedom of Association Act of 1901, but also, for the left, it referred to the Act of 1905 separating the Church and State, whilst some

---

[3] Ponthoreau M-C, and Ziller J, (2002) 'The Experience of the French *Conseil constitutionnel*: Political and social Context and Current legal-theoretical Debates' in Sadurski, W (ed), *Constitutional Justice, East and West – Democratic Legitimacy and Constitutional Courts in Post-communist Europe in a Comparative Perspective*, Kluwer, 119-142.

Christian democrats had in mind some sentences of other statutes which provided for financial support for free schools.

This has two consequences. First of all, it means that fundamental rights are still potentially a pretext for debates based on party-politically based interpretations, far more so than in a country like Germany. This gives a highly political content to all debates on the interpretation of the Constitution. Technically speaking the only means by which France can claim a list of constitutionally protected rights under the 1958 constitution is through the very short paragraph 1 of the Preamble according to which 'the French People solemnly proclaims its faithfulness to the rights of man and to the principles of national sovereignty as defined in the Declaration of 1789, confirmed by and with additions from the Preamble of the Constitution of 1946, and to the rights and duties as defined in the Charter for the Environment of 2004'. According to the established interpretation, this refers to the Declaration of Human Rights of 1789, a list of 17 articles, very representative of the first generation of rights; the Preamble of the Constitution of 1946, a list of 16 paragraphs of a declaratory nature, and representative to a large extent of the second generation of rights; and the famous 'fundamental principles' recognised by the Republic's laws for which there is not the slightest indication of content, and even less a list. Principles about the environment are a contested amendment of the Preamble, but the Council has recognised constitutional values for all these principles (decision n° 2008-564 DC of 19 June 2008). French scholarship refers to these texts as the *'bloc de constitutionnalité'*, for example the texts and principles that have constitutional value even if they are not directly embedded in the document called *'Constitution de la République française'*. There is a continuing debate about the precise limits of the *bloc de constitutionnalité* (see below).

The legacy of parliamentary sovereignty

From the Revolution of 1789, French public law has been dominated by two fundamental concepts: the general will is the only source of law (*la loi, expression de la volonté générale*), and the principle of representative democracy. The first concept introduced the sacred character of statute law, without much attention being given to the difference between the Constitution and acts of parliament. A century later, with the institution of parliament firmly rooted, the second concept led to a monopoly on decision-making by members of parliament, through a combination of two supposedly opposed theories of sovereignty. According to the theory of *souveraineté nationale* the only sovereign was the Nation, embodied by its representatives. According to the theory of *souveraineté populaire* the

People were the only sovereign, and expressed themselves through their elected representatives and through direct consultation. Under the 3rd Republic (1875–1940), the golden age of classical French constitutionalism, those concepts helped to support the unlimited power of parliament. This was enhanced by the fact that the three 'constitutional laws' of 1875 had been conceived as a transitional constitution and thus contained only arrangements for the functioning of state institutions. This firmly established parliamentary sovereignty, and therefore French constitutional law was opposed to the concept of constitutional review. Parliamentary sovereignty was not a principle as such, only the result of the combination of the two dominant legal concepts. Only a small part of legal scholarship tried to undermine theoretically this unlimited power of members of Parliament: Raymond Carré de Malberg was most representative of this view. In his pamphlet, *La Loi, expression de la volonté générale* (1931),[4] he demonstrated how the initial revolutionary theories had been unduly diverted by politicians and recommended introducing elements of direct democracy and constitutional review in order to balance parliamentarianism.

Parliamentary instability during the last decades of the 3rd Republic and even more during the 4th Republic (1946–1958), as well as the lack of courage of most members of parliament in 1940, were the grounds for a dramatic change. This was also prompted by the unsolved crisis of the Algerian war which helped General de Gaulle to come back into power in 1958. At that time there was an important consensus amongst scholars and politicians about the need to reduce the power of members of parliament. This resulted in the Constitution of 4 October 1958 which contained a number of technical constraints limiting the power of parliament, including a system of review of statute law by the newly created CC. The aim of the system was clearly to avoid parliament going beyond the competencies which were distinctively attributed by the Constitution. The purpose was not to check how parliament exercised legislative power, but to see that it restricted itself to adopting statute law in the most important fields and did not interfere with the executive power of the cabinet.

Furthermore, the CC developed as an institution which should not review statutes on merit, but only check if the right procedures had been followed. Until 1971 decisions focused on this issue. It was mechanical review and without interest. The most interesting decision deals with the review of the rules of procedure of the Houses of Parliament. The decision 59-2 DC (17, 18, 24 June 1959) is really important here because it is the consequence of the break with parliamentary sovereignty: because

[4]   Economica, 1984 reprint.

of constitutional review, it is impossible to amend the Constitution by a convention between the legislative and the executive via the rules of procedure of the Houses of Parliament. In particular, the aim was to avoid the Government risking its political life by way a motion of no confidence at any moment in the legislative process, as in the 4th Republic which was known for its enormous governmental instability.

This has two consequences. For more than ten years, there was hardly any link between the French system of constitutional review and fundamental rights, as these were not at stake in the numerous cases submitted to the CC. The main problem with this change has been that the whole system of mechanisms imagined in 1958 was designed to prevent excessive occurrence of the continental type of parliament with coalition governments, which had developed in France as also in Germany under the Weimar Republic. The personality of General de Gaulle and the constitutional reform of 1962, providing for the direct election of the President of the Republic, created the conditions for a majoritarian parliament on the Westminster model, and thus those mechanisms tended to become important weapons used by the government against the opposition. Until 1971 the CC was mainly seen as one of these mechanisms, thus not at all as a guardian of fundamental rights. This origin of the CC still accounts for an important part of the current debates about constitutional review in France.

THE SINGULARITY OF FRENCH CONSTITUTIONAL REVIEW

Fifty years after its birth, the CC is still the subject of heated debates about the issue of its possible reform. In the 1970s and 1980s the main doctrinal debate about the CC referred to its nature: judicial or political? The discussion was unavoidable, be it only for the choice of the word 'Council' instead of 'Court' when it was established. Nowadays the judicial nature of the CC seems to be admitted by a large body of scholarship. However insisting on the fact that the CC is in line with the European model of constitutional courts might reinforce the idea that the CC is just as much a 'constitutional court' as the German Constitutional Court. This argument is more and more contested.[5] The comparison between the CC and the European constitutional courts shows the singularity of the French case.

---

[5] Fromont, M (2001) "La justice constitutionnelle en France ou l'exception française" *in* *Mélanges Conac*, Economica, 167.

The composition of the *Conseil constitutionnel*

The first singularity is that former Presidents of the Republic are *de jure* life members of the CC. This rule is actually applied: Valery Giscard d'Estaing and Jacques Chirac take part in the CC's activity.

The second singularity is that there are no professional qualifications for membership. So, the Constitution does not particularly require judicial experience or experience as a professor of law.

The third singularity is that members are appointed by the President of the Republic, President of the National Assembly and President of the Senate. So, the members of parliament do not take part in the process of nomination of CC members.

However the recent constitutional amendment has provided for parliamentary control of the nominations. The explanation is simple. The nominations are unrestricted. Thus, a number of commentators stress the fact that the French system enables the appointment of experienced politicians to the CC, which might account for a fine-tuned political sensitivity.[6] As a matter of fact, more than two thirds of the 60 members of the CC to date have been active in politics before joining it, as members of government (about one third), members of parliament, or direct advisers of major politicians. For instance, the President of the CC is Jean-Louis Debré, a former minister and former President of the *Assemblée nationale*. This has accounted for the acceptance of the CC's decisions by the political class. In any case, the most important thing is the behaviour of the member after his nomination: she or he has a '*devoir d'ingratitude*'[7] in regard to the appointing body.

Some other commentators underline how few academics have been members of the CC,[8] something which contrasts highly with the Italian experience, and also that of Germany. Only five members of the CC have been professors of public law: Marcel Waline, François Luchaire, Georges Vedel, Jacques Robert and Jean-Claude Colliard. Two of these were CC members together 1965-1971, and none during 1959–1962 and 1974–1980. Following the last appointment in March 2007, there is no professor of public law. The number of career judges (*magistrats*) is even smaller, and they have obviously been appointed for political reasons much more than for professional ones. A much higher number have been advocates, but most of the latter had also very quickly started a political career. Clearly

---

[6] Rousseau, D (2006) *Droit du contentieux constitutionnel*, Montchrestien, 38.

[7] Translates as 'duty of ingratitude', in other words the recipient is under a duty to demonstrate no favour towards the appointing body.

[8] Melleray, F (2007), 'Sur une exception française', *Actualité juridique. Droit administratif*, 553.

the authorities in charge of appointing the CC members have tried to send signals to society that legal technique should not be the most important element in the CC's reasoning. The lawyers on the CC are not to be found amongst the ranks of professors of public law, a characteristic that corresponds best to French public law tradition. Strikingly, the number of former members of the *Conseil d'Etat* in the CC is twice as high as that of professors of law.

Naturally, the appointments to the CC are political. But it remains difficult to estimate the political consequences of these appointments[9] and there is no direct correlation between political nominations and votes for or against statutes passed on the initiative of a particular political party.[10] It would be too simple to deduce from this procedure the political nature of the CC. According to Alec Stone, 'although being qualified as jurisdiction, the Constitutional Council remains a power'.[11] Indeed the politicization of constitutional review which he describes is also the case for other constitutional courts or supreme courts,[12] and extends as far as all the constitutional courts which have powers on the border of law and politics. On the contrary, as Louis Favoreu put it, the CC will allow politics 'to be seized' by the law.[13] So, in the decisions relating to nationalizations in 1982, or relating to privatizations in 1986, the CC pronounced on eminently political questions, characteristic of governments with left or right wing programmes. Nevertheless, although composed mainly of judges appointed by right-wing political parties, the CC did not negate these statutes: it decided they were congruent with the Constitution, but this was 'congruency conditioned by interpretation'. In short, the CC did not really prevent these big political reforms; it even facilitated political change.

Furthermore the day to day running of the CC is controlled by the *Conseil d'Etat*: the CC has been installed in the *Rue Montpensier* in the same block of buildings as the *Palais Royal* where the *Conseil d'Etat* sits. This may seem purely incidental but the Secretary-General of the CC is traditionally also a member of the *Conseil d'Etat*. He (the gendered pronoun is used deliberately as all Secretaries-General so far have been male) is not only in charge of the organization of the CC, but it seems that he has a more and more important role in the drafting of the CC's decisions.

[9] Hourquebie, F (2001) 'Les nominations au Conseil constitutionnel' (108) *Les Petites Affiches*, 9-15.

[10] Shapiro, M (1990) 'Judicial Review in France' (6) *Journal of Law and Politics*, 531

[11] Stone, A (1989), *The birth of judicial power in France*, Oxford University Press, 1992.

[12] See Stone, A (1999), 'La politique constitutionnelle' in Drago G, Bastien F, Molfessis N (eds.), *La légitimité de la jurisprudence du Conseil constitutionnel*, Economica, 117-140.

[13] Favoreu, L (1988), *La politique saisie par le droit*, Economica.

The lack of procedural rules

The first specificity here is that the procedure is exclusively written and inquisitorial. No parties are represented. This feature is not really original. However, it is particularly marked in France in contrast to other European constitutional courts.

The second specificity is that Acts of Parliament may be referred to the CC, before their promulgation, by the President of the Republic, the Prime Minister, the President of the National Assembly, the President of the Senate, 60 deputies or 60 senators. Unlike the other European constitutional courts, the political authorities are the only authorities allowed to refer bills to the CC. There is no organic relationship between the CC and the others judges, in particular the two supreme courts (*Conseil d'Etat* and *Cour de cassation*). This point is very important, being a big difference from other constitutional courts. For them, in comparison, certified questions are the main method of constitutional review: constitutional court proceedings begin with a certification order, whereby a judge suspends all proceedings and submits the question to the constitutional court. In some cases (the German and Spanish Courts), citizens who feel that their civil rights have been violated can initiate a constitutional complaint. This is impossible in the French system. Several proposals for reform have been put forward from time to time, particularly concerning the introduction of concrete constitutional review of laws. The first reform, in 1990, which was rejected by Parliament, foresaw the possibility for an administrative and judicial tribunal to send the certified question about an act to the two supreme courts. These reforms are not any more on the agenda.[14] The recent constitutional amendment brings about a real change: the introduction of certified questions.

However the uniqueness of the CC is still present, weakened but still preserved. The new article 61-1 of the Constitution provides that in case of the violation of constitutional rights by an article of statute law, the judge can suspend all proceedings but he cannot submit a question directly to the CC. He has to submit the question to one of the two supreme courts of the judiciary order (*Cour de cassation*) or administrative order (*Conseil d'Etat*). Thus the certified question is referred to the CC by one of the two supreme courts who will exercise a filter on the questions submitted by ordinary judges. The aim of this original screening, apart from fundamentally reforming the organisation, is clearly to avoid too many

---

[14] On the origins of the reform, see the work by the *Balladur Committee* for the reform of institutions; more information can be found at : http://www.comite-constitutionnel.fr/actualites/?mode=details&id=48.

pending questions before the CC. While we can understand the reason for this initial screening, this function is exercised by constitutional judges in several other European constitutional courts. There is a risk in the French system of tension between the CC and the two supreme courts arising from the latter submitting inappropriately certified questions.[15]

The powers of the *Conseil constitutionnel*

The powers of the CC can be divided into two categories.

First, there is judicial authority covering two types of disputes, normative and abstract proceedings which are optional in the case of ordinary laws or international agreements and mandatory for institutional acts and rules of procedure of the parliamentary assemblies and electoral and referendum disputes. The CC decides on the lawfulness of presidential elections and the conduct of referenda, the results of which are announced by it. It also decides on the lawfulness of parliamentary elections and the rules on eligibility and incompatibility of interests of members of parliament.

Second, there are consultative powers. The CC gives its opinion when officially consulted by the Head of State whenever article 16 of the Constitution is applied and thereafter on decisions taken within that context. Moreover, the Government consults the CC on texts concerning the organisation of voting in presidential elections and referenda.

The CC does not have a general power as 'guardian of the constitution', so that certain conflicts are not reviewed, i.e. conflicts between state powers, and general problems of constitutional interpretation. Control by the CC is limited: this difficulty can be clearly seen during the period of *'cohabitation'* (when the President of the Republic and the Prime Minister did not come from the same political party). During this period, the most important problem of interpretation concerned article 13 of the Constitution which provides: 'The President of the Republic signs *ordonnances* and decrees deliberated upon in the Council of Ministers'. In 1986 Jacques Chirac, as Prime Minister, wanted to use *ordonnances*[16] in order to resolve some national problems speedily. However, François Mitterrand, President of the Republic, decided not to sign the *ordonnances*.[17] In making such a constitutional interpretation, the President is not subject to any reviewing

---

[15] Roux, A (2008) 'Le nouveau Conseil constitutionnel. Vers la fin de l'exception française ?' *JCP La semaine juridique*, 54.
[16] The Government has the possibility of securing a delegation of power under article 38 to pass legislation by *ordonnance*, thus avoiding further parliamentary battles and saving time.
[17] During the first *cohabitation*, F. Mitterrand refused to sign two very important *ordonnances*: one about privatization and the other one about electoral reform: see Bell, J (1992), *French Constitutional Law*, OUP, Clarendon Press, 107.

court. The only solution for the Prime Minister is that the draft *ordonnance* has to be passed by Parliament as a *loi*.

TWO IMPORTANT DATES: 1971 AND 1974

After decades of governmental instability, France became a prominent example of a strong executive, with a dominant party (the Gaullist party UNR, then the UDR replaced in 1976 by Chirac's RPR) which had no parliamentary tradition and thus little respect for the rights and status of opposition. Once De Gaulle had withdrawn from politics after having lost the 1969 referendum, the opposition parties, mainly those from the centre, started using the Constitution in order to develop better conditions for parliamentary democracy. Concerning the CC, the first clear case where this happened was in 1971 and the second in 1974. The two dates are closely linked and the cases determined the development of constitutional review.

1971, the birth of the *Conseil Constitutionnel* as the protector of fundamental rights

The President of the Senate for the first time took the initiative in asking the CC to review a bill on merit in a highly sensitive political context where the government was struggling for months with extreme left groups. In order to stop post-1968 unrest, the bill was intended to reform the famous Act of 1901 on Freedom of Association. The Senate had been strongly opposing General de Gaulle from 1962 to 1969 and the President of the Senate, Alain Poher, had been a candidate of the centre at the 1968 presidential election. In the same way as his predecessor, Gaston Monerville, he wanted to promote the image of the Senate as a defender of civil liberties. Monerville was very sceptical towards the CC, which had refused to acknowledge his request to review the 1962 Act instituting direct election of the President on the basis that it had been adopted by referendum.

It was quite a surprise for public opinion to discover that there was an institution called the *Conseil Constitutionnel* that was able to counteract government, even when the latter had an overwhelming majority in the National Assembly. For legal scholarship, the surprise was just as great, as there seemed to be nothing in the Constitution to prevent amendment of the 1901 Act. The 1789 Declaration did not recognise any freedom of association: on the contrary the Revolution abolished all 'intermediary institutions' (*corps intermédiaires*) as well as the system of corporatism which had been dominating professional life and obstructing the proper functioning of market mechanisms. One or more of the subtle legal minds amongst the members of the CC remembered the sentence about the fundamental principles recognised by the Republic's laws, of which the 1901 Act was the most prominent example. Interestingly the CC not only took a big risk in using such an unprecedented and extensive technique of interpretation, but also decided to quash the bill:[18] obviously there were not only subtle legal minds but also some very sensitive political minds amongst the members of the CC, who knew that they would be supported by an important part of the political class, which stretched beyond the divisions between government and opposition.

The constitutional amendment of 1974

It is quite clear that this case law would have remained quite exceptional without the political changes of 1974, where Valéry Giscard d'Estaing from the centre right won the presidential election, putting an end to Gaullist domination of the institutions of state. He very quickly prompted a series of reforms in order to modernise French political life by enhancing the status of the opposition. One of those reforms was the change in the list of authorities allowed to refer bills to the CC. In the 1958 Constitution only the President of the Republic, the Prime Minister, the President of the National Assembly and the President of the Senate could do so – only the latter could be close to the opposition. From 1974 on, 60 members of the National Assembly or 60 members of the Senate could refer a bill to the CC, a change of procedure that opened the door to a quite extensive jurisprudence. The origins of the 1974 reform seem to be quite often forgotten in contemporary debates. The lack of consensus on a possible charter of fundamental rights has always prevented a more comprehensive reform which would officially establish the CC as a major institution of the French system of rule of law. The constitutional sources of the institution may be found in the mechanism of parliamentary checks and balances, any further role being based on the actual content of the CC's case law, which would probably not have developed as it did if France had not been familiar for a long time with a system of legislative review which provided techniques to be taken up by the CC in reviewing acts of parliament. This reform and the decision of 1971 are also the origin of a recurrent problem concerning the extension of norms of reference for constitutional review.

---

[18] Decision n° 71-44 DC of 16 July 1971: the decision can be found at: www.conseil. constitutionnel.fr/decision/1971/7144dc.htm (no English translation).

RELATIONSHIP BETWEEN THE *CONSEIL CONSTITUTIONNEL* AND THE LEGISLATURE

The main problem here is the way constitutional justice is being exercised. In particular, there are three reasons which explain the tension between the CC and Parliament. First of all, discussion on the extension of norms of reference has always been very lively since the fundamental decision of 1971. The second discussion is about the extension of reviewing techniques, and the third is about reinforcing the protection of fundamental rights.

The extension of norms of reference

This problem is clearly summed up by the following quotation from Prime Minister Balladur to the Congress in Versailles – the *Congrès* in France is a plenary meeting of both houses of parliament – which convened for the first time in November 1993 in order to reverse a decision of the CC through constitutional amendment: 'Since the Council has decided to extend the scope of its review to the Constitution's Preamble, this institution has been inclined to check the congruency of Acts of Parliament with general principles which are sometimes more of a philosophical or political than a legal nature, sometimes contradictory, and furthermore conceived in times different to ours'. Unlike the Italian or Spanish constitutional courts, the CC is not bound by a fully-fledged catalogue of fundamental rights. Even the most critical commentators note that the CC has to face a difficult dilemma:

> If the constitutional judge were to apply only the letter of the Constitution, its review would be inefficient and useless because the text only exceptionally gives an answer to the question put to the Court. If on the contrary it tries to give life to the Constitution through a 'constructive' interpretation, it will be accused of arbitrariness and of wanting to act as a government.[19]

It is obvious that the CC has followed the second path in order not to be a useless institution.

In this framework legal scholars are debating the room for manoeuvre which the CC may enjoy while tracing the limits of the *'bloc de constitutionnalité'*. The main discussion is about the definition of *'principes fondamentaux reconnus par les lois de la République'*. It is still the CC that decides whether the conditions needed for the recognition of such 'fundamental principles' are met. By laying down more precise conditions

---

[19] Lochak, D (1991) 'Le Conseil constitutionnel, protecteur des libertés?'(13) *Pouvoirs*, 42.

(decision of 20 July 1988) the CC, however, puts limits on the development of its own interpretation, and its authority would suffer if it did not respect such interpretation. Certain legal scholars try to minimise the CC's power to create the norms of reference for the constitutional review. However, the judge's function is an interpretative activity. So, it would be better to improve the reasoning of the CC's decision even though this denies the Cc's law-making power.[20] The difficulty in admitting this explains the other discussion about the extension of reviewing techniques.

The extension of reviewing techniques

As soon as 1987, in the framework of a conference on 'the Constitutional Council and political parties,[21] members of parliament started to question the technique of 'congruency conditioned by interpretation' ('*conformité sous réserve d'interprétation*'). This method was described as 'the Constitutional Council treading on the legislator's ground' (P. Clément, centrist party) or leading to the 'slippery path of injunction' (J.-C. Martinez, extreme-right). This technique of congruency conditioned by interpretation, also used by the German and Italian constitutional courts, enables the Council to indicate to the executive and the judiciary what conditions are necessary to a constitutionally correct application of a statute. It may thereby subtract or add to the statutory text in order to make it congruent with the constitution. As a matter of fact, courts have tried to resist congruency conditioned by interpretation because it limited their own power to interpret (see below).

The CC competes with government and parliament in law-making. However constitutional scholarship is far less opposed to it, as it is conscious that the CC has to face a growing number of cases and thus needs to have a more flexible attitude towards congruency of a statute with the Constitution. Refusing to declare an act as void is not only motivated by the will to safeguard a text with high political content which includes questionable provisions, but is not contrary to the Constitution as a whole. It is also a way of avoiding the discontinuity in norms which would result from quashing the text, a sanction which would be disproportionate because of the gap that would remain in the text of the statute if only some words or sentences of the statute had to be deleted.

---

[20] Ponthoreau, M-C (1994) *La reconnaissance des droits non écrits par les cours constitutionnelles italienne et française. Essai sur le pouvoir créateur du juge constitutionnel*, Economica-PUAM.
[21] Favoreu, L (ed.) (1988), *Le Conseil constitutionnel et les partis politiques*, Economica.

Reinforcing the protection of fundamental rights

One of the most debated issues of the last decade is that of supra-constitutionality. This formulation is specific to French scholarship and linked to a debate that originated under the 3rd Republic. It was triggered by the formulation introduced into French constitutional law by the revision of 1884 (which is still applicable), according to which the republican form of government may not be amended. It points to natural law as being above the Constitution. The debate was very vivid in 1993 when the Government introduced a bill amending the constitution, which had the same content as a text which had been rejected by the CC's decision of 13 August 1993 concerning a bill on immigration. For the first time constitutional amendment was used in order to by-pass a decision of the CC. Far beyond the crisis, the issue was whether the power of constitutional amendment was unlimited and could thus give constitutional status to provisions that would violate fundamental rights.

It would be anti-democratic for a judge to overrule a decision that has been taken by the people according to established procedures. The CC's decisions of 6 November 1962 and of 23 September 1992, whereby the CC refused competence to review a bill approved by referendum, point in this same direction. This raises a familiar dilemma relating to the court's role: if one deploys the 'ultra-democratic' argument (what might otherwise be termed the parliamentary sovereignty position) the question arises whether even minimal review is justified once the democratic will has been expressed. On the other hand, how are minority rights going to be protected if one adopts a liberal argument which regards constitutional review as a fundamental safeguard against the abuse of power.

An important part of scholarly opinion saw the power of constitutional amendment as the expression of constitution-making power and thus needed the concept of supra constitutionality in order to limit this power. There has been some speculation since the constitutional decision of 2 September 1992 (mentioned below) whether the CC viewed itself as competent to review these limitations. A clear answer by the CC was given only in a 2003 case: it decided that the Constitution did not authorise it to examine provisions passed by the constitutional legislator in order to assess their compatibility with entrenched constitutional principles (decision of 26 March 2003).[22] This means that the constitutional legislator enjoys complete freedom of action: in others words, it has full discretion as to whether

---

[22]   Decision n° 2003-469 DC of 26 March 2003 can be found at:
www.conseil-constitutionnel.fr/decision/2003/2003469/index.htm (no English translation).

to modify the Constitution. A 2006 case confirms that the fundamental principles of constitutional identity are not untouchable (see below).[23] This is a strange understanding of the supremacy of the Constitution: on the one hand, the constitutional legislator is 'sovereign' and stands higher than the Constitution whilst on the other hand the Constitution (or more precisely some of its fundamental principles) stands higher than EC law.[24]

RELATIONSHIP BETWEEN THE *CONSEIL CONSTITUTIONNEL* AND OTHER COURTS

The CC is not situated at the summit of a hierarchy of judicial or administrative courts. In that sense it is not a supreme court in the meaning of the Supreme Court of United States. Indeed there was never any direct relationship between it and the two supreme courts, which are the highest court of appeal (*Cour de cassation*) and the Council of State (*Conseil d'Etat*). This situation will be changed because the recent constitutional amendments provide that in the case of the violation of constitutional rights by an article of statute law, the ordinary judges could suspend all proceedings and submit the question to one of these two supreme courts. It is at this point that one of these two supreme courts, having operated as a filter, returns the certified question to the CC. In a different sense, the CC comes into contact with the other jurisdictions through its jurisprudence and the authority given by the Constitution to its decisions.

Implicit relationships between the *Conseil constitutionnel* and other courts

First of all, the Constitution allows the CC to exert a real influence on the other courts' jurisprudence through article 62, which emphasizes the legal effect of the decisions meant as an absolute authority. The decisions of the CC are binding on the public authorities and all administrative and judicial authorities. No appeal lies against them. The legal force of the decision attaches not only to the judgment itself but also to the necessary reasoning supporting it. Consequently, an act of parliament which has been judged contrary to the Constitution cannot be promulgated and brought into effect.

---

[23] Decision n° 2006 240 DC of 27 July 2006, paragraph 19: 'The transposition of a Directive cannot run counter to a rule or a principle inherent to the constitutional identity of France, except when the constituting power consents thereto'.

[24] Ponthoreau, M-C (2008), 'Interpretations of the National Identity Clause: The Weight of Constitutional Identities on European Integration', in Baroncelli, S Spagnolo, C and Talani, L S (eds), *Back to Maastricht: Obstacles to Constitutional Reform the EU Treaty (1991-2007)*, CSP, 49.

However, to protect parliamentary sovereignty as much as possible against a decision of unconstitutionality and to indicate to the judiciary what conditions are necessary to a constitutionally correct application of a statute, the CC developed the technique of 'congruency conditioned by interpretation' ('*conformité sous réserve d'interprétation*'), also used by the German and Italian constitutional courts. Because the consequences of a decision that a law is unconstitutional could be very controversial and could be immediately understood as a political position, the CC prefers to adopt an intermediate solution which consists of declaring conformity subject to interpretation.

These '*réserves d'interprétation*' (reservations) are circulated, and are obvious to, all authorities made responsible for applying law, that is to say the Government and administration, but also to ordinary judges. When they are formulated, they define the power of the judges, and are therefore a significant element of their case law, as shown in a large number of decisions of the *Conseil d'Etat* and the *Cour de Cassation*. Thus reservations alert the judge applying the law, through the process of concrete review, to the risk of his decision turning out unconstitutional. However, such interpretation may lead to a very strong reaction by the authorities, fuelling the debate over government by judges. Reservations can also be understood as a means of strengthening the authority of a law by determining its constitutionality at the time it is brought into effect, thereby increasing the effectiveness of *a priori* review.

Independently of reservations, the case law of the CC exercises a profound influence on the case law of all other jurisdictions. Since the development of constitutional review - through the constitutional amendment of 1974 - there have been few aspects of individual rights untouched by this process. It is indeed certain that the ordinary jurisdictions are inspired more and more by the CC's case law. Besides, the more decisions of the CC serve the purposes of ordinary jurisdictions, the more this reception can take place. The CC must therefore be sensitive, when exercising its supervisory role, to the effect of its decisions on these jurisdictions. Reciprocally, the case law of the *Conseil d'Etat* and the *Cour de Cassation* influences that of the CC. Although the CC in *a priori* review does not exercise a similar jurisdiction to these courts, it must nonetheless envisage, in light of their case law, how cases might be disposed of by them. Moreover the CC is very much influenced by the advice given by the *Conseil d'Etat* as part of the process of drafting the legislation in question.

Finally, the dialogue among judges bears upon the '*contrôle de conventionalité*', that is, control of the law in respect to international standards. The CC exercises its control only with regard to the Constitution and to the '*bloc de constitutionalité*' and not with regard to treaties, as was established in a 1975 pivotal decision.[25] The reason for this is the difference in character between this control and the control of constitutionality. As a consequence, the '*contrôle de conventionalité*' is exercised by all the common jurisdictions, the *Cour de Cassation* declaring itself competent to exercise this jurisdiction in a decision of 1975[26] and similarly with the *Conseil d'Etat* in a decision of 1989.[27] In the field of fundamental rights particularly, because of the risk of being overruled, the ordinary judges are strongly aware of European law as interpreted by the Courts of Strasbourg and Luxemburg and are in danger of abandoning the Constitution as it has been interpreted by constitutional judges. There is thus a risk that these two kinds of review might result in conflicting positions. For this reason voices are heard today calling for better articulation of these two forms of review, which for the most part have the same object, namely the fundamental rights contained in the Constitution and the treaties. The issue is whether to confirm the current understanding of constitutional review or to widen it by reference to treaties containing fundamental rights, such as the EU Agreements, both pacts of the UN, and the proposed charter of the fundamental rights of the EU (Proposal of the President of Constitutional Council, Jean-Louis Debré).

THE MOST IMPORTANT DECISIONS

A '*grande décision*' (fundamental decision) was delivered by the CC on 16 July 1971 relating to freedom of association, which is fundamental in two ways. First, because it gave interpretative force to the preamble of the Constitution; and second, because it established the first stage in the emergence of the CC as a real defender of fundamental rights. This case[28] marked an acceleration of the process of recognition of fundamental rights by constitutional judges.

Decisions establishing essential liberties

In its decision 51 DC of 21 December 1973, the CC established for the first time the constitutional value of the principle of equality before the law. Since this decision, the principle of equality has been the object of more than 100

---

[25] '*Interruption volontaire de grossesse (IVG)*', Decision n° 74-54 DC, of 15 January 1975: English translation at http://www.conseil-constitutionnel.fr/langues/anglais/a7454dc.pdf.
[26] '*Jacques Vabre*', Cour de cassation, 24 May 1975, *Société Café Jacques Vabre*; the decision can be found atn: http://www.conseil-constitutionnel.fr/dossier/quarante/notes/vabre.htm.
[27] '*Nicolo*', Conseil d'Etat, of 20 October 1989, *Nicolo*; the decision can be found at: http://www.conseil-constitutionnel.fr/dossier/quarante/notes/nicolo.htm.
[28] Favoreu L, and Philip L, (2007) *Les grandes décisions du Conseil constitutionnel*, 14e Paris, Dalloz.

applications to the CC, and it has henceforth been the most invoked reason for unconstitutionality. In its decision 87 DC of 23 November 1977, the CC gave constitutional value to freedom of conscience as well as to freedom of education. The constitutional character of the respect for the rights of the defendant and the principle of the presumption of innocence were recognized in the decision 70 DC of 19-20 January 1981. Freedom of the press was established as a fundamental right in the decision 181 DC of 10-11 October 1984. The real constitutional status of foreigners was established in the decision 325 DC of 12-13 August 1993, which recognized the right to lead a normal family life and the immigration rights of dependents. At the same time as the constitutionalisation of individual freedom, the CC established certain number of economic and social rights such as: the right to strike (decision 77-105 DC of 25 July 1979); the freedom to join a trade union (decision 144 DC), the right to work (decision 156 DC) and the property rights of shareholders (decision 132 DC of 16 January 1982).

Decision 290 DC of 9 May 1991 relative to the status of Corsica[29]

The decision relating to the law-making status of Corsica was another *'grande décision'* which addressed the structure of the Republic. Indeed, the CC interpreted the provision of the indivisibility of the Republic as giving constitutional effect to the indivisibility of the 'French People'. By so doing, it negated the first article of the law which proclaimed the existence of 'Corsican people, the constituent of the French people', because the Constitution recognizes only the French people, consisting of all the citizens without distinction of origin, of race or religion. Echoing this ruling, the CC in its decision 99-412 DC of 15 June 1999 referred to the principle of uniqueness of the French people, to which it would give constitutional value.

Decisions 308 DC, 312 DC and 313 DC of 19 April, 2 and 23 September 1992: Maastricht I, II and III[30]

The year 1992 was marked by the debate on the Treaty of Maastricht which entailed a controversial constitutional amendment prior to the ratification of the treaty. Three related decisions allowed the court to exercise a real control over the constitutionality of international treaties based on the principle, 'the constitution, nothing but the constitution'. As a result they

---

[29] See notably Luchaire (F) (1991), 'A propos du statut de la Corse', *Revue française de droit constitutionnel*, 484.
[30] See *Les Grandes décisions du Conseil constitutionnel* n° 45.

required for the first time a prior amendment of the Constitution before ratification of the treaty and provided a specific constitutional foundation to the European framework (three articles of Title XIV called 'European communities and the European Union' are now Title XV and include five articles). More particularly the Treaty of Maastricht recognized the concept of European citizenship by proposing the right to vote and eligibility of community nationals in municipal and European elections. The CC supported this concept and the rights which are tied to it, but nevertheless recognized a constitutional exception relating to local councillors participating in the election of senators. Finally, the effect of the judgment in the Maastricht III decision is to allow the CC to decline jurisdiction to control a constitutional amendment act approved by referendum, in the name of the sovereignty of the constituent power and therefore avoid the path to 'supra- constitutionality'.[31]

Decision 98-408 DC of 22 January 1999, International Criminal Court[32]

This decision illustrates perfectly the involvement of the CC in questions of a political nature. Indeed, the CC settled the interpretation of the former article 68 of the Constitution, which limits the liability of the President of the Republic for actions performed in the exercise of his office except in cases of high treason. The question was whether this article prevented penal liability. The difficulty of interpretation appeared in a case concerning the former President Jacques Chirac, who was questioned regarding matters occurring before he took office. If the facts were to be considered as not associated with his office, he benefited from immunity; otherwise, he could be prosecuted before the ordinary criminal courts. As a consequence, the Council, then the *Court de Cassation*, on 10 October 2001, intervened to clarify the criminal liability of the Head of State. It decided that acts made prior to the beginning of the mandate should be considered as disassociated with it. Further, that prosecution for criminal malpractice would be suspended during the mandate in order to protect the presidential office and the privilege of immunity from the jurisdiction of the High Court of Justice. At the end of his mandate, the President could be brought before an ordinary court.

---

[31] See however the discussion of this decision above.
[32] See the except serie of the *Revue du droit public* (2003) and Favoreu L (2002), 'De la responsabilité pénale à la responsabilité politique du Président de la République', *Revue française de droit constitutionnel, 7.*

Decision 2004-496 DC of 10 June 2004, Law for the trust in the digital economy[33]

The CC considers that the transposition of European directives into French law is a constitutional requirement which must be respected. But the constitutional judge maintains the right to control standards stemming from community law if they become 'express dispositions contrary to the Constitution' (*'dispositions expresses contraires à la Constitution'*). In other words, the CC refuses to control the constitutionality of a law of transposition which is necessarily consequential on a European directive. However the supremacy of the Constitution would not be affected because the judge reserves the right to modify a law of transposition which becomes an express disposition contrary to the Constitution. An application of this case law was made in two recent decisions (2006-540 DC of 27 July 2006, Law relative to copyright; and 2006-543 DC of 30 November 2006, Law relative to the sector of the energy). The CC replaced the judicial mention of 'express disposition contrary to the Constitution' with the 'constitutional identity of France' (*'identité constitutionnelle de la France'*). They achieved this by considering that the transposition of a European directive could not go against a rule or principle inherent to the constitutional identity of France.

This type of control is new. It is not always easy to put into practice, but it fits in well with the logic of 'the French-style' of constitutional review, which is a priori control. This control allows the constitutionality of the law of transposition to be determined before it comes into effect.

In the same way as all French institutions, the CC has been the object of recurring attempts at reform in the name of a search for permanent legitimization; but few of these have been successful. The most important reform, approved on 23 July 2008, notably allowed change to the appointment procedure and to the conditions to refer bills to the CC. But the organic law which establishes the detailed provisions will not probably be published for several months. At this point it is not altogether clear how the constitutional review function is going to be exercised in practice, in particular, by which judges. In reality, much will really depend on the degree to which the *Cour de Cassation* and *Conseil d'Etat* act as a filter. The greatly enhanced regulatory role which the CC will play in the future of constitutional democracy also begs a more fundamental and more general

---

[33] See Levade A (2004), 'Le Conseil constitutionnel aux prises avec le droit communautaire dérivé', *Revue du droit public*, 889.

question: one that relates to the emergence of a countervailing power in the French constitutional system.[34]

Das Bundesverfassungsgericht: Procedure, Practice and Policy of the German Federal Constitutional Court

DONALD P KOMMERS* AND RUSSELL A MILLER** +

INTRODUCTION

Karlsruhe was the capital city of the Grand Duchy of Baden (1806–1918). During the Weimar Republic, Karlsruhe continued as the capital of the Republic of Baden (1918-1933). After the Allies crushed Hitler's Nazi regime, they reclaimed Baden from the centralizing and totalitarian policy of *Gleichschaltung* and used it as an Allied Occupation Zone that was shared by American and French forces. Karlsruhe was the Zone's hub. But Karlsruhe's run as a regional capital soon met its end. As the map of the Federal Republic of Germany was being drawn strong arguments were advanced for merging Baden with its neighboring rival Württemberg. The Federal Republic's founders could not settle the emotional and hotly contested question during the *Parlamentarischer Rat* (Parliamentary Council or constitutional convention) and left it to the states themselves to resolve the 'Southwest State' question.[1] When these rivals failed to

* Joseph and Elizabeth Robbie Professor of Political Science and Professor of Law, Notre Dame Law School.
** Associate Professor, Washington & Lee University School of Law. Professor Miller is grateful to Anna Ku (W&L 2008) for her research assistance and excellent proofreading.
+ This survey draws substantially on the first chapter of Donald Kommers's English-language treatise on the jurisprudence of the Federal Constitutional Court. See Kommers, Donald P. (1997) *The Constitutional Jurisprudence of the Federal Republic of Germany* (2d ed) at 3-29. The updates and changes to those materials reflected here draw substantially on work prepared in conjunction with the forthcoming publication of the third edition of the

reach a settlement, the federal government intervened and ordered a merger of the regions into the single state Baden-Württemberg, subject to approval in a federally coordinated referendum to be held in the relevant localities. Baden, fighting its demise by absorption, challenged the federal intervention and referendum before the new *Bundesverfassungsgericht* (Federal Constitutional Court).

The Court's *Southwest State Case* (1951), its first major decision, realized Baden's worst fears about its century and a half run as a regional capital.[2] The Court explained: 'In the case of the reorganization of federal territory consigned to the federation, it is the nature of things that people's right to self-determination in a state be restricted in the interest of the more comprehensive unit'.[3] The Second Senate of the Court allowed a federally orchestrated referendum to go forward, and the new, merged state of Baden-Württemberg resulted with its capital in Stuttgart. Karlsruhe, the proud and charming 'fan city', seemed fated to the ignominy of struggling on as Baden-Württemberg's 'second city'.

But out of the *Southwest State Case* came no small portion of redemption for Baden and, most especially, Karlsruhe. After all, Karlsruhe is the seat of the Federal Constitutional Court. And, as the Court's first major decision, *Southwest State* launched the Court into the prominent role it has played in the German polity. Some have gone so far as to describe the case as 'Germany's *Marbury v. Madison*',[4] analogizing it to the epochal US Supreme Court decision widely credited as the *fons et origo* of judicial review. From this perspective,

> *Southwest's* foundational character is rooted in the general principles of constitutional interpretation stated therein and in the clarity— and forthrightness—with which the Constitutional Court defined the scope of its authority under the Basic Law. The Court boldly asserted that its judgment and the opinion on which it rests are binding on all constitutional organs, even to the extent of foreclosing parliament from debating and passing another law of the same content.[5]

book. See Kommers, Donald P. and Miller, Russell A. (forthcoming 2009) *The Constitutional Jurisprudence of the Federal Republic of Germany* (3d ed).
1   *Grundgesetz* [GG] [Constitution] article 118 (F.R.G.).
2   Southwest State Case, *BVerfGE* 1, 14.
3   *Id.* at 49.
4   Kommers, Donald P. (1997) *The Constitutional Jurisprudence of the Federal Republic of Germany* (2d ed) Duke University Press at 66.
5   *Id.*

Southwest State was the first major sign of the significant role the Court would play in the new Federal Republic. The *Grundgesetz* (Basic Law or Constitution) itself virtually assured that the Court would play such a role, for it confers upon the Court wide-ranging powers that place it near the epicenter of Germany's political system. In the years since, armed with these powers, the Court has found itself banning political parties as unconstitutional, striking popularly enacted legislation, policing federal-state relations, monitoring elections, overseeing the dissolution of governments, and perhaps most significantly, defining and enforcing a regime of individual rights that fairly can be described as its most important contribution to the development of Germany's constitutional democracy.

HISTORY AND STRUCTURE

History

The Basic Law and the Constitutional Court

The Germans decided on their own to establish a constitutional tribunal, to vest it with authority to nullify laws contrary to the Constitution, and to elevate this authority into an express principle of constitutional governance.[6] In doing so, the Germans relied mainly on their own tradition of constitutional and judicial review.

Building on the groundwork laid by Professors Hans Nawiasky and Hans Kelsen, the establishment of a constitutional tribunal modeled after the Weimar Republic's *Staatsgerichtshof* was featured prominently in the draft constitution the Parliamentary Council debated. The draft plan envisioned a tribunal vested with both the competence of the *Staatsgerichtshof* (i.e., its constitutional review jurisdiction) and the authority to hear the complaint of any person alleging that any public agency had violated his or her constitutional rights. Aware of the potential power of the proposed court the conferees recommended a plan of judicial recruitment that would broaden its political support.

As the debate over the new court's structure continued in the Parliamentary Council attention turned to the new tribunal's character.[7] Should it be like Weimar's *Staatsgerichtshof* and serve mainly as an organ

---

[6] See Kommers, Donald P. (1976) *Judicial Politics in West Germany: A Study of the Federal Constitutional Court* Sage Publications at 70.

[7] For an excellent account of its proceedings in English, see Golay, John E. (1958) *The Founding of the Federal Republic of Germany* University of Chicago Press; Merkl, Peter H. (1963) *The Origin of the West German Republic* Oxford University Press.

for resolving conflicts between branches and levels of government (a court of constitutional review)? Or should it combine such jurisdiction with the general power to review the constitutionality of legislation (judicial review)? The framers finally agreed to create a constitutional tribunal independent of other public-law courts, but they disagreed over how much of the constitutional jurisdiction listed in the proposed constitution should be conferred on it as opposed to other high federal courts.

The controversy centered on the distinction between what some delegates regarded as the 'political' role of a constitutional court and the more 'objective' law-interpreting role of the regular judiciary. Some delegates preferred two separate courts—one to review the constitutionality of laws (judicial review) and the other to decide essentially political disputes among branches and levels of government (constitutional review). Others favored one grand multipurpose tribunal divided into several panels, each specializing in a particular area of public or constitutional law. Many German judges, alarmed by any such mixing of law and politics in a single institution, strenuously opposed this proposal. The upshot was a compromise resulting in a separate constitutional tribunal called the *Bundesverfassungsgericht* with exclusive jurisdiction over all constitutional disputes, including the authority to review the constitutionality of laws.

The final version of the Basic Law called the Court into existence in Article 92 and extended the Court's jurisdiction to twelve categories of disputes and 'such other cases as are assigned to it by federal legislation'. Originally, the Court's jurisdiction could be invoked only by federal and state governments, parliamentary political parties and, in certain circumstances, courts of law. However, the individual right to petition the Court was granted by legislation in 1951, just as the Court was summoned to life, and incorporated into the Basic Law as a constitutional guarantee in 1969.

The Basic Law's framers left other details of the Court's organization and procedure to later legislation.

The Federal Constitutional Court Act

Almost two additional years of debate were necessary after the promulgation of the Basic Law to produce the Federal Constitutional Court Act (FCCA),[8] the enabling statute creating the Court.

---

[8] Bundesverfassungsgerichtsgesetz [*BVerfGG*—Federal Constitutional Court Act], Aug. 11, 1993, BGBl I at 1473, last amended by art. 5 of the law enacted Nov. 23, 2007, BGBl I at 2614. For an excellent discussion of the FCCA's genesis, see Geiger, Will (1951) *Gesetz über das Bundesverfassungsgericht* Vahlen at iii-xxv; Laufer, Heinz (1968) *Verfassungsgerichtsbarkeit and*

In its current version the FCCA includes 105 sections that codify and flesh out the Basic Law's provisions relating to the Court's organization, powers, and procedures. Representing numerous political compromises the FCCA: (1) lays down the qualifications and tenure of the Court's members; (2) specifies the procedures of judicial selection; (3) provides for a two-senate tribunal; (4) enumerates the jurisdiction of each senate; (5) prescribes the rules of access under each jurisdictional category; (6) defines the authority of the Plenum (both senates sitting together); and (7) establishes the conditions for the removal or retirement of the Court's members.

Structure

The Two-Senate Structure

The most important structural feature of the Court is its division into two senates with mutually exclusive jurisdiction and personnel.[9] The Plenum — the two senates sitting together — meets periodically to resolve jurisdictional conflicts between the senates and to issue rules on judicial administration. Justices are elected to either the First Senate or the Second Senate, with the Court's President presiding over one senate and the Court's Vice President presiding over the other.

The bifurcation was the institutional expression of the old debate between those who viewed the Court in conventional legal terms and those who saw it in political terms. The original division of jurisdiction showed that the senates were intended to fulfill very different functions. The Second Senate was designed to function much like the *Staatsgerichtshof* of the Weimar-era. It would decide political disputes between branches and levels of government, settle contested elections, rule on the constitutionality of political parties, preside over impeachment proceedings, and decide abstract questions of constitutional law. The First Senate was vested with the authority to review the constitutionality of laws and to resolve

---

politischer Prozess Mohr at 97–139.

[9] The FCCA regulates the Court's organization, procedures, and jurisdiction. The Court's internal administration (i.e., budget, administrative duties of judges, authority and procedures of the Plenum, selection and responsibilities of law clerks, judicial conference procedures, and the rules governing oral argument and preparation of written opinions) is regulated by the Court's Standing Rules of Procedure. See Geschäftsordnung des Bundesverfassungsgerichts [*BVerfGGO*—Rules of Procedure of the Federal Constitutional Court], Dec. 15, 1986, BGBl I at 2529, last amended by the law enacted Jan. 7, 2002, BGBl I at 1171, § 1. The Court's organization and internal administration are treated at considerable length in Kommers, supra note 6 at 69–108.

constitutional doubts arising out of ordinary litigation. More concerned with the 'nonpolitical' side of the Court's docket and the 'objective' process of constitutional interpretation, the First Senate would hear the constitutional complaints of ordinary citizens as well as referrals from other courts.

This division of labor resulted initially in a significant imbalance between the workloads of the two senates. As a consequence, the *Bundestag* (Federal Parliament) amended the FCCA in 1956 to distribute the caseload more evenly. Much of the First Senate's work was transferred to the Second Senate, thus eroding the original rationale of the two-senate system. The Second Senate, while retaining its 'political' docket, would henceforth decide all constitutional complaints and concrete judicial review cases dealing with issues of civil and criminal procedure. The First Senate would continue to decide all such cases involving issues of substantive law.

The number of Justices serving on the two senates has also changed over the years. The FCCA originally provided for twelve members per senate. In 1956, the number was reduced to ten; in 1962, it was further reduced to eight, fixing the Court's total membership at sixteen.[10] Considerations of efficiency, coupled with the politics of judicial recruitment,[11] prompted these reductions.

Intrasenate Chamber System

To speed up the Court's decision-making process and ease the burden of an increasing number of cases, the FCCA changed the internal structure of the two senates in 1956 by authorizing each senate to set up three or more preliminary examining 'chambers', each consisting of three Justices, to filter out frivolous constitutional complaints.[12] This was necessary because, except under distinct circumstances, the FCCA obliges the Court to admit all constitutional complaints for decision.[13] A chamber may dismiss a complaint if all three of its members consider it to be 'inadmissible or to offer no prospect of success for other reasons'.[14] Under current procedure, if one of the three Justices votes to accept a complaint—that is, if he or she thinks it has some chance of success—it is forwarded to the full Senate.[15] At this stage, the 'rule of three' controls; if at least three Justices in the full

[10] *BVerfGG*, sec. 2 (a).
[11] See Kommers, supra note 6, at 128–44.
[12] Gesetz, July 21, 1956, BGBl I at 662. *BVerfGG*, sec. 93a (earlier version of the law). The procedures for establishing these chambers were initially laid down in the *BVerfGGO*, §§ 38 and 39.
[13] *BVerfGG*, § 93a(1).
[14] *BVerfGG*, § 93b (2).
[15] *BVerfGGO*, § 40 (1).

senate are convinced that the complaint raises a question of constitutional law likely to be clarified by a judicial decision, or that the complainant will suffer serious harm in the absence of a decision, the complaint will be held admissible.[16] Thereafter, and on the basis of more detailed examination, a senate majority could still reject the complaint as inadmissible or trivial.[17]

In 1986, on the Court's recommendation, the Federal Parliament enhanced the power of the three-Justice chambers. In addition to their normal screening function, the chambers were empowered to rule on the merits of a constitutional complaint if all three Justices agree with the result and the decision clearly lies within standards already laid down in a case decided by the full senate.[18] However, the authority to declare a statute unconstitutional or in conflict with federal law is reserved to the full senate.[19]

By separating the wheat from the chaff, the chambers dispose of more than 95 percent of all constitutional complaints, relieving the full senates of what would otherwise be an impossible task. Some form of gate-keeping procedure involving less than full senate review is necessary as a practical matter if the Court is to cope with a system that 'entitles [anyone] to complain to it about virtually anything'.[20]

Qualifications and Tenure

To qualify for a seat on the Constitutional Court, appointees must be forty years of age, eligible for election to the *Bundestag*, and possess the qualifications for judicial office specified in the *Deutsches Richtergesetz* (German Judges Act).[21] This means that prospective Justices must have successfully passed the first and second major state bar examinations. Additionally, Justices may not simultaneously hold office in the legislative

---

[16] *BVerfGG*, § 93d (3).

[17] See Spanner, Hans (1976) 'Die Beschwerdebefugnis bei der Verfassungsbeschwerde' in Starck, Christian (ed) *Bundesverfassungsgericht und Grundgesetz* at 374; Zacker, Hans H. (1976) 'Die Selektion der Verfassungsbeschwerden—die Siebftunktion der Vorprüfung, des Erfordernisses der Rechtswegerschöpfung und des Kriteriums der unmittelbaren and gegenwartigen Betroffenheit des Beschwerdeführers' in Starck, Christian (ed) *Bundesverfassungsgericht und Grundgesetz* at 396.

[18] *BVerfGG*, § 93b (2). Provided all three Justices agree, the FCCA authorizes the chambers to reject as 'inadmissible' referrals on concrete review from other courts. Only the full senate, however, may reject a referral for lack of admissibility if it originates in a state constitutional court or one of the high federal courts. *BVerfGG*, § 81a.

19 *BVerfGG*, § 93c (I).

[20] Singer, Michael (1982) 'The Constitutional Court of the German Federal Republic: Jurisdiction over Individual Complaints' (31) *Int'l & Comp. L.Q.* at 332.

[21] Deutsches Richtergesetz [German Judges Act], Apr. 19, 1972, BGBl I at 713, last amended by the law enacted Dec. 22, 2006, BGBl I at 3416, § 5.

or executive branch of the federal or a state government. Finally, the FCCA provides that the 'functions of a Justice shall preclude any other professional occupation save that of a professor of law at a German institution of higher education', and that the Justice's judicial functions must take precedence over any and all professorial duties.[22]

Justices enjoy single 12-year terms with no possibility of reelection.[23] Three of the eight Justices serving in each senate must be elected from the federal judiciary. All Justices must retire at age 68, even if they have not completed their 12-year term.

Machinery for Judicial Selection

The Basic Law provides that half the Court's members be elected by the *Bundestag* and half by the *Bundesrat* (Federal Council of States). The participation of the *Bundestag* in the selection of the Court's Justices underscores the significant role the Court plays in reviewing the content and democratic quality of the decisions of the popularly elected federal parliament. It seems appropriate, then, that the *Bundestag* plays some role in staffing the Court.[24] Similarly, the participation of the *Bundesrat* in the selection of the Court's Justices was meant to ensure that the Court was, at least with respect to its staffing, steeped in Germany's federalism.

Under the FCCA the *Bundestag* elects its eight Justices indirectly through a twelve-person Judicial Selection Committee (JSC) known as the *Wahlmännerausschuss*. Party representation on the JSC is proportional to each party's strength in the *Bundestag*; eight votes—a two-thirds super-majority—are required to elect.[25] The *Bundesrat* votes as a whole for its eight Justices, with a two-thirds vote also being required to elect.[26] The two chambers alternate in selecting the Court's president and vice president.

The process of judicial selection is highly politicized. The JSC, which consists of senior party officials and the top legal experts of each parliamentary party, conducts its proceedings behind closed doors and after extensive consultation with the *Bundesrat*. The two-thirds majority required to elect a Justice endows opposition parties in the JSC with considerable leverage over appointments to the Constitutional Court. Social and Christian Democrats are in a position to veto each other's judicial

---

[22] *BVerfGG*, § 3 (4).
[23] *BVerfGG*, § 4 (1).
[24] Schlaich, Klaus and Korioth, Stefan (2007) *Das Bundesverfassungsgericht — Stellung, Verfahren, Entscheidungen* CH Beck at 25.
[25] *BVerfGG*, § 6 (2).
[26] *BVerfGG*, § 7.

nominees, and the Free Democratic and Green parties, when in coalition with one of the larger parties, have won seats for their nominees through intra-coalition bargaining. Compromise is a practical necessity.

Compromise among contending interests and candidacies is equally necessary in the *Bundesrat*, where the interests of the various states, often independent of party affiliation, play a paramount role in the selection of the Justices. An advisory commission consisting of the state justice ministers prepares a short list of potentially electable nominees. The justice ministers on the commission, like certain state governors (*Ministerpräsidenten*) and members of the *Bundestag's* JSC, are often themselves leading candidates for seats on the Constitutional Court. Informal agreements emerge from the commission's proceedings, specifying which states shall choose prospective Justices and in what order. Throughout this process, the commission coordinates its work with that of the JSC. It is important to avoid duplicate judicial selections, and the two chambers need to agree on the particular senate seats each is going to fill and which of these seats are to be filled with Justices recruited from the federal high courts.

For all its opacity, the German process, largely as a consequence of the super-majority required for election, has consistently produced a Court reflective of Germany's most prominent political parties, regional divisions, and confessions.[27] In one respect, however, the Court has been less than representative of German society. The recently concluded Constitutional Court Presidency of Jutta Limbach, the first woman to hold the position, draws attention to the fact that the Court continues to be dominated by men. In 1951 the remarkable Erna Scheffler, who participated in the Parliamentary Council, was elected as one of the Court's first Justices. In the subsequent half-century, only ten other women have found their way onto the Court.

Jurisdiction

The Basic Law enumerates the totality of the Court's jurisdiction, with elaboration where necessary in the FCCA. The most important of these competencies are described briefly here.

Prohibiting Political Parties

The Court's function as guardian of the constitutional order finds its most vivid expression in Article 21(2) of the Basic Law. Under this provision,

---

[27]   (2004) *Uwe Wesel, Der Gang nach Karlsruhe* Karl Blessing Verlag at 41.

political parties seeking 'to impair or abolish the free democratic basic order or to endanger the existence of the Federal Republic of Germany shall be unconstitutional'.[28] The article goes on to declare that only the Federal Constitutional Court may declare parties unconstitutional. The Court has received only eight party-ban petitions from the other federal organs and it has decided just five of those cases. In only two, concluded early on, did the Court sustain the petitions: in 1952 when it banned the neo-Nazi Socialist Reich party,[29] and in 1956 when it ruled the Communist party unconstitutional.[30]

Disputes Between High Federal Organs

Conflicts known as *Organstreit* proceedings involve constitutional disputes between the highest 'organs', or branches, of the German Federal Republic.[31] The Court's function here is to supervise the operation and internal procedures of these executive and legislative organs and to maintain the proper institutional balance between them.[32] The governmental organs qualified to bring cases under this jurisdiction are the *Bundespräsident* (Federal President), *Bundestag* (Federal Parliament), *Bundesrat* (Federal Council of States), *Bundesregierung* (Federal Government), and units of these organs vested with independent rights by their rules of procedure or the Basic Law.[33] Included among these units are individual members of the *Bundestag*, any one of whom may initiate an *Organstreit* proceeding to vindicate his or her status as a parliamentary representative.[34] These units also include the parliamentary political parties.[35] An *Organstreit* proceeding is not available, however, to administrative agencies, governmental corporations, churches, or other corporate bodies with quasi-public status.

---

[28]   *Grundgesetz* [GG] [Constitution] art. 21(2); *BVerfGG*, § 13(2).
[29]   Socialist Reich Party Case, *BVerfGE* 2, 1.
[30]   Communist Party of Germany Case, *BVerfGE* 5, 85.
[31]   *Grundgesetz* [GG] [Constitution] art. 93(1)(1); *BVerfGG*, § 13(5).
[32]   See Lorenz, Dieter (1976) 'Der Organstreit vor dem Bundesverfassungsgericht' in Starck, Christian (ed) *I Bundesverfassungsgericht und Grundgesetz* Mohr at 255.
[33]   With respect to the Bundestag, these units would include the Committees on Foreign Affairs and Defense (GG, art. 45a), the parliamentary commissioner (GG, art. 45b), the Petitions Committee (GG, art. 45c), and even individual deputies deprived of rights or entitlements under GG, arts. 46, 47, and 48.
[34]   Abelein Case, *BVerfGE* 60, 374; Wüppesahl Case, *BVerfGE* 80, 188.
[35]   Party Finance III Case, *BVerfGE* 73, 40. See Kretschmer, Gerald(1992) *Fraktionen: Parteien im Parliament* (2d ed) von Decker.

Das Bundesverfassungsgericht

Federal-State Conflicts

Constitutional disputes between a *Land* (state) and the *Bund* (federation) ordinarily arise out of conflicts involving a state's administration of federal law or the federal government's supervision of state administration.[36] Proceedings may be brought only by a state government or by the federal government.

Concrete Judicial Review

Concrete, or collateral, judicial review arises from an ordinary lawsuit.[37] If an ordinary German court is convinced that a relevant federal or state law under which a case has arisen violates the Basic Law, it must refer the constitutional question to the Federal Constitutional Court before proceeding to a resolution of the case. Judicial referrals do not depend on the issue of constitutionality having been raised by one of the parties. An ordinary court is obliged to make such a referral when it is convinced that a law under which a case has arisen is in conflict with the Constitution.

Abstract Judicial Review

The Court may decide differences of opinion or doubts about the compatibility of a federal or state law with the Basic Law on the mere request of the federal or a state government or of one-third of the members of the *Bundestag*.[38] Oral argument before the Court, a rarity in most cases, is always permitted in abstract review proceedings. The question of the law's validity is squarely before the Court in these proceedings, and a decision against validity renders the law null and void.[39]

Constitutional Complaints

A constitutional complaint may be brought by individuals and entities vested with particular rights under the Constitution. After exhausting all other available means to find relief in the ordinary courts, any person who claims that the state has violated one or more of his or her rights under the Basic Law may file a constitutional complaint in the Federal Constitutional Court. Constitutional complaints must be lodged within a certain time,

---

[36] *Grundgesetz* [GG] [Constitution] art. 93(1)(3) and (4); *BVerfGG*, § 13(7) and (8).
[37] *BVerfGG*, § 13(11).
[38] *Grundgesetz* [GG] [Constitution] art. 93.
[39] *BVerfGG*, § 31 (2).

identify the offending action or omission and the agency responsible, and specify the constitutional right that has been violated.[40] The FCCA requires the Court to accept for decision any complaint if it is constitutionally significant or if the failure to accept it would work a grave hardship on the complainant.[41] 'Any person' within the meaning of this provision includes natural persons with the legal capacity to sue as well as corporate bodies and other 'legal persons' possessing rights under the Basic Law.[42]

The procedure for filing complaints is relatively easy and inexpensive. No filing fees or formal papers are required. Most complaints are prepared without the aid of a lawyer (attorneys prepare about a third). No legal assistance is required at any stage of the complaint proceeding. As a consequence of these rather permissive standing rules, the Court has been flooded with complaints, which have swelled in number from well under 1,000 per year in the 1950s, to around 3,500 per year in the mid-1980s, and rising from around 5,000 per year in the 1990s to nearly 6,000 in 2006. The Court grants full review to barely more than 1 percent of all constitutional complaints, but such complaints result in some of its most significant decisions and make up more than 50 percent of its published opinions.

Process

Internal Administration

The Court achieved a major victory when it won the authority early on to administer its own internal affairs. Administrative autonomy had the notable consequence of arming the Court with the power to prepare its own budget in direct consultation with Parliament and the Ministry of Finance. This, in turn, allowed the Court to plan its own future. In 1975, Parliament enacted a set of standing rules of procedure governing the Court's internal operations. The new rules charge the Plenum, over which the Court's president presides, with preparing the budget, deciding all questions pertaining to the Justices' duties, and formulating general principles of judicial administration. Overall judicial administration is the responsibility of the Court's director, the highest administrative official

---

[40] *BVerfGG*, § 93. See Singer, supra note 20, at 331–36; see also Seuffert, Walter (1971) 'Die Verfassungsbeschwerde in der Verfassungsgerichtsbarkeit' in Schmücker, Kurt (ed) *Bundesverfassungsgericht 1957–1971* (rev ed) C.F. Müller at 159–69.
[41] *BVerfGG*, § 93a (2).
[42] See, e.g., Factual Determination Case, *BVerfGE* 3, 359; Treasury Bonds Case, *BVerfGE* 23, 153. The Court has also granted standing to public broadcasting stations claiming free speech rights under GG, art. 5. See Television II Case, *BVerfGE* 31, 314.

in the Court, who answers only to the Court's president.[43] The director, like the Justices themselves, must be a lawyer qualified for judicial office. Finally, each Justice is entitled to four legal assistants or clerks of his or her own choosing. Legal assistants usually have embarked already on legal careers as judges, civil servants, or professors of law. Most serve for two or three years, although some legal assistants have stayed on for longer periods.[44]

Decision-Making

The Court's deliberations are secret, and the Justices render their decisions on the basis of the official record. The rules require that an official opinion signed by all participating Justices (six Justices constitute a quorum) justify each senate decision.[45] Recording the Justices' participation is vastly different than confirming their unanimity; the FCCA grants the senates the discretion to disclose or withhold information about the number of votes for or against the final decision. Oral arguments are the exception; they are limited to cases of major political importance. In 2006, the Court decided only six cases with the benefit of oral argument. A decision handed down on the basis of an oral proceeding is known as an *Urteil* (judgment); a decision handed down in the absence of oral argument is labeled a *Beschluss* (order or ruling). The distinction is formal; whether an *Urteil* or a *Beschluss*, the judgment binds all state authorities, and decisions have the force of general law.

Assignment

Specialization is a major feature of the judicial process within the Court. As noted earlier, each senate has a specified jurisdiction. Incoming cases are channeled to the appropriate senate and then passed on to the various Justices according to their areas of expertise. Before the start of the business year, each senate establishes the ground rules for the assignment of cases. By mutual agreement, and in consultation with his or her senate's presiding officer, each Justice agrees to serve as the rapporteur (*Berichterstatter*) in cases related to his or her particular interest or specialty. At least one Justice of the Second Senate, for example, has a background in international law and serves as the rapporteur in cases involving international legal issues. Another Justice might take charge of cases involving tax and social security

---

[43]   *BVerfGG*, § 13.
[44]   See Schalich & Korioth, supra note 24, at 27–28.
[45]   *BVerfGG*, § 30.

law. Still another might be assigned cases dealing with issues arising from family law.

The rapporteur's job is to prepare a *Votum*, which amounts to a major research report. The preparation of the *Votum* is a crucial stage in the decisional process. In it the rapporteur describes the background and facts of the dispute, surveys the Court's previous decisions and the legal literature, presents fully documented arguments advanced on both sides of the question, and concludes with a personal view of how the case should be decided. A *Votum*, which may be well over 100 pages long, may take weeks, even months, to prepare, and often it forms the basis of the first draft of the Court's final opinion.[46] In any one calendar year, each Justice prepares several major *Votums*, studies another 30 to 40 that are authored by his or her colleagues, drafts shorter reports (mini-*Votums*)—about two hundred per year—for his or her two colleagues on the three-Justice chambers, writes the opinion in cases assigned to him or her as rapporteur, and prepares for the weekly conference.

Oral Argument

As already noted, formal hearings before the Court are rare. Each senate hears oral argument in three or four cases annually, usually in *Organstreit* and abstract judicial-review cases, in which oral argument is mandatory unless waived by the major organs or units of government bringing these cases. The rapporteur, who by this time has nearly completed his or her *Votum*, usually dominates the questioning. The main function of the oral argument is less to refine legal issues than to uncover, if possible, additional facts bearing on them. For this reason, the Court may hear from fact experts during the oral argument in order 'to establish the truth',[47] as well as the lawyers, law professors, or public officials formally advocating for the parties. In spite of this genuine commitment to transparency, openness, and inclusion, the Court's oral arguments cannot be taped or broadcast.

Conference and Opinions

The presiding officer of each senate schedules regular meetings to decide cases and dispose of other judicial business. *Votums* and draft opinions of cases already decided dominate the agenda. In considering a *Votum*, the presiding Justice calls on the rapporteur to summarize the case and state

---

[46]   Kommers, supra note 6, at 178.
[47]   *BVerfGG*, § 26(1).

the reasons for his or her recommendation. The rapporteur's role is crucial here, for a carefully drafted and well-organized *Votum* usually carries the day in conference. In addition, the pressure of time often prompts Justices to defer to the rapporteur's expertise and judgment.[48] The rapporteur has the task of writing the Court's opinion. A rapporteur with strong dissenting views may request that the writing of the opinion be assigned to another Justice, but this rarely happens.

The well-settled tradition of the Court is to speak as an institution and not as a panel of individual Justices. Collegiality and consensus are the norm; despite the introduction of signed dissenting opinions in 1970, the Court continues unanimously to decide more than 90 percent of its reported cases. Although the FCCA requires the disclosure of the identities of the Justices participating in every case, authorial responsibility for unanimous and even majority opinions remains undisclosed. In the rare instances when the Court's institutional unanimity fractures, the Court is not required to identify which Justices voted with the majority and which voted with the minority. Only the publication of a signed dissenting opinion, an even rarer departure from the Court's prized institutional unanimity, might provide formal insight into the Court's voting constellations.

The institutional bias against personalized judicial opinions has tended to minimize published dissents. There have been only 134 since they were first allowed in 1970.[49] The prevailing norm seems to be that personalized dissenting opinions are proper only when prompted by deep personal convictions. As one commentator remarked, '[i]n their justification, style and intent, dissenting opinions are a departure from the Court's unanimity … [T]hey can draw attention to the dissenting Justice as a public figure, who may dissent in order to highlight his or her ethical or jurisprudential differences with the majority … Such dissenting opinions can endanger the Court's majority opinion'.[50]

Caseload and Impact

In a given calendar year, the Court receives 8,000-10,000 letters, notes, or communications from citizens throughout the Federal Republic. When these poorly articulated 'constitutional complaints' are obviously inadmissible or hopeless, they are provisionally assigned to the Court's General Register's

---

[48]   Kommers, supra note 6, at 179–81.
[49]   Bundesverfassungsgericht, Aufgaben, Verfahren und Organisation—Jahresstatistik 2006—Entscheidungen mit / ohne Sondervotum, grafisch, *available at* http://www.bverfg.de/organisation/gb2006/A-I-7.html (last visited Feb. 26, 2008) (on file with the authors).
[50]   Schlaich & Korioth, supra note 24, at 30–31 (authors' translation).

Office, which reviews the submissions and responds on behalf of the Court with an explanation of the legal nature of the matter that was the subject of the submission and, in light of this clarification, the General Register's view on whether a judicial decision is at all necessary or appropriate.[51] Of course, if the General Register's Office finds that a judicial treatment of the submission is necessary, the case is lodged for review in the ordinary admissibility process of the appropriate senate. If, in response to the General Register's clarification, the petitioner writes back demanding to be heard, his or her submission is lodged with one of the senates.[52] This process highlights the fundamental aim of the General Register's review, which is to give the petitioner an informed characterization of the submission while underscoring his or her ultimate responsibility for the 'complaint'. In 2006, the Court received 8,536 communications. The General Register's Office classified the great majority of them as 'petitions' or 'constitutional complaints'. In all, the General Register lodged some 46 percent of these communications with the Senates for ordinary admissibility review. However, a total of 3,332 communications merited only an explanatory letter from General Register's Office and were not passed along to the senates.[53] The General Register, thus, serves as an important checkpoint. Through it pass only the most insistent of complainants.

Constitutional complaints and concrete judicial review references make up the bulk of the Constitutional Court's very heavy docket. The General Register, along with the chamber review process described earlier, seem to have given the Court the flexibility it needs to cope with its caseload. The legal assistants each Justice is able to employ, recently increased to four, also help the Court manage its docket.

The number of concrete review references has not contributed to the Court's heavy docket. The number is surprisingly low in light of a judiciary consisting of twenty thousand judges. The apparent reluctance of judges to refer constitutional questions to the Court may be attributed to the strong tradition of legal positivism that continues to hold sway in the ordinary judiciary. Jealous of their own limited power of judicial review, judges usually resolve doubts about the constitutional validity of laws at issue in pending cases by upholding them or interpreting them so as to avoid questions of constitutionality, thus obviating the necessity of appeal to the Federal Constitutional Court.

[51] BVerfGGO, § 59.
[52] BVerfGGO, § 60.
[53] Bundesverfassungsgericht, Aufgaben, Verfahren und Organisation—Jahresstatistik 2006—Geschäftsanfall Allgemeines Register, *available at* http://www.bverfg.de/organisation/gb2006/D.html (last visited Feb. 26, 2008) (on file with the authors).

At the same time, the constitutional complaint procedure has served as an escape hatch for litigants upset with the performance of the judiciary. More than 90 percent of all constitutional complaints are brought against judicial decisions. The remaining 10 percent focus on legislative or executive infringements of basic rights. Nearly all complaints alleging that court decisions have violated the procedural guarantees of the Basic Law are disposed of by the Second Senate. The First Senate has jurisdiction over most complaints involving claims to substantive constitutional rights such as human dignity (Article 1); life, liberty and personality (Article 2); equal protection (Article 3); the freedom to choose a trade or profession (Article 12); and property (Article 14).[54] Even though the full senate decides a mere handful of such cases—15 of 5,918 complaints filed in 2006—the constitutional complaint procedure is now deeply rooted in Germany's legal culture.

In general, however, the Court is most politically exposed when deciding cases on abstract judicial review. These cases are almost always initiated by a political party on the short end of a legislative vote in the Federal Parliament or by the national or a state government challenging an action of another level of government controlled by an opposing political party or coalition of parties. The apparent manipulation of the judicial process for political purposes in these cases has led some observers to favor the abolition of abstract judicial review.[55] But those who decry the judicialization of politics—or, alternatively, the politicization of justice— have not gained much parliamentary support for the constitutional amendment that would be necessary to abolish abstract review. Equally disconcerting for those who would eliminate the thin line between law and politics trod by the Court in these cases is the failure of the Justices themselves to mount any opposition to abstract judicial review. Indeed, the elimination of abstract review would run counter to the view of constitutionalism currently prevalent in the Federal Republic; the Court, as guardian of the constitutional order, is expected to construe and enforce the Constitution whenever statutes or other governmental actions raise major disputes over its interpretation.

---

[54] Kommers, supra note 6, at 173.
[55] See Dolzer, Rudolf (1972) *Die staatstheoretische und staatsrechtliche Stellung des Bundesverfassungsgerichts* Duncker und Humblot at 114-18.

The Federal Constitutional Court and the Polity

Practice of Judicial Review

Federal Constitutional Court Justice Hans G. Rupp once noted: 'The only marshal there is to enforce the Court's ruling is its moral authority, the conscience of the parties concerned, and in the last resort, the people's respect for law and good government. It is mainly this limitation that renders it less objectionable to let a court settle legal issues that are closely connected with domestic or international politics'.[56] As it turns out, the Court has accumulated a considerable store of moral authority and public approval. A series of public opinion polls taken in recent years shows that the Court enjoys substantially more public trust than any other major political or social institution, including parliament, the military establishment, the regular judiciary, the television industry, and even churches and universities.[57] It relies on this goodwill when, as it often does, it wades into Germany's most contentious issues.

Among the many reasons for the widespread acceptance the Court enjoys are its passive posture in the scheme of separation of powers and the restraint is has typically shown when it does act.

With respect to its passive posture, it is often noted that, although the Court enjoys equal standing alongside the other 'high' federal organs that have principle responsibility for governing Germany (*Bundestag, Bundesrat, Bundesregierung* and *Bundespräsident*), it is unique in that it cannot call itself to action. It is bound, instead, to dispose of the cases and controversies that find their way to its door.

Even when summoned to service, in numerous ways the Court shows considerable restraint. First, the Court traditionally has refrained from anticipating a question of constitutional law in advance of the necessity for deciding it. While every case properly before the Court involves a constitutional question, the Court usually refrains from deciding ancillary constitutional issues not yet ripe for decision. Second, the approach the Court takes towards statutory interpretation exemplifies its reserve. A leading principle of judicial review in Germany obliges the Court to interpret statutes, when possible, in conformity with the Basic Law (*Pflicht zur verfassungskonformen Auslegung*). Additionally, the Court frequently has stated that it will not substitute its judgment of sound or wise public policy for that of the legislature.[58] The Court also will not overturn

---

[56] Rupp, Hans G. (1960) 'Some Remarks on Judicial Self-Restraint' (21) *Ohio St. L.J.* at 507.
[57] Conradt, David P. (2005) *The German Polity* (8th ed) Pearson Longman at 254.
[58] See, e.g., Saar Treaty Case, *BVerfGE* 4, 157 (168) and Conscientious Objector II Case,

statutes simply because the legislature may have inaccurately predicted the consequences of social or economic policy. Third, the Court abides by several rules that limit the number of concrete judicial review referrals from ordinary courts. Fourth, while the Court does not enjoy discretion akin to the *certiorari* power of the United States Supreme Court, it does have limited control over its docket through the three-Justice chambers. This admissibility review can, to no small degree, be instrumentalized to serve the Court's interests, including its interest in preserving its moral authority.

The Court's Impact

The Court's record, in spite of the modesty just described, reveals a self-confident tribunal deeply engaged in Germans' lives and politics. By 1 January 2007 the Court had invalidated 596 laws and administrative regulations (or particular provisions thereof) under the Basic Law. The large majority of these rulings admittedly involved minor legal provisions, but a fair number featured important public policies.[59] The number and range of cases in which the Federal Constitutional Court has acted to dramatically impact German politics are too great to systematically or comprehensively recount in this brief introduction. As already noted, the Court has banned political parties as unconstitutional,[60] policed federal-state relations, monitored the democratic process,[61] overseen the dissolution of parliament,[62] supervised the unification of West and East Germany,[63] shaped education policy,[64] delineated Germany's social market economy and cradle-to-grave welfare regime,[65] and defined and enforced a regime of basic liberties.

BVerfGE 48, 127 (160).

[59] See Benda, Ernst (1979) *Grundrechtswidrige Gesetze* Nomos Verlagsgesellschaft at 64-75; von Beyme, Klaus (1991) *Das Politische System der Bundesrepublik Deutschland nach der Vereinigung* Taschenbush Piper at 382.

[60] See Socialist Reich Party Case, *BVerfGE* 2, 1; Communist Party of Germany Case, *BVerfGE* 5, 85.

[61] See, e.g., Apportionment II Case, *BVerfGE* 16, 130; National Unity Election Case, *BVerfGE* 82, 322; Maastricht Case, *BVerfGE* 89, 155;

[62] See Parliamentary Dissolution I Case, *BVerfGE* 62, 1; Parliamentary Dissolution II Case, *BVerfGE* 114, 121.

[63] See, e.g., East-West Basic Treaty Case, *BVerfGE* 36, 1; Land Reform II Case, *BVerfGE* 94, 12; Stasi Questionnaire Case, *BVerfGE* 96, 171; Wall Shootings Case, *BVerfGE* 95, 96.

[64] See, e.g., Concordat Case, *BVerfGE* 6, 309; Hessen Mixed Ability School Case, *BVerfGE* 34, 165; Interdenominational School Case, *BVerfGE* 41, 29; 'LER' Conciliation Proposal Case, *BVerfGE* 104, 304; Junior Professor Case, BVErfGE 111, 226.

[65] See, e.g., Family Assistance in the Miners' Guild, *BVerfGE* 40, 65; Alimony Case, *BVerfGE* 53, 257; Geriatric Case, *BVerfGE* 76, 256; Homemaker's Pension Case, *BVerfGE* 87, 1; Sickness

The selection of any single field of the Court's expansive activity as representative of its significant influence and impact must necessarily be arbitrary. Uwe Wesel's recent book *Der Gang nach Karlsruhe (The Path to Karlsruhe)*,[66] an affectionate and accessible tour through the Court's history and many of its most remarkable decisions, suggests two possibilities: security policy and European integration.

Regarding security policy, Wesel concludes that the Court's interference with Chancellor Konrad Adenauer's early post-war efforts at remilitarization as the first of the Court's most inflammatory moments.[67] The politicized and highly strategic role the Court played in the question of the ratification of the European Defence Community Treaty reportedly prompted Adenauer to underscore his role as President of the West German constitutional convention and complain: 'That is not what we imagined'.[68] Contrary to this characterization of the founders' intent, the Court consistently has been involved in security policy and Germany's engagement with Europe's supranational undertakings.

The potential constitutional impediments to Germany's participation in the European Defence Community that were highlighted by the opposition's appeals to the Federal Constitutional Court had to be resolved by amendments made to the Basic Law in 1954. These amendments allowed West Germany to join the North Atlantic Treaty Organization in 1955. Germany's NATO membership would, in turn, give the Court occasion frequently, and sometimes dramatically, to enter the field of security policy. In two decisions in the 1980s the Court refused to credit constitutional challenges to the deployment of nuclear missiles in Germany under NATO auspices.[69] The missile deployment had galvanized strong pacifist sentiment among many Germans, leading to demonstrations that sometimes involved thousands of protesters 'blocking truck and tank traffic traveling up the main road to the Pershing missile base'.[70] This protest movement, and the lingering disappointment over the Court's rulings,

---

Benefits Case, *BVerfGE* 97, 378; Nursing Care Insurance III Case, *BVerfGE* 103, 242.

[66] Wesel, supra note 27. For English language surveys, see Kommers, Donald P. and Miller, Russell A. (forthcoming 2009) *The Constitutional Jurisprudence of the Federal Republic of Germany* (3rd ed) Duke University Press; and Currie, David P. (1994) *The Constitution of the Federal Republic of Germany* University of Chicago Press.

[67] Germany Treaty Case, *BVerfGE* 1, 396; EDC Treaty Case, *BVerfGE* 2, 143.

[68] Wesel, supra note 27, at 76 (authors' translation). Wesel explained: 'The Court, at least as Adenauer anticipated it, should render decisions against communists and fascists, but not against them, the representatives of a democratic government', *Id*. at 12-13 (authors' translation). See Limbach, Jutta (2001) *Das Bundesverfassungsgericht* CH Beck at 7.

[69] Arms Deployment Case, *BVerfGE* 66, 39; Atomic Weapons Deployment Case, *BVerfGE* 68, 1.

[70] Quint, Peter E. (2008) *Civil Disobedience and the German Courts* Routledge at 11.

solidified Germany's Green Party as a credible political force. Since reunification the Court has given the constitutional imprimatur to a gradual expansion of the role of Germany's armed forces. To the great frustration of governments of all political stripes the Court has repeatedly insisted, first and foremost, that every foreign troop deployment be authorized by the *Bundestag*. This proved to be so significant a barrier to Chancellor Gerhard Schröder's plans to support the U.S. invasion of Afghanistan in 2001 that he was compelled to couple the request for *Bundestag* approval with a no-confidence vote. But the very possibility of *foreign* troop deployments was the Court's handiwork. In 1994 the Court broke with the settled, Cold War understanding that the Basic Law envisioned a strictly defensive role for Germany's armed forces.[71] The Court has since upheld the expansion of the geographic range of foreign troop deployments to include actions taken outside NATO territory.[72] The Court has issued several rulings with respect to German involvement in the war in Iraq.[73]

Still in the realm of security policy, the Court has played a fundamental role with respect to the German 'front' in the so-called 'War on Terror'. Like most countries, following the 11 September 2001 terrorist attacks in the United States, German policymakers sought to implement a series of domestic security reforms that were aimed at equipping authorities to better detect and interdict the growing threat of global terrorism. Almost without exception, the Federal Constitutional Court has invalidated these reforms, perhaps most spectacularly with its ruling striking down the provisions of the Air Security Act that authorized the German Air Force to shoot down hijacked airplanes that might be crashed into buildings, population centers or other contexts that would increase the number of casualties.[74] Coming on the heels of the Court's refusal to endorse other provisions of the post-9/11 security regime, the *Air Security Act Case* prompted some policymakers to propose amendments to the Basic Law that would deprive the Court of the constitutional bases for its defiance.

With respect to European integration, the Court has exercised a degree of caution lacking in the enthusiasm exhibited by Germany's policymakers. Starting with the *So Long As I Case* in 1974 the Court articulated the strict but not insurmountable constitutional conditions on Germany's deepening participation in the European project.[75] As governing authority is shifted to the supranational European institutions, the Court reserved the right

---

[71] Military Deployment Case, *BVerfGE* 90, 286.
[72] NATO Strategic Concept Case, *BVerfGE* 104, 151.
[73] See, e.g., AWACS II Case, *BVerfGE*, 108, 34.
[74] Air Security Act Case, *BVerfGE* 115, 118.
[75] So Lang As I Case, 37, 271.

to determine whether Europe would exercise that authority in line with the fundamental principles outlined in the Basic Law. This restriction was repeatedly affirmed by the Court[76] and eventually became the content of the 1992 amendment to Article 23 (1) of the Basic Law: 'With a view to establishing a united Europe, the Federal Republic of Germany shall participate in the development of the European Union that is committed to democratic, social, and federal principles, to the rule of law, and to the principle of subsidiarity, and that guarantees a level of protection of basic rights essentially comparable to that afforded by this Basic Law'.[77]

These and many other decisions have inspired strong criticism of the Court from across the political spectrum, which is perhaps the best indication that it is fulfilling its mandate to serve as the 'Guardian of the Constitution'.

CONCLUSION

Karlsruhe, it seems, has benefited from a Faustian bargain implicit in the Court's *Southwest State Case*. As a result of that case, Karlsruhe traded its historical role as a regional capital for the title 'the capital of German justice'. From its home in Karlsruhe, the Federal Constitutional Court enjoys a breathtaking mandate, both in scope and depth; its jurisdiction is unlike any German court that has preceded it and remains unique when compared with other courts around the world.[78] The Federal Constitutional Court is often regarded as the 'most powerful constitutional court in the world'[79] and the 'most original and interesting institution' in the German system.[80] Symbolic of Karlsruhe's triumph, it was not an exaggeration for Gerhard Casper to suggest in his keynote address at the state ceremony commemorating the fiftieth anniversary of the Court's founding that modern Germany might properly be called the 'Karlsruhe Republic':

> If cities are to define German republics, then please allow me — at least for today and on this occasion — to choose the city of Karlsruhe, where the Federal Constitutional Court is located, as the symbol of German constitutional *continuity* ... [T]he constitutional history of the past fifty years, as it has been shaped by the Federal

[76] See, e.g., So Long As II Case, *BVerfGE* 73, 339; Maastricht Case, *BVerfGE* 89, 155.
[77] *Grundgesetz* [GG] [Constitution] article 23 (F.R.G.).
[78] Schlaich & Korioth, supra note 24, at 1–2.
[79] Wesel, supra note 27, at 7.
[80] von Beyme, Klaus (2002) 'The German Constitutional Court in an Uneasy Triangle between Parliament, Government and the Federal Laender' in Sadurski, Wojciech (ed) *Constitutional Justice, East and West* Kluwer at 101, 102.

Constitutional Court, continues as unassailable constitutional tradition. It is this fact that I first and foremost have in mind when I refer to the 'Karlsruhe Republic'.[81]

---

[81] Casper, Gerhard (2001) 'The 'Karlsruhe Republic', Keynote Address at the State Ceremony Celebrating the 50th Anniversary of the Federal Constitutional Court' (2) *German L.J.* at ¶¶ 3–4, available at http://www.germanlawjournal.com/article.php?id=111.

The Italian Constitutional Court: Towards a 'Multilevel System' of Constitutional Review?

TANIA GROPPI *

INTRODUCTION

The Constitutional Court was introduced for the first time in Italy in the 1948 Constitution, enacted by the Constituent Assembly after the fall of the Fascist regime and the end of the World War II. The Constitution establishes a 'constitutional democracy',[1] that is, a form of government in which the sovereignty belongs to the people, but which has to respect a 'rigid' constitution, entrenched by a difficult amendment process. The previous Italian Constitution, the '*Statuto Albertino*' 1848, was a flexible Constitution, such as most of the European Constitutions of the 19th century; thus the problem of judicial review of legislation was never raised in the Kingdom of Italy, in which the doctrine of supremacy of Parliament was largely accepted both by state institutions (including the judiciary) and by scholars.[2]

The framers of the Italian Constitution, having opted for a 'rigid' constitution, decided to introduce a system of constitutional review that was ranked among the various 'guarantees of the Constitution' (articles 134-139).[3] They rejected the few proposals oriented towards the

---

* Professor of Public Law, University of Siena.
[1] Among Italian scholars, the concept of 'Constitutional Democracy' has been developed mainly by Zagrebelsky, G (1992) *Il diritto mite*, Einaudi.
[2] See Watkin, TG (1997) *The Italian Legal Tradition*, Ashgate Publishing.
[3] The important link between a democratic state governed by law, a rigid constitution, and constitutional review, in the Italian experience, was pointed out in Rolla, G and Groppi, T 'Between Politics and the Law: The Development of Constitutional Review in Italy' in

introduction of a decentralized system, American-style, and, in accordance with the dominant constitutional trends in post-war Europe (particularly as expressed by Hans Kelsen), they designed a system of centralized review, with the creation of an 'ad hoc' organ of constitutional justice separate from the judiciary.[4]

The experience of more than 50 years of judicial review in Italy (the Court was only actually established, as will be underlined in the following pages, in 1956) has seen an evolution towards a much more decentralized system, as the article will try to point out, a system in which the ordinary judges also play an important role in constitutional review.

This article is composed of four parts. Part II provides some basic features of constitutional review in Italy, dealing with the composition and competences of the Constitutional Court. In this part the limitation of competences and the importance of certified questions as the main gateway to invoke the Court's jurisdiction will be pointed out. Part III illustrates the evolution of the Italian model of judicial review towards a concrete model, by emphasizing the creativity of the Constitutional Court and the relations with the judiciary and the legislature. Part IV explores the performance of the Constitutional Court in the development and protection of constitutional values, by focusing on four main stages of the experience of the Court. Finally, Part V provides some final remarks on the present role of the Court and some considerations on its possible future evolution.

BASIC FEATURES OF CONSTITUTIONAL REVIEW IN ITALY

Composition and competences of the Constitutional Court

The Constitutional Court's composition reflects the effort to balance the need for legal expertise, the characteristic of a judicial body, against the acknowledgment of the inescapably political nature of constitutional review:[5] fifteen judges, chosen from among legal experts (magistrates from the higher courts, law professors, and lawyers with more than 20

Sadurski, W (ed) (2002) *Constitutional Justice, East and West,* Kluwer Law International.

[4] The debates in the Italian Constituent Assembly are summarized in Pizzorusso, A; Vigoriti, V and Certoma, CL (1983) 'The Constitutional Review of Legislation in Italy' *Tem. L.Q.* 56 at 503.

[5] This balance has been pointed out by Zagrebelsky, G (1988) *Giustizia costituzionale,* Il Mulino, that remains the most complete study on the Italian Constitutional Court. It is interesting to notice the early study of the US Supreme Court Justice Samuel Alito: Alito, SA (1972) *An Introduction to the Italian Constitutional Court* (unpublished undergraduate Woodrow Wilson School Scholar Project prepared for Professor Walter F. Murphy, on file with Mudd Library, Princeton University), available at: http://www.princeton.edu/~mudd/news/Alito_thesis.pdf.

years of experience), one-third of whom are named by the President of
the Republic, one-third by Parliament in joint session and one-third by the
upper echelons of the judiciary.[6]

One of the main features of proceedings in the Italian Court, the
prohibition of dissenting (or concurring) opinions by judges (and the
related principles of secrecy of deliberation and collegiality) has also been
linked by scholars to the same necessity of finding a balance between
politics and the law. According to them, the principle of collegiality is a
way of protecting the Court from the pressures and interferences of politics,
giving to the judges the opportunity to express their opinion freely, without
having to justify their position outside the Court.[7] On the other hand, the
prohibition on disclosing the individual opinions of the judges has been
criticized because it may result in opaque, non-transparent motivation.
Over the years some attempts to introduce dissenting opinions have been
made by the Court itself, but all failed due to lack of consensus.

The powers of the Constitutional Court, defined in article 134 of the
Constitution, are typical of constitutional tribunals.

The Court has the power:

a)   to adjudicate on the constitutionality of laws issued by the national
     and regional governments;
b)   to resolve jurisdictional conflicts between organs of the state,
     between the state and the regions, and between regions;
c)   to adjudicate crimes committed by the President of the Republic
     (high treason and attempting to overthrow the Constitution).
     Article 2 of Constitutional Law n. 1 of 1953 added a further power
     beyond those listed in the Constitution:
d)   to adjudicate on the admissibility of requests for referenda to repeal
     laws, which may be promoted by 500,000 voters, or five regional
     councils, pursuant to article 75 of the Constitution.

[6] This tripartite model has been used later in other countries: see for example Chile,
Columbia, Dominican Republic, Ecuador, Guatemala, Indonesia, Korea, Mongolia, Paraguay.
[7] This is the point of view of Zagrebelsky, G (2005) *Principi e voti,* Einaudi.

Limitations on the competences of the Constitutional Court and the importance of indirect review

Compared to other models of constitutional adjudication, especially the most recently established,[8] these competences seem notable for being so apparently limited and minimalist.[9]

On the one hand, the Italian Constitutional Court does not have some competences which are present in other systems of constitutional law, and which could be labeled as political: for example, in many systems Constitutional Courts have powers relating to electoral issues, supervision of political parties and ascertaining the incapacity of the President of the Republic.

On the other hand, with regard to the Court's main competence of reviewing the constitutionality of laws, several limitations arise from articles 134-137 of the Constitution, Constitutional Law n. 1 of 1948 and Law n. 87 of 1953. These limitations concern the means of triggering constitutional review, the object of review and the types and effects of the Court's decisions.

First of all, access to constitutional review is rather circumscribed: the Italian system offers only *a posteriori*, indirect review, which arises mainly out of a separate judicial proceeding. The keys that open the door to constitutional review are primarily in the hands of ordinary judges, who therefore perform the important function of screening the questions that the Court will be called upon to answer. The constitutional proceeding begins with a 'certification order' whereby the judge suspends all proceedings and submits the question to the Constitutional Court. In that order, the judge must indicate the relevance and plausibility of the question, the law challenged, and the constitutional provision that it allegedly violates.

---

[8] See for example the competences of the Constitutional Courts in Central and Eastern Europe countries: see in this book the essay of Lach and Sadursky. See also Favoreau, L 'Constitutional Review in Europe' in Henkin, L and Rosenthal, AJ (eds) (1990) *Constitutionalism and Rights: The Influence of the United States Constitution Abroad* Columbia University Press at 52-53.

[9] For a general overview of the competences of the Constitutional Court see Cerri, A (2001) *Corso di giustizia costituzionale*, Giuffrè; Ruggeri, A and Spadaro, A (2004) *Lineamenti di giustizia costituzionale* Giappichelli; Malfatti, E; Panizza, S and Romboli, R (2003) *Giustizia costituzionale*, Giappichelli. Among the publications in English see Baldassarre, A (1996) 'Structure and Organization of the Constitutional Court of Italy' *St. Louis U. L.J.* 40 at 649; Pizzorusso, A (1988) 'Constitutional Review and Legislation in Italy', in Landfried, C (eds) (1988) *Constitutional Review and Legislation: an International Comparison*, Nomos Verlagsgesellschaft at 111; Dengler, DS (2001) 'The Italian Constitutional Court: Safeguard of the Constitution' *Dick. J. Int'l L.* 19 at 363.

There is also an avenue of direct review, according to article 127 of the Constitution, but it is rather circumscribed. The national government and the regional government may challenge, respectively, a regional or a national statute within 60 days of its publication. In this way, direct review is only a tool for the guarantee of the constitutional separation of powers as between national and regional governments. Neither private citizens nor parliamentary groups nor local (sub-regional) governments can directly invoke the Court's jurisdiction.

Secondly, the 'object' of constitutional review is represented exclusively by laws. Delegated or administrative legislation is not reviewed by Constitutional Court, but by ordinary Courts.

Furthermore, the Court may not wander from the '*thema decidendum*' (that is, the object and parameter of review) identified in the application to the Court. As stated in article 27 of Law n. 87 of 1953, 'The Constitutional Court, when it accepts an application or petition involving a question of constitutionality of a law or act having force of law, shall declare, within the limit of the challenge, which of the legislative provisions are illegitimate.' In other words, constitutional review is limited to the question presented and must be carried out 'within the limit of the challenge.' Article 27 itself carves out an exception to this general principle: the Court may also declare 'which are the other legislative provisions whose illegitimacy arises as a consequence of the decision adopted'. At issue here is 'consequential unconstitutionality.'

Thirdly, there is a limited range of decisions that resolve the process of constitutional review. Aside from decisions that are interlocutory or reject a question on procedural grounds, decisions either *accept* or *reject* constitutional challenges, known respectively as *sentenze di accoglimento* and *sentenze di rigetto*. The consequences of these two sorts of decisions, including their temporal effects, are rather straightforwardly defined by law. Decisions that *reject* a constitutional challenge do not declare a law constitutional. They merely reject the challenge in the form in which it was raised. These judgments are not universally binding, that is, they are not effective *erga omnes*. Thus, the same question can be raised again, on the same or different grounds; only the judge who has certified the question cannot raise it again in the same lawsuit. For this reason, such judgments are said to be effective only as between the parties, that is, *inter partes*. On the other hand, judgments that *accept* a constitutional challenge are universally binding and are retroactive (*ex tunc*), in the sense that the law declared unconstitutional cannot be applied from the day after the judgment has been published. This retroactivity is limited by what are called '*rapporti esauriti*,' which might be translated as 'concluded relationships' or '*res iudicata*'. For reasons of convenience and legal certainty, judgments do not affect situations that were already resolved by final judgments, claims that are barred by statutes of limitation, or the like. Yet there is an exception to this rule where a final criminal conviction has been entered pursuant to the law now declared unconstitutional: the law provides that such a conviction and any related punishment should cease.

Moving from a simple list of the Court's powers to statistics about its activities, the limited nature of its powers becomes even clearer. The vast majority of the Court's activity is dedicated to constitutional review of laws, overshadowing its other powers, in particular with regard to jurisdictional disputes between the State and the Regions.

Within this category of constitutional review, particular importance is assumed by 'incidental' review or certified questions, which has absorbed most of the Court's energy during its more than fifty years, and which therefore deserves the bulk of our attention.[10]

EVOLUTION OF THE ITALIAN MODEL OF JUDICIAL REVIEW

A centralized and concrete model of constitutional review

An analysis of the powers granted by the Constitution and a glance at the procedures used are indispensable for understanding the mechanics of the Italian Constitutional Court, yet they are not sufficient for comprehending the role it plays in the legal system. To this end, one must consider other aspects, taking account of history and considering the provisions governing constitutional review in the light of the dynamism of its jurisprudence.

It is hard to understand the current system simply by looking at the statute books. Theory traditionally distinguishes between the American model of judicial review of legislation, which is diffuse, concrete, and binding as between the parties, and the Austrian model (*Verfassungsgerichtbarkeit*) which is centralized, abstract, and binding universally.[11] Judged against this backdrop, the Austrian model clearly had the greatest influence on the framers of the Italian Constitution.

---

[10] Data about the work of the Court may be found in Celotto, A (2004) *La Corte costituzionale,* Il Mulino; Romboli, R (eds) (1990, 1993, 1996, 1999, 2002, 2005) *Aggiornamenti in tema di processo costituzionale,* Giappichelli and on the annual report of the President of the Court, published on the website of the Court: www.cortecostituzionale.it.
[11] See Cappelletti, M (1971) *Judicial Review in the Contemporary World,* Bobbs- Merrill; in this book see Gamper, A and Palermo, F, *Austria.*

Undoubtedly, the implementation of the Italian system has not maintained the purity of Kelsen's Austrian model, having introduced some features that approach the American model of judicial review.[12]

As an initial matter, the centralization of review has been mitigated by endowing ordinary judges with two important powers: first, as we already stated, the decision whether or not to raise a constitutional question; second, the constitutional review of secondary legislation.

Furthermore, the requirements that the question be relevant and explained by the certifying judge have introduced into the process features similar to those contained in systems of 'concrete review',[13] although the Court will review the constitutionality of the statute, but it will not decide the case: the decision is up to the ordinary judge, that has to wait (as the ordinary trial is suspended) the decision on the constitutionality of the statute, before reassuming the proceedings.

The nature of the Italian system is highlighted by the Court's practice which, in some phases, has helped to increase the degree of concreteness of its judgments. In this regard, one can emphasize the following developments:

a) The drastic reduction of time taken to decide a case and the consequent elimination of pending questions, that occurred in the early 1990s, means that a constitutional decision increasingly has concrete effects for the parties in the case at bar;[14]

b) The Constitutional Court has increasingly employed its evidence-gathering powers before deciding questions.[15] As a result, it can better understand the practical aspects of the question that gave rise to the constitutional challenge, the effects that would flow from the Court's judgment, and the impact of a judgment on the legal system;

c) An interpretative continuum has arisen, in two respects, between the Constitutional Court and ordinary courts (in particular, the Court of Cassation and the supreme administrative court, called the 'Council of State'). On the one hand, the legal principles and

---

[12] See Pizzorusso, A (1990) 'Italian and American Models of the Judiciary and of Judicial Review of Legislation: A Comparison of Recent Tendencies' *Am. J. Comp. L.* 38 at 373; Pasquino, P (1998) 'Constitutional Adjudication and Democracy. Comparative Perspectives: USA, France, Italy' *Ratio Juris* 11 at 38.

[13] Concrete review in the meaning given by Cappelletti, M (1971) *Judicial Review in the Contemporary World*, Bobbs-Merrill.

[14] On this new phase of constitutional justice in Italy see the essays published in Romboli, R (eds) (1990) *La giustizia costituzionale a una svolta*, Giappichelli.

[15] As I tried to show in my book: Groppi, T (1997) *I poteri istruttori della Corte costituzionale nel giudizio sulle leggi*, Giuffrè.

interpretations of the Constitution provided by the Constitutional Court acquire force for all legal actors, especially courts that must directly apply the Constitution or review rules that are subordinate to statutes. On the other hand, when resolving constitutional questions, the Constitutional Court tends to address the legal provision in question not in the abstract, but as it has been concretely applied. The Court tends to rule on the 'living law', or the rule as it has been interpreted in case law. In this way, there seems to have been a tacit division of labour between the Constitutional Court and ordinary courts, so that each endorses and approves the other's interpretation within its own sphere. This tendency may be broken by the excessive speed of the Court in deciding cases: the object of the proceeding may very well be a statute for which the 'living law' has yet to be consolidated.[16]

According to these developments, one can undoubtedly affirm that the Italian system still remains a centralized system, but with an increasing presence of elements of a diffuse system.

Procedure and Practice of the Constitutional Court, 'Interpretative' and 'Manipulative' Judgments and Relations with Courts and the Legislature

The powers of the Italian Constitutional Court and the process of constitutional review were regulated in the years immediately after the entry in force of the Constitution and have not changed much since then.[17] It should be noted, however, that unlike the procedure and practice of the ordinary courts, which are regulated in detail in the civil and criminal procedure codes those of the Constitutional Court are more flexible. The reason for this flexibility is due to the fact that, unlike the ordinary courts, the Constitutional Court has a much greater discretionality in interpreting its procedure and practice thus allowing it to modify the latter in order to achieve a desired goal or to more fully implement constitutional values.

This 'discretion' enjoyed by the Constitutional Court has divided scholars: some authors claim that the Constitutional Court's activity should be subjected to detailed rules of procedure that are spelled out with precision, while others believe that a certain measure of discretion is unavoidable, given the nature of judicial review. This disagreement mirrors the larger debate between those who emphasize the judicial nature

---

[16] See Pugiotto, A (1994) *Sindacato di costituzionalità e "diritto vivente"*, Cedam.
[17] See Const. Law 1/1948, Law 1/1953 and Law 87/1953.

of constitutional review and those who instead focus on its necessarily political nature.[18]

This flexibility is reflected most prominently in the way the Constitutional Court has devised different types of judgment which, as we shall see, have significantly influenced the development of Italy's legal system.[19] One should note that the Constitution[20] and subsequent constitutional and statute laws governing the Constitutional Court only provide for judgments that accept or reject a constitutional challenge, however, the Constitutional Court has since developed a rich variety of judgments, which again as we shall see, are based on the necessity to respond to specific practical needs rather than drawing on abstract theory.

In particular, the various types of judgments arise from the necessity, recognized by the Constitutional Court, to consider the impact its decisions have on the legal system and on other branches of government, in particular Parliament and the judiciary.

This result was made technically possible by the theoretical distinction between '*disposizione*' and '*norma*,' or legal 'texts' and 'norms'.[21] A 'text' represents a linguistic expression that manifests the will of the body that creates a particular legal act. A 'norm,' on the other hand, is the result of a process of interpreting a text. By use of hermeneutic techniques, one can derive multiple norms from a single text or a single norm from multiple texts. This distinction between text and norm is particularly important in that it permits the separation of the norm from the literal meaning of the text, in a way cutting the umbilical cord that link them at the moment the text is approved. This distinction allows the system to evolve, facilitating the interpreter's creative activity and helping to reduce the 'destructive' activity of the Court, with its consequent gaps in the legal system, giving it the ability to operate with more surgical precision.

---

[18] This debate has been summarized in the essays published in Romboli, R (ed) (1990) *La giustizia costituzionale a una svolta*, Giappichelli.

[19] On this judicial creativity see Pinardi, R (1993) *La Corte, i giudici ed il legislatore. Il problema degli effetti temporali delle sentenze di incostituzionalità*, Giuffré; Pinardi, R (2007) *L'horror vacui nel giudizio sulle leggi. Prassi e tecniche decisionali utilizzate dalla Corte costituzionale allo scopo di ovviare all'inerzia del legislatore*, Giuffré and exemples cited by Pinardi. In English see Vigoriti, V (1972) 'Admonitory Functions of Constitutional Courts – Italy: The Constitutional Court' *Am. J. Comp. L.* 20 at 404.

[20] See Art. 136 It. Const.

[21] This distinction was introduced by Crisafulli, V (1956) 'Questioni in tema di interpretazione della Corte Costituzionale nei confronti con l'interpretazione giudiziaria' *Giurisprudenza costituzionale* at 929 et seq.

Relationship with the courts

The need to establish a relationship with the courts, which are charged with interpreting statutory law, has led the Constitutional Court to issue two kinds of decisions, 'corrective' decisions and 'interpretative' decisions (which can come when the Court either strikes down or upholds a law). These two kinds of decision have allowed a division of labour between the ordinary courts and the Constitutional Court and have mitigated conflicts that arose during the Court's early years.[22]

a)   With its so-called *'corrective'* decisions, the Constitutional Court avoids the merits of the constitutional question and simply states that the statutory interpretation of the certifying judge is incorrect, in that he failed to consider either the teaching of other courts, a consolidated interpretation of the law in question, of the plain meaning of the text or, increasingly, of a possible interpretation that would conform to the Constitution.

b)   With *'interpretative'* decisions, the Constitutional Court distinguishes between the text and the norm (see above) and either indicates to the certifying judge an alternative interpretation (norm) that is in pursuance of the Constitution thus rejecting the constitutional challenge (i.e. a *sentenza interpretativa di rigetto*) or it judges the interpretation given by the certifying judge to be contrary to the Constitution and strikes down that specific norm, but not the text itself (i.e. a *sentenza interpretativa di accoglimento*).

More specifically, in the case of a *sentenza interpretativa di rigetto* the Constitutional Court offers the ordinary courts an interpretation that would render the statute consistent with the Constitution, thereby saving it from unconstitutionality. With such an interpretative judgment the Constitutional Court declares the challenge 'unfounded' insofar as the law can be attributed a meaning consistent with the Constitution, which is different from the one given to it by the certifying judge or the petitioner. Among the possible meanings of the text, the Court chooses the one that is compatible with the Constitution, putting aside those which could conflict with the Constitution.

Such an interpretation offered by the Court is not, however, universally binding because these judgments reject the challenge and therefore they only have an *inter partes*.[23] It is effective only insofar as its opinion is

---

[22]   See Merryman, JH and Vigoriti, V (1967) 'When Courts Collide: Constitution and Cassation In Italy' *Am. J. Comp. Law* 15 at 665.

[23]   The reason for this, as pointed out by an eminent constitutionalist and former President of the Italian Court Livio Paladin, is that Art. 136 of the Italian Constitution only deals with the generally binding effect of judgments that *accept* the challenge, but it is tacit with regard to the binding effects of judgments that *reject* a challenge. This 'silence' has been interpreted by the ordinary courts and by most legal scholars as signifying that the latter only have an

persuasive or its authority as constitutional arbiter is convincing. A legal duty is created only in relation to the judge who raised the question, who cannot follow the interpretation he initially submitted to the Court.

c) Due to this fact ordinary judges can ignore the Constitutional Court's interpretation, thereby persisting in an interpretation of the provision that is not in pursuance of the Constitution, thus demonstrating some of the underlying tensions between the Constitutional Court and the judiciary. Over time the Constitutional Court has thus increasingly delivered interpretative judgments that *accept* a challenge. In such judgments, the Court acknowledges the fact that the ordinary judges are interpreting the provision in an unconstitutional manner (even though other interpretations in pursuance with the Constitution would be possible) and it thus declares that specific interpretation unconstitutional. Because this is a judgment that *accepts* the constitutional challenge it is binding *erga omnes* therefore the provision can no longer be interpreted in that way, however all other interpretations remain valid, therefore the Constitutional Court does not strike down the text itself, but only one of the norms it gives rise.

Relationship with the legislature

While *'interpretative'* judgments seem designed to address the relationship between the Court and ordinary courts, other sorts of decisions have instead affected the relationship between the Court and the legislature.[24]

a) An especially delicate issue has been the use of *'additive'* judgments, whereby the Court declares a statute unconstitutional not for what it provides but for what it fails to provide. In this way, the Court manages to insert new rules into the legal system which cannot be found in the statutory text. This kind of decision runs contrary to Kelsen's model of constitutional review, according to which a constitutional court ought be a *'negative legislator'*. With these judgments, the Constitutional Court transforms itself into a creator of legal rules, thereby playing a role that in the Italian system belongs principally to Parliament. Yet in many cases, the mere nullification of an unconstitutional law would not solve the problem posed by the constitutional question, and the addition of a missing rule is

---

inter partes effect. It is worth pointing out, in the context of this book that this constitutes an important difference with respect to two other countries with a constitutional justice system similar to Italy i.e. Germany and Spain. In these two countries *both* judgments that *accept* and judgments that *reject* the challenge are binding *erga omnes*, see Paladin, L (1988) 'La tutela delle libertà fondamentali offerta dalle Corti costituzionali europee: spunti comparatistici' in Carlassare, L (ed.) (1988) *Le garanzie costituzionali dei diritti fondamentali,* Cedam, 11-25.

[24] Details and examples may be found in the books of Pinardi, quoted above at note 18.

the only way to remedy the violated constitutional value and, therefore, offers the only way for constitutional law to perform its task.

A first effort to limit the interpretative scope of such judgments is the principle that they are appropriate only where it is said, to use a poetical metaphor, as the Court did, that the judgment inserts only *'rime obbligate'*, or 'obligatory verses', into a statute. That is, the norm proposed by the Court is regarded by it as logically necessary and implicit in the normative context, thereby eliminating any appearance of discretionary choice.

b)   A second effort to eliminate the interference with the parliamentary domain implied by these judgments has led, in recent years, to the development of a slightly different type of judgment, which is described as adding only 'principles' rather than 'norms' (see above). These are known as *'additive di principio'*. In these decisions, the Court does not insert new rules into the legal system, but only principles, rather like framework legislation, that the legislature must give effect to with statutes that are universally effective, indicating a deadline within which the legislature must act.[25] In this way, the Constitutional Court strives to strike a balance between safeguarding the Constitution and preserving the discretionary powers of the legislator. In fact, as with additive judgments, the Court declares the statute unconstitutional, but in this case it leaves it up to Parliament to actually decide how to amend the provisions rather than itself providing a detailed set of rules. The problem is that these judgments pose problems with regard to their effectiveness vis-à-vis ordinary judges. In most cases judges have deemed it essential for Parliament to legislate on the basis of the guiding principles indicated by the Constitutional Court; however, on the other hand, in some cases they have considered the Court's decision to be directly applicable to the case at bar (i.e. they treat it like a standard additive judgment).

c)   Another type of decision deriving from the necessity of caution in relation to the legislature is the so-called 'admonitory' decision or *'doppia pronuncia'* – what one might call 'repeat' or 'follow-up' judgments. The Court has adopted this approach when it has faced highly politicized questions.

---

[25]   See, i.e., the decisions n. 185/1998, n. 26/1999, n. 32/1999, n. 61/1999; n. 179/1999, n. 270/1999, n. 526/2000. As examples, the decision n. 26/1999 may be quoted. In that case, the Court declared unconstitutional that part of the law on the organisation of the prison system which provided immunity for the prison administration from actions for damages by prisoners when their rights have been infringed. The Court expressly declared 'that the statute is unconstitutional due its defect in not providing jurisdictional guarantees, but the rules of judicial review of legislation do not allow for the introduction of the legislation needed to remedy such a defect. Thus, in order to carry out the principles of the constitution, the Court's only option is to declare the unconstitutionality of the omission, and, at the same time, call for Parliament to exercise its legislative function to remedy the defect'.

In these cases, it has preferred to bide its time and hint at its decision that the challenged norm is unconstitutional, without explicitly declaring it so. The Constitutional Court has introduced a logical distinction between its judgment and its opinion: the former announces that the constitutional question is 'inadmissible'; the latter, however, clearly indicates that the constitutional doubts are well-founded. Structurally, *'doppie pronuncie'* imply that in the first instance the Court will reject the certified challenge, asking the legislature to act. If Parliament does not act and the question is raised again, the Court will respond with a judgment that accepts the constitutional challenge, declaring the law unconstitutional.

d)   A further point is that the highly political nature of some issues, combined with the need to balance the defence of social rights against the state's financial exigencies, has obliged the Constitutional Court to moderate the effects of its decisions that strike down laws as unconstitutional. In this way, the Court tries both to assure that the Government and Parliament have the time needed to fill the gap created by its nullification of a law, and to strike a balance between the constitutional rights central to the social welfare state and the limits to economic resources.

This problem is not unique to the Italian legal system. Comparative study offers several solutions. The Austrian Constitutional Court can postpone the effects of a judgment nullifying a law for up to one year, thereby letting parliament regulate the area and avoid legal gaps.[26] The German Federal Constitutional Court can also declare laws simply 'incompatible' (*Unvereinbarkeit*), without declaring them nullified, or can declare that a law is 'still' constitutional. In that case, the law is declared only temporarily constitutional. The Court retains its power to declare the law unconstitutional if the legislature does not modify the law to conform with its judgment.[27]

In Italy, by contrast, the implications of the timing of a judgment that accepts a constitutional challenge are more rigidly established.[28] The Constitutional Court has tried, through its case law, to spread over time the effects of its decisions in two ways. First of all, it has imposed limits on the retroactive effects of its decisions accepting constitutional challenges (in order, for example, to protect certain trial proceedings) through what have been labeled judgments of 'supervening unconstitutionality'. In these cases, the norm is not nullified *ab initio*, but only from the moment it is held to be invalid. The simplest example is when a new constitutional

[26]   See the article on Austria in this issue.
[27]   See the article on Germany in this issue.
[28]   In fact, Art. 30.3 of Law 87/1953 clearly states that 'norms that have been declared unconstitutional cannot be applied the day following the publication of the decision'.

norm takes effect, but one could also imagine a change in the economic or financial environment, in social attitudes, or in a more general change in conditions that leaves a norm incompatible with the Constitution.

Finally, the Court can postpone the effects of a declaration of unconstitutionality (for example, where judgments lead to expenses for the public treasury), leaving the legislature a fixed amount of time to act before the statute is nullified. These are decisions of 'deferred unconstitutionality', where the Court itself, based on the balancing of various constitutional values, pinpoints the date on which the law is nullified. Such decisions pose serious problems of compatibility with the Italian system of constitutional review, in that they do not affect the case in question, thereby detracting from the concrete nature of review that characterizes the system.

THE MAIN STAGES OF DEVELOPMENT OF ITALIAN CONSTITUTIONAL REVIEW IN THE LAST FIFTY YEARS

To evaluate the role played by the Constitutional Court in the Italian constitutional system, its relationship with other branches of government and with parliamentary democracy, one can delineate (at the risk of oversimplification) several stages in its development[29].

Promotion of reforms

The first period (from the 1950s, when the Court was established, to the early 1970s)[30] could be described as 'implementation of the Constitution' or 'promotion of reforms'. This period was characterized by the central role played by the Constitutional Court in the modernization and democratization of the Italian legal system, as well as in the affirmation of the values contained in the new republican Constitution. In this process

---

[29]   We will follow the periods proposed by Cheli, E (1996) *Il giudice delle leggi*, Il Mulino. For an overview of the experience of the Court, see Volcansek, ML (2000) *Constitutional Politics in Italy: the Constitutional Court*, MacMillan. The decisions of the Court are available on its website, already quoted supra at note 8, and on the website www.giurcost.org, where it is possible to search for subject or words.

[30]   The Constitutional Court was not established until 1956, with a delay of eight years. The difficulty of establishing the Court was due to the resistances of the government, which tried to avoid the counter- majoritarian limitation always determined by constitutional justice. During this period of time, according to the VII transitional provision of the Constitution, judicial review had to be carried out by the ordinary courts, following the decentralized system. The lack of the 'constitutional sensibility' of the ordinary judges explains the small number of cases in which a statute was set aside because unconstitutional. See Adams, JC and Barile, P (1953) The 'Implementation of the Italian Constitution' *Am. Pol. Sc. Rev.* 61 at 66 *et sequitur*; Dietze, G (1958) 'America and Europe – Decline and Emergence of Judicial Review' *Va. L. Rev.* 44 at 1258.

of systemic reform, the Court acted as a stand-in for Parliament, which was slow and timid in modifying statutes inherited from earlier times. In this phase, the Constitutional Court took on what might be described as a 'didactic' function, in that it breathed life into the Constitution's principles and brought them to the attention of society, as well as a catalyzing function, as it renewed the legal system by eliminating norms contrary to the Constitution.

The Constitutional Court found itself constantly filling in for Parliament, which pursued statutory reform slowly and hesitatingly, and found itself in conflict with the highest levels of the judiciary, in particular with the Court of Cassation and the Council of State, according to whom programmatic constitutional norms did not provide grounds for judicially reviewing legislation. Beginning with its first judgment (n. 1 of 1956), which constitutes a landmark decision in Italian constitutional law, the Court affirmed the binding nature of all constitutional norms (thereby overriding the classic distinction between preceptive and programmatic norms), specifying their binding character not only in relation to the government, but also private parties, and reiterated its power to review laws that predated the Constitution.[31] In this way, thanks also to the stimulus provided by progressive elements of the judiciary, which raised numerous constitutional challenges to laws enacted before the Constitution concerning liberty as well as social and economic rights, the Constitutional Court was able to purge the legal system of numerous unconstitutional norms dating back to the 19th century as well as to the fascist era (1922-1943). Worthy of note are the Court's actions to protect personal liberty (such as its judgments in connection with the public security law of 1931 and the old system of unlimited pretrial detention, judgment n. 11 of 1956); freedom of expression (which was purged of the worst lingering traces of fascism such as the multiple permits to be obtained from the police, judgments n. 9 of 1965 and n. 49 of 1971); freedom of assembly (the Court declared unconstitutional a law that required prior notice for assemblies in public places, judgment n. 27 of 1958); and gender equality (the Court declared unconstitutional, in judgment n. 33 of 1960, a 1919 law that excluded women from a vast array of public positions).

---

[31]   On the first decision see Adams, JC and Barile, P (1957-1958) 'The Italian Constitutional Court in Its First Two Years of Activity', *Buff. L. Rev.* 7 at 250. Cf. also here the article by Harding and Leyland in this issue, which adverts to a similar critical decision in Indonesia. On the first years see Evans, M (1968) 'The Italian Constitutional Court' *Int'l & Comp. L. Q.* 17 at 602; Farrelly, DG (1957) 'The Italian Constitutional Court' *Italian Quarterly* 1 at 50; Farrelly, DG and Chan SH (1957) 'Italy's Constitutional Court: Procedural Aspects' *Am. J. Comp. L.* 6 at 314; Treves, G (1958) 'Judicial Review of Legislation in Italy' *Journal of Public Law* 7 at 345.

In this initial phase, the Constitutional Court was considered, both by legal scholars and public opinion, the principal (if not the only) interpreter and defender of the Constitution and of the values it embodied. It is this stage that explains how the Constitutional Court garnered its authority and prestige within the Italian legal system and laid the foundations of its legitimacy.

Mediation of social and political conflicts

The second stage ran from the mid-1970s to the mid-1980s and has been described as that of 'mediation of social and political conflicts'. This was a period in which, after the 'cleansing' of pre-constitutional legislation, the object of constitutional review was no longer pre-constitutional legislation, but recent laws that had been drafted and approved by the republican Parliament. For this reason, the Court took on a more politicized role characterized by balancing techniques, essentially in the search for equilibrium and mediation among the various interests and values involved in constitutional questions. The Court slowly changed the nature of its judgments. No longer was it simply a question of applying the traditional syllogism that compared an inferior norm to a superior one. Instead, it became a matter of considering all the constitutional values at stake, of weighing them and establishing not which would prevail, but what was the best balance possible among them. In sum, one can say that at this stage the Constitutional Court evaluated the choices of the legislature to determine whether it had adequately taken into account all the values and constitutional principles that might affect a certain issue. This operation was made technically possible by an evolving interpretation of the principle of equality. From article 3 of the Constitution, according to which all are equal before the law, can be drawn a duty of reasonableness imposed on the legislature, so that it not only must regulate different situations differently, but must also refrain from using arbitrary criteria. In order for a norm not to be unconstitutional, one must avoid contradictions between the goals of a law and the concrete normative rules, between the objective pursued and the legal tools used to achieve it. In sum, one must avoid irrational contradictions between the goals of the law and the content of its text.[32] In these years, the Court acted in numerous areas that characterize a secularizing society. It is enough to mention its judgments regarding divorce; abortion (see judgment n. 27 of 1975, which sought to strike a difficult balance between protecting the fetus and safeguarding the

---

[32] An earlier example of this technique is judgment n. 46 of 1959.

mother's health); church-state relations; family rights; the right to strike (the Court declared political strikes unconstitutional, judgment n. 290 of 1980); and numerous issues connected with the right to work and social welfare. In this way, the Court struck down what it termed 'unjustified discrimination' in the salaries of public employees (judgment n. 10 of 1973); upheld the 'Workers' Statute' (judgment n. 54 of 1974); and issued innumerable additive judgments that increased state spending that aimed at equalizing (upward) welfare and wages (judgments n. 141 of 1967 and n. 103 of 1989). Emblematic of this stage are also the many decisions concerning radio and television, decisions in which the Court found itself hounding and scolding the legislature in the name of freedom of expression, yet without ever succeeding in completely guiding its choices into conformity with the Constitution (see, among the many decisions, judgment n. 202 of 1976, which definitively opened the doors to local radio and television broadcasting).

The elimination of the case backlog

Paradoxically, the Constitutional Court's tremendous success during the first stages of its activity turned out to be one of the principal factors that rendered the system of constitutional review ineffective. The massive quantity of questions raised made it rather difficult to issue decisions at an acceptable pace. The increase in the number of questions gave rise to a significant backlog and a prolongation of the process. This spiral threatened not only to swamp the Constitutional Court, but also to impair its institutional functioning. The time factor, the length of the proceeding, is crucial for the impact of constitutional decisions on the legal system. Fortunately, the members of the Court, aware of these risks, dealt with this problem through a series of reforms of the Court's procedural rules.[33] These reforms gave rise to a third stage known as 'operational efficiency' that ran from the mid-1980s to the mid-1990s. The main goal of this new phase was to reduce the time taken for a constitutional decision and the number of pending cases, through declarations of inadmissibility in summary orders (*ordinanze*) of a large number of cases that were obviously inadmissible or trivial, as well as through the selection of cases on which the Court could focus its attention. To this end, the Constitutional Court adopted numerous procedural innovations (organization of work, streamlining of debate, deciding cases by summary order, and so on) that helped to reach

---

[33] See La Greca, G (1997) 'Current Situation and Planned Reforms in the Light of Italian Experience' *The Supreme Court and the Constitutional Court: Third Meeting of Presidents of Supreme Courts of Central and Eastern European Countries,* Council of Europe at 9.

these goals. At the beginning of the 1990s, the number of pending cases was significantly lower and the length of constitutional review cases had been reduced to nine months.

In order to reach this result some sacrifices had to be made, as pointed out by scholars who during these years focused their attention on constitutional procedure. For example, the number of decisions increased, but often at the expense of more summary opinions. The method for organizing work reduced the collegiality of decision-making and the importance of the parties' arguments, simultaneously increasing the procedural discretion of the Constitutional Court. In sum, operational efficiency does not always equate to effective decision-making. Insufficiently explained opinions are less persuasive and carry the risk of reducing consensus, both among scholars and the public and, as a consequence, of reducing the Court's legitimacy. Various procedural ideas have been advanced to promote more carefully reasoned opinions, in particular the introduction of dissenting opinions.[34] Likewise, some have proposed allowing interested parties to participate in constitutional proceedings even though they are not involved in the lawsuit giving rise to the constitutional question, in order to offer the Court more viewpoints in evaluating constitutional claims.[35] Yet none of these attempts has so far produced any change in constitutional procedure.

The Court during the 'transition years'

Once the case backlog had been eliminated, the Italian system of constitutional review entered a new stage, whose features are still unclear.

First, the brief time that passes between the raising and determination of a question means that the object of the Court's review is ever more frequently neither a law of the fascist period nor a law passed by a previous legislature, but a law that has just been adopted: that is, one supported by a current political majority. This rapidity has important consequences for the relationship between the Constitutional Court and Parliament as well as the judiciary. As for the former, the Court is inevitably drawn into current political conflicts. When politically and socially important issues are at stake, connected with recently approved laws that are often the result of delicate compromises and long debates, it is unavoidable that the Court's decisions are politically influenced and that its legal judgments are viewed both by the public and scholars as decisions of mere political convenience.[36]

---

[34] Panizza, S (1998) *L'introduzione dell'opinione dissenziente nel sistema di giustizia costituzionale,* Giappichelli.

[35] D'Amico, G (1991) *Parti e processo nella giustizia costituzionale,* Giappichelli.

[36] See Rolla, G and Groppi, T 'Between Politics and the Law: The Development of

The difficulties in these cases are obvious. In order to preserve the authority of their decisions, the Court's opinions take on special importance, particularly in their ability to persuade on the rhetorical rather than the logical level. As regards relations with the ordinary courts, the Court's rapid turnaround and the fact that it confronts 'new' laws means that the Court is forced to rule on the constitutionality of laws that have not yet received a consolidated judicial interpretation, the so-called 'living law'. The Court is therefore called upon to perform the task of interpreting the law subject to review, a task that belongs to the judiciary rather than the Constitutional Court. This raises afresh the problem of relations with the judiciary that the use of the 'living law' was thought to have overcome.

Second, the Constitutional Court finds itself interpreting constitutional texts that embody principles of the welfare state, that is, that recognize social rights, in an environment marked by the financial crisis of the state and by economic austerity policies. The Court is trapped between Scylla and Charybdis: between the danger of abdicating its role of supreme guarantor of the Constitution and the social rights it protects, and the danger of provoking serious economic repercussions with its decision. The Court's concern for the financial consequences of its decisions is readily perceptible from a survey of its activity. Indeed, it frequently issues evidence-gathering orders to acquire information about the costs of possible judgments striking down laws. Furthermore, a look at the Court's case law shows its tendency to significantly reduce, compared to the earlier stages, the number of decisions based on the principle of equality and designed to equalize unequal situations upward. On the contrary, on some occasions the Court has chosen the opposite path; faced with challenges raised in the name of equality, it has decided to equalize the situations downward, raising before itself *sua sponte* the question of the constitutionality of the baseline offered by the certifying judge (the *tertium comparationis*). This was the situation with regard to the personal income tax on pensions of parliamentary deputies. The favourable treatment they received was invoked as the baseline for all citizens in a case involving the income of employees. The Court did not hesitate to question *sua sponte* the favorable treatment accorded to these pensions, and declared them unconstitutional (n. 289 of 1994).

In the hope of balancing these two goals – on the one hand to fulfil its role of constitutional guardian, in particular of social rights, and on the other hand not to directly create state budgetary burdens without

---

Constitutional Review in Italy' in Sadurski, W (eds) (2002) *Constitutional Justice, East and West*, Kluwer Law International.

adequate financial support – the Constitutional Court has from the mid-1990s developed the innovative decisional techniques mentioned earlier, in particular judgments that 'add principles' rather than norms. These decisions are aimed at recognizing rights, but leaving it to the legislature to choose the means for implementing them and the funds to meet their costs. Illustrative of this tendency is judgment n. 243 of 1993. In that decision, the Court declared unconstitutional norms that excluded a cost-of-living adjustment from the calculation of severance pay benefits, but held that its decision could not take the form of the mere nullification of a law, or of an additive judgment. Rather, it fell to the legislature to choose the appropriate means 'in view of the selection of economic political choices needed to provide the necessary financial resources'.

Third, the constitutional reform of the State-regions relationship in 2001 created an unexpected increase in the number of direct complaints. The consequence was an increase in the number of decisions enacted in this kind of review from 2% in 2002 to 24.41% in 2006. For some years (between 2003 and 2006), most of the activity of the Court was devoted – independently of the will of the Court itself, but simply as a consequence of the number of state-regions disputes – to the solution of problems of division of competences between different levels of government, more than to the guarantee of fundamental rights.[37]

Finally, the current stage of constitutional jurisprudence is occurring in an unstable political and institutional context characterized, since 1992, by the weakening of the established balance of political power, with the collapse of the old party system, the change in the electoral system, the birth of alliances and alignments that have not yet sufficiently consolidated their positions, and the emergence, after 40 years of a consociational political system, of a majority system based on the alternation in government of two main coalitions.

These elements have resulted in an increase in the political role played by the Court. There has been an increase, both quantitative and qualitative, in the competences of the Constitutional Court with strong political ramifications, such as those related to conflicts over the attribution of powers among the branches of government and the admissibility of referenda to repeal laws. As a result, there has been a tendency to emphasize the Constitutional Court's role as an arbiter in political and constitutional conflict, a role from which the Court has not sought to extract itself. In this vein, it is worth noting its judgment concerning votes of no-

---

[37] See Del Duca, LF and Del Duca, P (2006) 'An Italian Federalism? The State, Its Institutions and National Culture as Rule of Law Guarantor' *Am. J. Comp. L.* 54 at 799.

confidence in individual ministers (which the Court found constitutional, even in the absence of express constitutional provisions, on the ground that they are inherent in the form of parliamentary government: judgment n. 7 of 1996); the cases regarding decree-laws (the Court went so far as to declare the unconstitutionality of reissuing them, in judgment n. 360 of 1996, because they violate legal certainty and would change the structure of government; see also n. 171 of 2007); the case law governing the immunity of parliamentary deputies for statements made in the performance of their official functions (in this regard, after many years of uncertainty, the Court annulled a parliamentary vote of immunity deemed to have been adopted in the absence of any functional nexus between the declaration of the deputy and his parliamentary activity: judgment n. 289 of 1998); the case related to the power of mercy of the President of Republic and his relationship with the Minister of Justice (judgment 200 of 2006, in which the Court ruled that this is a typical presidential power and that the Minister cannot influence the decision); and the case regarding the immunity of the higher power of the state (judgment n. 24 of 2004, in which the Court ruled the unconstitutionality of the statute that determined a complete immunity).

CONCLUSIONS

More than 50 years of constitutional review in Italy have brought about a consolidation of the position of the Constitutional Court. It is an important institutional actor, well accepted by public opinion and respected by the political system.[38]

In the last few years, however, something has changed. The traditional sources of legitimacy of the Court (the Constitution itself and the dialogue with public opinion) seem weaker than in the past, having been dried up by the loss of legitimacy of the Constitution itself, testified by the need, more and more widely acknowledged, of reform,[39] and the apathy of the public.

In order to preserve its legitimacy and to defend itself against an increasingly aggressive political power, the attitude of the Court has been very cautious: so far the Court has decided not make a direct link with public opinion. Instead, it preferred to 'disappear' from the headlines, devolving a large part of its job to other actors.[40]

---

[38] As it is testified by the fact that only in very few cases does Parliament reenact a law already set aside by the Court.

[39] An important constitutional reform, aimed at amending more than 50 articles of the Constitution, was passed by Parliament in 2006, but rejected by the people in a national referendum.

[40] On this attitude see Nardini, WJ (1999-2000) 'Passive Activism and the Limits of Judicial Self-Restraint: Lessons for America from the Italian Constitutional Court' *Seton Hall L. Rev.*

We can point out two main paths that have been followed by the Court towards this new, low-profile role.

First of all, the Court tries to decentralize its work maximally, involving ordinary judges more deeply in constitutional review than the European model of judicial review normally provides for, in order to share with them the task of safeguarding the Constitution. Before referring a question to the Constitutional Court, an ordinary judge is expected to look for an interpretation of the statute that will preserve its constitutional validity. Although ordinary judges cannot disregard statutes on constitutional grounds, they can interpret them. But it is obviously difficult to identify the conditions that a reading of a statute must satisfy to qualify as 'interpretation'. The European model is thus based on an unstable distinction between the power to interpret (for ordinary judges) and the power to set aside (for the Constitutional Court): in Italy the distinction is changing, in favor of the judiciary, by request of the Constitutional Court itself.

Secondly, the Court looks increasingly to supranational jurisdictions. The shift of Italian case-law in this regard in 2007 and 2008 was extremely significant. In judgments n. 347 and 348 of 2007 the Court established that the ECHR and the interpretation given to it by the European Court of Human Rights are 'intermediate law' (*norme interposte*) which falls between mere statute and the Constitution, and can be used as a parameter in reviewing the constitutionality of a national statute. In judgments n. 102 and 103 of 2008 the Court defined itself for the first time as a 'court or tribunal of a Member State' for the purposes of Article 234 (formerly Article 177) of the EC Treaty, in order to apply to the European Court of Justice and ask for a preliminary ruling on the interpretation of European Community law.[41] It should be remembered that in its previous case law, particularly in the ordinance n. 536/ 1995, the Italian Constitutional Court had always excluded that possibility in broad terms.

Both tendencies imply a transfer of power from the Constitutional Court to other bodies: ordinary judges on one hand, supranational judges on the other hand. The Court chooses to devolve many of its powers, to become 'the last resort' in defending the Constitution against extraordinary attacks.

Thus, as a consequence of this evolution, the question today in Italy concerns the very future of the centralized constitutional review.

On the one hand, the search for legitimacy might determine its impoverishment and even its disappearance. In that case, the price to

30 at 1.
[41] On the previous jurisprudence of the Court in relation to the EC law, see Cartabia, M (1990) 'The Italian Constitutional Court and the Relationship Between the Italian Legal System and the European Community' *Mich. J. Int'l L* 12 at 173.

be paid in the name of legitimacy would be too high. In addition, there are no guarantees that the legitimacy of the ordinary judiciary or of the supranational courts is better established than that of the Constitutional Court. The Constitutional Court, with its visibility, its history, its roots and its powerful resources is still more suitable than any other court in order to face the 'democratic objection'. On the other hand, we might witness not at a disappearance but a transformation, from a centralized system of judicial review towards a 'multilevel system', in which ordinary courts and supranational courts also contribute to the guarantee of the national Constitution, but under the direction and the control of the Constitutional Court. In that case, the Constitutional Court would play a new role: not the sole guarantor of the Constitution, but a kind of signalman (*'manovratore di scambi'*) in a system with many actors.

This new trend has just begun. We will see in the next years where this evolution will bring the Italian Constitutional Court.

The Constitutional Court of the Russian Federation: the Establishment and Evolution of Constitutional Supervision in Russia

JANE HENDERSON *

INTRODUCTION

Russia has transformed during the past 20 years. Before that, she was the Russian Soviet Federated Socialist Republic (RSFSR), one of 15 Socialist Republics in the vast empire of the Union of Soviet Socialist Republics (USSR). Now she is a 'democratic federated rule-of-law State with a republic form of government' (1993 Constitution of the Russian Federation article 1).[1] Then she had a parliamentary system, although with the Communist Party of the Soviet Union (CPSU, the Party) as the 'iron hand in the velvet glove of state'.[2] Now she has a presidential system with separation (although not balance) of powers (Constitution article 10), ideological diversity (article 13), and the principle that 'man, his rights and freedoms are the highest value' (article 2).

---

* King's College London. I would like to thank Alex Prezanti and Ksenya Kolpatchi for their materials, even if constraints of space precluded inclusion.

[1] English translation in Butler, WE (2005) *Russian Public Law* Wildy, Simmonds & Hill at 4.
[2] To paraphrase Professor Tumanov (later Chairman of the CCRF) giving evidence at the CC RSFSR hearing on the constitutionality of the CPSU that 'our state was merely a glove on the party hand', cited in Feofanov, Y (1993) 'The Establishment of the Constitutional Court in Russia and the Communist Party Case' (19) *Review of Central and East European Law* 623 at 627.

Part of the transformation has been the establishment of a Constitutional Court.[3] As with any major transformation, it has not been an easy passage and within three years of its founding the new Court endured suspension and resurrection with revised terms. Nevertheless it has successfully established itself as a key player in Russia's polity, not only as an important tribunal but also as an educator of judges, politicians, and the general population on the requirements for the rule-of-law state to which Russia aspires.

ESTABLISHING A COURT

The USSR Constitutional Supervision Committee (1990-91)

Soviet constitutions[4] were not directly applicable, and there was virtually no mechanism for testing the constitutionality of legislation. The legislature had the formal power to conduct 'constitutional oversight' but this was ineffective.[5]

Change came under the leadership of Mikhail Gorbachev, the Party General Secretary from 1985-91. The first lawyer since Lenin in the Party Politburo, he ushered in the era of перестройка (perestroika; restructuring) and the aspiration to set up a socialist rule-of-law state (социалистическое правовое государство; sotsialisticheskoe pravovoe gosudarstvo).[6] This included establishing the USSR Constitutional Supervision Committee (CSC) in 1990, to ensure 'conformity [...] to the USSR Constitution and [...] the protection of the constitutional rights and freedoms of the individual'.[7]

---

[3] For a thorough full-length analysis of the Russian Constitutional Court, see Trochev, A (2008) *Judging Russia: Constitutional Court in Russian Politics, 1990-2006* Cambridge University Press.

[4] 1918, 1925, 1937 and 1978 RSFSR Constitutions, 1924, 1936 and 1977 USSR Constitutions ; texts available at: <//www.constitution.garant.ru/DOC_8005.htm>.

[5] There are two minor exceptions: during the 1920s, the first USSR Supreme Court did have power of constitutional review, but only in an advisory capacity, reporting to the Presidium of the Central Executive Committee; see Solomon, PH (1990) 'The USSR Supreme Court: History, Role, and Future Prospects' (38) *American Journal of Comparative Law* 127. From 1977 the USSR Presidium had a duty based on 1977 USSR Constitution article 121(4) to 'exercise control over the observance of the USSR Constitution'; used for example against Estonia: see Henderson, J (1990) 'The Soviet constitutional reforms of December 1 1988: an analysis of the changes from draft to law' in Plender, R (ed) (1990) *Legal History and Comparative Law: Essays in Honour of Albert Kiralfy* Frank Cass 73 at 89.

[6] Resolution on Legal Reform of the 19th Conference of the CPSU, *Izvestiia* 5 July 1988.

[7] Law on Constitutional Supervision in the USSR of 23 December article 1 (1989) *Ved. SND SSSR* №29 item 572, translated in Butler, WE (1991) *Basic Documents on the Soviet Legal System* (2nd ed.) Oceana at 185.

A key motivation to create the CSC was to regulate relations between the Soviet Union and its constituent Socialist Republics.[8] This was problematic, not least because the Republics were reluctant to have a federal body ruling on disputes between themselves and the Union. It was politically unfeasible to give this role to a federal court, so the resultant body was labelled a Committee.[9] Nevertheless, it was hoped that the CSC would be taken seriously; those elected as members were highly regarded academics, not judges, who in the social milieu of the time were rarely afforded respect.

The Soviet Presidency was established in March 1990, after the law on the CSC had already been passed, so it did not provide for supervising presidential activity. However, as Gorbachev was appointed Soviet President by the legislature, rather than being directly elected, he qualified as an 'official' and was therefore subject to CSC control.[10]

Despite its short existence (May 1990 to 23 December 1991), the CSC worked hard to protect individual rights, including taking cases on its own initiative.[11] It acted as an important trailblazer for the Russian Constitutional Court.[12]

The Constitutional Court of the RSFSR (1991-93)

The law creating Russia's first Constitutional Court was passed on 12 July 1991.[13] The need for such a court was explicitly linked to the new Russian Presidency.[14] When Sergei Shakhrai, the Chairman of the Committee on Legislation, introduced the draft to the Supreme Soviet[15] he emphasised

---

[8] Middleton, J (1998) 'The Soviet experiment with constitutional control: the predictable failure of the USSR Constitutional Supervision Committee' in Müllerson, A, Fitzmaurice, M and Andenas, M (eds) (1998) *Constitutional Reform and International Law in Central and Eastern Europe* Kluwer 133. See also Hausmaninger, H (1992) 'The Committee of Constitutional Supervision of the USSR' 23 *Cornell International Law Journal* 287 and Trochev supra note 4 at 55ff.

[9] See Hausmaninger, H (1992) 'From the Soviet Committee of Constitutional Supervision to the Russian Constitutional Court' (25) *Cornell International Law Journal* 305 at 306.

[10] Point made at Anglo-Soviet Symposium, University College London, March 1990 by Professor Larin, chief draftsman of the law on the CSC.

[11] Maggs, P (1991) 'Enforcing the Bill of Rights in the twilight of the Soviet Union' *University of Illinois Law Review* 1049.

[12] Hausmaninger supra note 9 at 330.

[13] 'On the Constitutional Court of the RSFSR' (1991) *Ved SND i VS RSFSR* №30, item 1017. English translation in (1994) *Statutes and Decisions* (30(6)) 42. See also Trochev supra note 3 at 66 ff.

[14] Law on the President of the RSFSR, 24 April 1991. Boris Yel'tsin decisively won the contested election on 12 June.

[15] The Supreme Soviet was the 'organ of the CPD and permanently functioning legislative, administrative and control agency of state power of the Russian Federation' (article 107 RSFSR Constitution as amended).

that the court would be 'an important instrument in the balance of the three powers; legislative, executive and judicial'[16] necessitated by the introduction of an executive President. Indeed, the Court's first case involved overenthusiastic exercise of presidential power.[17]

There was provision for 15 judges with tenure for an unlimited term subject to retirement at 65. Candidates were nominated to the full Russian legislature, the Congress of People's Deputies (CPD), by political factions or committees of the legislature.[18] Approval was by majority vote. Only 13 out of the 15 seats were filled, but that provided a sufficient quorum. The sole woman, Morshchakova, was the only judge who had never been a Party member.[19]

The CC RSFSR had two main tasks. It considered constitutionality of 'international treaties and normative acts' (article 1(2)(1); ch.2) including taking cases on its own initiative (article 74). It also could receive individual appeals on 'the practice of application of law […] in accordance with custom' (article 1(2)(2); ch. 3), provided other procedures had been exhausted. This controversial power enabled the Court to look beyond the text of a legislative act to the impact of its actual (and regular) application. However, the Court could refuse jurisdiction if it found such an appeal 'to be inexpedient (*нецелесообразное; netselesoobraznoe*)' (article 69(14)).[20]

The court design borrowed from foreign experience, 'including the United States, but primarily by German, Austrian and Italian constitutional models',[21] with the Court's power of concrete review of the practice of application of law 'inspired by the German experience'.[22]

The CC RSFSR began work at the end of October 1991. By the end of December the USSR had dissolved, leaving its constituent Socialist

[16] (1991) *VS Biulleten'* №26 at 13. Cited in Henderson, J (1998) 'The first Russian Constitutional Court: hopes and aspirations' in Müllerson, A, Fitzmaurice, M and Andenas, M (eds) (1998) *Constitutional Reform and International Law in Central and Eastern Europe* Kluwer at 105.
[17] To merge the successor to the KGB with the Ministry of Internal Affairs. See Knechtle, J (2000) 'Isn't every case political? Political questions on the Russian, German, and American high courts' (26) *Review of Central and East European Law* 107 at 112.
[18] See Wishnevsky, J (1993) 'The Constitutional Court' 2(20) *Radio Free Europe/Radio Liberty Research Report* 14 May at 14. Wishnevsky gives tables at 12 and 13 setting out the judges' prior roles and which groups nominated them. See also Trochev supra note 3 at 70-71.
[19] Fein, E (2007) 'Re-defining justice and legitimacy in the post-Soviet space. The case of the first Russian Constitutional Court' in Fischer, S, Pleines, H and Schröder, H-H (eds) (2007) *Movements, Migrants, Marginalisation. Challenges of societal and political participation in Eastern Europe and the enlarged EU* Ibidem Publishers 15 at 18.
[20] More detailed discussion in Henderson supra note 16.
[21] Hausmaninger supra note 9 at 332.
[22] Burnham, W and Trochev, A (2007) 'Russia's war between the courts: the struggle over the jurisdictional boundary between the Constitutional Court and regular courts' (55) *American Journal of Comparative Law* 381 at 394.

Republics, including Russia, as independent states. At that stage the Russian Constitution was the much amended 1978 RSFSR Constitution, a clone of the 1977 USSR Constitution.

In 1993 the Constitutional Court, under its charismatic chairman Zor'kin, became embroiled in disputes between Yel'tsin and the Supreme Soviet. Zor'kin's attempts to mediate in April backfired; Yel'tsin doubted the Court's neutrality and in October he suspended its activity. He had already used force to close the legislature, under siege in the White House. Because of Yel'tsin's distrust of the Court he considered abolishing it and transferring constitutional supervision to the Supreme Court.[23] However, he was persuaded that a separate court was preferable, and the existing judges were set to draft themselves a new law. Meanwhile, Yel'tsin presented a draft constitution to the public for approval.

The 2003 Constitution

The new Constitution of the Russian Federation (RF) was adopted by national plebiscite on 12 December 2003. For the first time a Russian Constitution stipulated separation of power,[24] and direct effect.[25] The President is defined as head of state and 'guarantor of the Constitution [...] and the rights and freedoms of man and citizen'.[26] He may issue edicts and regulations, provided they do not contradict the Constitution or federal law.[27]

The new bicameral legislature, the Federal Assembly, consists of the State Duma and the Federation Council (also known as the Soviet or Council of the Federation).[28] The Federal Assembly adopts federal law and on particular issues specified in the Constitution adopts federal constitutional laws, which require qualified majorities.[29] The President may veto federal law (but can be overridden by a qualified majority) but cannot veto federal constitutional law.[30]

The President appoints the Chairman of the Government (Prime Minister), with the consent of the Duma.[31] If the Duma rejects three times

---

[23] Schwartz, H (2000) *The Struggle for Constitutional Justice in Post-Communist Europe* University of Chicago Press at 142.
[24] Article 10.
[25] Article 15.
[26] Article 80.
[27] Article 90.
[28] Article 95.
[29] Two-thirds in the Duma and three-quarters in the Federation Council.
[30] Articles 105-9.
[31] Article 83.

the candidacies submitted, the President appoints his Chairman, dissolves the Duma and designates new elections.[32] The Prime Minister proposes to the President candidates for deputy chairman and federal ministers.[33]

The President submits candidates to the Federation Council (FC) to appoint as judges to the Constitutional Court, the Supreme Court, and the Highest *Arbitrazh* (Арбитраж) Court (Commercial Court).[34] Other federal judges are appointed by the President 'in the procedure established by federal law' (article 128). The FC also has the power to suspend a Constitutional Court judge, although only for cause.[35] This has not yet occurred.

THE CONSTITUTIONAL COURT OF THE RUSSIAN FEDERATION (CCRF)

The Federal Constitutional Law 'On the Constitutional Court of the Russian Federation' (FCLCC) was passed on 21 July 1994.[36] The revised Court has 19 judges who sit in two chambers. The 13 original judges continued in office under their terms of appointment, so six new judges were needed. The Federation Council refused to accept a number of Yel'tsin's nominees despite excellent credentials because they were felt to be too close to the President. It was only when the FC realised that the longer they agonised about their choices, the longer they lacked a court with power to restrain Yel'tsin's actions that they acceded to proposed candidates. The final appointment allowing the Court to resume was in February 1995.[37]

Judicial Tenure

As we saw, the 1991 law gave the first judges an unlimited term until retirement at 65. The 1994 FCLCC established a once-only 12 year term,

---

[32]   Article 111.

[33]   Article 112.

[34]   Ovsepian, Z (1996) 'Constitutional judicial review in the Russian Federation' (34) *Russian Politics and Law* 46 at 54 notes that involvement of both executive and legislature branches in judicial appointment was borrowed from US practice; at 59 that it brings an element of balance of powers as the Court supervises those two branches.

[35]   FCLCC article 18(6) 'the commission by a judge of an offence defaming the honour and dignity of a judge'; Reglament paragraph 56: a majority of at least 10 votes at a plenary session of the court must adopt a decision before submitting the issue to the Soviet of the Federation.

[36]   (1994) *Sobranie Zakonodatel'stva Rossiskoi Federatsii* №13, item 1447. English translation in Butler, WE (2005) *Russian Public Law* Wildy, Simmonds & Hill at 454.

[37]   See Henderson, J (1995) 'The Russian Constitutional Court' 3(6) *Russia and the Successor States Briefing Service* 18 at 25 and Trochev supra note 3 at 82-85.

or retirement at 70, whichever came first. In February 2001 an amendment extended the term to 15 years and removed the fixed retirement age, but only for judges appointed between 1994-2000. The 70 year age limit was reinstated for those judges in December 2001, to come into force from 1 January 2005. The issue of retirement age was particularly sensitive, as a number of judges including the irrepressible Morshchakova were facing mandatory retirement. In fact, Morshchakova's time on the bench was extended despite her formal resignation on 31 March 2001 and her increasingly-exercised freedom to express opinions to the media, because she could only stand down once she had finished any ongoing cases and a suitable replacement had been appointed. This was delayed for some months until April 2002. Finally, in April 2005 all existing and future judges were given unlimited tenure until retirement at 70. This whole episode of 'Tinkering with Tenure'[38] when other judicial reforms were on the agenda showed 'short-term preferences of the rulers and clashes over judicial personalities'.[39] However, as Trochev evidences, this is 'anything but a unique Russian experience'.[40]

Jurisdiction

The 1993 Constitution (article 125) and the 1994 FCLRF define the CCRF's jurisdiction, although the Court may be granted other powers 'by the Constitution, Treaty of the Federation and Federal Constitutional Laws' (FCLCC article 3(7)). This has happened; the Federal Constitutional Laws 'On the Referendum' and 'On the Plenipotentiary for Human Rights in the RF' both establish a power to apply to the Court. The Court itself has also extended its jurisdiction through interpretation, discussed below.

There are three overriding jurisdictional principles. The Court does not have discretion but must consider all cases which fall within its remit and are properly presented. Secondly, it deals exclusively with issues of law, not fact.[41] And finally, the general grounds for consideration is 'indefiniteness' [*неопределенность; neopredelennost'*] or ambiguity in the normative act under review.[42] This allows the Court to refuse jurisdiction if it deems that there is no such 'indefiniteness'.

---

[38] See Trochev, A (2007) '"Tinkering with Tenure": the Russian Constitutional Court in a Comparative Perspective' in Feldbrugge, F (ed) (2007) *Russia, Europe, and the Rule of Law* Kluwer 47.
[39] Trochev supra note 3 at 87.
[40] Id at 87 and chapter 8 258ff, and supra note 38 at 71.
[41] FCLCC article 3.
[42] FCLCC article 36.

The Court has seven areas of competence, and the legislation imposes specific requirements for each. The seven are: abstract review of the constitutionality of certain legislation; settling separation of power disputes; reviewing the constitutionality of a law applied in a concrete case; constitutional interpretation; verifying impeachment procedure; and exercising legislative initiative.

Abstract review of constitutionality

There is a closed list of bodies empowered to initiate abstract review.[43] These are the President, the two chambers of the legislature, and a group of at least one fifth of the members of their legislative chamber, the Government, the Supreme Court and Highest *Arbitrazh* Court, and the agencies of legislative and executive power of subjects of the Federation. This is a narrower ambit than under the 1991 law, which also allowed an individual legislative member, the Procurator General, and 'social organisations in the person of their republican agency' to request such review.[44] The only courts that can ask for review under this heading are the Supreme Court and the Highest *Arbitrazh* Court; the CCRF cannot initiate cases itself and other courts may only bring reference in respect of concrete review discussed below.[45]

Article 125(2) lists the normative acts subject to review: (a) 'federal laws, normative acts of the President, the Federation Council, State Duma, and Government'; (b) constitutions of the republics, charters, and also laws and other normative acts of subjects of the RF issued in respect to questions relegated to their jurisdiction (see Constitution article 73 giving residual power) or to joint jurisdiction of a subject of the RF and the central authorities (listed in Constitution article 72); (c) treaties between RF authorities and the authorities of the subjects of the RF, and treaties between authorities of subjects of the RF; and (d) international treaties of the RF which have not entered into legal force. Note that except for international treaties, review is of enacted legislation, not draft. This contrasts with the USSR CSC which could consider both drafts and enacted legislation.

Matters under the exclusive jurisdiction of subjects of the Federation would go to subject level constitutional courts, if such exist.[46] This is

---

[43] Constitution RF article 125(2), FCLCC chapters IX and X.

[44] 1991 Law on the CC RSFSR article 59(1). One example of an appeal by a single member of the legislature was the countersuit in the 'Communist party case'; see Henderson, J (2007) 'The Russian Constitutional Court and the Communist Party Case: Watershed or Whitewash?' (40) *Communist and Post-Communist Studies* 1.

[45] Noted by Burnham and Trochev supra note 22 at 402.

[46] For an overview of the 15 existing courts, see Henderson, J (2008) 'Regional Constitutional Justice in the Russian Federation' (14) *European Public Law* 21; Bogdanovskaia, I (2003)

obviously problematic as the majority of subjects do not have the requisite courts. However, the same facts might give rise to consideration by both the subject and federal court if both respective constitutions are breached. There is no hierarchy of constitutional courts so cases are only heard at first instance, although there are channels for informal discussions between the judges of the different constitutional courts in Russia (similarly CCRF judges also liaise with their equivalents in Western European states).[47]

Separation of powers - issues of competence

Constitution article 125(3) and FCLCC Chapter XI specify which separation of powers disputes are subject to Court consideration. These concern the competences of (a) federal agencies of state power; (b) agencies of state power of the RF and agencies of state power of subjects of the RF; and (c) the highest state agencies of subjects of the RF. The Constitution is not explicit, but article 92 of the FCLCC makes clear that 'any of the agencies of state power specified in [this paragraph] of the Constitution of the RF and the President of the RF' are empowered to appeal to the CCRF on this issue. Other bodies or individuals do not have such power.

Concrete Review

Constitution article 125(4) specifies:

> The Constitutional Court of the RF shall verify the constitutionality of a law being applied or subject to application in a concrete case [...] in respect to appeals against the violation of the constitutional rights and freedoms of citizens and at the requests of courts.[48]

This particular power has huge significance as it is now the only routeway for citizens to obtain redress by the CCRF against infringement of their constitutional rights by unconstitutional legislation. Citizens (and others) do have power to bring to any other court (i.e. not the Constitutional Court) a 'citizen's complaint' seeking judicial review of infringement of their rights.[49] Such judicial review of administrative acts is regarded in Russia

---

'The Constitutional Court in Russia: the hard way to the "Rule of Law State"' (10) *Journal of Constitutional Law in Eastern and Central Europe* 171 at 175; Trochev, A (2001) 'The Constitutional Courts of Russia's regions: an overview' 6(44) *EastWest Institute Russian Regional Report* 12 December.

[47] See Reglament on the Constitutional Court chapter X paragraphs 66 and 67.

[48] Detailed in FCLCC Chapters XII and XIII.

[49] Based on the law 'On Appealing to a Court Actions and Decisions Violating the Rights

as an administrative rather than a constitutional proceeding, so is heard by an ordinary court or an *arbitrazh* court rather than the Constitutional Court. It follows that the court resolving the 'citizen's complaint' may rule on the legality but not the constitutionality of a piece of legislation; such a ruling does not carry as much precedential impact as a Constitutional Court decision.[50]

Concrete review is also the routeway for a judge to make a reference to the Constitutional Court querying the constitutionality of legislation applicable in a case. The practical implementation of this has been a serious and ongoing source of dispute between the CCRF and in particular the Supreme Court. Constitution article 15(1) declares the Constitution to have:

> highest legal force, direct effect, and be applied throughout the entire territory of the Russian Federation. Laws and other legal acts applicable in the Russian Federation must not be contrary to the Constitution of the RF.

On this basis, judges in the domestic court system have felt justified in refusing to apply legislation they judged to be inconsistent with the Constitution, without first asking the CCRF. On 31 October 1995 a decree of the Plenum of the Supreme Court confirmed this direct application of the Constitution.[51] The Supreme Court took the view that FCLCC article 101 specifying that a court make a request to the CCRF for a ruling on constitutionality was permissive not mandatory. The Constitutional Court took the contrary view. In a decree of 16 June 1998 it declared that it had the sole competence to rule whether legislation conformed to the Constitution;[52] a domestic court did not have the right to apply a law that it deemed to be unconstitutional but it must bring a reference to the Constitutional Court.[53] This dispute over jurisdiction has not yet been satisfactorily resolved.

and Freedoms of Citizens' *Ved RF* 1993 №19 item 685 as amended. See Henderson, J (1998) 'Defending the Rights and Freedoms of Citizens in the Russian Federation' (3) *Sudebnik* 293.
[50] See e.g. Solomon, P (2004) 'Judicial Power in Russia: through the prism of administrative justice' 38(3) *Law and Society Review* 549.
[51] *Biulleten' Verkhovnogo Suda RF* (1996) №2.
[52] *VKS RF* (1998) №5, relating to interpretation of Constitution articles 125, 126 and 127.
[53] See Di Gregorio, A (1998) 'The evolution of constitutional justice in Russia: normative imprecision and the conflicting positions of legal doctrine and case law in the light of the Constitutional Court decision of 16 June 1998' (24) *Review of Central and East European Law* 387; Krug, P (2000) 'The Russian Federation Supreme Court and constitutional practice in the courts of general jurisdiction: recent developments' (26) *Review of Central and East European Law* 129; Burnham, W and Maggs, P (2004) *Law and Legal System in the Russian Federation* (3rd ed) Juris Publishing at 82ff.

The CCRF has broadened its powers of concrete review through interpretation.[54] It has interpreted the word 'law' to include a range of normative acts, although it still does not cover sub-law such as ministerial rules. It has also expanded the right to bring appeals through non-literal interpretation of the word 'citizens' (justified by the principles of fairness and equality) to include non-citizens and legal entities. To some extent this has counterbalanced the reduction in the Court's jurisdiction. As we saw, under the 1991 law, individuals (not just citizens) could appeal directly to the court where a 'customary application of a law' infringed their constitutional rights but this possibility was not carried over into the 1994 law.[55]

Interpretation of the Constitution

The power to give authoritative binding interpretation of the Constitution was an innovation in the 1994 FCLCC (Chapter XIV). It has been particularly useful as the 1993 Constitution has stringent amendment procedures and there was no period of grace after its adoption for any textual infelicities to be ironed out (as there had been for example in relation to the Irish constitution). Three chapters are strongly entrenched and require an extraordinary process including convocation of a Constitutional Assembly even to consider the possibility of amendment (Constitution art 135). The rest can only be amended as a result of special majorities in the Duma and the Federation Council (two-thirds and three-quarters respectively) and subsequent approval by the local legislatures in at least two-thirds of the subjects of the federation (article 136).[56] The CCRF's ability to give authoritative interpretations has been invaluable to the practical application of the Constitution. Article 125(5) lists those who may request interpretation: the President, the Federation Council, State Duma, Government, and agencies of legislative power of subjects of the RF. Interpretation is made at a plenary session of the Court (article 21(2)) and is 'binding upon all representative, executive, and judicial agencies of state power, agencies of

---

[54] See Lomovtseva, M and Henderson, J (2009) 'Constitutional justice in Russia' forthcoming in (34) *Review of Central and East European Law.*

[55] Regretted by Pashin who drafted the 1991 Law: Pashin, S (1994) 'A second edition of the Constitutional Court' 3 (3/4) *East European Constitutional Review* 82 at 84.

[56] At the time of writing this process is underway for changes to the term of office of the President and the Duma. Exceptionally, amendments to constitutional article 65 relating to subjects of the federation can be made comparatively easily. Article 66 (5) allows their status to be altered by mutual consent under procedure specified in a federal constitutional law. Voluntary amalgamation has reduced the number of subjects from 89 to 83.

local self-government, enterprises, institutions, organisations, citizens, and associations thereof' (FCLCC article 106).

Unfortunately, the issue of interpretation has also become another battleground between the CCRF and the Supreme Court, over the extent to which the Constitutional Court can interpret legislation other than the Constitution. The CCRF has in recent years taken an extremely expansive view on the scope of this power, to the annoyance of the Supreme Court which feels that this trespasses on the domestic courts' remit.[57]

Verification of impeachment procedure

The President of the RF may be impeached on grounds of commission of treason or another grave crime. Accusation is made by the State Duma with the substantive issue being decided by the Federation Council. The Supreme Court must confirm the President's actions contain the elements of the alleged crime, and a plenary session of the CCRF must confirm compliance with the required procedure (Constitution article 93(1); FCLCC article 21(3) and Chapter XV). So far the Court has not been called on to fulfil this role.

Legislative initiative

Constitution article 104 lists the CCRF (along with the Supreme Court and Highest *Arbitrazh* Court) as having 'legislative initiative [...] with regard to questions of their jurisdiction'.[58] In Soviet times it was common practice for a wide range of bodies to have the power of legislative initiative, but it may be thought that in a rule-of-law state with separation of powers it is inappropriate for a Court to have this right. In practice it has been exercised minimally. The Court drafted its own 1994 law, and for example made suggestions for amendments to the Federal Constitutional Laws 'On the Judicial System' and 'On the Referendum'.[59]

---

[57]   See generally Burnham and Trochev supra note 22, and Trochev supra note 3 at 135.

[58]   FCLCC article 3(6). See also FCLCC article 21(5); paragraph 45 Reglament of the CCRF in Butler supra note 1 at 507.

[59]   (2003) *Konstitutsionnyi Sudebnyi Protsess* Norma 76. The USSR Constitutional Supervision Committee 'occasionally made formal use of its right of legislative initiative', Hausmaninger supra note 9 at 327.

Types of Court Ruling[60]

Rulings after contested hearings are issued in the form of a decree [*постановление; postanovlenie*]. The Court issues a determination [*определение; opredelenie*] on other matters, eg when refusing jurisdiction.[61] This might nevertheless be invaluable to an applicant, despite the Court's refusal to hold a hearing, if it gives reasons for deciding that there is one single (and constitutional) interpretation of the disputed legislative text.[62] Decisions are made by open vote. A decree must include supportive reasoned argument. Individual judges are allowed to give a 'separate opinion' if they wish. This may dissent from the majority decision, or agree but for different reasons. Publication of separate opinions is a novelty in Russia and not without controversy.[63] However, it may be an important factor in the development of the Court's jurisprudence. One Russian scholar suggests that the Court's discursive style of judgment with its 'past reasoning part' and the possibility of separate judicial opinions is 'similar to the structure of the decisions of the courts in common law countries'.[64] This view is reinforced by the fact that the Court follows its own previous reasoning; particularly although not exclusively in relation to interpretation of the Constitution. If it has established a 'legal position' [*правовая позиция; pravovaia pozitsiia*][65] this is binding on it unless overruled by a plenary court session.[66] In his major study of judicial law-making in Russia, Vereshchagin

---

[60]   Sources in English include summaries of the first 10 years' cases in van den Berg, G (2001) *Review of Central and East European Law* (27) and (2002-3) *Review of Central and East European Law* (28). Full translations of selected cases are in Reynolds SJ (ed) (1994) *Statutes and Decisions* (30) 3-6, (1995) *S&D* (31) 4, (1998) *S&D* (34) 1-2, (1999) *S&D* (35) 1-6, (2000) *S&D* (36) 1-6, (2001) *S&D* (37) 1-6, (2002) *S&D* (38) 1, 6, and (2005) *S&D* (41) 6. Some cases are in Burnham, W and Maggs, PB (2004) *Law and Legal System of the Russian Federation* (3rd ed) Juris, and Oda, H (2007) *Russian Commercial Law* (2nd ed) Nijhoff. For sources in Russian, see van den Berg (2001) at 88-192.

[61]   For a complaint that the Court website http://www.ksrf.ru/doc/index.htm has *postanovlenii* but not all *opredelenii*, see Simons, W (2002/3) 'Russia's Constitutional Court and a decade of hard cases: a postscript' (28) *Review of Central and East European Law* 655 at 659 ff.

[62]   The author would like to thank Dr Marina Lomovtseva for pointing out this possibility.

[63]   See Vereshchagin, A (2007) *Judicial Lawmaking in Post-Soviet Russia* Routledge-Cavendish at 161 and Barry, D (2001) 'Decision-making and dissent in the Russian Federation Constitutional Court' in Clark, R, Feldbrugge, F and Pomorski, S (eds) (2001) *International and National Law in Russia and Eastern Europe* Kluwer 1 at 16.

[64]   Bogdanovskaia supra note 46 at 180.

[65]   See discussion in Vitruk, N (1999) 'Pravovye pozitsii Konstitutsionnogo Suda Rossiiskoi Federatsii: poniatie, priroda, iuridicheskaia sila i znachenie' in Shablinskii, IG (ed) (1999) *Konstitutsionnoe Pravosudie v Postkommunisticheskikh Stranakh* Tsentr konstitutsionnykh issledovanii MONF at 88.

[66]   Requirement specified in FCLCC article 73. See Fogelklou, A (2007) 'Interpretation and accommodation in the Russian Constitutional Court' in Feldbrugge, F (ed) (2007) *Russia, Europe, and the Rule of Law* Kluwer 34 for examples of change in *pravovye pozitssii.*.

goes so far as to say that a CCRF decision sets precedent: 'It is binding upon the entire court system, its legal force is even higher than that of a law, it has both retroactive and prospective effect, decides the question of law, not fact, and is subject to publication.'[67]

Impact of International Law

International law is having an increasing influence in the Russian judicial system, encouraged by the CCRF. The Constitution article 15(4) states that 'generally recognized principles and norms of international law and international treaties of the RF shall be an integral part of its legal system'. This, combined with articles 17(1) and 18, establishes that international legal instruments, and indeed customary international law, can be directly applied in Russian courts,[68] including the Constitutional Court. However, the CCRF cannot strike down legislation as being inconsistent with international law.[69]

An early study of the CC RSFSR showed comparatively little use of international law.[70] There were some citations of international legal instruments but whilst welcome these were window-dressing than dispositive. Russia has been a member of the Council of Europe since 1996, so not only have Russians been increasingly taking cases to the European Court of Human Rights (ECtHR)[71] but the court's jurisprudence has direct application in Russia. The extent to which this is having a practical outcome is debatable. After a detailed study of citations of ECtHR judgments in Russian courts, Anton Burkov remained unimpressed because of the lack of sophistication in the arguments used in decisions, and the courts' failure to engage with ECtHR case law.[72] Nevertheless, given Russia's isolation during most of the 20th century from developments in international human rights law, it is should be a cause for optimism that its courts are attempting

---

[67] Vereshchagin supra note 63 at 118.

[68] See Decree №5 of the Supreme Court 'On the application by courts of general jurisdiction of generally recognized principles and norms of international law' of 10 October 2003 in Butler supra note 36 at 58.

[69] Pointed out by Burnham and Trochev supra note 22 at note 102.

[70] Henderson, J (1998) 'Reference to international law in decided cases of the first Russian Constitutional Court' in Müllerson, A, Fitzmaurice, M and Andenas, M (eds) (1998) *Constitutional Reform and International Law in Central and Eastern Europe* Kluwer at 59.

[71] See e.g. Bowring B (1997) 'Russia's Accession to the Council of Europe and human rights: compliance or cross purposes?' (6) *European Human Rights Law Review* 628, id. (2000) 'Russia's Accession to the Council of Europe and human rights: four years on' *European Human Rights Law Review* (4) 362, Jordan P (2003) 'Russia's accession to the Council of Europe and compliance with European human rights norms' (11) *Demokratizatsiya* 281.

[72] Burkov A (2007) *The Impact of the European Convention on Human Rights on Russian Law: Legislation and Application in 1996-2006* Ibidem.

to keep track of ECtHR developments; certainly the CCRF is supplied with the materials to allow it to do so. The flood of Russian cases to the ECtHR has more recently lead to suggestions that Russian citizens should enforce their European Convention rights more locally.[73]

Problems of enforcement

In its relationship with other agencies of state the CCRF must walk a tightrope. In many cases it will be ruling on the activities of the other branches of state power, however it may be dependent on those branches for enforcement of its rulings. Enforcement problems dogged the Court from the outset. In its very first case where it found a presidential decree unconstitutional, Court Chairman Zor'kin spent an hour persuading President Yel'tsin to accept the ruling, explaining that failure to accept the Court's decision would irreparably undermine its credibility.

Not long afterwards the Court declared as unconstitutional plans by the Republic of Tatarstan to hold a referendum asserting its sovereignty. Nevertheless Tatarstan went ahead, ignoring the Court, which was powerless to object.[74] According to Sharlet's assessment this was 'the one major setback for the court in its first year of work'.[75]

> During the first year of its existence, the Court tried to chart a course between the groves of law and the dense political thickets of Russian transitional politics. [...] In only one instance [the Tatarstan case] was the Court's authority defied - in the case most overtly fraught with politics.[76]

Amendments to FCLCC article 80 in December 2001 specified time limits within which relevant state bodies must act following adverse CCRF decisions. The Government has three months, the President two months, a subject of the Federation six months, and the executive of such a subject two months to comply. Failure may result in sanctions, such as dissolution of the local legislature or dismissal of the regional Governor. Whether these measures will solve the problem of enforcement in a state where rule-of-law is not deeply embedded remains to be seen. Trochev suggests

---

[73] See (2007) 'Putin endorses proposal to shift cases from Strasbourg to Russian courts' *Radio Free Europe/Radio Liberty Newsline* (11(185)) 5 October.
[74] See Schwartz supra note 23 at 122 ff and below text to note 95.
[75] Sharlet, R (1993) 'The Russian Constitutional Court: the First Term' (9) *Post-Soviet Affairs* 1 at 7.
[76] Id at 5-6.

that the 2001 provisions will actually further undermine court decrees by suggesting they are not self enforcing.[77] Certainly non-enforcement remains a live issue. In April 2008 the Federation Council instituted an inquiry into lack of governmental response to CCRF rulings,[78] and in May a CCRF judge publicly chastised 'authorities including judicial authorities' for flouting the Court.[79] President Medvedev's first 'state of the nation' address in November 2008 also drew attention to the 'huge problem' of the execution of court decisions. 'It is a problem for all courts, including the Constitutional Court'[80] although he did not yet propose specific remedies.

The Court Moves

Without consultation, the decision was taken in 2003 to transfer the Court from Moscow to St. Petersburg.[81] President Putin decided to distance it from the political centre, and noted that 'the Germans had placed their Constitutional Court outside the capital.'[82] Disputes over cost persuaded Prime Minister Kasianov against the move, but the plans were resurrected in late 2005 and approved shortly after with an estimated cost of eight million US$. The judges, averse to the move, lobbied for improved housing and working conditions which increased the cost to US$300 million. They also asked to keep the Court's Moscow office, to be allowed to hold sessions away from St Petersburg and to negotiate the timing of the move. The Duma agreed but then succumbed to presidential administration pressure and reneged. The judges complained to the Federation Council and the President. The relocation law as passed met the judges' demands, although they further negotiated a delay, to begin work at their new venue on 21 May 2008, rather than just before the March 2008 Presidential elections as proposed. Trochev concludes, 'In summary, Putin's initiative to move the RCC to his hometown confirmed the perception that both the internal clashes behind Kremlin walls over large sums of money trumped judicial

---

[77] Trochev, A (2002) 'Implementing Russian Constitutional Court decisions' (11(1/2)) *East European Constitutional Review* 95

[78] Romanov, I and Samarina, A (2008) 'Mironov Stands Up for Zorkin' *Nezavisimaia Gazeta* reported under title 'Russia: Putin Expected To Rocket Backsliding Government Officials' *World News Connection* 7 April accessed via Westlaw.

[79] (2008) 'Russia: Judge complains that ruling of Constitutional Court are being ignored' *BBC Monitoring Former Soviet Union* 23 May accessed via Westlaw.

[80] (2008) 'Russian president Medvedev's first annual address to parliament' *BBC Monitoring Former Soviet Union* 5 November accessed via Westlaw.

[81] See Trochev supra note 3 at 89-90.

[82] Id at 89.

independence and that judges became hostage to this exercise in routine pork-barrel politics.'[83] Even with the delay the move was not unproblematic.

> Several sources [...] commented that although the Court had met in its new building for the first time since its move on 21 May 2008, it was a 'half-baked court', working without the necessary means. The administrative and support staff had all resigned; the houses for the judges were not ready; and there was not even paper.[84]

THE CC RSFSR AND CCRF IN ACTION

Herman Schwartz summarised the CC RSFSR's first two years. It received:

> over 30,000 petitions from all sources: 16,000 during its first year alone. It decided twenty-seven cases, of which eight were based on individual complaints. [...] over 40 percent of its rulings (including the two 'opinions' on Yel'tsin's decrees not formally submitted to the court) dealt with separation of powers issues, 25 percent with federalism issues, and about a third to a half with human rights, either alone or with some other issue, the Court frequently finding human rights issues in separation of powers, or federalism contexts.[85]

In 2001 Robert Sharlet estimated that the CC RSFSR's rulings numbered 30% on individual rights, 28% on federalism, and 42% on separation of powers.[86]

By 1998 Baglai, the then CCRF Chairman, estimated that 60% of the caseload concerned individual rights, 30% federal issues and 10% disputes between legislative and executive branches.[87] In 2001, celebrating the Court's 10th anniversary, he said that 'since its founding, the Court has received more than 105,000 appeals from citizens and government agencies, held public hearings on 188 cases, and considered the constitutionality of 195 pieces of federal and regional legislation'.[88]

---

[83] Id at 90.

[84] Professor Bill Bowring, personal communication to author, citing <http://www.vedomosti.ru/newspaper/article.shtml?2008/05/27/149495>.

[85] Supra note 23 at 117-18.

[86] Sharlet, R (2001) 'Russia's second constitutional court: politics, law, and stability' in Bonnell, V and Breslauer, G (eds) (2001) *Russia in the New Century: Stability or Disorder?* Westview 59 at 71.

[87] Cited in Schwartz supra note 23 at 300 in note 349.

[88] (2001) *Radio Free Europe/Radio Liberty Newsline* (5(205)) 29 October.

Comparing the percentages calculated by Schwartz and Sharlet for the CC RSFSR and Baglai for the CCRF, we can see that federalism cases kept at approximately the same proportion during the period under review (around 30%) but there was a change in respect to the other two categories. Individual rights went up from around 30% to 60%; separation of powers down from around 40% to 10%. The first Court had 'more cases than it could handle' on separation of powers[89] but more recently individual rights cases have become a major focus. Chairman Zor'kin noted in 2006 that the Court received 15,000-17,000 complaints a year; most concern pension, labour and other social rights. Next come tax disputes, protection of property, and complaints over civil and criminal trials.[90]

Why the change? Separation of powers issues under the 1978 Constitution were problematic because it originally posited a parliamentary system, but had been amended to institute a presidential regime. The 1993 Constitution was clearer, although not perfect, but after more than a decade since its adoption many separation of powers issues have been resolved.

We may also note that Presidents Putin and Medvedev have followed the pattern begun by Mikhail Gorbachev of having had legal training. Apart from Lenin himself, no previous former leader in Russia, either pre- and post-revolutionary, had such expertise. This contrasts with, for example, the USA 'in which 26 out of 43 presidents have been lawyers, or the United Kingdom, in which 11 of 38 prime ministers since Pitt the Younger have been legally trained.'[91] Prior Soviet practice had tended to favour engineers, for example Brezhnev and his Dnipropetrovsk Faction. Yel'tsin had been a construction engineer. But since 2000 Russia has been led by someone who could understand the significance of legal provisions and would not need, as Yel'tsin had, an hour's lecture from the Constitutional Court chairman on the importance of acceding to a court decision. Both Putin and Medvedev would be in a better position to appreciate the subtle difference between working around legal rules and direct breach, and therefore be better equipped to avoid overt unconstitutional activity. More practically, the fact that both Putin and Medvedev have enjoyed a complaisant Federal Assembly means that they could get presidential policy put into action without excessive resort to ruling by decree, a favourite pastime of President Yel'tsin.

---

[89] Korkeakvi, A (1994) 'The Russian Constitutional Court and human rights' (1) *Parker School Journal of East European Law* 591 at 594.

[90] (2006) 'Interview with constitutional court chairman Valery Zor'kin' (25(3)) *Argumenty I Fakty Weekly* June 21.

[91] Kahn, J (2008) 'Vladimir Putin and the Rule of Law in Russia' (36) *Georgia Journal of International and Comparative Law* 511 at 523 in note 44. As of 20 January 2009, the figure for the USA will be 27 out of 44 – over 60%.

With fewer federation and separation of powers cases the Court has been able to intensify its defence of individual rights, which successive judges have explicitly highlighted as an important role. Indeed, Trochev suggests that focussing on individual rights was initially a deliberate ploy to avoid serious political controversies when the Court resumed work after its suspension.[92]

THE COURT'S PERFORMANCE: CASE LAW

In this section a number of cases are discussed which will provide some insight into the Court's performance and the issues which come before it. We can see that the Court may endeavour to be principled and astute in its decisions, but neither its judges nor commentators always agree that it has succeeded. The cases are grouped to roughly reflect the three categories already mentioned: federalism, separation of powers, and individual rights, although it must be noted that it is a feature of the Court's cases that there is significant overlap between these categories and the cases also indicate that the Court's activity reaches into all corners of Russian life. We see an example of this overlapping of issues in the *Udmurt* case below, which involved the delineation of local autonomy within the federation, but was resolved using the separation of powers principle. It is also part of the Court's strategy to highlight individual rights where possible, making 'persistent efforts to "constitutionalize" social justice … based on the notion that the 1993 Constitution protects individuals from both the state and other individuals.'[93]

Cases on Federalism[94]

We saw above[95] that the CCRF was petitioned by a group of deputies claiming that a planned referendum in Tatarstan was unconstitutional.

---

[92] Trochev supra note 3 at 207, 228 and 288.

[93] Trochev, A (2008) 'Russia's constitutional spirit: judge-made principles in theory and practice' in Smith, GB and Sharlet, R (eds) (2008) *Russia and Its Constitution: Promise and Political Reality* Nijhoff at 69.

[94] See Pomeranz, W (1997) 'The Russian Constitutional Court's interpretation of federalism: balancing centre regional relations' (4) *Parker School Journal of East European Law* 401, and Sharlet, R (2008) 'The Russian Constitutional Court's Long Struggle for Viable Federalism' in Smith, GB and Sharlet, R (eds) (2008) *Russia and Its Constitution: Promise and Political Reality* Nijhoff 23, and generally Kahn, J (2002) *Federalism, Democratization and the Rule of Law* Oxford UP.

[95] See text to note 74 above and van den Berg, G (2001) 'Tatarstan_referendum_ruling_130392 No. 3-P' (27) *Review of Central and East European Law* 201. English translation in (1994) *Statutes and Decisions. The Laws of the USSR and its Successor States* (3) 32.

In the *Tatarstan* case the Court had to balance the two international law principles of the right to self determination and a state's right to integrity.[96] In its view (with one dissent) the latter principle prevailed. The terms of the referendum question[97] rendered it unconstitutional by suggesting Tatarstan was independent of Russia. This ruling issued on 13 March 2002 did not stop the referendum on 21 March. It gained 62% support.

The Court also attempts to preserve the federal structure, as may be seen with the *Udmurt* case of 1997.[98] In April 1996 the Udmurt State Council passed a law to abolish the local elected agencies of self-government, including the mayoralty of its capital Izhevsk, with transfer of their power to newly appointed legislative bodies. It also claimed power to appoint the heads of local administrations. This reorganization involved reclassifying population centres. President Yel'tsin and others appealed to the CCRF about this abolition of local autonomy. The Court issued a careful ruling which reaffirmed earlier decisions[99] that the subjects of the Federation could decide their own local government structure, provided they preserved separation of powers. Further, the organisation of local government was in joint jurisdiction of central and subject- level authorities (Constitution article 72(1)(m)). Absent federal law, subjects of the Federation could pass their own legislation on the matter, provided they did not contradict the Constitution. But the CCRF ruled (with two dissents) that the local heads of administration should not be appointed by the State Council as that would breach the principle of separation of powers, and the proposed reclassifications should only have been made after consultation of the affected population. The prior system of local self-government was restored pending such consultation.

These are two of the early cases, amongst many, where the Court has taken the rather brief constitutional provisions on the Russian Federation and tried to forge a workable system out of Russia's unusual federal structure.

[96] See Henderson supra note 70.
[97] van den Berg supra note 95, cites the referendum question: 'Do you agree that the Republic Tatarstan is a sovereign state and a subject of international law that builds its relations with the Russian Federation and other republics or states on the basis of co-equal compacts? Yes or No?'
[98] Id at 423. van den Berg 'Udmurtia_local_self_government_ruling_240197 No. 1-P' supra note 95 at 266. English translation in (2000) (1) *Statutes and Decisions. The Laws of the USSR and its Successor States* 51.
[99] Relating to Altai and Kaliningrad; Pomeranz supra note 94 at 426.

Cases on Separation of Powers and Presidential Authority

An especially difficult area for the Court to handle, especially during its early days, has been the delineation of presidential powers in a system adhering to the principle of separation of powers. This can be seen particularly in the 'Party' case and the *Chechen* case.

The CC RSFSR spent almost a quarter of its existence on the Party case.[100] Communist deputies claimed that Yel'tsin had acted *ultra vires* by banning the CPSU and the Russian Communist Party following the abortive putsch against Gorbachev in August 1991.[101] The Court was not empowered to consider political cases,[102] but through a constitutional amendment gained jurisdiction to consider the constitutionality of political parties. This enabled a cross-petition by Yel'tsin's supporters that the CPSU was anti-constitutional. The protracted hearing allowed a public airing of the realities of Party repression, but the final Court majority ruling was a compromise: the Court found against Yel'tsin on eight points, but for him on 13.[103] The vexed issue of the constitutionality of the Party was sidestepped; it remained moot as regards the CPSU, which no longer existed; and as regards the Russian CP, which technically never existed, not having been registered. The outcome was generally regarded as politically and practically astute, and the Court's efforts 'affirmed that the establishment of a legal order in Russia was becoming a reality'.[104] There were, however, three strong dissents: one that the Party was criminal, one that the President acted completely *ultra vires*, and one that the Party was unconstitutional but the President was not empowered to ban it.

During the hiatus after the closure of the CC RSFSR, in 1995, President Yel'tsin issued orders sending troops into Chechnia. In the resulting *Chechen*[105] case the Court reviewed the legality of these orders, although only after procedural problems were resolved including non-payment of the requisite fee.[106] The majority found the President's actions constitutional on the grounds of 'reasons of state'. There were eight strong dissents, covering both procedural and substantive issues. In his thorough review of the case

---

[100] van den Berg 'CPSU_ruling_301192 No. 9-P' supra note 95 at 205.

[101] See Henderson, J (2008) 'Making a Drama out of a Crisis: The Russian Constitutional Court and the Case of the Communist Party of the Soviet Union' (19) *King's Law Journal* at 489.

[102] 1991 Law article 1(2)(3).

[103] Henderson supra note 101 at 500.

[104] Feofanov supra note 2 at 623.

[105] van den Berg 'Chechnia_ruling_310795 No. 10-P' supra note 95 at 230. English translation in (1996) *Human Rights Law Journal* (3-6) 133 ff.

[106] See van den Berg supra note 95 at 224, footnote 17.

Pomeranz[107] makes analogy with the American 'political question' doctrine and Lomovtseva[108] suggests that the CCRF borrowed the US doctrine of implied powers in a number of cases, particularly this one.[109]

A more novel query over exercise of presidential power arose[110] after Yel'tsin in 1998 presented the same candidate to the Duma three times. We saw above that the President appoints the Prime Minister, but with Duma consent, and that 'triple rejection by the State Duma of the candidacies submitted'[111] allows the President to dissolve the Duma. The CCRF decided (with three dissents) that 'candidacies' could encompass an individual's repeated candidacy, so Yel'tsin's action was constitutional. Commenting, Luryi persuasively argues that the Court decision was 'inherently self-contradictory; it is also in obvious conflict with the practice of democratic states'.[112]

Another critical issue arising in this area is judicial independence. The turf war between the Supreme Court and the CCRF did not stop the latter coming to the former's aid in its dispute with the Government over judicial salaries. An economic crisis in 1998 lead to a 26.6% cut in funding to courts. The Supreme Court alleged that the cut violated the Constitution (article 124) and the Federal Constitutional Law 'On the Judicial System' (article 33(5)). The CCRF agreed. Shortly afterwards a federal law confirmed the requirement that the federal budget sufficiently finances the courts. However as Fogelklou pointed out 'This is a faint response to the fact that regional authorities often provide financial support to the courts'[113] thus undermining independence. The CCRF maintains strong protection of the special position of the judiciary. In 2008 it ruled that the terms for removal of judges' housing benefit unconstitutionally breached the separation of powers: 'the financing of judges cannot be determined by the will of the legislative or executive branches'.[114]

---

[107] Pomeranz, WE (1997) 'Judicial review and the Russian Constitutional Court: the Chechen case' (23) *Review of Central and East European Law* 9 at 18.

[108] Established in *McCulloch v Maryland* 1819 17 U.S. 316. See Lomovtseva and Henderson supra note 54.

[109] Decree of 31 July 1995 №10-P. See (1995) 31(5) *Statutes and Decisions* 48; Pomeranz supra note 107; Fogelklou supra note 67 at 37, and Sharlet, R (1995) 'Reinventing the Russian state: problems of constitutional implementation' (28) *John Marshall Law Review* 775 at 781.

[110] van den Berg 'appointing_Premier_Article_111_interpretation_111298 No. 28-P' supra note 95 at 337.

[111] Translation in Luryi, Y (1999) The appointment of a Prime Minister in Russia: the President. The Duma. The Constitutional Court' (25) *Review of Central and East European Law* 585 at 588.

[112] Id at 606.

[113] Fogelklou, A (2000) 'Constitutional order in Russia: a new territory for constitutionalism?' (26) *Review of Central and East European Law* 231 at 238.

[114] 'Constitutional Court Stands up for Independence of Judges' (2008) *Radio Free Europe/*

Individual Rights

A third area of obvious interest is individual rights.

The Propiska (residence registration permit) cases[115] dealt with an enduring problem arising from the requirement imposed on individuals to be registered to reside in certain cities.[116] This requirement was declared unconstitutional by the USSR CSC in October 1991,[117] but persisted nonetheless. In 1995 the CCRF held that a refusal to grant a permit to an unmarried cohabitee was unconstitutionally arbitrary; in 1996 it invalidated five regional statutes imposing charges for residence; and in July 1997 it struck down a Moscow residential tax. In a further case in February 1998 the Court found that existing registration rules violated the Constitution. However, to quote Rubins, 'There is little sign that the constitutional court decisions have had a significant effect upon local practices'.[118]

There have also been a number of important criminal justice decisions. For example in February 1999 the Court banned the imposition of the death penalty unless the constitutional right to trial by jury was available in all areas,[119] and ensured that judicial oversight of pre-trial detention would come into force with the rest of the 2001 Code of Criminal Procedure.[120]

Not all the Court's decisions have, however, been welcomed by human rights activists. In July 2005 the CCRF surprised legal analysts by ruling that the period of limitation in relation to back payment of tax did not run in the case of deliberate evasion of payment.[121] The case arose over a fine levied against YUKOS for non-payment of value-added tax in 2001, and continued a dispute with the tax authorities and the *Arbitrazh* Court over

---

Radio Liberty Newsline (12(22)) 1 February.

[115] van den Berg 'Sitalova_ruling_250495 No. 3-P' supra note 95 at 224, (1995) (4) *Statutes and Decisions*; van den Berg 'propiska_fees_in_Moscow_ruling_040496 No. 9- P' supra note 95 at 253, (1999) (1) *Statutes and Decisions* 42; van den Berg 'propiska_Moscow_Province_ ruling_020797 No. 10- P' supra note 95 at 281, (1999) (1) *Statutes and Decisions* 79; van den Berg 'propiska_or_registration_ruling_020298 No. 4- P' supra note 95 at 301.

[116] See Maggs, P (1995) 'The Russian Constitutional Court's decisions on residence permits and housing' (2) *Parker School Journal of East European Law* at 561; Karanian, K (1998) 'The propiska and the Constitutional Court' (7(2)) *East European Constitutional Review* at 52; Rubins, N (1998) 'The demise and resurrection of the propiska: freedom of movement in the Russian Federation' (39) *Harvard International Law Journal* at 545.

[117] van den Berg 'propiska_system_opinion_111091 No. 26 2-1' supra note 95 at 198.

[118] Rubins supra note 116 at 564.

[119] van den Berg 'jury_death_penalty_ruling_020299 No. P-3' supra note 95 at 344.

[120] See Lediakh, I (2005) 'Russia's Constitutional Court and human rights' in Sharlet, R and Feldbrugge, F (eds) (2005) *Public Policy and Law in Russia: in Search of a Unified Legal and Political Space* Koninklijke Brill at 213.

[121] 'Constitutional Court buttresses Tax Police in battles with business?' (2005) *Radio Free Europe/Radio Liberty Newsline* (9(132)) 15 July.

the rights of 'good faith' taxpayers.[122] By this stage the Court appears to have capitulated to the executive. A similar hard line was evident in May 2007 when the Court ruled that cases against convicted criminals may be reviewed and sentences made more severe when new evidence appears. This restricts the already limited protection against double jeopardy.[123]

The more recent Aslamazian case of 2008[124] (the first heard by the Court sitting in St Petersburg) gives grounds for more optimism about the Court's role in defence of individual rights. In January 2007 Manana Aslamazian, Head of the Educated Media Foundation, attempted to bring into Russia money in excess of the permitted quota. Her actions were categorised both as the administrative offence of failure to declare under the Code of Administrative Violations article 16(4) and as smuggling under the Criminal Code article 188(1). Aslamazian argued that her criminal persecution was only possible because the law was insufficiently precise. The Court agreed; the principles of equality and justice, and *nullum crimen sine lege* were breached, so article 188(1) was unconstitutional and therefore Aslamazian's conviction unlawful. 'Her lawyer, Viktor Parshutkin, said [...] that the judges "have sent a signal to society, to the authorities: let's build life in this country a little differently. Enough persecuting people, enough repression, enough imprisoning people for no reason."'[125]

CONCLUSION

In less than two decades the Russian Constitutional Court has established its place in the Russian political and legal landscape. In a state where for decades the role of law had been distorted by Marxist ideology, it was striking how quickly political actors seized the chance to use the new institution of constitutional control.

In its brief span, the USSR CSC took a significant stand for human rights. As we noted, it declared unlawful the requirement for residence registration (*propiska*) and on its own initiative it nullified unpublished legislation which infringed individual rights.

The CC RSFSR was working at a time of transition, when the concept of legality was changing from 'application of the rules' irrespective of content,

---

[122] See Trochev supra note 3 at 235-40.
[123] 'Constitutional Court rules that criminal cases may be revisited'(2007) *Radio Free Europe/ Radio Liberty Newsline* (11(90)) 17 May.
[124] Decree of the CCRF of 27 May 2008 №8-P 'On verification of the constitutionality of article 188(1) of the Criminal Code RF in connection with the appeal of citizen MA Aslamazian' <http://www.ksrf.ru:8081/SESSION/S__zbxhF3cC/PILOT/main.html>.
[125] *Internews Press* release 27 May 2008 <http://www.internews.org/prs/2008/20080527_russia.shtm>.

to a more cohesive notion of fairness, equality and the recognition of inherent inalienable human rights. The Court's subsequent embroilment in the 1993 power struggle between Yel'tsin and the chairman of the Russian Supreme Soviet, Khasbulatov, was unfortunate. Court Chairman Zor'kin gained a reputation of too much involvement in the political fray, possibly inevitable in the overall circumstances.[126]

Back in action under the 1994 law, the CCRF settled down to avoid obvious controversy. It continued the struggle to make sense of Russia's asymmetric federalism. During the time of Putin's Presidency, the Court was at some pains to interpret legislation to minimise conflicts between it and the other branches of state.[127] Trochev notes that generally it had good relations with Putin, who 'never brought a case to the Constitutional Court'.[128] The CCRF has shown sensitivity to its position of simultaneously having stewardship over, yet dependent on, the other branches of state power. However, involvement in political life is inevitable; 'constitutional judicial review [...] is [...] a political activity undertaken through a jurisdictional form.'[129] The FCLCC (article 11) has very broad and open-ended restrictions against judges' individual direct political activities, but the Court's role brings it into the political sphere. Its centrality is pointed up, for example, by press speculation about whether Putin would end up as Constitutional Court Chairman,[130] and the extent to which President Medvedev might place friends onto the bench.[131]

The Court's status means that it is more than merely a mechanism to resolve specific cases. It also has a systemic role as educator and mentor, encouraging constitutionality and respect for law.[132] The Court's decisions must contain reasoned argument and this assists the formation of a coherent jurisprudence. Trochev observes that the Court has developed a hierarchy of implicit constitutional principles which assist it to achieve consistency.[133] However 'As the Constitutional Court renders more and more "legal

---

[126] See Sharlet, R (1993) 'Chief Justice As Judicial Politician' (2) *East European Constitutional Review* 32; Schwartz supra note 23 at 144.

[127] See Fogelklou supra note 66 at 29.

[128] Trochev supra note 38 at 54.

[129] Ovsepian supra note 34 at 46.

[130] Uglanov, A (2008) 'Arrival of the "Jurassic" Period' *Moscow Argumenty Nedeli* English translation under title 'Speculation of Putin as Possible Constitutional Court Chairman Reported' *World News Connection (Newswire)* 24 January.

[131] Tulskiy, M (2008) 'Taking Control of the Court in Two Moves' *Moscow Argumenty Nedeli* English translation under title Possible Medvedev Takeover of Constitutional Court Outlined *World News Connection (Newswire)* 18 August.

[132] Many of the Court's judges have published scholarly legal works.

[133] Trochev supra note 93 at 53.

positions" and directives, parliament and the judiciary may have trouble understanding and following them'.[134]

The Constitutional Court has taken a very broad view of its role and thus raises expectations that it strives to meet. It has matured quickly in the hothouse of the Russian political system to become a leading institution that has built considerable theoretical legitimacy, even if compliance remains a practical concern. Its fosters a grand vision to bring constitutionality to Russia, acting as a compass for the ship of state as it sails into new waters.[135]

[134] Trochev supra note 77 at 102.
[135] Sergei Pashin's image when presenting his draft law to the Supreme Soviet on 6 May, see Henderson supra note 16 at 121.

The Spanish Constitutional Court: Time for Reforms

VICTOR FERRERES COMELLA*

The Constitutional Court, which was set up in 1980, is a fundamental institution in the Spanish political and legal system. Both the emergence of a politically decentralized state, with the establishment of 'Autonomous Communities' in different regions, and the commitment to respect fundamental rights, led to the creation of this special body. The Constitution of 1978 devotes a specific title (Title IX, articles 159-165) to regulate its structure and functions. A more detailed regulation is established in the *Ley Orgánica 2/1979 del Tribunal Constitucional* (hereinafter: LOTC), which has been amended several times.[1]

In this article, I will give an overview of the origins, structure and functions of the Court; the problems it has encountered in its interactions with other branches; its openness to international and foreign legal materials; the strengths and weaknesses of the Court's actual performance, and the reforms that have been tried, or proposed, in order to correct some of its deficiencies.[2]

---

* Professor of Constitutional Law, Universitat Pompeu Fabra (Barcelona, Spain).
[1] The most important commentary on the LOTC is Requejo, JL (editor) (2001) *Comentarios a la Ley Orgánica Del Tribunal Constitucional* Madrid: Boletín Oficial del Estado. For an interesting and influential set of studies, by a former Vice-President of the Court and the current Secretary General, on the theoretical foundations of this institution, see Rubio, F and Jiménez, J (1998) *Estudios Sobre la Jurisdicción Constitucional* Madrid: McGraw-Hill. See also, Rubio, F. "Constitutional Review and Legislation in Spain", included in Landfried, C (editor) (1988) *Constitutional Review and Legislation. An International Comparison* Baden-Baden: Nomos Verlagsgesellschaft. For a general description of the Spanish constitutional system, one can consult Prakke, L "The Kingdom of Spain", included in Prakke, L and Kortmann, C (editors) (2004) *Constitutional Law of 15 Eu Member States* Deventer: Kluwer.
[2] Information about the Court can be obtained from its website (www.tribunalconstitucional. es), which also publishes its decisions (in Spanish). Every year, the Court issues a useful report (*Memoria*) with information and statistics about the different types of cases it has dealt

THE REASONS FOR SETTING UP A CONSTITUTIONAL COURT

When a new Constitution was discussed in Parliament after the first democratic elections of June 1977, there was not much disagreement among political parties as to who should be in charge of enforcing the new fundamental law: a Constitutional Court.[3] This is not surprising. First of all, various European nations at that time already had such an institution. In particular, Germany, France and Italy[4] did, which were the three countries whose political systems were most influential in the framing of the Spanish Constitution. The reasons that are usually offered to justify the centralization of judicial review of legislation in a single body were applicable to Spain too: legal certainty is deemed to be better protected if a single court is in charge of checking ordinary law against constitutional norms, instead of conferring that power on all courts. To the extent, moreover, that statutes are enacted by a democratic Parliament, the general feeling is that their validity should only be reviewed by a special institution whose members are selected in more democratic ways than are ordinary judges.[5]

Secondly, Spain had already set up a Constitutional Court during the Second Republic (1931-1936). At that time, Spain was one of the few countries (together with Czechoslovakia and Liechtenstein) that followed the so-called 'Austrian' (Kelsenian) model of constitutional review.[6] General Franco's dictatorship (1936-1975) abolished this republican institution, but it served as a historical precedent for the constitution-framers of 1977-78.

Thirdly, the ordinary judges that had been appointed under Franco's dictatorial regime were not replaced when democracy came, in spite of the fact that the liberal-democratic commitments of most of them were rather weak. Given this historical circumstance, it made no sense to grant them the power to check the validity of the laws enacted by the new democratic

---

with.

[3] See Pérez, P (1985) *Tribunal Constitucional y Poder Judicial* Madrid: Centro de Estudios Políticos y Constitucionales at 97-109.

[4] See the articles on these three countries in this book, as well as Sweet, AS (2000) *Governing with Judges. Constitutional Politics in Europe* Oxford University Press.

[5] For an elaboration of these and other arguments in support of the centralized model, one may wish to read my two articles, (2004) "The European model of constitutional review of legislation: Toward decentralization?" 2 *International Journal of Constitutional Law* at 461 and (2004) "The Consequences of Centralizing Constitutional Review in a Special Court: Some Thoughts on Judicial Activism" 82 *Texas Law Review* at 1705.

[6] For a general study of the emergence of the "European model" of judicial review between the First and the Second World Wars, with a specific examination of the Spanish version of it as it operated during the Second Republic, see Cruz, P (1987) *La Formación del Sistema Europeo de Control de Constitucionalidad (1918-1939)* Madrid: Centro de Estudios Políticos y Constitucionales. See also the article on Austria in this book.

Parliament. The constitution-framers preferred to ascribe the task of legislative review to a separate body, whose members would be selected by the political branches.

COMPOSITION

The Constitutional Court has 12 members. Although these judges are formally appointed by the King, the decision to select them is actually in the hands of other institutions: the Congress of Deputies (which selects 4); the Senate (4); the Government (2); and the General Council of the Judiciary (2). Parliament (which consists of the Congress of Deputies and the Senate) has thus an important say in the appointment process: most judges on the Court (8 out of 12) are chosen by it. The General Council of the Judiciary, moreover, has an indirect democratic legitimacy, for its members are also elected by Parliament. The Government too is connected to Parliament, for the Prime Minister is chosen by the Congress of Deputies.

In spite of this strong link between the Constitutional Court and Parliament, it is impossible for a transient majority to appoint a Court of its liking. A super-majority of three fifths is necessary for both the Congress and the Senate to nominate the judges. This means that the governing majority must negotiate the names of the candidates with the main party in the opposition. The two appointments in the hands of the General Council of the Judiciary must also be made by a super-majority of three fifths, which requires some consensus among its members.[7]

The LOTC has recently been reformed (in 2007) in order to change the specific procedure the Senate must follow to fill the four seats that are allotted to it. Up to now, the Senate could freely choose the judges among prestigious jurists with at least 15 years' experience. Under the new system, in contrast, the legislative assemblies of the 17 Autonomous Communities will propose the names of possible candidates, and the Senate must select four of them.[8] This reform has been defended by the current Socialist Government as a necessary step to reinforce the character of the Senate as a

---

[7] The Constitution does not impose this super-majoritarian requirement on the Council. The *Ley Orgánica del Poder Judicial* (LOPJ) does, in article 107.2.

[8] The LOTC delegates the details of regulation to the standing orders of the Senate (*Reglamento del Senado*), article 184 of which specifies that each Autonomous Community will propose two candidates. It also provides that if the total list does not include a sufficient number of them, the Senate can appoint additional ones. It seems clear, however, that if the number of candidates is sufficient (that is, if at least four names are included), the Senate cannot choose someone who is not in the list. Of course, the candidates must satisfy the general legal requirements: a candidate proposed by a Community who is not a prestigious jurist with at least 15 years of experience can be rejected, and the Senate can ask for a replacement.

representative body of the Autonomous Communities, but it is controversial from a constitutional point of view. The Constitution explicitly grants the Senate the power to select four judges. May the LOTC constrain this power by requiring the Senate to choose from a list that is drawn by external institutions? The *Partido Popular* argued that this is unacceptable, and decided to file a challenge before the Constitutional Court. In its decision 49/2008, the Court has finally upheld the new law, but has read into it some exceptions, so that the Senate has still some room for manoeuvre. In particular, if all the candidates proposed by the Autonomous Communities fail to obtain the required super-majority to fill a given seat, the Senate is then free to select others.

The judges on the Court do not serve for life, or until the age of retirement. They sit for a fixed period of nine years. Their terms, however, cannot be immediately renewed: judges can only be re-appointed once there has been a partial renewal of the Court, which takes place every three years. For these purposes, the twelve judges are distributed in three different groups, depending on the institution that appointed them (the Congress; the Senate; the Government and the General Council of the Judiciary).

One of the judges is appointed President of the Court. Another is appointed Vice-President. The latter presides over the Second Chamber of the Court, while the former presides over the First Chamber, as well as the Court as a whole. The election is made by the judges themselves. Since four new judges are sent to the Court every three years, the term of the President and the Vice-President is also three years. They can be reappointed for a second term (of the same length). One of the important functions of the President, apart from organizing the agenda of the Court and taking care of its administrative matters, is to break ties when votes are taken (article 90.1 of LOTC). The Vice-President has also this power in his capacity as President of the Second Chamber. This puts them in a very delicate position when a highly controversial case is to be decided. In 1983, for example, the Court had to examine a governmental *decreto-ley* (a kind of emergency decree) that expropriated an important set of banks and industries that were in crisis. The Court was divided 6-6, and the vote of the President was decisive to uphold the decree (STC 111/1983). More recently, this power of the President has given rise to an intense battle in connection with a challenge brought by the *Partido Popular* against the new Statute of Autonomy of Catalonia. Since the Court seems to be divided over some key issues in this case, the President may have to cast the decisive vote. This has led to a complicated set of moves, both outside and inside the Court, in order to decide who will be the President.[9]

JURISDICTION OF THE COURT

The Court decides different types of cases through different kinds of procedure: it controls the constitutionality of legislation; it decides conflicts between certain public institutions; and it examines complaints of violation of fundamental rights. For these purposes, the Court is divided into two chambers (*Salas*) of 6 judges each. The latter are further organized in two sections (each comprising 3 judges).[10] Decisions are made by a majority of judges, and dissenting and concurring opinions are allowed.

Constitutional Review of Legislation

To begin with, the Court has the authority to pass judgment on the constitutionality of statutes. This is the most important function that has historically led to the creation of constitutional courts in Europe. The Court has a 'monopoly' when it comes to legislative review: only this special body is entitled to hold a legislative provision to be invalid on constitutional grounds.

It should be noted that this monopoly applies equally to the statutes enacted by the national Parliament and to those enacted by the regional

---

[9]   When the terms of office of the President and the Vice-President expire, the practice so far has been to wait for the appointment of the new four judges, if there is a delay in the renewal of the Court. The four judges whose terms have expired remain on the Court, but it has seemed unfair to let them participate in the decision as to who should be the President and the Vice-President, for this would deprive the new appointees of the right to vote on this matter. In order to make sure that this traditional practice is respected in connection with the current President, the 2007 reform of the LOTC introduced an explicit provision to this effect (article 16.3). The *Partido Popular*, however, filed a constitutional challenge against it, on the grounds that the Constitution establishes that the term of office of the President is three years (article 160), and that this categorical rule cannot be excepted, even if the political branches have not yet appointed the new judges. There was an intense battle within the Court over whether or not the current President should abstain from this case. She finally chose to do so. In its decision 49/2008, the Court has finally upheld the legal provision against the constitutional challenge. It bears emphasizing that all these complicated political and judicial quarrels would certainly not have taken place if the President lacked the power to break ties.
[10]   Depending on the cases, the Court decides en banc (*Pleno*), or through its chambers or sections. Until the 2007 reform of the LOTC, the basic division was roughly this: the Court as a whole exercised constitutional review of legislation and resolved conflicts of competences; the chambers were concerned with deciding individual complaints for violation of fundamental rights; and the sections were responsible for admissibility decisions over the latter. Under the new regime, there has been a delegation of tasks from the Court as a whole to the Chambers, and the sections have been given wider discretion to reject complaints.

legislative assemblies. An ordinary judge cannot disregard a regional statute on the grounds that it clashes with the Constitution or with a piece of national law: only the Constitutional Court can react against such a statute (STC 163/1995). Moreover, there are certain types of laws (*Decretos-leyes, Decretos legislativos*) that originate in the executive, but are awarded the same 'rank' as statutes in the legal hierarchy. The Court's monopoly extends to them too.

Different procedures can be resorted to in order to trigger legislative review. One is the 'constitutional challenge' procedure (*recurso de inconstitucionalidad*), which permits the Prime Minister, the Ombudsman, 50 Deputies or 50 Senators to challenge laws in the abstract. There is a deadline for this: 3 months since their official publication. When the law has been enacted by the national Parliament, the regional governments or their legislative assemblies can also institute such actions.[11] In practice, the 50 Deputies or 50 Senators belong to the parliamentary opposition: they disagree with the majority and, since they take the statute to be problematic from a constitutional point of view, they decide to bring an action to the Court. When a regional government or a regional assembly files a challenge, the objections it usually adduces against the national law are related to federalism questions. Whatever the source of the attack, the effects of the Court's decision are always *erga omnes*: they bind all branches of government.[12]

Another avenue whereby the Court rules on the constitutionality of legislative provisions is the 'constitutional question' procedure (*cuestión de inconstitucionalidad*), which is triggered by ordinary courts.[13] When the latter have to decide a particular case, and doubts arise as to the validity of the applicable statute (or any other norm with the same rank), they are required to petition the Court to rule on the issue. Since the Constitutional Court has a monopoly in this area, the ordinary judge must certify the question, even if he is confident that the law is unconstitutional. Even in the extreme case in which a law is very similar or almost identical to another that has already been struck down by the Court, the ordinary judge must still refer the law to the latter (see STC 23/1988). If the ordinary judge decides to raise a constitutional question, the proceedings in the instant case are suspended until the Court resolves it. It will then be for that judge to finally decide the

---

[11] In this case, the deadline of 3 months can be extended to 9 months, if a bilateral commission composed of state and regional representatives has met to negotiate an agreement.
[12] On constitutional challenges, see García, A (1992) *El Recurso de Inconstitucionalidad* Madrid: Trivium.
[13] For a comprehensive treatment, see López, JM (2000) *La Cuestión de Inconstitucionalidad en Derecho Español* Madrid: Marcial Pons.

case, in light of the answer that the Court has given to the constitutional issue. The Court's opinion, however, has *erga omnes* effect.

The objections against the statute that is applicable to a case may be advanced by one of the parties. But it is also possible for the ordinary court to raise the objection *sua sponte*. In both instances, the parties to the case (as well as the prosecutor) are always asked to express their views as to whether or not a question should be certified to the Constitutional Court. And it is always the ordinary court's responsibility to finally decide what to do. Thus, if the ordinary court concludes that the statute is valid, or if it deems it unnecessary for the resolution of the case to inquire into its validity, it applies the statute to resolve the dispute, even if one of the parties has requested to petition the Constitutional Court.[14]

Before an ordinary judge sends a statute to the Constitutional Court for its review, however, the judge must try to find an interpretation of that statute that makes it consistent with the Constitution (article 5.3 of the *Ley Orgánica del Poder Judicial* explicitly imposes this duty). That is, if the applicable legal provision can be read in different ways, the judge must choose that reading that harmonizes it with constitutional principles. The Court should intervene only when this attempt at *interpretación conforme* has been unsuccessful. This does not mean, of course, that judges are entitled to distort a statutory provision through interpretive means. The constitutionally-inspired reading of the statute should not be at odds with its clear textual meaning and the underlying legislative intention. As the Court has held, the judge should not use the Constitution to support an interpretation of the statute that is *contra legem* (STC 138/2005). The problem, however, is that it is not always easy to determine whether a particular reading of the statute is still possible as a fair interpretation of it or is, on the contrary, so strained a reading that it should count as a prohibited, *contra legem* interpretation.

An important question arose soon after the Court was set up in 1980: what about statutes that were enacted *before* the Constitution of 1978 entered into force? What happens if there is a contradiction between that statute and the new Constitution? May an ordinary court set it aside on its own authority, or is it required to certify the question to the Constitutional Court? The latter soon held that the ordinary court has a choice: it can directly disregard the statute, or, in case of doubt, refer it to the Court for purposes of determining its constitutionality (STC 4/1981). Of course, in the first case, the statute is merely disregarded in the particular dispute, while

---

[14] What the ordinary court must do in the latter case, however, is to explain the reasons why it refuses to raise a constitutional question: STC 35/2002.

in the second case the Constitutional Court can formally eliminate it from the legal system, through a decision that has general effects.

Apart from constitutional challenges and questions, a third procedure exists, in order to test the constitutionality of international treaties (article 95.2 of the Constitution). Once treaties are signed by Spain, but before they are finally consented to, the Court can be requested to determine whether they respect the Constitution. The Congress, the Senate and the Government can petition the Court to rule on the issue. This is currently the only instance of *a priori* review of legal norms in Spain.[15] The justification for this special rule is that it is particularly useful to clarify the constitutional issue before Spain ratifies a treaty that will affect third parties on the international level. The Court's decision is binding: if an incompatibility is found, Spain will have to amend the Constitution if it wants to ratify the treaty. It should be mentioned, however, that the Court is also entitled to review a treaty once it has been ratified, through an ordinary constitutional challenge or question. The preventive mechanism complements, but does not replace, the general procedures that are available to impugn the validity of statutes and legal norms of equivalent force.

This procedure of article 95.2 has been used in only two instances so far: in connection to the 1992 Maastricht Treaty (Declaration 1/1992), and the 2004 Treaty establishing a Constitution for Europe (Declaration 1/2004). In the first case, the Court held that the Spanish Constitution would have to be amended, if foreign citizens of the European Union were to be granted, as they were under the Maastricht treaty, the right to vote and to run for office in local elections. The Constitution was consequently amended: article 13.2 expanded the political rights of foreigners. (This is the only reform, by the way, that the Constitution has undergone so far). In the second case, the Court ruled that there was no incompatibility between the idea that the Spanish Constitution is the 'supreme law' of the land, and the clause in the proposed European Constitution (article I-6) that provided that European Union law would have primacy over national law.

Conflicts

A second head of jurisdiction relates to conflicts between public institutions. The most important conflicts arise in the area of regionalism. The Constitution (together with the Statutes of Autonomy that were enacted to create Autonomous Communities, as well as certain 'organic laws' that

---

[15] In the past, organic laws and Statutes of Autonomy could also be reviewed before their promulgation. This preventive mechanism was abolished in 1985, through a reform of the LOTC.

specify some relevant matters) distributes legislative and executive powers between the state and the regions. Conflicts of competences are likely to arise between the two levels of government (or, less often, between different regions). Almost always, the conflict is 'positive', in that both parties claim competence over a disputed subject-matter. In such cases, the dispute can be initiated by one of the executive bodies involved (state or regional). When the source of the dispute is a statute (or any other norm that has the same rank), the procedure the Court follows is the same that applies to constitutional challenges. If the conflict is 'negative', which means that both organs assert that they lack competence over a particular item, the conflict may be instituted by the state executive, or by an affected person.[16]

The Court has also been given the authority to settle controversies between various organs at the national level. However, only the Government, the Congress, the Senate and the General Council of the Judiciary are relevant for these purposes. In a parliamentary democracy, it is unlikely that deep tensions will emerge between these institutions. Actually, very few cases of this type have been brought to the Court.[17]

A third kind of conflict, which is also of marginal importance, was introduced in 1999 through a reform of the LOTC, in order to protect local institutions (*municipios* and *provincias*). When the latter consider that a statute (or another norm of equivalent rank) enacted by the state or by an Autonomous Community violates its constitutionally protected 'local autonomy', a certain number of them can bring an action to the Court.[18]

Complaints of violation of fundamental rights

A third function of the Court is linked to fundamental rights. The Spanish Constitution includes a rather long list of rights (as well as duties and social principles) in Title I. All the rights that are mentioned in articles 14 to 38 are 'fundamental', in the sense that they protect a certain 'core' (*contenido esencial*) that the legislature cannot destroy. But some of these rights (those mentioned in articles 14 to 30.2 of the Constitution) also benefit from a special procedural guarantee: public actions (or omissions) that violate any of these rights can be attacked through a 'complaint' (*recurso de amparo*) to be

---

[16] See García, J (1993) *Los Conflictos de Competencias Entre el Estado y Las Comunidades Autónomas* Madrid: Centro de Estudios Políticos y Constitucionales.

[17] See Gómez, ÁJ (1992) *El Conflicto Entre Órganos Constitucionales* Madrid: Centro de Estudios Políticos y Constitucionales.

[18] It should be mentioned that while the Court's authority to resolve the regional conflicts is directly established in the Constitution, it was the LOTC that expanded the Court's jurisdiction to cover, first, the conflicts between constitutional organs of the state (in 1979), and, later on, the conflicts to protect local autonomy (in 1999).

lodged before the Constitutional Court.[19] The actions that can be impugned in this way may originate in the executive, the judiciary or a parliamentary assembly.[20] A person who claims to be harmed by the infringement of any of these privileged rights (as well as the Ombudsman and the public prosecutor) is entitled to file a complaint.

It is necessary, however, first to exhaust all judicial remedies, which means that, in practice, the person must go to the ordinary judiciary to seek legal protection. The Constitutional Court is thus a sort of 'special court of appeals': it is the really supreme judicial body in Spain, for it can quash the decisions of any other court, even the Supreme Court. It cannot decide, however, all the factual and legal issues that a case poses. Its *amparo* jurisdiction is limited to checking whether or not the relevant fundamental right has been infringed. If it concludes that there has been such a violation, it so declares, and it normally invalidates the action that has caused the violation. It can also establish measures to protect the right against future infringements.

In the vast majority of cases, the action that is found to offend a fundamental right rests on an incorrect interpretation and application of the relevant body of law: the law as such is fine, but the relevant authority has not read it in a proper way, or has exercised its discretion in the wrong direction. Sometimes, however, it is the applicable statutory provision that is at fault, in that it violates the fundamental right invoked. If the Court so concludes, it can declare its invalidity in a separate procedure, where the provision can be struck down with general effects.[21]

RELATIONSHIPS AND TENSIONS WITH OTHER JUDICIAL BODIES

Given the procedures described above, it is clear that there are strong links between the Constitutional Court and the ordinary judiciary. First of all, legislative review can be triggered by ordinary judges in the context of concrete disputes. From the very beginning, scholars in Spain

---

[19] For detailed information on the many legal issues that the *amparo* jurisdiction has given rise to, it is useful to consult Fernández, G (1994) *El Recurso de Amparo Según la Jurisprudencia Constitucional* Madrid: Marcial Pons, and Pérez, P (2004) *El Recurso de Amparo* Valencia: Tirant lo Blanch. Compare the article on Latin America in this book.

[20] Laws enacted by a legislative assembly cannot be directly challenged through this procedure, however. Only decisions that do not have the form of law can.

[21] This is regulated in article 55.2 of the LOTC, which has been amended in 2007. Before its reform, this article provided that the procedure of legislative review would be initiated *after* the decision on the complaint had been rendered. It now establishes that the complaints procedure will be suspended until the Court passes judgment on the constitutionality of the applicable law in the second procedure.

have emphasized that ordinary judges are expected to play an important role in this connection: they are not supposed to passively accept the applicable statutes, but must instead activate the 'constitutional question' procedure, if they conclude that those statutes are problematic in light of the Constitution.[22] An internal 'dialogue' between courts is supposed to take place in this context: ordinary judges can offer their views about the Constitution; the Constitutional Court accepts or rejects those views; if the Court finally upholds a statute, it is still possible for judges to raise further objections against it in future cases, if circumstances have changed or new arguments are constructed. This is generally taken to be an interesting arrangement, to compensate for the rigidity of constitutional challenges, which are brought by non-judicial bodies, without any connection to cases (in the abstract), and within a short period of time after the publication of the relevant statute. In the context of such questions, which can be certified by ordinary judges at any time, the Court can be more sensitive to the evolution of legal debates and to the change of social circumstances.

In general, this procedure has not generated any serious tension between the Constitutional Court and the ordinary judiciary. Ordinary judges (including the Supreme Court) have generally accepted the Constitutional Court's rulings on the validity of legislation. If the Court strikes down a statute, ordinary judges cease to apply it, for the simple reason that the Court, acting as a 'negative legislature', has expelled the statute from the legal system. When the Court does not strike down the statute, but imposes a particular understanding or reconstruction of it, in order to save its constitutional validity, ordinary judges have also been respectful. In contrast to what happened in Italy for a long while, the Spanish Supreme Court has not disregarded such interpretive rulings.[23] Since the Constitutional Court is the only institution that is authorised to invalidate statutes, the general consensus is that it is also entitled to fix the particular conditions under which a particular law can be maintained in the legal system. The LOTC, moreover, ascribes *erga omnes* effects, not only to the Court's decisions that declare a statute unconstitutional, but also to those that uphold it (article 38.1). This has helped reinforce the authority of the Court's 'interpretive' decisions: even if the latter are not, technically speaking, decisions that declare a statute unconstitutional, they are binding on all courts nevertheless.[24]

---

[22] The most influential scholarly work that soon emphasized this point was García, E (1983) *La Constitución Como Norma y el Tribunal Constitucional* Madrid: Civitas.

[23] See the article on Italy in this book.

[24] On this difference between the situation in Spain and Italy, see Díaz, FJ (2001) *Las Sentencias Interpretativas del Tribunal Constitucional* at 80 and 99 Valladolid: Lex Nova.

The interactions between the Constitutional Court and the ordinary judiciary get more complicated in the field of complaints for violation of fundamental rights (*amparo*). The Court is supposed to confine its attention to the question whether the action complained of has caused an infringement of a fundamental right. It has no jurisdiction to check whether the ordinary courts have properly decided the factual and ordinary legal issues that the case poses. In practice, however, it has been difficult to specify the boundaries that define this division of labour.[25]

To begin with, fundamental rights are not regulated in detail in the Constitution. Legislation has to be enacted to establish a more precise and complete legal regime for each right. If ordinary judges make a mistake when interpreting and applying such legislation, is that mistake of 'constitutional' import, or is it merely 'statutory'? One cannot maintain that any interpretive error is a direct violation of the Constitution, for many statutory details are not imposed by the Constitution. On the other hand, some of those details are important aspects of the legal regime that is currently in force to protect the relevant fundamental right. The Court has not laid down clear criteria to define the scope of its control in this area. Some scholars have suggested that only direct infringements of the Constitution should be dealt with by the Court, but they are aware of the restrictive consequences of their proposal, which may be too harsh in some cases.[26]

Things get even more complicated with some fundamental rights that are special in the following sense: what they guarantee, basically, is that the ordinary law will be applied in the right way. Article 25 of the Spanish Constitution, for example, safeguards the right not to suffer any punishment for actions (or omissions) that were not defined as a crime (or misdemeanour or administrative infraction) by the laws that existed at the time of their commission. Of course, it is ordinary law that creates crimes and imposes penalties. What the Constitution guarantees in this clause is the correct interpretation and application of criminal laws. Should the Constitutional Court, however, review all criminal convictions that are attacked on the grounds that they are based on an incorrect reading of those laws? If it did, it would be the truly supreme court in criminal matters, thus interfering with the institutional function of the Criminal Chamber of the

---

[25] For a systematic study of the tests and doctrines that the Court has constructed in order to define its own jurisdiction vis-à-vis ordinary courts, see the collection of articles edited by Viver, C, former Vice-President of the Constitutional Court (2006) *Jurisdicción Constitucional y Judicial en el Recurso De Amparo* Valencia: Tirant lo Blanch.

[26] See, e.g., Díez-Picazo LM (2008) *Sistema de Derechos Fundamentales* 126-128 Madrid: Civitas.

Supreme Court. On the other hand, the Court cannot completely decline to intervene in those cases, for the Constitution does give it jurisdiction to protect article 25. The Court has tried to find a middle ground between these two extremes, defining the particular kinds of interpretive errors that can be examined by it. The idea is that only the most egregious mistakes permit the Court to quash a judicial decision on article 25 grounds (see, for instance, STC 111/1993). A similar intermediate position has been defined by the Court to handle criminal cases where the convicted person claims that the evidence against him was not sufficient to destroy his right to the presumption of innocence, which the Constitution protects as a fundamental right in article 24 (STC 31/1981).

The difficulty of drawing the boundaries between the Constitutional Court and the ordinary judiciary has given rise to tensions in some cases. Are ordinary judges bound by the Court's rulings, if they think that the latter has overstepped the limits of its jurisdiction? The Court, for example, has spoken to the question, when exactly the action to bring criminal charges against someone has the effect of interrupting the applicable statute of limitations (STC 63/2005, and STC 29/2008). The thesis it has maintained runs counter to the dominant case law of the Supreme Court. It is not clear whether this is really a matter for the Constitutional Court to decide, or is instead an ordinary question of statutory interpretation. Both the prosecutors and the Supreme Court have decided, for the moment, not to apply this new doctrine, and wait and see future developments from the Constitutional Court.[27] Similar tensions arose in the past concerning the amount of damages that must be granted to a public figure whose fundamental right to privacy is found to have been infringed. The Constitutional Court once quashed a Supreme Court's ruling on the amount of compensation to be awarded to the plaintiff (STC 186/2001). The Supreme Court expressed its strong disagreement with that decision.

It must be borne in mind, moreover, that, although ordinary courts must respect the Constitutional Court's decisions in the particular cases, the authority of those decisions as *precedents* is not clear.[28] Are ordinary courts strictly bound by the jurisprudence that the Court generates, even in the field that is clearly 'constitutional'? This question is very similar to the more general question in many *civil law* countries as to whether lower courts are legally bound by the statutory interpretations announced by

---

[27] See *Instrucción* 5/2005, issued by the *Fiscalía General del Estado*, and decision by the Supreme Court (Second Chamber), number 331/2006, March 24, 2006.

[28] A careful treatment of this question can be found in Santos, JM (1995) *Doctrina y Jurisprudencia del Tribunal Constitucional. Su Eficacia Respecto de los Tribunales Ordinarios* Granada: Comares.

the Supreme Court. Lower courts tend to respect the latter, but are they really bound by them? Given the principle of judicial independence, are courts empowered to deviate from such interpretations? There is no legal consensus in Spain about this question.[29] It is not surprising that there is no consensus either as to the authority as precedent of Constitutional Court decisions that resolve complaints for violation of fundamental rights (*amparo*). If, as many scholars and judges in Spain believe, lower courts are not bound by the doctrines laid down by the Supreme Court in the ordinary legal field, why should they be under a duty to follow the jurisprudence of the Constitutional Court (even assuming that the latter has not gone beyond its 'constitutional' jurisdiction)? It is one thing, it is asserted, for ordinary judges to be constrained by the specific decisions that strike down a statute (or uphold it, with or without conditions), in a procedure of legislative review. It is quite another for them to be bound by the interpretations that the Court establishes when deciding concrete cases in its *amparo* jurisdiction.

All these boundary problems and tensions are probably inevitable in a system that super-imposes a new Constitutional Court on an extant Supreme Court.[30] What happened in 2004, however, was more extraordinary - almost surrealist. To make the story short, the facts were basically these:[31] a lawyer who wanted to challenge the way the Constitutional Court appoints its own legal staff brought an action before the Third Chamber of the Supreme Court, which specializes in administrative law. Since he did not succeed there, he afterwards lodged a complaint before the Constitutional Court itself, asking all judges, on partiality grounds, to abstain from participating in the case, and to request the government to create a new Constitutional

---

[29]   To get a sense of the diverse views held by different judges and scholars in Spain on this controversial issue, see the collection of essays edited by the General Council of the Judiciary (2001) *La Fuerza Vinculante De La Jurisprudencia* Madrid: Consejo General del Poder Judicial. For a good, general overview, see Laporta, F and Miguel, AR "Precedent in Spain", included in MacCormick, N and Summers, R (editors) (1997) *Interpreting Precedents: A Comparative Study* Ashgate. For my own views on this question, see Ferreres, V (2002) *El Principio de Taxatividad en Materia Penal y el Valor Normativo de la Jurisprudencia* Madrid: Civitas at 153, where I give arguments to support the binding character of the Supreme Court's rulings.

[30]   For many years, the Constitutional Court has been viewed by culturally conservative ordinary judges in Spain as a "political" institution that is artificially constraining the jurisprudence of the "truly judicial" Supreme Court. As Francisco Rubio Llorente points out, the fact that the Constitution regulates the Constitutional Court in a different title (Title IX) than the ordinary judiciary (Title VI), as if there were a political-judicial dualism at work here, has facilitated this misunderstanding of the nature of the Constitutional Court. See (2004) "El Tribunal Constitucional" 71 *Revista Española de Derecho Constitucional* at 30.

[31]   For a description in English of this episode, see Turano, L (2006) "Spain: Quis Custodiet Ipsos Custodes?: The Struggle for jurisdiction between the Tribunal Constitucional and the Tribunal Supremo" 4 *International Journal of Constitutional Law* at 151.

Court that would be in an impartial position to decide. The Court rejected the complaint, giving reasons why it was not possible for it to do what the plaintiff had asked. This was not the end of the story, however, for the plaintiff then went to the First Chamber of the Supreme Court (which deals with 'civil matters'), seeking damages against the judges of the Constitutional Court, on the grounds that their decision to reject his constitutional complaint was based on insufficient reasons, and that this had caused him a moral harm: he no longer trusted courts! Incredibly, the Supreme Court agreed, and condemned each judge to pay 500 euros to the plaintiff (decision number 51/2004, January 23, 2004). Although the Supreme Court made clear that it had no jurisdiction to review the validity of the order to reject the complaint, it insisted that it had jurisdiction to impose liability for damages on the judges who issued it. The Constitutional Court made a public statement criticizing the decision. What's more, the judges themselves filed an *amparo* against the decision! (The Constitutional Court has admitted it, but has not yet decided it). This episode has seriously poisoned the relationships between the two high courts in Spain, and has introduced an additional element of complexity in the system.

RELATIONSHIPS AND TENSIONS WITH THE POLITICAL BRANCHES

The main source of potential tension between the Court and the political branches is the Court's power to strike down laws. Maybe because the Court is aware of this, it has tended to focus on rather 'technical matters' when invalidating statutes or other norms that have the same rank as statutes. An important part of its jurisprudence in the field of legislative review has been devoted to the problem of defining the boundaries between different sources of law: 'ordinary statutes', 'organic statutes', 'statutes of autonomy', emergency decrees (*decretos-ley*), decrees issued by the government in the exercise of delegated legislative power (*decretos legislativos*), budgetary laws, and so on. Another significant part of its case law has centred on the legislative conflicts between the state and the Autonomous Communities, an area where there is usually a clash of parliamentary wills, and the Court is asked to decide who is competent to regulate what. Even the opinions in the field of fundamental rights have often addressed rather technical questions, such as, for example, whether a criminal law on terrorism was sufficiently precise (STC 89/1993); or whether the statutory definition of *flagrante delicto*, for purposes of police searches in private homes, was in accordance with the constitutional meaning of this term (STC 341/1993).

Of course, the Court's decisions can have significant political consequences, even if the reasons for invalidating legislative enactments are rather technical. Thus, one of the most politically relevant opinions ever written by the Court concerned a 'law of harmonization' (the so-called LOAPA) that tried to clarify and harmonize the exercise of the competences held by the different Autonomous Communities. The Court struck parts of it down on the grounds that the constitutional conditions for using this kind of legal instrument were not met, and that a law cannot pretend to fix an authoritative interpretation of constitutional terms: this would interfere with the judicial function (STC 76/1983). Similarly, the Court's decision invalidating a statute that defined *flagrante delicto* too broadly, for purposes of police home searches, caused the resignation of the Minister of the Interior who had sponsored it. Actually, in response to pressure, he had publicly announced that he would do so if the law were invalidated. The Court's ruling had an important political effect, even though its justification was rather technical.

There certainly have been decisions striking down laws in morally controversial matters. The abortion case is the most prominent example (STC 53/1985). The Court held that the foetus is entitled to constitutional protection, even though it is not a person, and that abortion should therefore in principle be a crime. The Court accepted some exceptions, however, concerning extreme circumstances under which it would be against the woman's fundamental rights to prohibit abortion. In particular, the Court accepted as valid the three types of situation where the law being examined had decriminalized abortion (rape, malformation of the foetus, and health risks for the mother). The Court found that the law was nevertheless deficient for lack of sufficient safeguards that would guarantee that the abortions performed as legal really fell in practice under one of those exceptions. In spite of the public criticisms that the decision generated, some of them voiced by leading political figures like the Vice-President, Parliament accepted the constitutional ruling and changed the law accordingly.

The degree to which a constitutional case gets 'politicized' depends, in part, on who invokes the Court's jurisdiction. There is a clear contrast in this respect between the parliamentary opposition (50 Deputies or 50 Senators) bringing a constitutional challenge against a law, on the one hand, and an ordinary judge certifying an issue to the Court, on the other. In the first case, the Court is closer to the terrain where political battles are fought. A decision upholding the statute will count as a political victory for the government and a defeat for the opposition, while a decision against the statute will be read in the opposite way. The risk exists that the Court will be too worried about the political reading of its decisions.

This does not mean, however, that when ordinary judges raise questions to the Constitutional Court, there is no potential conflict with the political branches. The latter may be very upset if an important piece of legislation is struck down, even if the parliamentary minority cannot claim a victory. Actually, sometimes ordinary judges have asked the Court to intervene in connection with statutes that no important political party has chosen to challenge, either because all of them support the statute, or because it would not be very popular to insist on certain criticisms. Thus, both the majority and the parliamentary opposition were in favour of a legal provision enacted in 1995 (article 607.2 of the Criminal Code) that makes it a crime for someone to deny or justify past genocides, or to defend political regimes that committed such acts. When criminal charges were brought against a person who sold books that denied the existence of gas chambers in Nazi concentration camps, the criminal court in Barcelona that handled the case on appeal decided to certify a question to the Constitutional Court, on the grounds that the applicable provision offended freedom of speech. The Court's decision (STC 235/2007) declares article 607.2 unconstitutional in part. It holds that it is constitutionally possible to criminalize speech that seeks to *justify* past genocides, but it is not possible to do so with speech that simply *denies* their commission.

Similarly, the Criminal Code was amended in 2004 in order to establish harsher penalties for certain crimes of domestic violence, but it did so in a way that treats the convicted persons differently depending on whether they are men or women: men receive higher penalties than women for the same kind of conduct (see, for instance, article 153). The law was passed unanimously in Parliament.[32] Given this unanimity, and given that it is not very popular to challenge a law whose explicit goal is to reduce the level of violence against women, no constitutional challenge by political actors was to be expected. Instead, a significant number of ordinary judges in charge of enforcing the new provision concluded that it is unduly discriminatory, and chose to petition the Court to review it. In a very controversial decision, however, the Court has finally upheld the new law (STC 59/2008).

The most politically controversial case that is presently in the Court's docket concerns the new Statute of Autonomy of Catalonia. This is a new basic law for the region of Catalonia, whose Parliament proposed in 2005 a reform of the existing 1979 Statute of Autonomy, in order to enhance its self-government. With some important amendments, the Statute was passed by the Spanish Parliament in 2006, with the support of the governing *Partido Socialista*, over the strong opposition of the *Partido Popular*, and was finally

---

[32] The *Partido Popular*, however, had expressed some objections against this sort of "'reverse discrimination' in the criminal field, and tried to soften the inequality to a certain extent through an amendment to the original bill. The amendment was accepted, but the final draft of the law was still discriminatory in important respects.

approved by the Catalan citizens in a referendum (the victory was clear: 74%, yes; 21%, no; but the turnout was quite low for Spanish standards: around 49%). The Statutes of other regions have also been modified, or are currently in the process of modification, following, in part, the Catalan example. The *Partido Popular* decided to bring a constitutional challenge against many legal provisions of the Catalan Statute. One of its basic claims is that many of the political choices that the Statute expresses could only be validly introduced if the Spanish Constitution were first amended. For such an amendment, a super-majority of the Spanish Parliament is required, which means that the agreement of the *Partido Popular* would be necessary. The Socialist majority, this party asserts, is trying to do by means of the new Statute what can only be done through a constitutional amendment.[33]

Those who support the Catalan Statute have been very critical of the *Partido Popular's* strategy. Many of them, moreover, have claimed that it would be undemocratic for the Court to invalidate a law that has been passed, not only by two parliaments (the regional and the national), but also by the people themselves in a referendum. There is certainly no genuine doubt among scholars that the Court does have jurisdiction to review the Statute under the Constitution. It is absolutely clear that all Statutes of Autonomy must respect the Constitution, and the LOTC explicitly gives the Court the power to review them (article 27.2). There is also no doubt, however, that the case is delicate from a democratic perspective. Even if the citizens that have spoken in the referendum are not the sovereign Spanish people, but only Catalan citizens, the Court cannot easily disregard the potential political consequences of a ruling that is strongly critical of the Statute. Still, in a recent opinion (STC 247/2007) dealing with a relatively minor clause that figures in the Statute of Autonomy of another region (Valencia), the Court has established a general doctrine that will have to be applied to the Catalan Statute. If the Court is consistent with what it unanimously holds in this opinion (in spite of the existence of an internal division as to the way such a holding must be applied), the Catalan Statute will not pass constitutional muster as it currently reads, for it regulates matters that can only be dealt with by the state through 'organic laws' such as those providing for the organization of the judiciary, or the public finance system. Quite likely, the Court will try to save the Statute to the extent it is possible to do so, through an 'interpretive decision' that will readjust many of its clauses in light of existing constitutional constraints. If so, an interesting question will arise: what will happen with other Statutes

---

[33]   It should be noted that the Ombudsman has also brought an abstract challenge against the Catalan Statute.

of Autonomy that have introduced similar clauses, but which have not been impugned? Technically, they will not be directly affected. In practice, though, it will be hard to accept this inequality, all of which adds a new layer of complexity to this politically charged case.

CONSTITUTIONAL BORROWINGS AND OPENNESS TO INTERNATIONAL LAW

'Spain is the problem, Europe is the solution', asserted the Spanish philosopher José Ortega y Gasset. The transition of dictatorship to democracy in 1975-1978 was strongly connected with the wish to overcome Spain's isolation from the rest of Europe. The dominant ideas in European democratic nations thus acquired a special epistemic authority in Spain. It is therefore not surprising that the Constitutional Court has been eager to draw inspiration from foreign and international legal materials when interpreting the Spanish Constitution. This openness is facilitated by article 10.2 of the Constitution, which provides that the Bill of Rights will be interpreted in accordance with the Universal Declaration of Human Rights, as well as the international conventions on human rights that Spain ratifies. Chief among these is the European Convention on Human Rights of 1950, which the Court has often resorted to in order to read the text of the Spanish Constitution. Actually, the Court has paid increasing attention to the case-law of the Strasbourg Court.[34]

The Court has also been sensitive to the jurisprudence of the European Court of Justice (in the area of gender equality, for example). It has actually gone further than this: it has recently shown its willingness to ensure that ordinary judges in Spain make a correct use of the preliminary reference procedure that is established in article 234 of the Treaty of the European Community. In an important opinion (STC 58/2004), it quashed a decision of an ordinary court that had resolved a dispute in a way that contradicted the extant case law of the European Court of Justice, without having raised a preliminary reference to the latter. The Constitutional Court held that, under certain conditions, a failure to raise a preliminary question of EC law can be regarded as an indirect violation of the Spanish Constitution (article 24: due process), and that, consequently, the Constitutional Court may be entitled to intervene through its *amparo* jurisdiction. As was noted earlier, the Court has also been eager to facilitate the introduction in Spain

---

[34] For a systematic study of the way the Court has used article 10.2, see Alejandro Saiz (1999) *La Apertura Constitucional al Derecho Internacional y Europeo de los Derechos Humanos. El Artículo 10.2 de la Constitución Española* Madrid: Consejo General del Poder Judicial.

of the principle of primacy of EU law over national law. In its Declaration 1/2004, it concluded that there was no need to amend the national Constitution for Spain to validly ratify the proposed Treaty establishing a Constitution for Europe, article I-6 of which enshrined the principle of EU law primacy. In its reasoning, the Court gave much weight to article 93 of the Spanish Constitution, which permits the country to join supranational organizations[35]

It should also be mentioned that although the Constitutional Court is particularly attentive to legal developments at the European level, it has also drawn inspiration from other jurisdictions. Thus, for example, it has clearly been sensitive to American ideas on the exclusionary rule in criminal cases,[36] or on the protection of false information that affects public figures when the journalist does not act with malice (STC 6/1988). Although the Court has shaped its own version of these American doctrines, there is no doubt that it has learned much from them.

ACTUAL PERFORMANCE AND PROPOSALS FOR CHANGE

When one evaluates the general performance of the Court since its creation, the first thing one is authorized to note is that the Court has done a remarkable job at 'constitutionalizing' the interpretation and application of the law. One of the historical missions of this institution has been to instil the new constitutional values into the legal minds of ordinary judges. In this connection, the *amparo* jurisdiction has been of crucial importance: by this means the Court has been able to explain how cases must be decided in light of constitutional liberties, and to quash judicial decisions that deviate from its rulings.

The Court has also played a significant role in checking the validity of legislation under the Constitution. However, while its role as arbiter in the clashes between state and regional legislation has been quite prominent (for its intervention is inevitable when such clashes emerge), its performance as a counterweight to the parliamentary majority at the national level has been more marginal. The Court has been so overwhelmed with *amparo* cases that it has not had much time and energy left to decide constitutional challenges and questions of validity of statutes.[37] The Court has usually

---

[35] For various comments on this Declaration, see López, A, Saiz, A and Ferreres, V (2005) *Constitución Española y Constitución Europea* Madrid: Centro de Estudios Políticos y Constitucionales, and García, RA (2005) "The Spanish Constitution and the European Constitution: the script for a virtual collision and other observations on the principle of primacy" 6 *German Law Journal*.

[36] See, e.g., STC 114/1984, citing *United States v. Janis* 428 US 433 (1976).

[37] In 2006, for example, the Court received 11,741 applications, of which 97.7% were

taken a long time (up to eight, nine, ten, and even eleven years in some instances) to render a decision.[38] As a result of these extraordinary delays, it is often the case that the law has already been repealed or modified by Parliament when the Court finally lays down its decision, which gives rise to the sometimes difficult question whether a decision is still necessary, given that the law that was attacked no longer exists.

There is a general consensus among experts that the Court should play a more prominent role as guardian of the Constitution against the legislature: those delays are unacceptable. The problem, of course, is how to reduce the workload that the *amparo* jurisdiction has generated. A recent 2007 reform of the LOTC has given the Court more flexibility, both from a procedural and a substantive point of view, in order to more quickly dispose of cases and concentrate on those that raise important questions of constitutional interpretation. Whether this reform is really sufficient, in order to give the Court the breathing space it needs to exercise legislative review, remains to be seen. Some voices have advocated more radical changes, such as eliminating the *amparo* jurisdiction, at least in its original conception: the Court should focus on the constitutionality of legislation exclusively, even when individual complaints are filed.[39]

Other proposals to modify the Court's organization and functions are also on the political table. The *Partido Popular*, for example, has recently advocated the need to introduce *a priori review* of Statutes of Autonomy. It feels that these norms are so basic to the constitutional structure that the Court should be allowed to speak to the validity of their reforms at an early stage, before the citizens have expressed their vote in a referendum. This party has also proposed to extend the terms of office of the future judges on the Court: instead of sitting for nine years only, as is currently the case, they should sit until they reach a specified age of retirement. While the first proposal does not require an amendment of the Spanish Constitution, the latter does (for article 159.3 fixes the nine-year term), which makes it very unlikely that it will be implemented in the near future. It is nevertheless a reasonable change to introduce, for purposes of strengthening the independence of the judges on the Court. The latter should not count on the possibility that the political branches may reward them with further appointments, once they leave the Court. It is true that, other things being equal, longer terms can generate a gap between the Court's jurisprudence and the mainstream convictions in the political sphere. But if the judges

---

constitutional complaints (*amparo*). See *Memoria 2006*, available at the Court's website.
[38] See, e.g. SSTC 194/2000, 10/2002, 193/2004, 138/2005, 111/2006.
[39] See Cruz, P (2006) "Tribuna abierta: Qué hacer con el amparo" 15 *Actualidad Jurídica Uría Menéndez* at 7.

are selected through super-majoritarian parliamentary procedures, as is true in Spain of most judges on the Court (8 out of 12), the risk of having judges with rather extreme ideological views is rather low, and, therefore, the danger of a democratic deficit drastically diminishes.

The Constitutional Court of Turkey: The *Anayasa Mahkemesi* as the Protector of the System

ESİN ÖRÜCÜ *

INTRODUCTION

Heir to the Ottoman Empire, the Turkish Republic is a relatively young constitutional parliamentary democracy, which embraced laws and cultures from various sources, and endeavoured to build a monolithic legal and cultural system by using law and legalism as formative tools to reflect a particular vision for the country.[1] Judges try to balance divergent interests within the official framework which is there to safeguard the six pillars of the Republic, called at their inception the six arrows of Kemalism: nationalism, laicism, republicanism, populism, statism and reformism often referred to as westernisation. Today, in addition are: a democratic state, human rights, a social state and the rule of law. All are protected by the Constitution and by laws whose constitutionality cannot be challenged. Turkey's institutions, political and legal systems are captive to past and present political and social problems and live within the restraints imposed by these. The role of the Constitutional Court (*Anayasa Mahkemesi*), set up in 1962, in the preservation of the vision and the building up of a modern Turkey is regarded as perhaps more important than the protection of individual rights.[2]

---

* Honorary Senior Research Fellow and Professor Emerita of Comparative Law, University of Glasgow and Professor Emerita of Comparative Law, Erasmus University Rotterdam.
[1] See Örücü, E (2006) 'A Synthetic and Hyphenated Legal System: the Turkish Experience' (2) *The Journal of Comparative Law*, 261- 281.
[2] A wide range of human rights, fundamental freedoms and civil liberties, and social rights, were entrenched for the first time in the 1961Constitution, and at present, are in the 1982

The first Constitution of the Republic (1924), concentrated political power in a single legislative Assembly. There was no constitutional review, no effective guarantees for fundamental rights and liberties and the judiciary did not have full independence. Parliament (the Turkish Grand National Assembly) had the exclusive right to define the limits of the classical civil liberties cited in the Constitution. The 1961 Constitution, which followed the 1960 military take-over, was a reaction to past events and the majoritarian form of democracy of the previous period. It introduced extensive innovations including a Constitutional Court and a liberal model of democracy. After a second military take-over in 1980, a new Constitution was adopted in 1982, which has been amended many times since then in response to political and social events. Substantial amendments are being discussed today.

It is important to note that articles 1 to 3 of the 1982 Constitution are 'immutable provisions' protected by article 4, which states that articles 1-3 'shall not be amended nor shall their amendment be proposed'. These set the form of the State as a Republic and pose the characteristics of the Republic as democratic, laic,[3] social, governed by the rule of law, respecting human rights within the concepts of public peace, national solidarity and justice, loyal to Atatürk nationalism and based on the fundamental tenets set forth in the Preamble.[4] They further lay down that the State is an indivisible whole with its territory, nation and language. In addition, protection is afforded to certain Laws, noted above, passed at the time of the formation of the Republic by article 174 of the Constitution. These are the İnkilap Kanunları (Laws of Radical Reform), which were, and still are, regarded as a *sine qua non* of modernisation, westernisation and laicism - the major aims of the Republic.[5] This means that at the very outset the

---

Constitution. Looking at the Index of Cases decided in 2006 by the *Anayasa Mahkemesi*, we see the following rights and freedoms subject to decisions: legitimate expectations, university autonomy, freedom to form associations, right to education, principle of equality, right of action, legality of offence and punishment, proportionality in punishment, presumption of innocence, individuality of criminal responsibility, the principle of respect for vested rights, property rights, respect to privacy, right to social security, freedom of the press, sexual discrimination, freedom of expression and dissemination, right to protection of the home, freedom of contract. (*Anayasa Mahkemesi Kararlar Dergisi* (*AMKD*): 42 & 43, 2006).

[3] Secularism as understood in its French version of laicism.

[4] As re-written in 1995 and amended in 2001, the Preamble includes: '[N]o activity to be defended which is opposed to Turkish national interests, the principle of the indivisible integrity of Turkish existence with its State and territory, Turkish historical and moral values, the nationalism, principles, reforms and modernisation of Atatürk, and that as demanded by the principle of laicism, sacred religious feelings being in no way permitted to interfere with State affairs and politics.'

[5] The general aim was for modernisation and national integration, and to become European legally, socially and culturally. The eight principal reform laws established secular

Anayasa Mahkemesi is restricted in the issues it can deal with and the way it can use its powers of interpretation.

Important consequences of the above are the strict control on political parties and the use of freedoms such as those of expression, the press, association and religion, and a self-referential legal system. The concept of sovereignty has a strong hold in Turkey.

Until October 2001, when Parliament repealed the provisional article 15/3 of the 1982 Constitution, another limitation was that claims of unconstitutionality of laws and decrees with the force of law passed between 1980-1983 could not be brought to the *Anayasa Mahkemesi*.[6]

Since 1961, the Turkish Constitutions have embodied almost all the human rights and freedoms covered by the ECHR and other Conventions on related issues, as well as the principle of review of constitutionality. Nevertheless, the specific socio-cultural and political problems Turkey faces give a peculiar twist to these, to be seen below.

THE *ANAYASA MAHKEMESI*

Reasons for setting up a Constitutional Court

Demand for a constitutional court was first expressed in 1957 after the Republican People's Party (*Cumhuriyet Halk Partisi*) lost the elections. However, the party that then came to power (*Demokrat Parti*) enjoyed the advantages of majoritarian democracy and did not support this view. A number of laws passed in the period 1957-1960 had dubious constitutionality and led to the political climate calling for military intervention in May 1960.

The 1960-61 Constituent Assembly, dominated by the secular elite establishment, accepted constitutional review without much debate. The 1961 Constitution was adopted after referendum and contained a detailed Bill of Rights, which put rights and liberties, including social rights, under effective judicial guarantees. Its basic philosophy was the replacement of majoritarian democracy with liberal democracy. The scope of legislative action with respect to civil liberties was substantially limited through the

---

education and civil marriage, adopted international numerals, the Turkish alphabet and the new calendar, introduced the hat, closed the *dervish* convents, abolished certain titles and prohibited the wearing of certain garments.

[6] See for example, 1999/23; 1999/18; 25.5.1999 *AMKD*: 35, 2000, 446, where the Court declared lack of competence and said that in order to review laws passed in this period, the ban introduced by art. 15 must be lifted by Parliament (Art. 87) (repealed on 3.10.2001 as part of the harmonization package with the EU). However, there are a few cases where the Court gave direct effect to the constitutional provision to sidestep (by neglect) laws passed during this period.

principles of constitutional supremacy, constitutional review ensuring this supremacy, separation of powers and the independence of the judiciary.

The Constitutional Court (*Anayasa Mahkemesi*) that became operative in 1962, was established on the German and the Italian models, following debate as to the type of court, its composition, method of selecting judges and access to the court. The concept of the 'core of rights' was brought in (article 11), which meant that the *Anayasa Mahkemesi* had additional ammunition to use when reviewing violation of rights. This article was construed by the Court as 'prohibiting any infringement which would make the exercise of a right or liberty impossible or particularly difficult'.[7]

The 1982 Constitution, born after another military coup and the product of similar elites and the army, came into effect with another referendum. It was inspired by the 1958 French and American Constitutions. Amendments to it over the years draw on Turkish social and political reality, and more recently, on the perceived demands of the European Union and the European Convention on Human Rights. This Constitution did not change the powers of the *Anayasa Mahkemesi* in essence (articles 146-153). However, though under the 1961 system, ordinary courts also had the power to render a decision on the constitutionality of a particular law applicable in a pending trial in exceptional cases and *inter partes* decisions were allowed, the system of the 1982 Constitution did not allow either.

In preference to protecting the rights of citizens, the Court was now conceived as an instrument to protect the fundamental values and interests of the establishment. The concept of 'core of rights' was dropped from the Constitution.[8] Instead the limit of limits was now 'the necessities of democratic social order'. The Court was seen as a protector and guardian of the basic ideology, Kemalism, reflected in the provisions of the Constitution. In fact, in the last three decades, the Court has acted essentially to fulfil the expectations of the elite that had empowered it. One of the examples of this attitude can be observed in cases related to the dissolving of political parties to be seen below. The Court, which protects the national and unitary state and the principle of laicism, the two basic pillars of the Kemalist vision, has been consistent in its attitude to ethnic Kurdish, separationist and Islamist political parties by using a rigid and narrow interpretation of the Constitution and the Law on Political Parties. Constitutional review thus

---

[7] Özbudun, E (2004) 'Constitutional Law' in Ansay T and Wallace D (eds) *Introduction to Turkish Law* 5th ed (Kluwer Law International, The Hague) 24. For an analysis of this concept see Örücü, E (1986)'The Core of Rights and Freedoms: The Limit of Limits' in Campbell, T, Goldberg, D, McLean, S and Mullen, T (eds) *Human Rights: From Rhetoric to Reality* (Basil Blackwell, Oxford) 37-59.

[8] This concept re-entered the Constitution with the 2001 amendments.

ensures adherence to the Constitution and supports its superiority and its binding force, the Court defending primarily the legal order and rule of law according to the Constitution.[9] This has been described as 'an ideologically-based paradigm' in contrast to 'a right-based paradigm'.[10]

A number of decisions of the *Anayasa Mahkemesi* protecting the rights of Parliament from the executive, also reflect distrust of the mechanisms of majoritarian democracy. [11] The Court does in fact act as a 'negative legislator'.

The structure of the Court

Under the 1961 Constitution, the majority of the *Anayasa Mahkemesi* judges (15 regular and five substitute judges) were chosen by the other High Courts: the Court of Cassation (*Yargıtay*), the Turkish Conseil d'Etat (*Danıştay*), the Military Court of Cassation (*Askeri Yargıtay*), the Court of Accounts (*Sayıştay*) and the Supreme Military Administrative Court (*Yüksek Askeri İdare Mahkmesi*). In addition, the National Assembly chose three, the Senate of the Republic two and the President of the Republic two members (one of whom from among the three candidates nominated by the Military Court of Cassation (*Askeri Yargıtay*).

The present 1982 Constitution provides that all eleven regular and four substitute judges are appointed by the President of the Republic (direct appointment system), the majority of judges to be nominated by judges of the High Courts, with each court nominating three for each vacant seat. The President appoints two regular and two substitute members from the *Yargıtay*, two regular members and one substitute member from the *Danıştay*, and one member each from the *Askeri Yargıtay*, the *Yüksek Askeri İdare Mahkemesi* and the *Sayıştay*. The President also appoints one judge from the three candidates put forward by the Supreme Council of Higher Education (*YÖK*) who are members of the teaching staff of institutions of higher education. The President can only choose freely three regular judges and one substitute judge from among senior civil servants and lawyers

---

[9]   Art. 11 of the Constitution states that: 'The provisions of the Constitution are fundamental legal rules binding upon legislative, executive and judicial organs, and administrative authorities and other institutions and individuals. Laws shall not be contrary to the Constitution.'

[10]   Arslan, Z (2002) 'Conflicting Paradigms: Political Rights in the Turkish Constitutional Court' *Critical Middle Eastern Studies*, 9-25.

[11]   Decisions limiting the scope of 'decrees with the force of law' and of martial law and emergency regime ordinances can be given as examples. See 1988/64; 1990/2; 1.2.1990 *AMKD*: 26; 1989/4; 1989/23; 16.5.1989 *AMKD*: 25; 1991/6; 1991/20; 3.7.1991 *AMKD*: 27/1; 1990/25; 1991/1; 10.1.1991 *AMKD*: 27/1.

(article 146). They must be over the age of forty, have completed higher education, or have worked at least fifteen years in the teaching staff of institutions of higher education, as administrators or lawyers. The Court has complete independence from the legislative and the executive branch. The Court assembles *en banque*.

The 1961 Constitution did not limit the term of office of the judges of the *Anayasa Mahkemesi*, which meant that changes in public opinion could not be easily reflected in the composition of the Court. The 1982 Constitutions foresees retirement of judges at the age of sixty-five. Apart from age, their office may be terminated *ipso facto* upon conviction of an offence entailing dismissal from the judicial profession or for reasons of health, in which case, the Court decides on termination (article 147).

As noted, the legislature is excluded from the selection process.[12] It has been often suggested that the legislature should be involved in the process. Some judges of the *Anayasa Mahkemesi* are of the opinion that this would politicise the Court and interfere with their independence, in the belief that the Presidential office is apolitical, neutral and above political parties.

Nonetheless, in 2004 the *Anayasa Mahkemesi* submitted to the Venice Commission a draft proposal on a constitutional amendment with regard to the Court, introducing a hybrid solution with a modest role for the legislature in the selection process, the Court to be composed of seventeen judges, eleven elected by the High Courts, four by Parliament and two directly by the President. However, Parliament would not be entirely free in their choice, and could only elect one member from the three candidates nominated by the YÖK, one member from the three candidates nominated by the Union of the Bar Associations and two members from the presidents and members of the *Sayıştay*.[13] There would be no substitute judges. The Court would be divided into two chambers. The minimum age requirement would be fifty and the retirement age 67. The proposal provided for a twelve-year term of office.

This proposal met with strong opposition from the presidents of the other High Courts. It is not known whether the present membership of the *Anayasa Mahkemesi* would still support this draft.

The new draft constitutional amendments, presently under discussion, transfer the competence to elect members of the *Anayasa Mahkemesi* from the President of the Republic to Parliament, with eight members to be

[12] This has been called a *sui generis* phenomenon, a 'Turkish type', resembling neither the European nor the USA models. See Arslan, Z (2004) 'Tartışma' *Anayasa Yargısı* No: 21, Anayasa Mahkemesi Yayınları : 51, Ankara, 132.
[13] See ibid for papers and discussion on this proposal presented at a Symposium organised by the *Anayasa Mahkemesi*.

elected by Parliament (at least three from among law professors), four by the *Yargıtay*, four by the *Danıştay* and one by the *Sayıştay*. They would be elected for one period of nine years. There would be seventeen members, no substitute members, the minimum age for election would be forty and retirement age 65.

The jurisdiction of the Court and gateways for invoking jurisdiction and developments

The jurisdiction of the *Anayasa Mahkemesi* extends to constitutionality of laws, decrees having the force of law, and the rules of procedure of Parliament (article 148). The Court examines their constitutionality as to substance and form. Constitutional amendments however, can only be examined with regard to their form. The review as to form means consideration of whether the requisite majority was obtained in the last ballot, and in the case of constitutional amendments, of whether the requisite majorities were obtained for the proposal and in the ballot, and whether the prohibition on debates under urgent procedure was complied with. Review of form can be requested by the President of the Republic or one-fifth of the members of Parliament. Such an application cannot be made more than ten days after the date on which the law was promulgated. Furthermore, if the parliamentary immunity of a deputy has been waived, the deputy in question, or another deputy, may, within seven days of the decision of Parliament, appeal to the *Anayasa Mahkemesi*, for the decision to be annulled for being contrary to the Constitution, law or procedure, whereupon the Court must decide on the issue within fifteen days (article 85).

The Court is not bound by the reasoning put forth by the parties.[14] The quorum for decisions is absolute majority. However a decision to invalidate a constitutional amendment on procedural grounds must be made by a three-fifths majority of the Court (articles 148, 149). This same quorum is required for decisions on the closure of political parties. All decisions are *erga omnes* and not *inter partes*.

There are certain restrictions on the jurisdiction of the Court: No action can be brought before the Court alleging unconstitutionality as to the form or substance of decrees having the force of law issued during a state of emergency, martial law or in time of war (article 148/1).[15] In addition, international agreements duly put into effect carry the force of law and no

---

[14] Art. 29 of Law 2949 on the Establishment and Procedure of the *Anayasa Mahkemesi*.
[15] However, see cases cited in footnote 11 supra. Another limitation in Art. 15 has been repealed (see footnote 6 supra).

appeal to the *Anayasa Mahkemesi* can be made with regard to them on the ground that they are unconstitutional (article 90). Furthermore, as noted above, no provision of the Constitution can be construed or interpreted as rendering unconstitutional the Reform Laws which aim to raise Turkish society above the level of 'contemporary civilisation' and to safeguard the laic character of the Republic, and which were in force on the date of the adoption by referendum of the Constitution of Turkey (article 174).

There are other restrictions: no appeal can be made to any legal authority, including the *Anayasa Mahkemesi*, against decisions and orders signed by the President of the Republic on his/her own initiative, against decisions of the Supreme Military Council (*Yüksek Askeri Şura*), and decisions of the Supreme Council of Judges and Public Prosecutors (*Hakimler ve Savcılar Yüksek Kurulu*) (articles 105, 125 and 159). In addition, the *Anayasa Mahkemesi* at times declares lack of jurisdiction regarding certain decisions of Parliament (article 87). Furthermore, when the legislature is negligent in passing laws in fulfilment of its obligations under the Constitution no remedy is allowed to the *Anayasa Mahkemesi*. Neither has the Court the right to prior preventive control but only to a posterior repressive control. Another restriction laid down in article 153/2 is that, while annulling the whole, or a provision, of a law, the Court cannot act 'as law-maker and pass judgment leading to a new implementation'. This signals the necessity of judicial self-restraint and may be regarded as an unnecessary provision, since the Court does not go into the merits of the cases and does not discuss political preferences of the legislature.[16]

Access to the Court can be through two gateways: The first is by an annulment action (*iptal davası*), a principal proceeding, an abstract norm control, which can be instituted by the President of the Republic, parliamentary groups of the governing party and the main opposition party, or at least one-fifth of the full membership of the Assembly (article 150).[17] Here, there is no need for a conflict or violation of a right, only a diverse opinion on constitutionality. Such suits of unconstitutionality for substantive review must be initiated within sixty days following the promulgation of the law in the Official Gazette (*Resmi Gazete*). In case of formal review, the period is ten days from promulgation.

The second gateway is by an incidental proceeding, the plea of unconstitutionality (*anayasaya aykırılık itirazı*), that is, the objection of unconstitutionality before other courts, leading to a concrete norm

---

[16] See 1984/1; 1984/2; 1.3.1984, *AMKD*: 20, 161; 1987/23; 1987/27; 9. 10.1987, *AMKD*: 20, 380-381.
[17] The draft constitution brings in a restriction in that the main opposition party alone will not be able to go to the *Anayasa Mahkemesi*.

control. This arises out of a pending trial in an ordinary civil, criminal or administrative court and can be raised by that court or any individual party to the pending trial and is not subject to any time limitation. The court trying the case must determine whether such a demand is serious and justified. If the court so decides, it adjourns the proceedings and refers the matter to the *Anayasa Mahkemesi*, which must decide the issue within five months. Otherwise, the regular court must render judgment on the basis of the existing law.[18] According to article 153, if the *Anayasa Mahkemesi* dismisses the case on substantive grounds, no plea of unconstitutionality for the same law can be put forward before a ten-year period has elapsed.[19] This Article was brought in for 'legal stability', however, 'it is, in fact, a serious limitation upon defendants' rights',[20] is contrary to the purpose of constitutional review and does not cater for changing social circumstances.

The Court gives two types of judgments: Annulment or dismissal of claim. However, over the years, the *Anayasa Mahkemesi* has developed further means not foreseen by the Constitution through its precedents. The first of these is the method by which the Court avoids annulment, and develops the law by opting for an interpretation compatible with the Constitution.[21] The second method, rarely used, is when the Court neglects the provision of a law that is incompatible with the Constitution, but gives direct effect to a constitutional provision. This way out is usually resorted to when the legislation in question cannot be challenged. The condition is that the constitutional provision must be clear, detailed and possible of direct applicability. The third means developed is an interim decision: 'stay of implementation'. The Constitution has not given the Court the power to declare stay of implementation in a case brought before it. However, though until 1993 the Court refrained from doing so, since then, there has been an increase in the number of cases where the Court has granted this plea.[22] There are strict conditions though: There must be serious indications that the law in question is contrary to the Constitution and that if implemented, this might give rise to damages that cannot be recovered. The Court has also developed the measure of 'proportionality',

---

[18] The 1961 Constitution allowed the trial court to decide on constitutionality in circumstances when the *Anayasa Mahkemesi* did not reach a decision within six months.
[19] The proposals of the *Anayasa Mahkemesi* and the new draft amendments to the constitution reduce this to five years. There was no such provision in the 1961 Constitution.
[20] Özbudun, supra note 7, 45.
[21] See 1984/18; 1984/10; 20.9.1984; AMKD: 20, 298.
[22] In 1994 there were 16 such pleas, increasing to 21 in 2003. See Kılıç, H (2004) 'Türk Anayasa Mahkemesi'nin Yeniden Yapılandırılmasına İlişkin Öneri', *Anayasa Yargısı* No: 21 Anayasa Mahkemesi Yayınları: 51, Ankara, 82. This interim decision has been given a place in Art. 153 of the draft proposal of the *Anayasa Mahkemesi* and the draft constitutional amendments under discussion (Art. 117/3).

which it uses widely, specifically in cases where article 13 (as amended in 2001) of the Constitution is implemented by Parliament to restrict rights and freedoms in accordance with article 15 'to the extent required by the exigencies of the situation': Accordingly, a fundamental right or freedom can only be restricted for the specific reasons set forth in the relevant article of the Constitution, without touching their 'cores', and only by legislation. These restrictions cannot be contrary to the wording and the spirit of the Constitution, the democratic social order and the necessities of the laic Republic and the principle of proportionality.

Upon invalidation, the law in question becomes ineffective as of the date of publication of the decision (*ex nunc*) in the *Resmi Gazete*. A date not later than one year from the date of the publication of the annulment decision may be set by the Court as the date the decision shall come into effect (Article 153).[23] In such a case, Parliament must debate and decide with priority on the draft bill or proposal designed to fill the legal void arising from the decision. Decisions of the Court cannot be retroactive and are final. Furthermore, according to the established jurisprudence of the Court, both the decisions and the reasoning are binding.[24] However, though the Court cannot act as law-maker and pass judgment leading to new implementation (Article 153), the legislature or the executive cannot modify or postpone the decisions of the Court, neither can a new law be passed to give life to an annulled provision.[25]

Neither the 1961 nor the 1982 Constitutions accepted an individual's right to constitutional complaint. Neither do the new draft constitutional amendments consider this option, the emphasis being on review of constitutionality of laws rather than review of the application of laws.[26] However, in spite of problems related to a considerable increase in workload, individual access through a 'constitutional complaint' to the Court has been proposed by the *Anayasa Mahkemesi* in 2004, following the German model.[27] One of the main reasons for the introduction of this gateway – though as an exceptional and subsidiary path – is so that the number of files against Turkey brought before the ECtHR would decrease. The scope of the complaint is limited to protecting basic rights in the Constitution, which are also regulated in the ECHR.[28] The *actio popularis* option has not been considered.

---

[23] See e.g. 2005/99; 2006/8; 19.1.2006 *AMKD*: 42, 2006, 93.

[24] See the Court's view of this e.g. in 2006/22; 2006/40; 22.3.2006 *AMK D*: 43, 2006, 219-220.

[25] Ibid.

[26] In many respects this type of review is undertaken by the Turkish *Conseil d'Etat*, the *Danıştay*.

[27] See for extensive discussion supra note 13, 163-313.

[28] The proposed Art. 148/6 reads: 'All individuals claiming that one of their constitutional

Under the 1961 Constitution, the Court based its decisions not only on the Constitution but also referred to international conventions and general principles of law. International conventions were not used as reference norms but as supportive norms. However, general principles of law were regarded as even a superior reference norm, though never used as an independent ground but considered as part of the '*Rechtsstaat*'.[29] Public interest has always been an important criterium. In assessing public interest 'core of rights' was the limit of limits, now, under the 1982 Constitution, the limit is the 'necessities of a democratic social order' and most decisions are based solely on the Constitution.

Concerning fundamental political choices and value judgements, the Court thinks strategically, with a view to the impact of its decisions on the public. The Court sometimes interprets the law to make it compatible with the Constitution, but often it decides on annulment and lays down a single possible interpretation of the law, putting the Court into the position of a 'positive legislator'.[30]

In April 2007, the *Anayasa Mahkemesi* was involved in the election of the Eleventh President of the Republic and had to decide a number of cases brought before it by the then President of the Republic and the opposition party. The opposition challenged the Parliamentary vote on the grounds that there was not the necessary quorum. The *Anayasa Mahkemesi* agreed and annulled the first round, which forced the government to hold early elections on July 22, 2007. In the process, Abdullah Gül, the new President elected after the general elections, accused the Court of acting as a Senate, a political organ, rather than as a legal one, in correcting political decisions taken by Parliament by its own political decisions.[31]

The *Anayasa Mahkemesi* can also try impeachment cases as a Supreme Court (*Yüce Divan*) and decide on unconstitutional activities of the political parties. The Chief Public Prosecutor of the Republic acts as public prosecutor in the Supreme Court.

---

rights or freedoms in the scope of the ECHR has been violated by public power are entitled to apply to the *Anayasa Mahkemesi* on condition that they have exhausted legal remedies. The principles and procedures on admissibility and competence of pre-review commissions and on judgments of the Chambers shall be regulated by law'.

[29] Some of the general principles used in the 1982 Constitution period are good faith, *pacta sunt servanda*, respect for vested rights, non-retroactivity of laws and respect for *res judicata*.
[30] This means that there is only one way to legislate after an annulment. An example of this is the second headscarf (*türban*) case to be seen below.
[31] Reported in the *Zaman* newspaper on 23.06.2007.

Problems encountered and how these are dealt with

One important problem arises as a result of the long time lag between reaching an annulment decision and its publication. The only rule is that if the Court decides to postpone the coming into effect of such a decision, the date cannot be more than one year from the date of publication (Article 153/3). However, since annulment decisions cannot be made public without written reasoning and both the decision and its reasoning are binding, sometimes in exceptional cases, the Court takes a much longer period before it publishes a decision.[32] Since usually, the decision is leaked to the public, in the interim period unconstitutional practices may continue.

Though binding on everyone, there are no sanctions for situations where the decisions of the *Anayasa Mahkemesi* are not followed by other High Courts in the system, and unfortunately the *Yargıtay* and the *Danıştay*, though to a lesser extent, at times give decisions contrary to the *Anayasa Mahkemesi* decisions purposefully, violating their Constitutional duty. This leads to a deep conflict of interpretations and there are no mechanisms to resolve this conflict.[33]

Again, unfortunately, the legislature may re-introduce a piece of legislation annulled by the Court, albeit with minor changes. According to the Court this amounts to rendering *Anayasa Mahkemesi* decisions ineffective.[34] Obviously this practice can be regarded as a violation of the Constitution (article 11). In such cases the *Anayasa Mahkemesi* simply annuls the new law.[35]

Until recently, in reaching its decisions, the *Anayasa Mahkemesi* seldom considered Strasbourg case law and other International Conventions which give additional rights to the people. Article 90 of the Turkish Constitution deals with international treaties. Article 90/5 reads:

> International agreements duly put into effect carry the force of law.
> No appeal to the *Anayasa Mahkemesi* can be made with regard to these agreements, on the ground that they are unconstitutional.

---

[32] See, for instance, 1997/61; 1998/59; 29.9.1998; *Resmi Gazete* No: 24937; 15.11.2002, related to a married woman's surname, discussed below. Also see 90/31; 29.11.1990, where the publication of the decision annulling the then Section 159 of the Civil Code, which stated that a wife needs her husband's permission to work outside the home, was delayed for two years, either because of the difficulty of composing a reasoning through which the Court could satisfy all sides, or in order to postpone the introduction of the change.

[33] For a discussion of this problem and some examples see Sağlam, F (1996) 'Yetki ve İşlev Bağlamında Anayasa Mahkemesi'nin Yasama Yürütme ve Yargı ile İlişkisi' *Anayasa Yargısı* No 13, Anayasa Mahkemesi Yayınlar: 32, Ankara, 53-60.

[34] See 1991/27; 1991/50; 2.9.1992; *AMKD*: 27, 700.

[35] See 1993/26; 1993/28; 16.9.1993; *Resmi Gazete* No: 21772; 8.10.

> In conflicts arising between different provisions of a domestic law and an international agreement related to fundamental rights and freedoms, the provisions of the international agreement will be taken as the basis.

In spite of the above, the last sentence of which entered the Constitution in 2004, there is continuing debate around this provision, and as to whether the ECHR has a special status, the future status of EU treaties, and what will be the hierarchical relationship between the Turkish Constitution and these agreements if Turkey joins the EU.[36]

A number of academics and the judges of the *Anayasa Mahkemesi* regard the ECHR, as they do any other international agreement. The only difference from ordinary legislation is that the constitutionality of the Convention cannot be challenged. Therefore, the *Anayasa Mahkemesi* should not review its decisions in the light of ECtHR judgments, as national sovereignty belongs to the nation unconditionally (*egemenlik kayıtsız şartsız milletindir*). This dominant view also found support in the decisions of the *Anayasa Mahkemesi* – which upheld the Turkish Constitution above all else – until March 2007.[37]

It has also been held that when a human right covered by the Convention but not by the Constitution is at issue, *lex posterior* (the Constitution for example) defeats *lex specialis* (the ECHR for example), and therefore the Constitution should prevail.

On the whole, the *Anayasa Mahkemesi* regards the extensive section on rights in the Constitution (articles 19-74) as the sole basis of review of constitutionality, and though at times it refers to articles of the ECHR, this is at the level of citing without analysis, showing parallels that exist between the provisions of the Convention and the articles of the Constitution. The review is one of constitutionality not of conventionality and there is a lack

---

[36] See the discussions and papers published in *Anayasa Yargısı* No: 17, Anayasa Mahkemesi Yayınları: 42, Ankara, 2000.

[37] Turkey introduced amendments to several Laws in August 2002. A clause has been added to the Code of Criminal Procedure, the Code of Civil Procedure and the Code of Administrative Procedure, departing from the long held official and academic views: When the ECtHR determines that a Turkish final decision has been given in violation of the European Convention or its Protocols, then the Minister of Justice, the Public Prosecutor for the *Yargıtay*, the applicant to the ECtHR or his/her representative can request a re-trial within one year of the judgment of the ECtHR, with the condition that in view of the quality and seriousness of the violation, payment of just satisfaction to be given under Article 41 would not redress the situation. These amendments came into force on 9th August 2003, and only apply to cases taken to the ECtHR after this date. The above interim decision was made in the first case where the process of re-trial has been extended to decisions of the *Anayasa Mahkemesi* by the Court itself. The case is pending.

of creative and extensive interpretation. A reading of the decisions shows that, traditional values and the social needs of the country usually override most other considerations.

THE TYPES OF ISSUE THE COURT HAS DEALT WITH AND ITS ACTUAL PERFORMANCE[38]

We will now consider a number of cases from some significant areas.[39]

(a) Dissolution of political parties

One group of cases dealt with by the *Anayasa Mahkemesi* relates to the permanent closure of political parties.[40] The Court is specifically empowered by the Constitution in this matter and must determine whether the party in question 'has become the centre for the execution of activities' banned by Article 69.

The majority of the dissolved parties are to the left in the political spectrum and/or parties advocating a separate homeland and/or autonomy for the Kurdish population. The *Anayasa Mahkemesi* bases its decisions on Law No: 2820 on Political Parties.[41] The political parties and their representatives base their cases partly on the two relevant Articles of the ECHR, 11 and 17. The public prosecutor – and the Court following – rejects the claims, based on the limitations introduced in 11/2 and 17/2. In such cases, the *Anayasa Mahkemesi* typically takes into consideration existing

---

[38] An analysis of the applications to the Court between 1982 and 2004, both in principal and incidental proceedings, show that in 1982 there were two, in 1983, 12; 1984, 17; 1985, 33 applications, This number gradually increased to 86 in 2000, peaked at 495 in 2001, 171 in 2002 and 113 in 2003. See Kılıç, supra note 22.

[39] All translations of Turkish court decisions are by this author.

[40] Samples are: 1992/1; 1993/1; 14.7.1993 *Resmi Gazete* No: 21672; 18.8.1993; 1993/2; 1993/3; 30.11.1993 *Resmi Gazete* No: 22016; 9.8.1994; 1993/3; 1994/2; 16.8.1994 *Resmi Gazete* No: 21976; 30.6.1994; 1993/4; 1995/1; 19.7.1995 *Resmi Gazete* No: 23148; 2210.1997; 1995/1; 1996/1; 19.3.1996 *Resmi Gazete* No: 23149; 23.10.1997; 1996/1; 1997/1; 14.2.1997 *Resmi Gazete* No: 23384; 30.6.1998; 1998/2; 1998/1; 9.1.1998 *Resmi Gazete* No: 23266; 22.2.1998; 1997/2; 1999/1; 26.2.1999 *Resmi Gazete* No: 24591; 22.11.2001; 1999/1; 2003/1; 13.2.2003 *Resmi Gazete* No: 25173; 19.7.2003, all brought to the Court by the Chief Public Prosecutor for the Republic. For an analysis of these cases see Koçak, M and Örücü, E (2003) 'Dissolution of Political Parties in the Name of Democracy: Cases from Turkey and the European Court of Human Rights' (9) *European Public Law*, 399-423.

[41] This Law was passed during the years 1980-83, a period protected by article 15 of the Constitution noted above, whose constitutionality could not have been challenged until 2001. However, in 2000, while dealing with a party dissolution case brought before it, the *Anayasa Mahkemesi*, in an incidental proceeding acting as the appellant, annulled an amendment to section 103/2 of Law No: 2820, claiming that it was narrowing the powers bestowed upon the Court by article 69. 2000/86; 2000/50; 12.12.2000 *Resmi Gazete* No: 24268; 22.12.2000.

Turkish laws first and then the prevailing political and social climate and conditions in Turkey.[42] One case involving the closure of the German communist party is discussed in more detail and comparatively – it was the only other case the ECtHR decided on this issue, and the closure was not found to violate the Convention. Such references are superficial.[43]

In two other cases related to the closure of religious parties, the *Anayasa Mahkemesi* discussed laicism in relation to democracy.[44] In the 1998 case closing the *Refah Partisi* (the Welfare Party), both the public prosecutor and the defenders brought extensive discussion of various international instruments, the concept of laicism as understood by doctrine, and the law in some foreign jurisdictions such as the USA, the UK, Switzerland, Germany, France and Yugoslavia with some reference to the case law of the US Supreme Court. Freedom of expression was the major issue here and these cases tried to balance this freedom with the protection of the existing system in keeping with the official vision discussed earlier. The Court regarded the matter as solely Turkish.[45] However, this case was supported by the ECtHR.[46]

(b) Right to education, religion and laicism

In one case related to Law No: 4307 of 1997 on Primary Education, extending education in primary schools from five to eight years, the claim was that this was contrary to a number of articles of the Constitution, and articles 9 and 10 ECHR and article 2 of its Protocol 1, as it would impede religious education. The appellant, the *Refah Partisi* (the main opposition party), made reference to foreign doctrine and decisions of the ECtHR on democracy, pluralism, equality, tolerance, fundamental rights and freedoms, conditions of social peace and laicism. There were references to a number of International Conventions, the ECHR, and foreign jurisdictions in the USA, France, Germany, Italy, the UK, Norway and even Japan. The *Anayasa Mahkemesi*, deciding solely within the framework of the Turkish Constitution held:

> On the other hand, though not a direct basis for constitutional control, the ECHR has value and effect as a supplementary norm

[42] 93/2; 93/3; 30.11.1993; *Resmi Gazete* No: 22016; 9.8.1994.
[43] See 1992/1; 1993/1; 14.7.1993; *Resmi Gazete* No: 21672; 18.8.1993.
[44] 1996/3; 1997/3; 22.5.1997 *Resmi Gazete* No: 24067; 2.6.2000.
[45] 2000/86; 2000/50; 12.12.2000 *Resmi Gazete* No: 24268; 22.12.2000, applying directly the Constitution.
[46] See Koçak & Örücü, supra note 40.

and its article 9 related to freedom of religion and conscience is in essence parallel to article 24 of the Turkish Constitution. There is no violation of Protocol 1 article 2, since there is no limitation or prohibition on the choice parents have on the child's religious education.[47] In this case nothing was found to be unconstitutional.

More important is the way the *Anayasa Mahkemesi* evaluates the headscarf (*türban*) cases in educational establishments within the context of laicism. The first decision reached on this issue was in 1989, annulling the amendment to the law lifting the ban on the wearing of the headscarf in such institutions.[48] The Court opined that,

> [T]he fact that the wearing of the headscarf, giving a woman the appearance of being anachronistic, is gradually spreading, has obvious drawbacks for the Republican reforms and the principle of laicism. ... A laic legal order, laic education and laic administration cannot be thought of as separate from one another. ... Educational establishments cannot be set up contrary to the requirements of article 42 of the Constitution ... and higher education institutions are no exception. To separate students on religious affiliation by symbols indicating which belief they support in classes, laboratories, clinics, policlinics and corridors, where students work together in a spirit of friendship and solidarity to reach the truth by being educated and applying scientific methods, would lead to conflict and hinder co-operation.

Later in 1991 in a second case[49] the *Anayasa Mahkemesi* decided that the regulation bringing 'freedom of attire' in higher education institutions did not apply to religious dress and 'covering the neck and hair with a scarf or *türban* due to religious belief', and that this regulation was unconstitutional and should be annulled. According to the Court, any symbol representing religious belief should be kept out of educational institutions and allowing the wearing of the *türban* in the universities cannot accord with a laic scientific environment.

---

[47]   1997/62; 1998/52; 16.9.1998 *Resmi Gazete* No: 24206; 30.10.2000; and *AMKD*: 36, 2001, 198.
[48]   This is usually referred to in Turkey as the 'First *Türban* Decision'. See, 1989/1; 1989/12; 7.3.1989; *Resmi Gazete* No: 20216; 5.7.1989. The appellant was the President of the Republic.
[49]   Referred to in Turkey as the 'Second *Türban* Decision'. See, 1990/36; 1991/8; 9.4.1991 *Resmi Gazete* No: 20946; 31.7.1991. The appellant was the *Sosyal Demokrat Halkçı Parti*, the main opposition party.

211

The reasoning of the *Anayasa Mahkemesi* has also been accepted by the ECtHR [50] and the ban on the wearing of the *türban* in public institutions and educational establishments is regarded as essential to laicism, a *sine quo non* of democracy.

(c)   Sexual equality

Equality before the law is regarded as one of the bases of the Turkish Republic and is the only fundamental right cited among the general principles in Part I of the Constitution as article 10 – an article widely referred to in Court.

For example, adultery used to be a punishable offence in the Turkish Penal Code in addition to being a ground for divorce in the Civil Code.[51] In 1996 the *Anayasa Mahkemesi* annulled section 441 of the then Penal Code concerning adultery of the husband, finding a violation of article 10 of the Constitution on equality.[52] Section 440 of the same Code regulated adultery of the wife saying that the penalty for a wife's adultery is imprisonment for from six months to three years. The same applied to a man who had sexual intercourse with a woman knowing that she was married. However, section 441 had additional conditions for a husband's adultery. Sexual intercourse, sufficient in the case of a wife's adultery, was not sufficient in the case of a husband.[53] This distinction in the requirement of fidelity was found unconstitutional, there being no legitimate reason to justify it, spouses being under the same obligation to be faithful to each other. Though there were references to the International Covenant on Civil and Political Rights, the ECHR and the Convention on the Elimination of All Forms of Discrimination Against Women, the decision was based solely on article 10. The Court adopted a purely 'legalistic approach'.

In cases related to equality in family law, one decision of the *Anayasa Mahkemesi* illustrates how cultural exceptionalism supported by the Constitution is the basis. Until amended in 2002, the Turkish Civil Code, modelled on the Swiss Civil Code, regarded the residence of the husband as

[50]   The Grand Chamber of the ECtHR, following the Chamber decision of 29.6.2004, decided in the *Leyla Şahin v. Turkey* on 10.11.2005 that such a ban can be regarded as 'necessary in a democratic society' and that those who agree to undertake university education are to be deemed as having agreed to accept the principles of laicism, one of the fundamental principles of the state. Turkey was found not to violate the Convention.

[51]   See Örücü, E (1987-88) 'Turkey: Reconciling Traditional Society and Secular Demands', in (26) *J.FAM.L.* 221-236 at 230

[52]   1996/15; 1996/34; 23.9.1996; *Resmi Gazete* No: 22860; 27.12.1996; 246.

[53]   He must have lived with another unmarried woman as if she were his wife either in his marital home or a place known to others. Only in this case would they both be imprisoned for from six month to three years.

the residence of the wife, and the court of his residence the competent court in divorce cases brought by either spouse. This provision was challenged as creating inequality for the wife and violating her freedom of choice of residence. The Court held:

> Some rights of individuals have been transferred to the family unit. ... Public interest justifies this regulation. Rights can be limited for public interest, public morality, public health and other special grounds mentioned in the pertinent article, when these limitations are proper in a democratic society.[54]

As to the right to one's surname, the wife takes the surname of the husband upon marriage. An option entered the then Turkish Civil Code in 1997, when section 153 (now 187) allowed the married woman to use her maiden name before that of her husband's surname, upon her written request.[55] A decision of the *Anayasa Mahkemesi* however, again helps us to reflect on the general attitude to equality between the spouses. Although the lower court saw the claims of violation of articles 10, 12, and 17 of the Constitution related to equality, personality rights and rights to development of personality, as serious, the *Anayasa Mahkemesi*, following a very conservative interpretation of the family and the place of the woman in it, and referring to long established traditions, saw no violation of the articles mentioned.[56] It took four years to publish this decision, which indicates how the *Anayasa Mahkemesi* finds it extremely difficult to pass judgement in cases related to equality of the sexes. Here again exceptionalism overrides universalism.

The same Court also decided on the issue of financial equality in marriage. A provision of the then Civil Code stated that a wife could only become a guarantor to her husband and a debtor to third parties in the interest of the husband with permission from a judge.[57] The claim before the *Anayasa Mahkemesi* was that this provision, which appeared at first glance to protect the rights of a wife, actually treated her as a minor since the husband in the same position did not need permission. The *Anayasa Mahkemesi* said that,

> The aim of this provision is to protect the wife from entering into obligations unwittingly as she may not know the consequences, the

---

54 1993/23; 1993/55; 2.12.1993; *Resmi Gazete* No: 23917; 25.12.1999.
55 This is still the case in the amended Civil Code (2002).
56 1997/61;1998/59; 29.9.1998; *Resmi Gazete* No: 24937, 15.11.2002.
57 This requirement has been removed from the amended Civil Code (2002).

scope and the aim of this debt. She may enter such an obligation under the husband's influence. This limitation is to protect the unity of the family and is in the public interest.[58]

There were dissenting opinions stating that any discrimination based on sex was illegal and that national provisions should be viewed in the light of the Convention on the Elimination of All Forms of Discrimination Against Women, not only on the Turkish Constitution.

CONCLUDING REMARKS

The form and characteristics of the Turkish State are at present static. Within such a framework there is little flexibility or possibility for judicial interpretation to change the existing normative legal order or the officially accepted value system, though, some significant additional Constitutional and legislative amendments are on the way. As far as the *Anayasa Mahkemesi* is concerned, these amendments aim to have an impact on its composition, election of members, procedures and on those who can apply for abstract norm control. The legislature sees a conflict of power between itself and the Court, and resents the Court's role, which it perceives as correcting legislative decisions. Few of the restrictions on its activities are to be removed.

The judicial response to social and legal problems in Turkey is highly national, the system remaining mainly self-referential, the target audience being domestic. Though significant developments in the fields of democracy and fundamental rights and freedoms, and review of constitutionality have found their way into Turkish law, the last with the 1961 Constitution, the *Anayasa Mahkemesi* acts more as a protector of the system. Nevertheless, the Turkish Court has been labelled as one of the most activist courts in the world.[59]

As judges begin to regard the member states of the EU as the audience to impress, in addition to the domestic audience of various shades, references to decisions of courts of foreign jurisdictions and the ECtHR and the ECJ may become more explicit and persuasive. Nevertheless, today, Turkish social and political needs and the cultural context, but above all the restraints posed by the Constitution, continue to carry more weight than any other consideration.

---

[58] 1997/27;1998/43; 30.6.1998; *Resmi Gazete* No: 23934; 15.1.2000; and 1999/47; 1999/46; 28.12.1999; *Resmi Gazete* No: 23989; 10.3.2000.
[59] Hazama, Y (1996) 'Constitutional Review and the Parliamentary Opposition in Turkey' *The Developing Economies*, XXXIV-3, 324-325.

AFRICA

Egypt's Supreme Constitutional Court: Managing Constitutional Conflict in an Authoritarian, Aspirationally 'Islamic' State

CLARK B. LOMBARDI *

Constitutional review in the Egyptian legal system is today carried out by a special constitutional court.[1] This court is the Supreme Constitutional Court of Egypt, often referred to by its acronym, the SCC. It is an important example of a puzzling phenomenon—a liberal court that is permitted to operate, at least for a time, in an authoritarian regime. Studying this Court helps us understand why such courts are created. It also helps to demonstrate the fragility of such institutions, once they emerge.

The SCC is Egypt's first effective institution of judicial review. Ironically enough, it owes its existence to an authoritarian regime's fear of independent judicial review. After the judiciary in Egypt asserted the right to exercise judicial review, the government of Jamal Abd al-Nasir feared it would exercise review in a manner uncongenial to the regime. The Nasir regime thus decided to take judicial review out of the hands of the judiciary and put it, instead, in the hands of a special constitutional court that he

* Associate Professor of Law, University of Washington School of Law, Carnegie Scholar 2006. The author is grateful to the University of Washington and the Carnegie Corporation for research support. The author thanks Greta Austin, Michael Feener, Andrew Harding, Victor Ramraj, Arun Thiruvengadam and some other generous friends for invaluable comments. Statements made and views expressed are those of the author and all errors are solely his responsibility.
[1] Transliterations follow the International Journal of Middle East Studies (IJMES)—without macrons for long vowels or dots under letters such as the aspirated 'h'.

intended to control. The decision to create a constitutional court, however, had unexpected consequences.

Nasir's successor, Anwar al-Sadat, modified the structure of the new constitutional court—retaining control over appointments, but giving it more independence. He also renamed it the Supreme Constitutional Court. Sadat's reform of the constitutional court coincided with a period of activism among the Egyptian bar and judiciary. The spirit of the age affected the new court. After a quiet first decade of operation, the SCC in the 1990s defied the wishes of the Egyptian president and became a liberal activist institution that was often in open confrontation with the executive. More surprising still, during this period, the Court's liberal majority, which was entirely composed of secular-trained judges, actively reached out to the Islamic opposition. They used Islamic legal arguments in support of their liberal vision and issued decisions that had the effect of empowering the Islamist opposition—thereby building support among Islamists for the court and its liberal commitments.

In the face of these unexpected challenges, the executive sought successfully to undermine the liberal majority on the Court. From 2001 to the present day, the SCC has arguably ceased to exercise any meaningful check on the executive. It remains to be seen whether the liberal SCC has been forever subdued or whether it is in hibernation, ready to awaken in the future.

HISTORICAL BACKGROUND

The Modern Egyptian Legal System

The modern Egyptian legal system took shape during the late nineteenth century.[2] Under considerable pressure from colonial powers, Egypt adopted in 1883 a civil code modeled on the French Civil Code and later adopted other codes based on continental European models. To apply these codes, the government established a new court system modeled on the French system. That system serves as the skeleton of Egypt's current system. In contemporary Egypt, the National Courts continue to be the courts of general jurisdiction for private actions and criminal law.[3] An entirely

---

[2] For a history of the Egyptian legal system, see Brown, Nathan J. (1997) *The Rule of Law in the Arab World* at 26-31. For a comprehensive introduction to the contemporary system, see generally Dupret, Baudouin and Bernard-Maugiron, Nathalie (eds) (2002) *Egypt and its Laws*. For a discussion of constitutional litigation in Egypt, see also Lombardi, Clark B. (2006) *State Law as Islamic Law in Modern Egypt* at 141-158.

[3] See Dupret, Baudouin and Bernard-Maugiron, Nathalie (2002) 'Introduction: A General Presentation of Law and Judicial Bodies' in *Egypt and its Laws* supra note 2 at xxviii-xxxi.

separate system of administrative courts (*mahakim al-idariyya*) operates within the Council of State (*Majlis al-Dawla*).[4] One also finds a number of courts with more specialized jurisdictions which problematically overlap with the jurisdiction of the national and administrative courts.[5]

Judicial Review in Egypt and the Creation of Constitutional Courts

For much of the twentieth century, it was unclear whether any Egyptian courts had the power to perform judicial review. After Egypt gained full independence over judicial matters in 1937, elite lawyers urged that courts be given the power of judicial review. In 1948, the High Administrative Court in the Council of State issued an opinion in which it definitively claimed for the judiciary the right to engage in a limited form of constitutional review,[6] and its position was supported by important legal academics.[7] However, Egyptian courts never got the opportunity to exercise freely their self-proclaimed powers of judicial review. After Jamal Abd al-Nasir took power in a military coup, the judiciary thought it unwise to exercise aggressively its newly-claimed right of judicial review.[8] Worried, though, that the judiciary's self-restraint might cease, Nasir stripped the courts of their jurisdiction to engage in constitutional review and lodged the power of review in a new institution firmly under the control of the executive. Law No. 81 of 1969 stripped the existing courts of any right to determine which laws were unconstitutional. Law No. 66 of 1970 placed the right of constitutional review in a new Supreme Court (*al-Mahkama al-`Ulia*) with little independence.[9] Thus, ironically, a constitutional court was established to ensure that no meaningful constitutional review took place.

---

[4]   See Dupret and Bernard-Maugiron, 'Introduction' supra note 3 at xxxi-xxxiii; Hill, Enid (1993) 'The Administrative Courts of Egypt and Administrative Law' in Mallat, Chibli (ed) *Islam and Public Law* at 207-28; Sherif, Adel Omar (1998-99) 'An Overview of the Egyptian Court System' in (5) *Yearbook of Islamic and Middle Eastern Law*.

[5]   On these courts, see generally el-Islam, Seif 'Exceptional Laws and Exceptional Courts' in *Egypt and its Laws*, supra note 3 at 359ff; Farhang, Michael (1994) 'Terrorism and Military Trials in Egypt: Presidential Decree No. 375 and the Consequences for Judicial Autonomy' (35) *Harvard International Law Journal* at 235-236.

[6]   Case 65, Judicial Year 1 (Feb 10, 1948). See also Hill, Enid (1997) 'Establishing the Doctrine of Judicial Review in Egypt and the United States' in Cotran, E. and Sherif, A. O. (eds) (1997) *The Role of the Judiciary in the Protection of Human Rights* at 323, 324-330.

[7]   Hill, 'Establishing the Doctrine' supra note 6 at 328-329. For the perspective of three SCC judges, see El-Morr, `Awad et al (1996) 'The Supreme Constitutional Court and Its Role in the Egyptian Judicial System' in Boyle, Kevin and Sherif, Adel Omar (eds) (1996) *Human Rights and Democracy: The Role of the Supreme Constitutional Court of Egypt* at 38-39.

[8]   See Brown, *The Rule of Law* supra note 2 at 69-92.

[9]   See Sherif, Adel Omar (1995) *Al-Qada' al-Dusturi fi Misr [Constitutional Justice in Egypt]* at 80-88; Brown, *The Rule of Law*, supra note 2 at 91-92; Moustafa, Tamir (2007) *The Struggle for Constitutional Power: Law, Politics and Economic Development in Egypt* at 65-67.

Egypt never felt the full impact of Nasir's Machiavellian strategy to create a non-independent and, ultimately, illiberal constitutional court. Nasir died in 1970, one year after establishing Egypt's first constitutional court, and Nasir's successor, Anwar al-Sadat, began a series of reforms that would lead to changes in the structure, staffing and, ultimately, the behavior of Egypt's constitutional court. Upon taking office, Sadat decided cautiously to liberalize the economy and to re-establish the state's formal ideology on a less rigidly socialist model. To help manage the new (and controversial) market economy and to help establish the dwindling popular legitimacy of the government, Sadat began to reform and liberalize the legal system. In the process, Nasir's constitutional court underwent subtle but significant changes.

Sadat's 1971 Constitution provided for the establishment of a new constitutional court, called the SCC. The Constitution did not provide, however, many details about the new court.[10] Ultimately, the process of drafting the legislation took the better part of ten years, during which time the old Supreme Court continued to operate on an interim basis. In 1979, a law was finally enacted that reflected the Sadat's government's cautious embrace both of economic liberalization and of some degree of judicial empowerment. It established the SCC as a constitutional court whose justices, once they had been appointed, would have considerable independence.[11]

Reasons for the creation of an independent constitutional court

A number of political scientists have asked in recent years why governments in countries without a tradition of judicial review would ever create independent institutions with the power of judicial review. Some favor evolutionary explanations, which propose that for ideological or administrative reasons states find it impossible to survive without institutions of judicial review.[12] In a challenge to such evolutionary theories, several scholars have argued that there is nothing mechanical about the

---

[10]   *Egypt Const.*, art. 174-178 (1971). Translations here follow that of Egypt's State Information Authority, available at www.Egypt.gov.eg/english/laws/Constitution/index.asp.

[11]   Law No. 48 (1979). A translation by Awad el-Morr (former Chief Justice of the SCC) was published in Boyle and Sherif (eds) *Human Rights and Democracy* supra note 7. Translations here will follow this translation. During those eight years, the existing Supreme Court continued to be a transitional organ.

[12]   For a review and criticism of arguments that modern states are delegitimized if they do not permit judicial enforcement of human rights, see Hirschl, Ran (2004) 'The Political Origins of the New Constitutionalism' (11) *Ind. J. Global Legal Stud.* at 71, 74-79. For a summary of arguments that modern regulatory states need independent courts to effectively set policy or police the bureaucracy, see, e.g., Moustafa, *The Struggle* supra note 9 at 198-201.

spread of judicial review. Looking at a range of countries that have recently introduced judicial review, for example, Tom Ginsburg, Ran Hirschl and Tamir Moustafa have each argued that elites will only empower judges with the power of judicial review when very specific circumstances exist.

Based on a study of Asian countries that created courts during the transition from authoritarian rule to democracy, Ginsburg argues that judicial review is often created by elites who feel they may imminently lose power in a democratic transition. By creating institutions composed of sympathetic unelected officials with the power of judicial review, these elites feel they will be able to influence policy long after they are removed from office.[13] Hirschl has developed a slightly different thesis, which he argues can account for the recent establishment of judicial review not only in transitional democracies but also in more mature democracies such as South Africa, New Zealand, Israel and Canada. Hirschl proposes that judicial review is granted as a form of 'hegemonic preservation' by elites committed to unpopular policies.[14] According to this theory, independent constitutional courts are created when hegemonic elites realize that (1) even if they retain power, democratic pressures will make it hard for them to impose cherished policies and (2) they find economic and judicial elites who can be appointed to courts and can be trusted to impose the blocked policies judicially.[15] Ginsburg and Hirschl's arguments provide an explanation for why elites *in democracies* will sometimes choose to vest judges with the power of judicial review and will sometimes not. Studying the creation of the SCC allows us to ask whether these theories can also help explain the rise of judicial review at particular times in authoritarian countries. It seems that if we modify these arguments slightly, they can indeed help.

As noted already, Jamal `Abd al-Nasir died in 1970, only a year after the creation of the toothless Supreme Court. When Anwar al-Sadat succeeded him as head of the ruling party and President, he inherited an authoritarian state in crisis. Nasirist policies had left Egypt in a ruinous economic condition.[16] Furthermore, a humiliating military defeat suffered at the hands of Israel in 1967 had led many to question Arab socialism of

---

[13] See generally Ginsburg, Tom (2003) *Judicial Review in New Democracies: Constitutional Courts in Asian Cases.*
[14] See generally Hirschl, Ran *Towards Juristocracy: The Origins and Consequences of the New Constitutionalism* or the abbreviated form of the argument published as Hirschl, 'Political Origins' supra note 12. See particularly 90-105.
[15] Hirschl, 'Political Origins' supra note 12 at 91.
[16] On Egypt's economic policies and performance under Nasir and Sadat, see generally Wahba, Mourad (1994) *The Role of the State in the Egyptian Economy*; Waterbury, John (1983) *The Egypt of Nasir and Sadat.*

the Nasirist variety and the Egyptian government was facing ideological challenges from both secular liberals and Islamists—each of whom demanded liberalization of the political and social sphere. Sadat proposed to revitalize the authoritarian Egyptian state by embarking upon an ambitious policy of economic liberalization and economic growth funded by foreign investment.[17] This was to be accompanied by a change in the ideological justification for the regime from one of Arab socialism to a controlled liberalism and Islamism.[18] The government's decision to give the SCC an increased amount of independence must be seen against this backdrop.

In an important monograph on the SCC, Tamir Moustafa has argued at length that at the time the SCC was created, Sadat's inner circle assumed private investment would not grow in the absence of judicial review.[19] This was not idiosyncratic. Prevailing wisdom held at that time that economic liberalization would fail to attract investment unless a strong independent court was available to hear property rights disputes. Noting this, Moustafa explains the creation of the SCC as a largely mechanical response to this perceived need: investors wanted a court that would define property rights expansively and protect them vigorously; therefore, the Egyptian government created a strong constitutional court whose judges, coming from a historically liberal profession, could be expected to do this.

Moustafa's careful argument is important and, to an extent, convincing. Nevertheless, it has not provided a complete explanation for Sadat's decision to create the type of constitutional court that he did. The SCC was paradoxically stronger and weaker than one would expect if the Court had been created simply to provide a forum for the vindication of investor's property rights. The SCC's jurisdiction encompassed more than property rights cases. Thus, the new Court was more powerful than it needed to be. Furthermore, it was a creation of the executive and, as we shall see, could be reined in by the executive. Thus it was too weak, by itself, to guarantee protection of property from an executive bent on expropriation. One can combine Moustafa's insights about Egypt, however, with Hirschl's insights about constitutional judicialization in other contexts. By doing so, one

---

[17] On the Islamist challenge and Sadat's response, see Beattie, Kirk (2000) *Egypt during the Sadat Years* at 200-210.

[18] The administration turned for assistance to Sufi Abu Talib, who published an ideological tract in 1978 in *al-Iqtisadi*, July 16, 1978 and then served as speaker of the captive legislature entrusted with the task of developing legislation that would realize the new ideology. See Beattie, *Egypt during the Sadat Years* at 168-171 and Reinich, Jacques (1977-78) 'The Arab Republic of Egypt' in (2) *Middle East Contemporary Survey* at 391-92.

[19] See generally Moustafa, *The Struggle* supra note 9.

can develop a more complete and persuasive explanation for the court's creation.

As Moustafa has amply demonstrated, an ascendant faction in Egypt felt that they would lose power if controversial economic reforms were not undertaken. Such reforms were, however, deeply unpopular. They were very hard to push through the legislature, in which skeptics were powerful.[20] The supporters of economic liberalism knew that any attempt to take consistent steps towards radical economic and political liberalization (and possibly Islamization) might lead to a revolt by important party factions and might cause reformers to lose control over the whole party. In this environment, the creation of an independent constitutional court had attractions beyond its role in comforting private investors. By empowering the constitutional court to hear claims under provisions of the constitution protecting civil rights and by guaranteeing Islamization, economic liberals tried to attract to their cause a number of disparate factions, some of which inclined towards political liberalism and some of which inclined to a moderate form of Islamism. In other words, the economic liberals who controlled the Sadat regime believed they could transfer responsibility for its unpopular economic liberalization plan to a court enjoying popular legitimacy because it was a guarantor not just of economic rights but also of political rights and of the right to live under a regime that respected Islamic norms. In short, the Court would not only facilitate economic liberalization, but it would immunize the decision to liberalize from reversal by anti-reform factions of the party.

Moustafa's explanation for the empowerment of the Egyptian constitutional court thus seems to become stronger if we consider that it may also reflect what Hirschl has called the 'judicialization' of controversial policy decisions. Looking at non-autocratic case studies, Hirschl predicts judicialization of the economic and political policies will occur when 'the judiciary's public reputation for professionalism, political impartiality and rectitude is relatively high'; judicial appointments are (or at least can be) controlled to a large extent by hegemonic political elites; and, arguably, judges 'mirrored the cultural propensities and policy preferences of these hegemonic elites'.[21] In autocratic Egypt, these conditions were generally

[20] Sadat's difficulties 'selling' his plan are evident in inconsistencies one finds in the 1971 Constitution enacted by a legislature completely dominated by the ruling party. On the legislature's schizophrenic policies towards private property, see Hill, Enid (1999) 'The Supreme Constitutional Court of Egypt on Property' in Bernard-Maugiron, Nathalie and Dupret, Baudouin (eds) (1999) Le Prince et son juge: droit et politique dans l'Égypte contemporaine at 55-92.
[21] See Hirschl, 'Political Origins' supra note 12 at 91. The ideological shift from socialism had the added advantage of being attractive to both Western and Gulf Arab nations—each a

met. In the face of intra-party debate about the wisdom of economic reforms, an ascendant faction of economic liberals wanted to design popular judicial institutions that would be inclined to carry out economic reforms in a way that the existing political institutions resisted.

Having empowered a constitutional court for largely instrumental reasons, Sadat and his allies tried to ensure that the Court did what it was supposed to—but no more. Concerned, apparently, that judges who protected private property might acquire broader liberal agendas, the SCC was eventually structured so that it could be reined in if it became too aggressive in promoting a political liberalization that would threaten the elite's hold on power. Sadat's successor eventually felt compelled to use these checks.

THE STRUCTURE, STAFFING AND PROCEDURES OF THE SCC

Law 48 of 1979 replaced the much derided Supreme Court with a new SCC which had broad jurisdiction and whose justices were, in comparison to the judges on the Nasir's original constitutional court, remarkably powerful and independent.[22] The executive, however, retained nearly total control over appointments to the court.

Jurisdiction

Article 25 of Law 48 of 1979 entrusts the SCC with three main duties. First, it is to serve as the final authority in case of a jurisdictional dispute between two Egyptian courts. Second, it has the power to issue authoritative interpretations of legislative texts if different judicial institutions (for example, the national courts and the administrative courts) have disagreed about their proper interpretation and 'they have an importance that necessitates their uniform interpretation'. Finally, Article 25 grants the SCC the right to perform constitutional review in certain cases, including ones where lower courts determine that a legitimate constitutional question needs to be resolved.

According to Article 29 of the Court's statute, if a court hearing a case has concerns about the constitutionality of legislation that is at issue in the case, it may *sua sponte* refer the case to the SCC. Alternatively, if a litigant in the course of litigation challenges the constitutionality of legislation,

---

source of foreign aid.
[22] Law No. 48 (1979), supra note 11.

pertinent to his or her case, the court hearing the case must determine whether the claim is 'plausible' and, if so, must either refer the case to the SCC on its own or, in the alternative, authorize the challenger to raise the constitutional issue before the SCC. In managing constitutional cases, then, a symbiotic relationship exists between the regular courts (or administrative courts) and the SCC. The SCC relies largely on judges in these other courts to refer cases to it; and the judges in these other courts themselves rely on the SCC to strike down legislation that they believe unconstitutional.[23] Theoretically, through this system, the public might be prevented from raising legitimate constitutional claims before the courts. With a few exceptions, however, the courts have been quite willing to refer constitutional claims to the SCC.[24] The discussion of cases in the next section will make clear that citizens have been able to bring an enormous number of constitutional claims, both minor and momentous, to the attention of the SCC. As a practical matter, then, courts have so far permitted citizens ample access to the SCC. Furthermore, the co-operative mode arguably adds to the legitimacy of the SCC's decisions and increases the odds of compliance.

Once a case has been properly referred, the SCC must hear it. That said, once a case is on the SCC's docket, the Court has the power to hear and decide the case quickly or to delay the process of hearing or deciding the case. Occasionally, the Court seems strategically to have chosen how quickly to decide cases—withholding decisions on some important cases in the hopes, thereby, of gaining leverage over the executive.

Procedures

Once a case has been referred to the SCC, it is examined by a special 'Commissioners Body', composed of highly respected jurists assigned to assist the Court.[25] The commissioners assist the justices in preparing

---

[23] For an analysis of the process, see Sherif, Adel Omar (2002) 'Constitutional Adjudication, in Dupret and Bernard- Maugiron, (eds) (2002) *Egypt and its Laws*, supra note 2 at 329-38.

[24] Some examples include the national courts' refusal to refer to the SCC the constitutional issues arising in the apostasy trial of Nasir Hamid Abu Zayd and the administrative court's (including the High Administrative Court's) refusal to refer to the SCC the constitutional issues arising in the constitutional challenge to a Ministry of Health order banning female genital mutilation. My thanks to Justice Adel Omar Sherif for drawing my attention to these cases.

[25] Articles 21-24 of Law 48 establish that these assistants must have the qualifications necessary to be justices on the SCC, and they get life tenure and salary protection. The preparation of the case by such jurists adds to court prestige and quality. Commissioners have often been appointed to be Justices, and some of the Court's best known judges have been former commissioners.

for cases. After the case has been prepared, it will be reviewed by some number of justices. Law 48 does not set the exact number of justices sitting on the SCC, nor the exact number who must hear a case. Article 3 of Law 48 merely requires that a quorum of at least seven members must decide each case. The ambiguity in the law regarding the number of justices seems to be deliberate, and its importance will become apparent below.

Article 49 of Law 48 provides that, once a majority has reached a decision, the Court must produce an opinion. If in the majority, the Chief Justice will write the opinion, and if not in the majority, he or she will assign it to a judge of his or her choosing.[26] Once seven justices certify that an opinion represents the views of a majority on the Court, the opinion becomes final. Pursuant to Article 49, it must then be published in Egypt's *Official Gazette* and any decision to void a law automatically becomes effective the day after publication. With respect to opinions, it is important to note that dissenting judges do not have a right to have their dissents recorded.[27] The power to write or assign opinions combined with the absence of dissents gives the Chief Justice extraordinary power to shape the Court's jurisprudence — particularly if the Chief Justice is in the majority.

Qualifications and protections for justices

Law 48 contains provisions designed to guarantee that the Court's justices are respected both for their qualifications and independence. Article 4 provides that, to be eligible for a position on the Supreme Constitutional Court, a justice must have extremely high qualifications. This helps to guarantee the prestige of the Court, the Court's position relative to other courts and, to a certain degree, its position relative to the executive. Articles 5 and 11-20 also provide the justices of the Court with significant guarantees of independence. Once appointed, justices cannot be removed prior to the mandatory retirement age except by consent. Judges also have salary protections. All disciplinary issues are to be handled by the SCC itself.

---

[26] If the justices cannot agree on a rationale, the majority will settle on one opinion. No dissent will be published. See Sherif, Adel Omar 'The Freedom of Judicial Expression: The Right to Concur and Dissent' in Boyle and Sherif (eds) *Human Rights and Democracy* supra note 7 at 137-58.
[27] On this practice, see Sherif 'The Freedom of Judicial Expression' supra note 26 at 144-45.

Appointment and Number of Justices

Given the wide jurisdiction of the Court, the considerable access that citizens have to date had to the Court,[28] and the prestige and independence of the SCC's justices, the executive has a strong interest in selecting who can ascend to the bench. Not surprisingly, therefore, Law 48 leaves the executive very tight control over appointments to the bench. Article 5 provides that the president appoints a Chief Justice by presidential decree. Outside of the requirement that the Chief Justice have the qualifications necessary to serve as a justice on the SCC, the President has absolute discretion in his choice. Article 5 provides that associate justices are also appointed by presidential decree. In appointing associate justices, however, the president must select from between two nominees: one nominated by the Chief Justice and one nominated by the general assembly of the Court. The provision apparently anticipates that the Chief Justice and the majority of his court may disagree about who is appropriate to serve on the Court, and it allows the President to favor the preferences of the Chief Justice.

As noted above, Law 48 of 1979 does not specify the number of justices on the Court. Arguably, if the Chief Justice and Court choose to nominate candidates and the President chooses to appoint them, there can be an infinite number of justices. The importance of this fact has recently become clear. If a Chief Justice and President both dislike the decisions of majority on the Court, they can collude to pack the court with justices sympathetic to their views. This is not merely a hypothetical power. As we shall see, in the early 2000s, the executive did seek to control the Court by packing it with friendly justices.

THE SCC AS A POLITICAL AND LEGAL ACTOR

Having seen the Court's independence, and its potential vulnerability to court-packing, we can turn to a discussion of the Court's behavior and its jurisprudence to date. During its first twenty years, the SCC evolved in significant ways. Beginning as a court with limited ambitions and policy preferences very much in keeping with that of the Egyptian president, the SCC developed into a court committed to reforming and liberalizing the entire Egyptian legal and political system, a policy entirely at odds with the wishes of the President.

---

[28] Given the ongoing willingness of lower courts to refer constitutional cases to the SCC.

1980 - 2000: From Economic Rights to Social and Political Rights

Sadat's willingness to create an independent constitutional court seems to have rested on his belief that, if appointments were made carefully, the Court could be trusted to provide credible guarantees of property rights—something that members of the legislature and bureaucracy were unwilling and, arguably, unable to do. Similarly, he believed that careful appointment of judges could ensure that the Court did not become a force for aggressive political liberalization. Sadat's confidence seemed at first to be well placed. In 1981, shortly after the SCC started operations, Sadat was assassinated and a subordinate, Husni Mubarak, took power in Egypt. As a policy matter, Mubarak was similar to Sadat in his commitment to economic liberalization and aversion to political liberalization. Thanks to Sadat's careful appointments, little in the Court's early jurisprudence gave Mubarak much cause for worry.

When the SCC was first set up, the Egyptian President had, for the most part, allowed judges who had already served on the Supreme Court to staff the SCC. These judges were appointed to the SCC precisely because their jurisprudential proclivities were known. Not surprisingly, the SCC began its life acting more or less as Sadat had expected. When the SCC began to hear cases in 1980, its jurisprudence showed a commitment first to establishing aggressively the Court's own broad powers and independence.[29] Having done so, the Court focused considerable attention on challenges to economic legislation, clarifying the meaning of the ambiguous constitutional guarantees of private property.[30] In a series of cases, the SCC identified in Articles 29-36 conflicting principles requiring the protection for private property but also a duty on the part of the executive to guarantee equitable distribution of wealth and government services. Asserting for itself the right to strike the proper balance, the Court quickly established a consistent and credible policy of protection for property rights. Thus, as Enid Hill and Tamir Moustafa have demonstrated, the Court provided invaluable support to the ruling party, in its attempts to move the nation away from a statist economy and towards economic liberalization.[31]

---

[29] See, e.g., Case No. 28, Judicial Year 2 (May 4, 1985), 3 SCC 195-208. (The Court's official reporter is officially named *Al Mahkama al-Dusturiyya al-`Ulia*, Abbreviated henceforth as "SCC.") On the SCC's increasingly ambitious assertions of judicial independence and power, see Sherif 'Constitutional Adjudication' supra note 23 at 339-40.

[30] See, e.g., the summary of cases by Chief Justice Awad El-Morr, published as 'The Status and Protection of Property in the Constitution' in *Human Rights and Democracy*, supra note 7 at 115-27; see also, Hill 'The Supreme Constitutional Court of Egypt on Property' supra note 20.

[31] See generally Hill 'The Supreme Constitutional Court of Egypt on Property' supra note

The Court did not remain content, however, to act as a champion of economic liberalism alone. In the late 1980s, the Court's old guard began to retire, and a new generation of judges came to be appointed. To the consternation of the President, these justices embraced a more expansive vision of the liberal state, one in which people enjoyed not only substantial economic rights but civil and political rights as well. Scholarship to date has not focused on explaining how these justices were selected, and thus it is not clear how the President ended up appointing justices (particularly Chief Justices) with views that were so threatening to his authority. The fact remains that such appointments were made.

By the mid-1980's the SCC was demonstrating a willingness to check the executive when it seemed unambiguously to violate explicit constitutional limitations on executive power—even if their decision touched upon sensitive issues. The SCC confronted the executive as early as 1985, when it issued a starting ruling setting limits on the executive's emergency powers.[32]

By 1985, Egypt had long been governed (and indeed is to this day is governed) by a seemingly interminable state of emergency, pursuant to which the executive has claimed extraordinary powers. Confident that his emergency powers could be invoked for whatever purpose he, in his discretion, thought wise, President Sadat in 1979 decided to enact controversial family law reforms by emergency decree. The reforms in question granted women a number of important new rights. Initially these reforms were supposed to be enacted through normal legislation. However, they were vigorously opposed by the religious establishment and, ultimately, by many Egyptians. The proposed reforms proved to be so controversial that Sadat's captive legislature was reluctant to enact them through the regular legislative process. Reluctant to court revolt within the ranks of the ruling party, Sadat enacted them as an Emergency Decree.

In 1985, the Supreme Constitutional Court stunned the new President, Husni Mubarak, by holding that his predecessor's 1979 actions had been unconstitutional, and by voiding the 1979 reforms.[33] The Court held that when legislating pursuant to his emergency powers, the President must demonstrate a reasonable nexus between the emergency decree and the security of the state. As the President had not demonstrated this, the

21 (see particularly the comments at 88); see also Moustafa *The Struggle* supra note 9 at 119-136 (particularly the comments at 136).
[32] Case No. 28 Judicial Year 2 (May 4, 1985), printed in SCC, Vol. 3, 195-208.
[33] Case No.28 of Judicial Year 2 (May 4, 1985), 3 SCC, 195-208. For an analysis of the case, an analysis that was co-authored by two justice of the SCC, see El-Morr, Awad and Sherif, Adel Omar (1996) 'Separation of Powers and Limits on Presidential Powers', in *Human Rights and Democracy* supra note 7 at 68-71. See also Lombardi *State Law* supra note 2 at 169-171.

family law reforms were void and would have to be re-enacted by regular legislative process. After this embarrassing rebuke, a reform bill was subsequently introduced and passed by the legislature, but the reforms therein were less ambitious. The new executive had also been warned that, at least in some cases, the SCC was willing to stand up to him.

In the late 1980s, the SCC made clear that its 1985 decision was not an aberration. It engaged in a series of striking opinions that tried to limit the executive's control over the political system. In a notable series of decisions (ones extremely embarrassing for the executive) the Court repeatedly struck down the laws under which local and national elections were held.[34] The last of these led to the dissolution of Egypt's national legislature and forced new elections.[35] In the 1990s, the SCC expanded its focus and began to protect an ever expanding range of individual rights. To do this, it had to come up with constitutional doctrines that would allow it to protect implied rights.

Incorporating International Human Rights Norms into Egyptian Constitutional Law

The Court's ability to uphold citizens' rights outside the area of property and political participation seemed at first to be limited by the nature of the Egyptian Constitution, which did not provide many unambiguous checks on government power. The extensive rights provisions of the Constitution are phrased in vague or contradictory ways. The Court thus found it difficult actively to restrain the President or his captive legislature without either interpreting the existing rights provisions expansively or developing a doctrine of implied rights.[36] In the mid-1990s, the Court began to do both.

In the early 1990s, the SCC identified within the text of the 1971 Constitution two overarching, somewhat ambiguous, constitutional principles that the majority argued should inform all others. The first principle consisted of a guarantee of 'the rule of law'. Article 64 of the Constitution makes the rule of law 'the basis of state rule'. Article 65 provides unequivocally that the state is 'subject to [the rule of] law', and

---

[34] Case No.131, Judicial Year 6 (May 16, 1987), Case No.23, Judicial Year 8 (April 15, 1989) printed in 4 SCC 205-217; Case No.14, Judicial Year 8 (April 15, 1989) printed in 4 SCC 191-204, Case No.37, Judicial Year 9 (May 19, 1990) printed in 4 SCC 256-293 . The cases are discussed by a justice of the SCC in Sherif, Adel Omar 'Constitutional Adjudication' in Bernard-Maugiron and Dupret *Egypt and its Laws* supra note 2 at 342-43 and in Moustafa supra note 9 at 98-100.

[35] Case No. 37 Judicial Year 9 (May 19, 1990), reprinted in 4 SCC 256-93.

[36] Nathan Brown has made this point perceptively in Brown *The Rule of Law* supra note 2 at 118-120.

declares that judicial independence is a necessary safeguard of liberties. The Court argued that these provisions permit and indeed require the Court to incorporate international human rights principles into Egyptian constitutional law. The second overarching principle was that all law should conform to Islamic legal principles. In the Court's opinion, the two principles were mutually reinforcing because, in a series of much discussed opinions, the Court interpreted Islamic legal principles in a creative manner to support its liberal rulings in the area of economic rights, civil and political rights and equal protection.[37]

At the start of the 1990s in the preface to volume IV of the SCC's official reporter, the sixth Chief Justice of the Court, Mamduh Mustafa Hasan, hinted that the Court intended to adopt an expansive interpretation of citizens' civil and political rights—one that was shaped by evolving international human rights law. Today, he said, individual rights 'take an international character which transcends the various regional limits. Their tendencies find their clear expression in a number of international documents and in the institutions of the international judiciary which is in charge of these rights'.[38] Shortly thereafter, in a seminal 1992 case, Hasan's Court interpreted the Constitution's 'rule of law' provisions to establish the principle that the Egyptian government was constitutionally bound to obey emerging international human rights standards—even when these were not specifically referenced in the Egyptian Constitution.[39]

From this point on, the SCC's judges actively tried to bring Egyptian law into line with emerging human rights norms. Justices and members of the Court's Commissioners Body promoted scholarship in the areas of comparative constitutional law and human rights law, and they sponsored conferences that promoted such scholarship by others.[40] In public speeches and published writings they argued that constitutional judges were required to draw upon this scholarship and incorporate into Egyptian

---

[37] See discussion below.

[38] 4 SCC, 4-5. Translation follows Johansen, Baber 'Supra-legislative Norms and Constitutional Courts: The Case of France and Egypt' in Cotran & Sherif (eds) *The Role of the Judiciary* supra note 6 at 37-38 (1997) at 367.

[39] Case No. 22, Judicial Year 8 (January 4, 1992), 5 SCC (Part I) 89. See also the analyses in Sherif, Adel Omar 'Unshakeable Tendency in the Protection of Human Rights: Adherence to International Instruments by the Supreme Constitutional Court of Egypt' in Cotran and Sherif (eds) *The Role of the Judiciary* supra note 6 at 37-38; Boyle, Kevin 'Human Rights in Egypt: International Commitments' in Boyle and Sherif (eds) *Human Rights and Democracy* supra note 7 at 89-90; Johansen 'Supra-legislative Norms' supra note 38 at 367-68.

[40] The Court sponsored in the 1990s a series of important international conferences in Cairo on international human rights and the judicial protection thereof. See Moustafa supra note 10 at 168-69. Papers were published in: Boyle and Sherif (eds) *Human Rights and Democracy* supra note 8 and Cotran and Sherif (eds) *The Role of the Judiciary* supra note 7.

constitutional law human rights principles that are widely shared among constitutional democracies.[41] These writings were sometimes published in appendices to the Court's own Reporter, giving them a peculiar status between academic commentary and an attempt at official clarification of the Court's decisions.[42]

A survey of Court opinions makes clear that the Court's discussions about the incorporation by Egypt of international norms represented more than empty theorizing. In the 1990s, the SCC regularly cited international human rights documents or the opinions of other constitutional courts in order to shed light on the rights that the Egyptian Constitution guarantees to Egyptians.[43] The SCC then applied their ever more expansive list of rights to restrain the executive and to expand in unprecedented ways a wide range of freedoms, including, *inter alia*, the freedom of the press, freedom of association, the sanctity of the home, and the right to marry. In so doing, the SCC's justices directly confronted the executive, which was not only opposed to expanding rights but was actually in the mid-1990s trying to take away previously recognized rights.[44]

The Justification of Liberal Jurisprudence in Islamic Terms

One intriguing development that occurred during the court's liberal heyday is that as the Court began to move into confrontation with the executive, it began to use Islamic legal arguments in support of its liberal vision.

Islamic law was very much part of Egyptian political legal and discourse in the 1980s and 90s. Responding to pressure from Islamists, Article 2 of the Egyptian constitution had been amended in 1980 to say that 'the principles of the Islamic *Shari`a*[45] are the chief source of Egyptian legislation'. Islamists and, indeed, most Egyptians believed that the 1980 amendments created a new constitutional requirement that all laws conform to 'the principles of

---

[41] See, for example, the extraordinary discussion in El-Morr, Awad (1997) 'Judicial Sources for Supporting the Protection of Human Rights' in Cotran and Sherif (eds) *The Role of the Judiciary* supra note 6 at 5-10.

[42] See, e.g., El-Morr, Awad 'Human Rights as Perceived by the Supreme Constitutional Court of Egypt' 7 SCC at 2-121.

[43] Anyone who reads the SCC Reporter in the 1990s will find numerous references to foreign and international law. One scholar found "Through the mid-1990s between one-quarter and one-half of all SCC rulings incorporated specific aspects of international legal or foreign rulings. Even more referred to 'accepted international standards,' broadly stated, and to the comparable judicial principles of other 'civilized nations.'" Moustafa *The Struggle* supra note 9 at 168.

[44] For an analysis of the Court's decisions in this area and the degree to which they interfered with newly restrictive state policies, see Moustafa *The Struggle* supra note 9 at 140-164.

[45] The term '*Shari`a*' here means 'God's law' as revealed in the Qur'an, and reflected in the Prophet's behavior.

the Islamic *Shari`a'*. Although secular liberals contested this interpretation, the SCC in 1985 agreed with the Islamists—at least in part. In Case 20, Judicial Year 1 (May 4, 1985), the Court held that Article 2 created a justiciable requirement that legislation enacted after the amendment of Article 2 in 1980 conform to the principles of the Islamic *Shari`a*.[46] Thereafter, the Court began with growing regularity and confidence to measure Egyptian laws not only for consistency with explicit constitutional rights guarantees and unwritten human rights norms, but *also* with the principles of the Islamic *Shari`a*, as interpreted by the SCC. The results were not, however, what secular liberals had feared.

After the Court's 1985 decision, some secularists fretted that the constitutionalization of *Shari`a* principles represented a capitulation to conservative Islamic forces in Egypt and suggested that it would prevent judges from endorsing a liberal interpretation of the Egyptian constitution.[47] These fears proved unfounded. Building creatively on classical and modernist theories of Islamic law, the SCC argued that the 'principles of the Islamic *Shari`a'* to which Article 2 refers are highly general principles that leave the political branches considerable legislative latitude. These principles do not require the government to enact into law many specific rules that classical Muslim jurists considered to be part of the *Shari`a*. Rather, according to the Court, Article 2 required the government, in most areas of legislation, to respect only a handful of specific Islamic rules. It would, however, have to respect general moral principles that reflected the overarching 'goals' of Islamic law.[48]

The Court's Article 2 jurisprudence realizes, in certain ways, the aspirations of a number of modern liberal Islamic thinkers—not only in Egypt but in countries like Pakistan as well. To understand this, it helps to

---

[46] Case 20, Judicial Year 1 (May 4, 1985), printed in 3 SCC 209-224. For an analysis, see Lombardi *State Law* supra note 2 at 159-73.

[47] See, e.g., comments in Mary Ann Weaver (informed by talks with Egyptian intellectuals) in (June 8, 1998) 'Letter from Cairo: Revolution by Stealth' *The New Yorker* at 38.

[48] For a monograph on Article 2, see Lombardi *State Law* supra note 2. See also Lombardi, Clark and Brown, Nathan 'Do Constitutions Requiring Adherence to Shari`a Threaten Human Rights? How Egypt's Constitutional Court Reconciles Islamic Law with the Liberal Rule of Law' (21) *Am. U. Int'l L. Rev.* For other perspectives, see Bernard-Maugiron, Nathalie 'La Haute Cour Constitutionelle Egyptienne et la Shari`a Islamique' (19) *Awrâq* 103; Bernard-Maugiron, Nathalie 'Les Principes de la sharia sont la source de la législation' in *Le Prince et son Juge*, supra note 21 at 107; Dupret, Baudoin (1995) "La Chari`a est la source de la législation': interpretations jurisprudentielles et theories juridiques' (34) *Annuaire de l'Afrique Nord* at 261; Johansen, Baber 'The Relationship between the Constitution, the Shari'a and the Fiqh: The Jurisprudence of Egypt's Supreme Constitutional Court' in (64) *Zeitschrift für ausländisches öffentliches Recht und Völkerrecht* at 881; Vogel, Frank (1999) 'Conformity with Islamic Shari`a and Constitutionality under Article 2: Some Issues of Theory, Practice and Comparison' in Cotran and Sherif (eds) *Democracy, The Rule of Law and Islam* at 525.

consider classical Islamic legal theory, the challenge that modern Islamic legal thinkers levied at classical theory and the way in which the SCC incorporates modern Islamic legal theory in the service of a liberal vision of law.

Classical Islamic legal theory assumed that a special class of trained Islamic scholars was uniquely qualified to interpret God's law.[49] When reasoning out law from the scriptures, these scholars identified two types of rule. The first type was those rules that were 'certain' to represent divine commands. These 'definitive' rules were found explicitly stated in texts that the scholars had determined to be definitively authentic. The second type was ones that a scholar had determined were probably (but not surely) divine commands. These non-definitive rules were found in texts of uncertain authenticity or else were presented in language that the scholars thought contained some subtle ambiguity. While classical Muslim scholars expected by and large to agree on the definitive rules, they understood that they would disagree on the probable rules of *Shari`a*.

In the modern era, several trends appeared that, together, led many Muslims to question the assumptions of classical Islamic legal theory.[50] First, many Muslims came to accept that Islamic legal interpretation could be carried out by people who had not received classical Islamic legal training. Second, many Muslims came to believe that those who interpreted Islamic law should use new methods of interpretation. Among the new methods were utilitarian methods of reasoning. Among them too were methods that saw traditional Islamic rules as merely the application in a particular time and place of underlying divine principles—principles that represented the timeless aspect of the divine command. These principles were the only norms that bound modern Muslims. One could identify these underlying principles by induction—inducing them from a study of the many different rules that had been laid down at different times and places. Working from their new methods of interpretation, lay interpreters around the world, including Egypt, came to question laws that had long been considered definitive and to develop novel interpretations of Islamic law. Some of these new interpretations were reactionary on some issues, being more restrictive than classical Islamic law, for example, on questions of women's rights. Other untraditional modern interpretations of Islamic law were extremely progressive.

---

[49] See Lombardi *State Law* supra note 2 at 13-17. Monographs discussing this phenomenon, include Hallaq, Wael (2005) *The Origins and Evolution of Islamic Law*, Stewart, Devin (1998) *Islamic Legal Orthodoxy: Shi'ite Responses to the Sunni Legal System.*

[50] See Lombardi *State Law* supra note 2 at 59-77; see also, Kurzman, Charles (ed) (2002) *Modernist Islam: 1840-1940* at 3-30.

Naturally, in twentieth century Egypt, 'Islamist' political groups were not monolithic. Some Islamists urged the government to 'Islamize' the law in accordance with the largely conservative views of the classically trained scholars; some urged the government to 'Islamize' the law according to liberal views espoused by liberal lay Islamic thinkers; and others urged the government to hew to the reactionary views of fundamentalist thinkers.[51] By the time Egypt agreed to Islamize its laws, the Muslim community had become deeply divided about what Islamization would entail.

Given the change in notions of religious authority in Egypt, the explosion of diverse new interpretations, and the balkanized nature of the Islamist political movement, judges on the SCC found themselves able in Article 2 cases to construct a theory of Islamic legal interpretation that was considered plausible by many Islamists and which permitted (indeed, it arguably required), the government to respect the liberal rights that the Court had committed itself to protecting.

The Court's theory evolved slowly. By the late 1980s, the Court had asserted without much explanation that Islamic law supported its rulings protecting property rights.[52] In the early 1990s, shortly after the SCC announced its ambitious effort to incorporate international human rights norms into Egyptian constitutional law, the judges on the Court elaborated upon their understanding of Islamic law. The method that the SCC eventually developed was subtle.[53] For the purpose of this article, the important points are the following: First, according to the Court, it was constitutionally required only to ensure that its rules did not violate (a) the definitive rules of *Shari`a* or (b) the 'goals' of the *Shari`a*. Like classical jurists, the SCC distinguished between definitive and non-definitive rules of *Shari`a*. However, using a modified form of modernist methodology, the Court concluded that there were very few definitive rules of *Shari`a*. And what definitive rules they found tended to be extremely general principles that could be interpreted and applied in a manner that was consistent with the justices' liberal assumptions about individual human rights. Similarly, when the Court identified a series of social 'goals' that the *Shari`a* tended to promote, it found a series of goals that were quite general and were capable of being understood to favor a liberal, rights-friendly society in which men and women enjoyed largely equal rights.

---

[51] See Lombardi *State Law* supra note 2 at 101-119.
[52] See id. at 175-78.
[53] See id. at 174-200. For other analyses, see generally Johansen 'The Relationship between the Constitution, the Shari'a and the Fiqh' supra note 48; Vogel 'Conformity with Islamic Shari`a' supra note 48.

As a result, the constitutional requirement that Egypt respect Islamic norms did *not* preclude the government from enacting laws that were inconsistent with classical Islam, but which improved the rights of women in questions of family law. For example, to the distress of conservative Islamists, the Court permitted the government to depart from traditional Islamic laws governing family relations. The Court held that an 'Islamic' legal system could (a) require a man who divorced his wife without cause to support the divorced wife, and (b) award the wife special custody of older children from the marriage.[54] Such a government could also allow a woman to sue for dissolution of her marriage if her husband took a second wife,[55] and it could allow a court to issue retroactive orders of child support.[56] Most dramatic of all, the Court held that the Egyptian government does not transgress the principles of the Islamic *Shari`a* when it adopts regulations banning school girls from veiling themselves. In each of these cases, the government rule was inconsistent with classical interpretations of *Shari`a* and was highly unpopular among conservative Islamists in Egypt.[57]

More intriguing still, the Court suggested, the constitutional command to respect Islam reinforced the recently announced constitutional requirement that the Egyptian Government must respect international legal norms—providing alternate grounds for rulings that protected international human rights. Thus, laws were occasionally struck down not only because they violated the property rights provisions of the constitution or the international human rights that had been incorporated into the Egyptian Constitution, but *also* because they violated, at the same time, the constitutional provisions requiring the state to respect Islamic norms. Thus, for example, a number of restrictions on private property were struck down on the grounds that they were inconsistent both with the Constitution's specific private property rights provisions *and* with Article 2's general requirement that the state respect Islamic norms.[58] Similarly, a

---

[54]   Case No. 7, Judicial Year 8 (May 15, 1993), printed in 5 SCC (part 2) 265-90; analysis in Lombardi *State Law* supra note 2 at 202-18.

[55]   Case No. 35, Judicial Year 9 (August 14, 1994) printed in 6 SCC 351-8; analysis in Lombardi *State Law* supra note 2 at 224-36.

[56]   Case No. 29, Judicial Year 11 (March 26, 1994), printed in 6 SCC 231-56. French translation by Baudouin Dupret (4) *Islamic Law and Society* 91-113 (1997). Analysis in Lombardi *State Law* supra note 2 at 218-224.

[57]   Case No. 8, Judicial Year 17 (May 18, 1996), 8 SCC 344-367. For an English translation, see Brown, Nathan J. and Lombardi, Clark 'The Supreme Constitutional Court of Egypt on Islamic Law, Veiling and Human Rights: An Annotated Translation of Supreme Constitutional Court Case No 8 of Judicial Year 17 (May 18, 1996)' (21) *Am. U. Int'l. L Rev.* at 437.

[58]   See, e.g., Case No. 68, Judicial Year 3 (March 4, 1989), 4 SCC 148-64 (striking down a government order expropriating not only the real property of a wealthy landowner subject to the law, but also the real property of all his adult children); Case No. 65, Judicial Year 4 (May 16, 1992) (striking down a law governing the de-sequestration of land); Case No. 25

restriction on certain government officials' right to marry foreign women was struck down on the grounds that it violated both international human rights norms guaranteed under the Constitution's general requirement that the government respect the rule of law *and* Article 2's command to respect Islamic norms.[59] Not only did Islamization fail to restrain the liberal Court, then, but Islamic arguments were occasionally used to support some of the Court's controversial human rights decisions.

1980-2000: The Court's Attempt to Insulate Itself from Executive Backlash

The justices on the SCC were not naïve. It was clear that their active protection of civil and political rights in the 1990s was as unwelcome to President Mubarak as their protection of economic rights had been welcome. Mubarak had total control over the legislature and bureaucracy and thus could revise laws or, if necessary, amend the Constitution, so as to destroy the Court. As they began to set out upon an activist liberal trajectory in the 1990s, the justices used a number of tools to try and insulate themselves from anticipated executive interference.

In his monograph on the Court, Tamir Moustafa has carefully explored the tools that the Court employed to protect itself and has explained why they were inadequate.[60] Among the tools was the tool of calculated self-restraint. As aggressive as the Court was in striking down laws in sensitive areas, it was not as aggressive as it could have been. For example, it conspicuously chose to uphold the regime's highly controversial use of Emergency State Security Courts to try politically sensitive cases.[61] Similarly, it never ruled on the constitutionality of President Mubarak's decision to declare and never renounce, for almost thirty years, a 'State of Emergency' that left him with extraordinary powers.[62] Some evidence suggests that the Court deliberately delayed issuing opinions on some cases that were potentially damaging to the executive—sometimes for up to ten years—with the implicit threat that, if the executive ignored SCC

---

of Judicial Year 11 (May 27, 1992), 5 SCC 408-428 (striking down laws regulating seizure of property); Case No. 6 of Judicial Year 9 (March 18, 1995), 6 SCC 542-566 (striking down restrictions on a landlord's right to choose his tenants). For an analysis, see Lombardi *State Law* supra note 2 at 175-178, 236-240 (2006).

[59] See. e.g., Case No. 23, Judicial Year 16 (Decided March 18, 1995) 6 SCC 567-96; Case No. 31, Judicial Year 16 (may 20, 1995) printed in 6 SCC 716-39 and Case No. 25, Judicial year 16, July 3, 1995, printed in 7 SCC 45-94. For analyses of all these cases, see Lombardi *State Law* supra note 2 at 255; Bernard Maugiron 'La Haute Cour' supra note 48 at 127-28.

[60] Moustafa *The Struggle* supra note 9.

[61] Case 55, Judicial Year 5 (June 16, 1984) printed in 3 SCC, 80-89.

[62] In interviews with several justices in 2001, this was described to me as one of the Court's greatest pieces of unfinished business.

rulings or interfered with the Court's liberal majority, a damaging opinion would be issued.[63]

The justices also sought to empower and build alliances with a number of institutions in civil society—both in Egypt and abroad.[64] They did this in part by the mechanism of judicial review itself—striking down laws restricting speech and assembly and thus allowing civil society groups to operate. When not on the bench, liberal justices also wrote and spoke regularly on the importance both of civil society and of judicial independence. As Moustafa has described, the alliance with NGOs and other civil society institutions served a number of important functions. For one, NGOs generated, funded and prosecuted the cases challenging state authority that were, at the end of the day, the SCC's reason for existence and the source of its power. The alliance also helped to increase the visibility and popularity of the SCC, both domestically and abroad—something that might raise the costs for Mubarak if he ignored the Court's rulings or used the power of appointment to break their majority.

Finally, as we have described already, the SCC came increasingly in the 1990's to rely on Islamic arguments. In numerous cases where a law was struck down on the basis of enumerated or un-enumerated constitutional rights, the SCC would explain why, based on its liberal interpretation of Islamic law, this law *also* violated Article 2's requirement that all law be consistent with the Islamic *Shari`a*. While the judges seem to have believed in good faith that they were interpreting the *Shari`a* properly, the willingness to hear Islamic cases and to attempt regularly to articulate an alternate 'Islamic' ground for aggressive liberal rulings can be seen as an effort to build support among the powerful Islamic opposition. The goal was, in part, to create broader support for its liberal understanding of the Constitution's individual rights provisions and to create a diverse constituency that would resist any attempt by the executive to interfere aggressively with the increasingly pesky liberal majority on the Court. The Court's aggressive moves to preserve its liberal majority and liberal outlook were not, ultimately, as successful as they had hoped.

2000-Present: The Taming of the SCC

In the late 1990's President Mubarak and his inner circle prepared an attack on the Court. They began by suppressing the institutions in civil society that were supportive of the Court. When the Court's Chief Justice died

---

[63] See Moustafa *The Struggle* supra note 9 at 181-82.
[64] See generally Moustafa *The Struggle* supra note 9 at 136-54, 169-72, 178-92. The discussion below draws on his analysis.

in 2001, the regime was confident it had neutralized the institutions that could mobilize effective domestic and international support for the Court. Using his carefully reserved powers of appointment, [65] the President appointed as Chief Justice an unapologetic political ally of the executive and an outspoken critic of the Court's earlier attempts to interfere with repressive executive action. This Chief Justice proceeded immediately to nominate (and the President proceeded to appoint) five new justices to the court. In a stroke, he eliminated the liberal majority. Not surprisingly, thereafter, the SCC revealed little of its previous appetite for confrontation with the executive. More troubling to some observers, in several cases the SCC invoked its rarely-used power to interpret statutes that had received inconsistent interpretations in the lower courts and overturned rights-protective opinions in the regular court system.[66]

To outsiders, at least, the Court had come full circle. Writing in the 1990s, Nathan Brown was struck by the ways in which the SCC had departed from its roots in Nasir's anti-liberal Supreme Court. He echoed the views of many when he said that the SCC had transformed itself 'from a check on the judiciary into the boldest judicial actor in the country'.[67] Brown, however, sounded a note of caution, wondering if it could continue to act so boldly.[68] This caution proved wise. Writing in 2007, Moustafa described in detail how the SCC had become once again, a tool to suppress activist liberal jurisprudence in the Egyptian courts.

With President Mubarak in his 80s, Egypt will soon change its head of state and potentially will undergo some deeper political reform. The memory of the SCC's liberalism has not disappeared. Some distinguished liberal constitutionalists remain on the court and others could theoretically be appointed. It remains to be seen what new shapes and roles, if any, the Court will take on in the future.

LESSONS FROM THE HISTORY OF THE SCC

Studying the SCC is interesting for a number of reasons. For students of comparative constitutional law, the history of the SCC provides a provocative example of judicial review being established in an authoritarian regime. One question is whether it occurs for the same reasons that it occurs in democratizing or established democratic countries. Moustafa

---

[65] On this event including telling interviews, see Moustafa *The Struggle* supra note 9 at 198-201.
[66] See generally, Moustafa *The Struggle* supra note 9 at 136-54, 169-72, 178-92.
[67] See Brown *The Rule of Law* supra note 2 at 104.
[68] Id. at 126-128.

has argued that in developing countries like Egypt, the explanation for the creation of the SCC is largely to be found in the executive's belief that independent courts will help the nation attract capital. Supplementing this, I have argued above that we should recalibrate theories of hegemonic preservation to account for intra-elite fighting in a one-party state. If we do, theories of hegemonic preservation may help to further explain why the Sadat regime created the SCC at the time that it did and with the structure that it did.

Studying the SCC also reminds us that autocrats are wise to fear constitutional courts and to retain emergency brakes over the process of judicialization. Courts are selected because their judges are likely to support the executive's most important policy objectives and probably will share them for a time. Yet, as the SCC demonstrated, independent judges, though they can help an autocratic executive in some ways, also tend over time to start acting in ways that are distressing to the executive. Such behavior is not unforeseeable.

This brings us to another point. Given the oedipal tendency of courts to rebel against the expectations of their founders, autocratic executives try to give judges enough independence to carry out the objectives for which they were created. But the executives also try to retain some ability to take control of the court if the court's behavior becomes too threatening to the executive. The history of the SCC is revealing on this point, showing the fragility of any judicial rebellion in an autocratic system. Although judicial review does at times arise in an authoritarian context, the power of independent judicial review in authoritarian countries often remains extremely weak and cannot be exercised in a robust manner without support from informal networks in politics and civil society that are themselves vulnerable.

Ultimately, the SCC, which had transformed itself from an illiberal institution to an active liberal one, was transformed by the executive back into a less active, and apparently less liberal, one. This suggests that the most significant challenge to evolutionary theories about the inevitable spread of judicial review may not lie in the stories of countries that have chosen to withhold independent judicial review. It may instead lie in the stories of authoritarian countries like Egypt that have been able indirectly to control how it is used and what its effect will be. There are still more chapters to be written in the history of the SCC. Nevertheless, the history of this institution to date leaves open the possibility that the SCC's tale will prove to be a cautionary one. If judicial review can be turned on or off when convenient, judicial review is liable to spread, but it is also liable to have few of the salutary effects that its champions suggest. What signs of hope are there? One ambiguous sign appears in an unlikely place.

One possible lesson from the history of the SCC involves the role of Islam in the constitutional jurisprudence of Muslim states. The experience of the SCC suggests that Muslim views about Islamic legal interpretation are far less rigid than people may realize. In nations that constitutionalize Islamic law, courts can assert the power to interpret Islamic law and, indeed, to interpret it creatively and liberally. In some cases, the Court chose to cite Islamization provisions as a justification for liberal decisions in the area of property rights and even human rights. We have mentioned above that liberal constitutional courts in authoritarian countries can gain power and freedom if they can build support networks in civil society. In light of this, the SCC's use of Islamic law for liberal purposes is provocative, and its ability to do so with minimal protest from the Muslim opposition (and indeed with some support) is intriguing.[69]

Muslim autocrats have long been successful at playing their Islamic opposition off against their secular liberal opposition, arguing that their respective interests are fundamentally misaligned. The SCC's Article 2 jurisprudence argues implicitly that the perceived misalignment is a chimera. The SCC was never able to forge a really effective secular/Islamist support network—or at least one that was effective enough to prevent the executive from destroying the SCC's liberal majority through its power over court staffing. Nevertheless, the SCC's overtures to Islamists were not entirely rebuffed. One wonders whether, in another country, a more effective alliance could be built. And indeed, one wonders whether in Egypt, a new alliance might arise that unites moderate Islamists and liberal judges—an alliance that might provide judges with popular support and enable a re-emergence of liberal judicial power and liberal constitutionalism in Egypt.

---

[69] For the lack of criticism, see the discussion in Lombardi *State Law* supra note 2 at 259-264. Nathan Brown and Amr Hamzawy report that when a handful of younger members of the powerful Muslim Brotherhood in Egypt championed stripping the SCC's jurisdiction over Article 2 cases (and instead giving them to a new institution), they were harshly criticized by leading Brothers—with the explicit comment that the SCC was the appropriate body to continue interpreting Article 2. See Brown and Hamzawy (2008) 'The Draft Party Platform of the Egyptian Muslim Brotherhood: Foray Into Political Integration or Retreat Into Old Positions?' (89) *Carnegie Papers, Middle East Series* at 7-8.

Models of Constitutional Jurisdiction in Francophone West Africa

BABACAR KANTE *

INTRODUCTION

Reasons for the creation of constitutional courts

One would have thought that the states of West Africa, former French colonies, would have conferred on themselves after independence the same metropolitan model of judicial organisation. Curiously enough, this did not occur. Contrary to received notions, the influence of the colonial system has not been as durable as one would normally have predicted in the political and judicial field; although it has left deeper traces in matters of administrative organisation. The first constitutions copied from the French parliamentary model were in fact quickly amended to the point of losing their character and the system of judicial organisation was completely overturned.

These countries have effectively opted initially for a type of judicial organisation which is delineated strongly on the French pattern. While in France there exist two jurisdictions with a Conseil d'Etat and a Cour de cassation, jurisdictional conflicts between which are decided by a Tribunal des conflits, and along side which sit a Cour des comptes and a Conseil constitutionnel; the newly independent francophone African states chose a system of united as opposed to divided jurisdiction. In this system all jurisdictions were placed under the authority of a single Supreme Court, situated at the apex of the judicial hierarchy, which is the regulator of the entire body of jurisprudence. This court had jurisdiction to decide, in the last resort, all private law, administrative and fiscal litigation. In francophone

Africa, constitutional justice was thus integrated in the Supreme Court, and entrusted to a specialised bench of the court.[1]

Constitutional justice had not begun to discover any kind of autonomy in francophone Africa until the beginning of the democratic transition at the end of the 1990s.[2] This process found its point of departure in the National Conference organised by Benin 19-28 February 1990, which could be considered, from some points of view, as having the same significance in Africa as the fall of the Berlin wall in Europe. This event was in fact a foundational element of a new juridical and political order in francophone Africa. It had the double objective of both reporting on the exercise of political power and laying down the basis for the new mode of its devolution. During its continuance the National Conference spread quickly to other francophone states, but curiously not to any anglophone states, to constitute indirectly afterward the point of departure for the renovation of constitutional justice in Africa.

It was starting at this moment that nearly all the African states rediscovered the French model of judicial organisation. One can observe precisely at this moment the creation, in a cascade as it were, of constitutional jurisdictions, under whatever name. Some are called *Conseils constitutionnels* while others are called *Cours Constitutionelles*. It was thus with Benin in 1990[3]; Mauritania in 1991[4]; Mali[5], Senegal[6] and Togo in 1992[7]; Ivory Coast first in 1994[8] then in 2000 after a suspension of the 1994 Constitution; and Burkina Faso in 2000[9]. Thus only Guinea amongst the old French colonies

---

* Translated from French by A. Harding, P. Leyland with assistance from Sonia Lamine and William Zilio.
[1] Cf. on this subject, G. Conac (sous la direction de), Les Cours suprêmes en Afrique, Tome II, Paris, Economica, 1969, 299.
[2] On what is usually called the democratic transition in Africa, see G. Conac (sous la direction de), L'Afrique en transition vers la pluralisme politique, Paris, Economica, 1993, 517.
[3] Cf. Law n.90-32 of the 11 December 1990 according to the Constitution of the Republic of Benin and law n.90-009 of the 4 March 1991 according to the organic law of the Constitutional Court modified by the law of the 31 March 2001.
[4] Cf. Constitution of the 20 July 1991 and ordinance n.92-04 of the 18 February 1992 modifying the organic law of the Constutional Court.
[5] Cf. Constitution of the 25 February 1992 and law n.97-010 of the 11 February 1997 modifying the Organic Law determining the rules of organisation and functioning of the Constitutional Court also of the procedures to follow before it.
[6] Cf. Constitution of the 7 March 1963 and Organic law n.92-23 of the 30 May 1992 modified by the Organic Law n.99-71 of the 17 Feburary 1999.
[7] Cf. Constitution of the 14 October 1992 and the organic law n.97-01 of the 8 January 1997.
[8] Cf. Law of the 16 August 1994 modifying revision of the constitution, Ordinance of the 27 December authorising suspension of the constitution, the Constitution of the 1 August 2000 and and the law n. 2001-303 of 5 June 2001 modifying the organisation and the functioning of the Constituional Council.
[9] Cf. Loi n. 003/2000 du 11 avril 2000 in regard to the reform of the constitution, loi n.

of the region was an exception to the rule. Guinea Bissau, not having been under French domination, did not follow the same trajectory as the other neighbouring states: it has a Supreme Tribunal of Justice.

The judicial reform which resulted from the installation of autonomous constitutional jurisdictions was realised by various means. In certain cases constitutional jurisdictions cohabited with a Supreme Court: this was the case with Benin, Burkina Faso, Ivory Coast, Mauritania and Mali, where it remained attached to the united jurisdiction model in which the Supreme Court was preserved. In other cases, the Supreme Court disappeared in favour of the new constitutional jurisdiction.[10] Senegal, however, recreated a Supreme Court in 2008.

There is no longer any doubt today, with the benefit of hindsight, that the political context of the time was a factor that determined the blossoming of constitutional justice in West Africa. Constitutional jurisdiction is in fact, rightly or wrongly, considered a basic element accompanying the new process in which African countries were involved thirty years after their independence. The states in question were for the most part characterized by an unstable political system not conforming to the minimal norms of Western democracy. Some operated without a national assembly; in others the constitution was suspended; and others had many constitutions within a short period of time.[11] In states such as Burkina Faso and Mauritania, for example, that experienced several coups d'Etat, and as a result a rupturing of the normal functioning of institutions, it was illusory to envisage the viability of constitutional justice. The issues confronting some of these states at the Benin National Conference were fundamental, and concerned not so much their governance as their governability. It was more a matter of providing a new basis for political society and attempting to promote the rule of law state and democracy. From this standpoint, the Constitutional Court, especially in these states, will act as a model for others, and will be considered as an essential engine of the project of democratic revival.

011/2000 AN du 27 avril 2000 in regard to the composition, organisation and attribution of functions of the Constitutional Council and the procedure applicable before it.

[10] Cf. M. Diagne, La mutation de la justice constitutionnelle. L'exemple du Conseil constitutionnel du Sénégal, in Annuaire International de Justice Constitutionnelle, 1996, Vol XII, p 99. I. Diallo, A la recherche d'un modèle de justice constitutionnelle, in Annuaire International de Justice Constitutionnelle, 2005, Vol XX, p 93.

[11] Cf G. Conac (sous la direction de), Les institutions constitutionnelles et politiques des Etats d'Afrique francophone et de la République malgache, Paris, Economica, 1979, 353 p.

The conception of constitutional justice

In general the new constitutional jurisdictions of all the West African former French colonial nations are all considered to different degrees as judges of electoral disputes, protectors of fundamental rights, and reviewers of the exercise of state powers. Nevertheless, they may be perceived differently, according to the specific circumstances in which they were created. One can therefore, simplifying somewhat their characteristics, attempt to categorize them. In this way it would be possible, according to criteria based on their purpose or remit, to attempt to group them together in three broad categories.

The first would correspond to the Senegalese model. Here, the Constitutional Council was perceived as being principally a judge of electoral disputes. The process of its creation and the deliberate limitation of the range of its competences, in comparison with the other courts, militates in favour of this classification. It was in fact following a contentious election that plunged the country into a very serious political crisis in 1988, and at the end of the drafting of a new Constitution, that the Council was created, confirming its role as the judge of national legislative and presidential electoral disputes.

On the other hand, the second would group together the countries that have decisively moved beyond a dictatorial or autocratic system, of which Benin is the prototype. In this case, the essential purpose of constitutional jurisdiction is to oppose all excesses of power. In these countries, the function of reviewing the exercise of state powers is the most important one. It is important to note that this function is expressly set out in the law creating the Court, in contrast to the position in Senegal. This role goes far in explaining the legitimate concern to place definitively limits on the arbitrary use of power that characterized the former system. The Court is considered by citizens, but also by itself, not so much in terms of analysis of its jurisprudence, but rather as being the ultimate bulwark against the violation of rights.

The third group would comprise other countries, less typical, but which followed the national conference movement by imitation or anticipation, and assigned a rather more symbolic role to constitutional jurisdiction. These countries are located somewhere between the first two first categories. In these cases, constitutional jurisdiction was given an important role by a process of imitation, but they were not in a position to fulfil this role for reasons linked to the political context. This is essentially a case of a country emerging from conflict or a grave crisis and hoping to find in constitutional jurisdiction a remedy for its problems. Constitutional jurisdiction appears here more or less as a panacea. This is often also the case in Central and East Africa.

ORGANISATION AND FUNCTIONING OF THE CONSTITUTIONAL JURISDICTIONS

What are the different heads of recognized competences of the constitutional jurisdictions?

Constitutional jurisdictions in West Africa, as with that of the French Constitutional Council from which they draw their inspiration, generally have the benefit of two types of competence – contentious and consultative.[12] The principal contentious competence could be summarized under three heads: checking that certain legislative acts are in conformity with the constitution; jurisdiction over elections and referenda; and judicial review of the actions of executive authorities and institutions. According to the political context, the importance of these types of competence can vary from one country to another.

With regard to the review of legislative acts one could quote a number of features common to almost all the cases studied: the verification of conformity to the constitution of laws, international conventions, and legislative assembly regulations. With regard to elections, jurisdiction generally applies to legislative and presidential elections and the announcement of their results. Regarding judicial review of executive acts, the constitutional jurisdictions were given the duty of supervision of their proper functioning, dealing with jurisdictional conflicts between different state organs, administering the oath of the president of the republic, and declaring the absence of power.

Thus, all constitutional jurisdictions in West Africa are competent to check the constitutionality of laws. However, in this area some differences in their powers should be noted. While some courts (the majority) are empowered to review the constitutionality of laws only *in abstracto*, others (not very numerous) also do this *in concreto*: the latter is the case in Senegal, Ivory Coast and Burkina Faso. Those states that have adopted this concept of unconstitutionality thereby distance themselves from the French practice that did not recognise this type of recourse despite attempts to introduce

---

[12] For a comparative table, see Association des Cours Constitutionnelles ayant en Partage l'Usage du Français (ACCPUF), Compétence et organisation des Cours constitutionnelles ayant en partage l'usage du français, Bulletin n° 2, numéro spécial, 2 vol.and the Association's webiste: www.accpuf.org.

it into contentious constitutional litigation.[13] France has introduced this possibility as part of its judicial system with the constitutional reforms of the 21st July 2008. Still on the subject of constitutional review of legislation, one can note also that regulations of national assemblies can be defined narrowly or broadly. In the narrow sense, these regulations include only those of the parliamentary assemblies; while in the broad sense they include also such organs as the High Council of Local Authorities and the Economic, Social and Cultural Council in Mali, and the High Broadcasting Communications Authority of Benin. Another difference between African and French-style jurisdiction relates to judicial review of administrative acts. Certain African jurisdictions in fact have this jurisdiction by virtue of their jurisdiction over fundamental rights, although these cases are rare – Benin is one. One can equally note cases where there is express jurisdiction to supervise the procedure for constitutional amendment, as in Burkina Faso.

With regard to electoral matters and referenda the principle applicable almost everywhere is that there was constitutional jurisdiction, ever since its creation, over elections and referenda. But in this area, as elsewhere, one notes nevertheless nuances in the manner in which the powers are granted. In a general sense, constitutional jurisdiction involves power to verify the regularity of the electoral process, dealing with election petitions and the role of confirming the final results of presidential and parliamentary elections. Jurisdiction in these matters is sometimes shared with other institutions; but the risk of conflict of jurisdiction is slight because the method of intervention differs in the details. The ordinary courts, for example, have jurisdiction over disputes regarding the electoral lists, while administrative jurisdictions often intervene during election campaigns. It is necessary also to mention, even if this is extremely rare, that in certain countries the constitutional jurisdiction also deals with local elections, as is the case in Burkina Faso. As for referenda, the constitutional arrangements and relevant organic laws are not always very clear; it is therefore hard to determine the range and the limits of the jurisdiction of constitutional courts and councils in this matter. It is therefore by a sometimes extended interpretation of their jurisdiction that some constitutional courts check the process relating to a referendum; this is the case notably in Senegal. The jurisprudence of public law has therefore been recognized as applicable right through the process up to the declaration of the results.

---

[13]   F. Delpérée (sous la direction de), Le recours des particuliers devant le juge constitutionnel, Paris, Economica- Bruylant, 1991, 221 p.

With regard to the regulation of the functions of public authorities, certain countries expressly confer this competence on the constitutional jurisdiction, while in others it has only been assumed implicitly. The express conferment occurs in states with a heavy democratic deficit. In these cases, it drives the courts in question to arbitrate disputes between the different decision centres in the State, ranging from the president of the republic to the prime minister and the national assembly. The attribution of this jurisdiction requires the interpretation of controversial constitutional powers, and the qualification of certain powers, but also the granting of authority to the body in question. Sometimes executive bodies have allowed this constitutional jurisdiction to intervene directly in their functions so that they play an auxiliary role. For example, this is the case in Benin and the Ivory Coast where the constitutional court can in fact declare a law binding because it conforms to the constitution and not because it is promulgated by the president of the republic. In Benin, the President of the Constitutional Court is even called upon to confirm the interim status of the president of the republic when he faces accusations before the High Court of Justice. A special characteristic of the Benin system is that the Court is forced to confirm the principle of the continuity of the state in all circumstances.

It should also be noted, however, that the regulation of the functioning of public authorities would not always be included as part of constitutional jurisdiction. For this reason some countries have not experienced serious disruption in the normal functioning of their institutions. This is the case in Senegal which already had democratic experience well before the creation of the constitutional council. But even in these states the balance of powers comes into play through litigation requiring interpretation of the limits to their powers. This applies at times to certain litigation on the margins of the electoral process.

For example, in Benin, the council deals with questions relating to the date of elections, their estimated budget and their organisation. On occasion the council also sends orders to the president of the republic for the organisation of elections. Others, on the other hand, have a restrictive conception of this issue. For example, this is the main difference between Benin and Senegal: Benin's judges have not hesitated to assume the court's competence in any law carrying a constitutional amendment and in all other contentious matters relating to the rule of law while the Senegalese Constitutional Court has excluded such laws from being within its field of competence. In fact, Senegalese jurisprudence has kept faith with the approach of the French Constitutional Council.

The consultative competences of these African constitutional jurisdictions are unfortunately less developed. The Senegalese Constitution had even been reduced in this respect from 21 January 2001 in comparison to how it was in 1963.[14]

But as a whole, these competences concern opinions which confer constitutional jurisdiction. In almost all the countries that are the subject of study, the constitutional court is called upon to give an opinion in two situations: when the president of the republic exercises special powers in periods of crisis and in relation to the organisation of a referendum. This is the position in Benin, Mali and the Burkina Faso. However there are specific situations in certain countries where the court is granted a consultative jurisdiction. In Benin for example, the Court hears cases of contempt of the national assembly by the president of the republic. In the Ivory Coast, the court is empowered to hear cases on bills, orders and regulatory decrees before their examination by the cabinet; or in the regulatory domain it can intervene to examine the text of legislation and delegated legislation before it comes into force as part of the constitution. This is a matter of consultative competence that is conferred in other countries on the council of state or on the executive.

Gateways to the constitutional jurisdictions

Given the importance of these jurisdictions, especially in light of the decisions that they reach, it is crucial to understand the avenues open to have access to these courts.

It is necessary to start by specifying that these courts do not generally have the power of self-submission, except in exceptional cases, and that the range of persons who have the power to submit a petition is strictly limited.[15] In addition, these persons might have the power to apply to the constitutional court in cases which might range from a matter related to an organic law, a regulation or basic rights and civil liberties. The extent varies with each state.

In regard to checking on questions of constitutionality, the generally accepted rule is that access to the jurisdiction is restricted to the president of the republic, the prime minister and sometimes to the president of the

---

[14] The new constitution of the 22 January 2001 did not any more anticipate the obligation of referring to the consitutional council in order for it to pronounce on the constitutionality of organic laws before their promulgation, which appeared in Article 2 to Article 67 of the previous constitution.

[15] Cf L'accès au juge constitutionnel, 2ème congrès de l'Association des Cours Constitutionnelles ayant en Partage l'Usage du Français, Libreville, septembre 2000, 796 p.

national assembly. The power can extend to individuals for exceptional cases of unconstitutionality. But even in this situation, it is sometimes a requirement placed on the organ whose decision is questioned to postpone the decision and refer the matter to the constitutional court. Nevertheless, in certain states different authorities are empowered to refer matters to the constitutional court. For example, the President of the High Council of Local Authorities in Mali, and the President of the High Broadcasting Authority and Communications in Benin.

On electoral matters, it is the candidates or their representatives that usually are in a position to act. Nevertheless, in certain countries voters are able to refer issues to an election judge. This is the case in Mauritania where all registered citizens can refer to a judge in order to challenge the electoral process and the provisional declaration of the election results.

The access to the constitutional court is even more widely available in other countries. Associations/NGOs and individuals may be able to refer matters to the court when human rights are threatened. This is notably the case in the Ivory Coast, which allows standing to NGOs, but in Benin standing is granted to individuals.

There are special avenues for referring matters to constitutional courts. The first type is concerned with the abstract control of constitutionality, while the second is a concrete form of control. Nevertheless, the latter is subjected to a number of conditions: the referral must be done by a sovereign jurisdiction in the same manner as the French Conseil d'Etat and Cour de Cassation. Despite many proposals and attempts, the exception to unconstitutionality was not introduced as part of French constitutional litigation until the reform adopted 23 July 2008. One could therefore say that, on this point, the African juridical systems such as Senegal were ahead of France, the supposed source of their inspiration.

ROLE AND POSITION OF CONSTITUTIONAL COURTS

The main reason that such constitutional jurisdictions were created in Africa in the early 90's was to reinforce the anchorage of the rule of law, rights and democracy in countries which have been subjected to autocratic systems whilst France responded to another concern. After around fifteen years of functioning, it is possible to sketch out a first report and to give an overview.

The factors determining their role and position

Naturally every jurisdiction has its own logic and its institutional forces that determine its evolution. For a certain number of years, despite everything, one can identify a tendency to internationalise constitutional rights especially in Africa. From the standpoint of these sources, this factor increasingly gives rise to norms originating in international conventions, particularly regarding matters to do with the protection of human rights and the organisation of elections. At the same time, in regard to institutions, one notes a similarity between the structures and organs that are set up by the different states for the organisation of public powers based on the principle of the separation of the powers.

It is regrettable that comparative law is not considered as a method for the creation of constitutional rights, even though African countries are faced with similar problems.[16] Given that the pleadings and the means of submission for the African constitutional courts are almost all the same, it is astonishing that their responses should be so different from one another. The main reason for the weak influence of foreign (i.e., European rather than African) human rights laws upon national courts is because constitutional courts are strongly influenced by events and by indigenous factors. One of the consequences of this position is that it is difficult to outline regional constitutional laws in West Africa or to talk about a reciprocal influence of the jurisprudences or of harmonisation between them, despite the resemblances between the constitutional jurisdictions themselves. The most important factor that influences the role and the purpose of these courts remains without a doubt the political context that created these courts. On the basis of this criterion, one could classify West African constitutional jurisdictions, from the standpoint of their role and of their purpose, into two major categories.

The first category has an essential role in guaranteeing the rule of law - to make sure that laws passed by Parliament are in conformity with the constitution. In this regard, some courts have fewer powers than the others but some are more positively active. These less powerful courts are generally the constitutional councils. They sometimes have a minimal conception of their role, giving themselves merely the role of verifying the hierarchy of laws and respect for the law. From the moment that they fail to detect any incompatibility or non conformity between the law and the constitution, essentially, they consider that the rule of law is intact and that their function is therefore exhausted. Moreover, in this capacity, the techniques of control in the field of public law litigation, such as the doctrine of manifest error,

---

[16] Cf. M-C. Ponthoreau, Le recours à « l'argument de droit comparé » par le juge constitutionnel. Quelques problèmes théoriques et techniques, Actes du colloque sur l'interprétation constitutionnelle (sous la direction de F-M. Soucramanien), Paris, Dalloz, 2005, p 155.

are not always used.[17] Faced with the requirement of more state controls and the constant quest for ever increasing democracy for African citizens, this type of jurisdiction sometimes gives rise to criticism and often to the mistrust of the opposition. It is necessary to specify that generally there are concerns about courts that do not evolve in a politically extreme context and which do not hesitate to cross the border between the overriding objective of constitutionality and that of the appropriateness of the law which is not within the remit of the constitutional judge. In other words, if the judge is going beyond the strict control of the constitutionality of the law and appreciating the appropriateness of the law, he or she risks substituting his or her own will rather than that of the legislature: that is something which is not within the court's competence. This tendency can be termed 'government by judges'. One finds that sometimes the jurisdictions concerned evolve in a more or less consensual environment where they can be the fruit of a compromise. Elsewhere, the system of judicial organisation is such that other ordinary jurisdictions exist and are in a position to supply what is considered by certain observers as a lack of constitutional jurisdiction. Senegal would fit into this first category.[18]

In a second category, one could classify the jurisdictions that were set up with the purpose of guaranteeing and promoting democracy. This has been about creating jurisdictions endowed with substantial strengths through the granting of wide competences or those which have assumed important prerogatives. In these cases, one is in the presence of true courts, the role of which is essentially to regulate the organisation of the political system. This position is often created in countries which have recently experienced autocratic regimes. Such systems also become visible in cases where the constitutional jurisdiction was created following a conflict. After establishing democratic transition, it becomes a matter of placing these states in a position to withstand the shifting of power and to prevent a return to the authoritarian system of the former regime. In these countries where the socio-political balance is again fragile, and/or they are in political crisis, the decisions of the courts have an eminently political function. Indeed they might be considered as stabilising elements or discordant factors, according to whether they go in the required direction or not. In these countries the declaration of election (especially presidential)

---

[17] M. Diagne, Le juge constitutionnel africain et la technique des réserves d'interprétation (in preparation).
[18] A. Kah, La loi Ezzan devant le Conseil constitutionnel du Sénégal : une amnistie au menu du juge, in Annales de l'Université des Sciences sociales de Toulouse, 2006, tome XLVIII, p 71.

results, always gives rise to moments of very strong political tension which confronts the constitutional court. The Constitutional Court of Benin is an example of this type of jurisdiction.

The composition of constitutional courts and the method of selecting their members is another factor which exercises an influence on the function which they must fulfil. In general, to respect the separation of powers and guarantee the independence of judges, the nomination of the judges is often made by different bodies, for example, from the president of the republic, the president of the national assembly and the president of the senate, and also on the basis of a list proposed by a number of professional bodies, such as judges, barristers or civil associations. In West Africa, Senegal, where all the members of the court are named by the President of the Republic, this in fact constitutes an exception.

Nevertheless, despite the variety of methods used for the selection of their members, the independence of the constitutional courts always remains a problem in the minds of political activists, when there are in opposition and from civil society. Logically therefore, this poses the question of whether an ideal method of selecting these judges exists. But more important than the methods of the nomination of judges, is the composition of the judicial panels. In fact it appears that these courts are largely composed of judges with a legal background. In addition, since the major concern of all those involved, including judicial and public authorities, is to guarantee the neutrality of the courts, the nomination of the judges generally excludes those having current or past political experience. This then poses less of a problem of technical competence, within these jurisdictions, and more of a problem of methodology and approach. Constitutional courts deal with issues often involving arbitrating between the general interest, which the law must protect, and the interests of private citizens. The challenge for the constitutional judge is to check the law without necessarily opposing the putting into operation of government policy which has been legitimated by universal suffrage. This boils down to studying the law without looking to any partisan political considerations. Such an approach requires a particular turn of mind, different from that required for resolving disputes between private litigants. Private law relationships are based on consensuality and autonomy. In order to arbitrate, the court adopts an accusatorial procedure which treats both parties equally. These methods and techniques are not always applied to political matters which are of a different nature. The court in its normal judicial capacity is in effect a 'servant of the law', while the constitutional jurisdiction is a 'critic of the law'. The transformation is not always easy. But when it is necessary for the constitutional court or council to detach itself from judicial practices and show originality it can contribute effectively to the balance of relationships in society and reinforce democracy. It is because of this that, in countries where democracy is still emerging, as in much of Africa, the constitutional judges have a reassuring influence and impose a degree of political stability.

African constitutional jurisdictions have sometimes succeeded in overcoming these obstacles and produced rulings to subject political power to the law to such a point that one can identify the revival of African constitutionalism.[19] One could thus quote a number of notable decisions and opinions.[20] By way of example in the field of elections the decision of the Constitutional Court of Senegal can be cited. The court prevented the political party of the President of the Republic from using his photo on election posters of coalition political parties of which his party was a member on the occasion of the legislative elections of 2001. This was on account of the fact that he was not a candidate.[21] On the subject of human rights, the Constitutional Court of Benin has also made a decision declaring contrary to the constitution a legal provision consisting of the family code authorising polygamy for all males.[22] In the same vein, the Senegalese Court held unconstitutional a legal provision making obligatory parity between men and woman in the lists of candidates to the elections for the legislature.[23] On the subject of the functioning of institutions, the Beninese Court not only considered itself to be competent to have special familiarity with the law but, in addition, it has declared the law extending the mandate of representatives unconstitutional.[24] The Ivory Coast went through a situation of crisis since 2002. The Constitutional Council has had to give opinions and to pronounce judgment over a certain number of important problems such as the extension of the mandate of members of the National Assembly. But these opinions and decisions at times passed unnoticed and still have not been the object of commentary by African jurists.[25]

The relationship with the other judicial institutions

Constitutional courts and constitutional councils are special institutions, which sometimes present a problem in Africa. This is due to the nature

[19] Cf Constitutionalism in Africa: a quest for autochtonous principles, edited by C.M. Zoethout, M.E. Pietermaat-Kross, P.W. Akkermans, Rotterdam, Sanders Institute, 1996, 94 p.
[20] For more details on the decisions and opinions given by constitutional courts along these lines, it will suffice to view the website of l'Association des Cours Constitutionnelles ayant en Partage l'Usage du Français (ACCPUF): www.accpuf.org.
[21] Decision n. 2/E/2001, n° 3/E/2001, n° 4/E/2001.
[22] Decision DCC 02-144 23 December 2004.
[23] Decision n. 1/C/2007 27 April 2007.
[24] Decision DCC 06-074 8 July 2006.
[25] See the jurisprudence of the constitutional council of the Ivory coast published on the website l'ACCPUF

of these bodies and because of their role in the state. It is relevant to ask what type of relations they have with the other institutions responsible for implementing the law.

In certain cases, this issue is expressly mentioned. For example, Article 114 of the Benin constitution states that the Constitutional Court is 'the highest jurisdiction of the state in constitutional matters'. In other cases, the jurisdiction occupies a place that only sometimes reveals the authority for its decisions. This is the situtation in Senegal where the Constitution and not organic law provides for the Constitutional Court. Article 92:2 provides that: 'The decisions of the Constitutional Council are not susceptible to any avenues of review. It imposes its authority over public power and on all administrative and jurisdictional authorities'. Besides, in serious cases of difficulties in the distribution of powers between the executive and judicial branches, it is the Constitutional Court that is empowered to determine the matter. Therefore, one can say with authority that the Constitutional Court is placed directly and implicitly at the summit of the judicial hierarchy.

The problem of the relationship between constitutional adjudication and the other judicial institutions is a little more delicate and the response is less evident in systems having retained a supreme court alongside a constitutional court. But even in such situations, the main decisions made by constitutional judges are not the subject of serious challenge by the supreme court. However, it can pose a difficulty relating to the application of the principle of the superiority of these decisions for practical purposes. Information does not always circulate correctly between judicial institutions, and therefore decisions on these subjects by the constitutional court cannot always apply in relation to the other jurisdictions. There is very little risk of this happening for decisions that are highly topical because of the interest of public opinion in the matter, such as on the Ezzan law of Senegal.[26]

Lastly, it is important to note that, as a rule, from the time the constitutional court or council is involved in a contentious matter, it has the final word. It is interesting to point out that in certain countries, curiously, it is even specified that the decisions of these courts are also imposed upon the military authorities. This is generally the case in nations which have experienced military coups and, as a consequence, instability of their political system, for example, Benin, the Ivory Coast and Togo. The

---

[26] This law, approved by the National Assembly of Senegal on the 7 January 2005, brought amnesty for all the criminal offences or penalties committed in politics, applying between the 1st January 1983 and the 31 December 2004, whether committed by Senegalese as well as foreigners and irrespective of whether the perpetrators had been tried or not. The application of this law included granting amnesty in relation to the facts relating to the assassination of senior vice-president of the constitutional council. Cf A. Kah, op cit.

constitutional court in these nations is designed to ultimately subject the military to political power. At the same time, this brings to our attention evidence in some countries such as Senegal where the military have never been required to arbitrate over the political game to the extent of exercising powers of this nature.

The relationship with other state institutions

The constitutional jurisdiction often plays a part in regulating the functions of other state institutions. The court oversees the establishment of the institutions and then their functioning.

It is generally the constitutional court judges who install the President of the Republic in office by taking the oath of office and, and in certain cases, the declaration of loyalty to the state, but at the same time oversees the impeachment procedure. In regard to the legislature the court's jurisdiction may concern matters of incompatibility, ineligibility and forfeiture of seats of members national assembly. Equally, in regard to the functioning of other institutions the court decides on the principles and rules which determine their operation.[27] This often results in determining matters of confict which arise directly or indirectly between public bodies. It is also an arbitrational function which takes up the court's attention when they are called upon to determine the legality of contested legislation or delegated legislation. But on this point, another feature of Benin is that the court presides over cases of contempt of the National Assembly by the President of the Republic.

Sometimes this jurisdiction goes beyond the simple function of arbitrating and intervening to determine institutional functions. This is when the court can declare whether a law that has been passed by the legislature has been promulgated in the correct way, as is the case in Benin and in the Ivory Coast. This formidable power is not found in all these constitutions.

Some of these jurisdictions adopt the French doctrine of '*les réserves d'interprétation*'.[28] Under this doctrine the constitutional judge decides on the constitutionality of a law on condition that this law will be interpreted in the sense which the court has indicated in the decision. This technique is sometimes used by judges to rewrite the law and thus to impose a judicial interpretation over that of the legislature. In certain cases it assists in putting

---

[27] Cf O.B. Ahmed Salem, Les juridictions constitutionnelles en Afrique. Evolution et enjeux, Annuaire International de Justice Constitutionnelle 1992, Vol VIII, p 111. Le développement de la justice constitutionnelle en Mauritanie, in Annuaire International de Justice Constitutionnelle 1993, Vol IX, p 31.

[28] Cf M. Diagne, op cit.

into effect the true power of substitution of the constitutional court judge. In other words, the consequence of the *réserve d'interprétation* is that at times it results in imposing a power of judicial substitution over the legislature which turns the court into the real law maker in place of the legislature. This is a power which risks overriding the legislative branch. According to some commentators, this tendency is revealed by the analysis of certain decisions of the constitutional Court of Benin.[29]

CONCLUSION

Before concluding this study of constitutional courts in West Africa two questions remain. The first one concerns making a general assessment and the second relates to wider future perspectives.

How can one assess constitutional courts?

Although belonging to the same geographic zone and having identical problems, the constitutional courts of West Africa have not always assumed the same level of participation in the development of law and democracy. Some have in fact been more active and more productive than others. Any assessment however should not only be based on the though put of cases; in practice, one should also equally take account of the quality of the constitutional jurisprudence produced and its capacity to stabilise the political system.

Over the past 15 years, African states have taken a new step in their political evolution. At the outset constitutional courts can be considered as elements taking their part in this process. Their function, expressed explicitly or implicitly, was to constitute a counterweight to the power of the executive (contrary to what occurred in France) and to regulate the power of public bodies. The majority of laws passed voted by African parliaments are in fact of presidential origin. Having reviewed the results, can it be said that the objective has been achieved?

In overseeing the declaration of results of presidential and parliamentary elections constitutional courts have sometimes contributed to the consolidation of the legitimacy of political authorities which comes from the ballot box. However, on some occasions, they have delivered judgments that have stirred up public unrest. Otherwise, constitutional courts have often managed to arbitrate between public bodies and thereby

---

[29] Cf S. Bolle, Le code des personnes et de la famille devant le Conseil constitutionnel du Bénin. La décision DCC 02-144 du 23 décembre 2004 ; in AFRILEX 2004, n°4, pp 315ff.

avoided an explosion into institutional crisis. To achieve this result, it has been necessary for them to assume a number of prerogatives that were not expressly included in the laws which created these jurisdictions.

In the area where constitutional courts or councils were supposed to bring a major contribution by the development of a constitutional rights jurisprudence, especially regarding the protection of basic human rights, their contribution has been negligible. But certain courts in countries lagging behind in the field of civil liberties have compensated for this omission. This is unquestionably the case in respect of Benin. Thus one notes that as a whole the constitutional jurisdictions are still in a phase of gestation and that only gradually do they contribute to defining the political principles that govern the life of African society. Case law jurisprudence, which should be the most vibrant part of constitutional law, is still in an embryonic state of formation in West Africa. For this reason, the existence of these courts in West Africa is a response to a necessity.

Turning to analyse their day to day functioning, it appears that the legal work of these jurisdictions is of variable importance. One cannot identify a real will on the part of these courts to develop general principles of natural law governing the relationship between governmental bodies and citizens. Constitutional law itself is still more institutional than substantive. The definition of a new concept of citizenship by these jurisdictions, through systematic development and the rigour of a judicial regime of fundamental rights, again lacks substance. Rather, the major contribution of these courts has revolved around the arbitration of political conflicts between public bodies and the confirmation of election results. Nevertheless, the Constitutional Court of Benin can be singled out on account of the fact that it often intervenes in matters concerning rights. However, these decisions, since they have concerned administrative acts, have been more to do with civil liberties than basic human rights. This is no less reason for governmental authority to respect its decisions. But it contributes to a style of decision making adopted by the state where governmental bodies remain subjected to judicial control, despite the legitimacy invested in them following an election.

What are the challenges which will confront these courts in the future?

Accounts of outside observers, notably the political classes and civil society, regard the independence of these courts as the main problem which has arisen. But despite their best efforts it would be more accurate to say that this is often a matter of bias from which they suffered since their creation. In fact even before any analysis of the content of the decisions made by these courts, it appears this problem often originates from the method of selection.

Although this concern is well founded, it should not be exaggerated. In practice, it rarely happens that published decisions are overturned and that clearly ideological judgments are delivered. In reality, such critical observations are more often made by politicians and by organisations defending human rights and rarely by lawyers and political scientists. All the same one should recognise that the situation keeps changing with the increase in the quantity of research work undertaken into constitutional justice.[30]

In any case, no method of selection of constitutional courts is entirely satisfactory. With the passage of time the systems cited above, as also in the French example, have revealed their limits. Thus in France, despite the variety of nominating bodies, of the eleven current members of the Constitutional Council, nine are appointed by people belonging to the same political party. The lesson that can be learned for African nations is that independence is mainly a personal matter, requiring a personality holding to a certain set of values.

On the other hand, another problem rarely referred to that is nevertheless fundamental in determining the future of these courts, relates to their methods and techniques of working. Constitutional law in the advanced democracies is mainly jurisprudential. On the other hand, in Africa, a literal application of the law is widely predominant. Furthermore, in the final analysis, questions concerning the struggle to gain power or retain it take up the bulk of the litigation which comes before the courts. The other aspects of national law, dealing with the relationships with citizens, notably guarantees of legal security before the law, do not receive the consideration that they deserve in these African systems. But with the development of political relationships, one can foresee that this type of question will be posed more and more often in the future. This will be an issue for the African judge to confront as part of the new situation.

In the light of the current case law, one might ask oneself whether these young constitutional courts and councils will be in a position to fulfil the function of the protection of individual rights confronted by all the power of the State. This forms the new requirement of contemporary constitutional law and it is mainly by this route that these courts will succeed in subjecting politics to law. The challenge for constitutional judges is in finding a balance between, on the one hand, the necessity to subject power

---

[30] Cf S. Bolle, Le code des personnes et de la famille devant le Conseil constitutionnel du Bénin. La décision DCC 02-144 du 23 décembre 2004 ; in AFRILEX 2004, n°4, pp 315ff.

to a rigorous system of control, while, on the other hand, avoiding this oversight function paralysing the executive and ensuring that it does not contradict the popular will expressed by the legislature. It seems doubtful whether all African constitutional courts are prepared to take on this task. To allow them to correctly rise to these challenges, a number of measures can be envisaged. Some are external to the courts, whilst others are internal.

A first measure not relating necessarily to constitutional courts themselves would consist in modernising the teaching of constitutional law by providing education in greater depth and breadth. The essentials of this education are exempted in the first year in law faculties and covered mainly under the general theory of the state and the political system. The parts relating to justice and to civil liberty are still neglected in African syllabuses. Universities and schools in the training of judges must make up for this omission in making deeper provision for constitutional law in their courses. This has been a weakness that prevents the renewal and progress of constitutional law.

A second measure would concern the greater development of collaboration between constitutional courts. There is an association that groups them together as l'Association des Cours Constitutionnelles ayant en Partage l'Usage du Français (ACCPUF). However, the cooperation between the African members inside this association is not very developed. As a result comparative law is not sufficiently used as a source of constitutional law.[31] Thus, one finds a position in which nations belonging to the same region, having identical legal organisations as a result of their common membership of the same regional organisations, and confronted with similar problems, have no reciprocal contact with one another. This is quite the opposite to what happens in Europe. The reinforcement of collaboration between judges could help with the harmonisation and the integration of constitutional law.

A third series of measures would be internal to the constitutional courts. The first would be a need to redefine the exact scope of their jurisdiction. A comparative examination of the jurisdictions of these courts reveals that there are differences in the sensitivity threshold depending on the subject coming before the court. It would be an illusion to believe that expanded jurisdiction will better guarantee the rule of law and democracy. In reality, to allow them to perform this role more effectively it would be even more interesting to put the emphasis on the prevention of such litigation. In order to do this, it is naturally important to augment their competence over contentious matters, but it is also all important to increase their consultative

[31]   Cf M-C. Ponthoreau, op cit.

role and their constitutional jurisdiction. Allowing different state bodies, such as the president of the republic, the prime minister and the presidents of the national assembly and the senate, to refer to the constitutional court to determine the interpretation of controversial provisions of the constitution, puts them in the position of regulating the exercise of public power and anticipating potential conflicts, the opinions and decisions of this type being therefore dressed up in the highest authority. Without any doubt the court's intervention would contribute not only towards reducing the risks of institutional crisis, but also, in reinforcing the belief in law as a method of peaceful regulation of such disagreements. This consultative competence exists almost everywhere, but only in a residual state. It needs to be developed.

With regard to the control of litigation, it would be interesting, without going so far as opening up the constitutional court to all individuals and making referral on grounds of unconstitutionality generally available to the public, to envisage broadening access to argue unconstitutional claims in all the West African jurisdictions. The first positive consequence of the exception to unconstitutionality would be to permit the contestation in front of a judge of a law which has become definitive. The second would be that thanks to this process, it would be possible to contest some laws contrary to the constitution passed as a result of collusion in the bosum of parliament which has allowed the required majority to be obtained.

The same type of idea, but in a different sense, concerns acts which can be challenged before constitutional courts. In order to avoid making all legal acts referable to constitutional courts, it would be conceivable to make the referral of laws concerning human rights obligatory. Such an obligation exists in certain states and also encompasses organic laws before their promulgation, but this requirement should nevertheless be increased.

Finally, we come to the potential of constitutional justice. Constitutional law has become one of the most important branches of public law. For some years it has been moving forward on the continent at a prodigious speed complicated by three important factors: the trend towards democracy in Africa; the quantity and qualitative development of international conventions, notably in the domain of human rights; and economic integration. This evolution has called into question classic sources of law, and its principles and techniques. Therefore, it is now important that constitutional justice follows these trends by adapting efficiently within each national context. In order for this to happen, the courts must be given the staff and resources to allow them to follow the evolution of constitution law which is increasingly becoming an internationalised constitutional law. However, it appears that some courts are presently staffed with unqualified personnel and are otherwise ill-equipped. Constitutional courts in Africa have sometimes been supported by bi-lateral or multilateral financial partners. But the efforts supplied by the rulers and the states concerned have not yet reached the level of combating the risk to the rule of law and democracy on the continent and satisfying the expectations of citizens.

From this standpoint, there is a strong temptation to call for the strengthening of constitutional courts, to push them to take further steps and become bolder in their checking of the exercise of political power. However, one might come to regret this. *This is because, at the same time, the courts must be careful to take account of the national context, not to raise themselves to a divinity, to enforce the allocation of cases coming before the court and not to oppose the will of the people at times when this is validly expressed by universal suffrage.* This is not a matter of limiting the power of constitutional courts, but only to appreciate that in law-making there are opportunities, but also relative constraints in the application of decisions. This search for a balance between that which, politically, is desirable and that is possible in African states is one of the sternest challenges confronting constitutional courts in consolidating their authority.

South Africa's Constitutional Court: Enabling Democracy and Promoting Law in the Transition from Apartheid

HEINZ KLUG

INTRODUCTION

South Africa's Constitutional Court is a product of the country's democratic transition away from Apartheid in the early 1990s. The democratic transition was achieved through a two-stage process of constitutional change. In the first stage an 'interim' constitution was adopted and a democratic election held to both elect a new government as well as legislative body whose two houses met jointly to form a Constitutional Assembly that produced a 'final' Constitution for post-apartheid South Africa. This two-stage process was facilitated by an agreement to adopt a set of Constitutional Principles that would be attached as a schedule to the negotiated 'interim' Constitution providing the framework within which the democratically-elected Constitutional Assembly would formulate a 'final' Constitution. While the new constitutions both introduced extensive bills of rights as a response to the country's history of colonialism and apartheid, the Constitutional Principles promised those who would loose power in a democratic election that their fundamental concerns would still be addressed in the final constitutional dispensation. It was in order to guarantee this outcome that the negotiating parties agreed that there would be a Constitutional Court and that it would serve the unique function of certifying whether the 'final' constitution produced by the Constitutional Assembly was in conformity with the parameters set by the Constitutional Principles.

The Constitutional Court's power is based on both the Constitution's proclamation that it is the supreme law of the land and its explicit grant

263

of authority declaring the Court the final arbiter of the meaning of the Constitution. As a direct product of the political negotiations that ended apartheid, the Constitutional Court, provided for in the 1993 'interim' Constitution, was established in the first half of 1995, about a year after South Africa's first democratic election, with the appointment of 11 justices to the Court. The Court was formally opened in October 1995. Empowered to exercise both concrete and abstract review, as well as to take direct applications and to serve as a court of final review, the Constitutional Court has had a broad scope of authority within which to establish its role. On average the Court decided about 25 cases per year during its first decade and ruled against the government in about 40 percent of cases. Of the cases that the Court decided approximately 60 percent were based on claims of violations of rights, 30 percent arose out of criminal cases and about 78 percent of all cases were decided by a unanimous Court.

In order to appreciate the emergence of the South African Constitutional Court and its contribution to constitutional law in South Africa and around the globe, this article will first discuss the origins of the Court and the role it played in the transition to a constitutional democracy in South Africa. Second, it will consider how the Court's early rights jurisprudence provided the institution with a high degree of legitimacy while the Court adopted a strategic approach to its own role, both as an interpreter of the Constitution and arbiter of power between the different regional and institutional locations of power in the new South Africa. Finally, the paper considers how the Court has begun to address issues that touch on the fundamental relations of power in South African society – effecting gender, land and traditional authorities – while also becoming increasingly embroiled in the complex and high stakes power struggles that have roiled the government and ruling party, from the corruption trials of the ANC President to the problems of judicial independence.

ORIGINS AND CREATION OF THE CONSTITUTIONAL COURT

Rejection of tyranny and the embrace of rights is a logical reaction to their systematic violation, yet it does not explain why a particular society would choose to turn to the judiciary as the ultimate protectors of such rights. This is particularly so when the judiciary and the law in general was intimately associated with the construction and maintenance of a prior oppressive regime. In South Africa judicial review of legislative authority had historically been explicitly rejected, and in the period just prior to the democratic transition all the major parties remained committed to notions of democracy which assumed that a democratic South Africa would continue to embrace parliamentary sovereignty. In fact, the struggle against apartheid was always understood as a struggle against racial oppression and minority rule, and conversely, as a struggle for majoritarian democracy. This history makes the empowerment of judges in a democratic South Africa not just unnecessary to the goals of democratization, but a rather unexpected outcome of the democratic transition.[1]

Despite this legacy, the origins of the Constitutional Court as well as the legitimacy of the justices appointed by a newly elected President Nelson Mandela, brought an extraordinary degree of legitimacy to this new institution. Prior to the 1994 Constitution the South African high court system was composed of a Supreme Court, the architecture of which provided for a number of provincial and local divisions exercising both original and review jurisdiction with a final appeal to an Appellate Division. The judiciary was appointed by the executive and as a matter of custom its members were drawn from the ranks of senior Advocates, the equivalent of barristers, in South Africa's divided bar. As a result of both the reluctance of a number of senior advocates who considered the apartheid judiciary to be tainted as well as the increasing tendency of the Apartheid regime to appoint judges sympathetic to its world view, the integrity of some justices, particularly Chief Justice Rabie, was increasingly called into question. FW De Klerk's appointment of the more liberal Justice Corbett at the beginning of the democratic transition seemed to acknowledge the importance of shoring up the legitimacy of the judiciary in this period. At the same time the liberation movement was suggesting that there needed to be a complete replacement or at least vetting of Apartheid judges.

As attention shifted to the negotiation of a new constitution a debate began over the role of the judiciary in a new South Africa. While there was early agreement in the negotiations on the principle that there should be a competent, independent and impartial judiciary that should have the 'power and jurisdiction to safeguard and enforce the Constitution and all fundamental rights',[2] the parties remained far apart in their proposals for the structure and functioning of a new court. While there seemed at first to be agreement that the appointment of new judges more representative of the population would be an important benefit of establishing a new constitutional court, a number of other issues continued to separate the parties, including: whether a constitutional jurisdiction would be a parallel system of courts or integrated into the existing court system; whether the judges who would exercise this jurisdiction had to be senior judges from

---

[1] See, Klug, H (2000) *Constituting Democracy: Law, Globalism and South Africa's Political Reconstruction*, Cambridge University Press.

2 Third Report to the Negotiating Council, Kempton Park, May 28, 1993, p2.

within the existing judiciary or possibly new appointees with little or no judicial experience; whether it would be a court of appeal or have first and final jurisdiction over the validity of laws; whether it would have sole jurisdiction or serve as the court of final appeal in a system of review that was integrated into the jurisdiction of the existing courts; and finally, would the Chief Justice in an integrated court or the Constitutional Court itself, as a separate body, decide whether a particular matter was constitutional in nature or not, and hence who would have the power to exercise jurisdiction in the particular case.[3]

Responding to the South African Law Commission's earlier proposal that a specialist Constitutional Court be created to uphold a Bill of Rights, the apartheid government argued that such a court should not be a separate institution but rather a special chamber within the existing Appellate Division of the Supreme Court. This position was strongly supported by the newly appointed Chief Justice Corbett who felt that a separate Constitutional Court would undercut the prestige and authority of the Appellate Division. He was also concerned that a separate Court would be considered political and thus would undermine the 'evolution of a human rights culture in South Africa and the legitimacy of the Constitution as the Supreme Law'.[4] Another concern was expressed by Etienne Murenik, who as advisor to the opposition Democratic Party, supported the creation of a separate Constitutional Court but argued that 'the values of the Bill of Rights [should] permeate every corner of our law', building a 'culture of justification ... in which every lawmaker and every official can be called upon to justify his or her actions in terms of the values for which the bill of rights stands'.[5] Despite these arguments the Technical Committee's Report was adopted by the two major parties accepting the creation of a separate Constitutional Court with final jurisdiction over constitutional matters.

JURISDICTION AND RELATIONSHIP TO THE COURTS OF GENERAL JURISDICTION

Despite distrust of the old judicial order, the idea of superimposing a constitutional court as the final interpreter of a new constitution gained early acceptance among participants in the political transition while the exact parameters of its power was left to subsequent negotiation. In fact, the Constitutional Court first created under the 1993 'interim' Constitution was

3 See, Spitz, R and Chaskalson M, *The Politics of Transition: a hidden history of South Africa's negotiated settlement*, Hart Publishing, 2000, pp.191-198.
4 Id at 194.
5 Id 194-195.

initially placed in a co-equal position with the old Appellate Division of the Supreme Court of South Africa which retained final jurisdiction over all non-constitutional matters but had no jurisdiction at all over constitutional questions. The 1996 'final' Constitution retained this basic jurisdictional division, but integrated the courts into a new hierarchy: the Constitutional Court is now the highest Court, retaining original jurisdiction over direct constitutional applications[6] and serving as the final court of appeal on the Constitution.[7] The Supreme Court of Appeals, which hears appeals from the High Courts, now has appellate jurisdiction over all matters, including constitutional issues,[8] but since constitutional jurisdiction is very far reaching, including not only all government related activity[9] but also certain private activity,[10] as well as the duty to develop the common law and indigenous law in conformity with the requirements of the Bill of Rights,[11] the Constitutional Court increasingly serves as a final Court of appeal on most important questions.

When it comes to direct access however the Constitutional Court has in practice applied rather strict criteria to those seeking direct access,[12] preferring to allow a case to be argued up through the lower courts so as to get as full a development as possible of the facts and legal arguments before the case reaches the Court. While the lower courts (including the Supreme Court of Appeals) may hear constitutional challenges to law and actions under the law, including legislative and executive acts, there is an express limit to their power in this regard. Any lower court decision declaring National Legislation or an act of the President in violation of the Constitution must be forwarded to the Constitutional Court for confirmation before it can take effect. As a result all challenges to acts of the President or national legislation are considered by the Constitutional Court. In addition to these cases the Constitutional Court is also the final court of appeal on all other constitutional matters, including the question of whether an issue is a constitutional issue or not.

---

[6]   S. Afr. Const. (1996) section 167(6)
[7]   S. Afr. Const. (1996) sections 167(3)-(5)
[8]   S. Afr. Const. (1996) section 168(3)
[9]   S. Afr. Const. (1996) section 8(1)
[10]   S. Afr. Const. (1996) section 8(2)-(3)
[11]   S. Afr. Const. (1996) section 39(2)
[12]   See, Dugard, J 'Court of First Instance? Towards a Pro-Poor Jurisdiction for the South Afircan Constitutional Court', 22 *South African Journal of Human Rights* 261 (2006).

APPOINTMENTS TO THE CONSTITUTIONAL COURT

Initially, little attention was paid to the proposal by the technical committee to the Multi-Party Negotiating Process that Constitutional Court Judges be nominated by an all-party parliamentary committee and be appointed by a 75 percent majority of both houses of parliament. However, as the significance of the Constitutional Court became increasingly clear, a major political conflict exploded.[13] In fact conflict over this process brought the multi-party negotiations, once again, perilously close to deadlock. Despite this inauspicious beginning, the resolution of this conflict was with minor changes retained in the 'final' constitution. The resolution involved an elaborate compromise in which the newly elected President was required to follow three distinct processes in appointing members of the Constitutional Court for a non-renewable period of seven years.[14] First, the President appointed a president of the Constitutional Court in consultation with the Cabinet and Chief Justice.[15] Second, four members of the court were appointed from among the existing judges of the Supreme Court after consultation between the President, Cabinet and the Chief Justice.[16] Finally, the President, in consultation with the Cabinet and the President of the Constitutional Court, appointed six members from a list submitted by the Judicial Service Commission (JSC),[17] a newly created body dominated two-to-one by lawyers.[18]

The final Constitution extended the period of non-renewable appointment from 7 to 12 years but also imposed a mandatory retirement age of 70 years. A subsequent constitutional amendment provides that the term of an individual justice may be extended by an Act of Parliament.[19] Appointments to the court are made by the President, either in consultation with the JSC and the leaders of the political parties represented in the National Assembly — in the case of the Chief Justice and the Deputy-Chief Justice — or for the remaining positions on the court, from a list of nominees prepared by the JSC after the President consults with the Chief Justice and the leaders of political parties. The JSC is required to provide three more nominees than the number of appointments to be made and the President

---

[13] See, Mureinik, E 'Rescued from illegitimacy?' *Weekly Mail & Guardian, Review/Law,* Supplement, Vol. 1, No. 5, Dec. 1993 at 1; and Haysom, N 'An expedient package deal?' *Weekly Mail & Guardian, Review/Law,* Supplement, Vol. 1, No. 5, Dec. 1993 at 1.
[14] S. Afr. Const. 1993, section 99(1)
[15] S. Afr. Const. 1993, section 97(2)(a)
[16] S. Afr. Const. 1993, section 99(3)
[17] S. Afr. Const. 1993, section 99(3)
[18] S. Afr. Const. 1993, section 105(1)
[19] S. Afr. Const. 1996, section 176(1).

may refuse to appoint any of these by giving reasons to the JSC why the nominees are unacceptable — requiring the JSC to provide a supplemental list. The President's power of appointment is further restricted by the requirement that 'at all times, at least four members of the Constitutional Court must be persons who were judges at the time they were appointed'.[20] The President is required to remove a judge from office if the JSC 'finds that the judge suffers from an incapacity, is grossly incompetent or is guilty of gross misconduct' and the National Assembly votes by a two-thirds majority for that judge's removal.

Appointment to the Constitutional Court is also determined by the requirement that the person must be a South African citizen and that consideration must be given to the '[n]eed for the judiciary to reflect broadly the racial and gender composition of South Africa'.[21] In practice the Constitutional Court has, despite its young age, experienced a regular change in the composition of its panel. This has occurred as a result of a number of developments, including: the transfer of the first Deputy-President of the Court to become Chief Justice (then head of the Supreme Court of Appeal exercising final appeal jurisdiction over non-constitutional matters); the death of Justice Didcott, numerous retirements and the fairly frequent use of acting Justices when permanent members were either seconded to international organizations or on leave. The *Judges Renumeration and Conditions of Employment Act of 2001* now provides that although it is a single 12 year term of office, justices may continue until they have completed fifteen years of total judicial service or reached the age of 75, which ever comes first, in order to ensure that those who have not previously held judicial office may still retire from the Court with a full judicial pension. While the first appointments to the Constitutional Court were dominated by lawyers, judges and legal academics who had gained high stature during the struggle against apartheid or whose integrity was recognized nationally and internationally, concern for the need to achieve or maintain racial and ethnic representivity on the panel seems to have determined more recent appointments. Ten years after its inauguration the Justices of the Constitutional Court reflect the diversity of South Africa with two female, four white, six African, one Indian and two physically-disabled justices on the eleven person panel.

---

[20] 1996 Constitution, section 174(5).
[21] 1996 Constitution, section 174(1) and (2).

EARLY DECISIONS AND THE TRIUMPH OF RIGHTS

In its first politically important and publicly controversial holding the South African Constitutional Court struck down the death penalty.[22] Although there had been a moratorium placed on executions from the end of 1989, as part of the initial moves towards a negotiated transition, as many as 400 persons were awaiting execution at the time of the Court's ruling. In declaring capital punishment unconstitutional the Court emphasized that the transitional constitution established a new order in South Africa, in which human rights and democracy are entrenched and in which the Constitution is supreme. The court's declaration of a new order based on constitutional rights was forcefully carried through in the adoption of a generous and purposive approach to the interpretation of the fundamental rights enshrined in the Constitution.

The unanimous opinion of the court, authored by the President of the Constitutional Court Justice Arthur Chaskalson, was however, judiciously tailored. Finding that the death penalty amounted to cruel and unusual punishment under most circumstances Chaskalson's opinion declined to engage in a determinative interpretation of other sections of the bill of rights that may also have impacted upon the death penalty, such as the right to life, dignity and equality. The individual concurring opinions of the remaining ten justices were not as restrained. Despite their concurrence in Justice Chaskalson's opinion each of the remaining ten members of the court went far beyond the majority opinion in their interpretation of other rights and in their prescriptions on the future trajectory of the courts jurisprudence.

All ten justices joined Constitutional Court President Chaskalson in giving explicit and great weight to the introduction of constitutional review. They emphasized that the court 'must not shrink from its task' of review,[23] otherwise South Africa would be back to parliamentary sovereignty and by implication back to the unrestrained violation of rights so common under previous parliaments.[24] Even the recognition that public opinion seemed to favor the retention of the death penalty was met with a clear statement that the Court would 'not allow itself to be diverted from its duty to act as an independent arbiter of the Constitution',[25] and that public opinion

---

[22] *S v Makwanyane and Another* 1995 (3) SA 391 (CC); 1995 (6) BCLR 665 (CC) [hereinafter *Makwanyane*].
[23] *Makwanyane* at para. 22, quoting the South African Law Commission *Interim Report on Group and Human Rights Project* 58 (August 1991) para 7.33.
[24] *Makwanyane* at para 88.
[25] *Makwanyane* at para 89.

in itself is 'no substitute for the duty vested in the Courts to interpret the Constitution and to uphold its provisions without fear or favour'.[26] If public opinion were to be decisive, Chaskalson argued, 'there would be no need for constitutional adjudication'.[27]

A similarly strong stand was taken by the court in its early cases striking down legislation in violation of the equality clause, although the ability of the court to move beyond formal equality and to fulfill the transformative promise of substantive equality remains in question.[28] The Court also took up numerous criminal cases involving both procedural and substantive rules that the Court found in violation of the Bill of Rights. In its first year over 64% of the Court's case load involved criminal matters although this dropped to around one-third in the following two years. In considering the willingness of this new court to strike down legislation and reverse official decisions it is important to note that the vast bulk of legislation struck down in this early period as well as official decisions and acts that were reversed were based on laws and regulations inherited from the Apartheid era. While the old regime had insisted on legal continuity – the idea that all laws would remain in place until either reversed by new legislation or found to be inconsistent with the new constitution by the Court – the outcome of this approach was to indirectly empower the new Constitutional Court as it proceeded to strike down old laws and regulations without any resistance from the new democratic government. What might under other circumstances have been perceived as a counter-majoritarian and hence anti-democratic power was instead embraced as the triumph of human rights standards over the legacies of apartheid.

INTERNATIONAL RECOGNITION AND THE COURT'S INNOVATIVE JURISPRUDENCE

It was the same boldness in the upholding of rights that brought international attention to the new Court. From the moment the Court struck down the death penalty it was being held up around the world as a shining model, a new and progressive institution arising out of the ashes of apartheid. When it first reversed a decision made by President Mandela, he welcomed the decision and publically thanked the Court for doing its duty. By the time the court was faced with making decisions at odds with the policies of the new government, it had garnered a significant amount of international support

[26] *Makwanyane* at para 88.
[27] Ibid.
[28] See, Albertyn, C 'Substantive Equality and Transformation in South Africa', 23 *South African Journal on Human Rights* 253 (2007).

and recognition as well as local respect, which ensured that its opinions would not face overwhelming resistance in the new order. International interest in the Constitutional Court's jurisprudence has been particularly acute in relation to the Constitution's guarantee of socio-economic rights as well as opinions in which the Court has addressed cases involving religious and cultural conflict through its particular articulation of the relationship between these forms of individual and collective identity and how these interact with the Constitution in the 'rainbow' nation.

The inclusion of justiciable socio-economic rights in the 1996 Constitution has been heralded as a mark of the Constitution's extraordinary status and has raised questions about how these provisions would be interpreted in a situation of vast socio-economic inequalities and limited governmental capacity. Responding to concerns about the justiciability of these rights in the *First Certification* case the Constitutional Court rejected the rigid distinction between different types of rights and instead argued that '[a] t the very minimum, socio-economic rights can be negatively protected from improper invasion'.[29] In the now famous case addressing the scope of socio-economic rights — *Grootboom*[30] — the Court was called upon to define both the negative and positive obligations that the constitutional right to housing imposed on the government. In this case the Court reviewed a local government's action in evicting squatters from private land that was to be used for low income housing. In the process of eviction the homes the squatters had erected were destroyed and much of their personal possessions and building material had also been deliberately destroyed.

While the Constitutional Court upheld the claimant's argument that the municipality's action violated the negative obligation – the duty not to deprive them of shelter – owed to them under section 26(1) of the Constitution, the Court proceeded to extrapolate on the positive duties placed on the state. Although the government was able to present a well documented national housing policy which met the obligation to 'take reasonable legislative and other measures, within its available resources, to achieve the progressive realization of this right',[31] the Court found that the failure to have a policy to address the needs for emergency shelter meant that the policy failed 'to respond to the needs of those most desperate' and was thus unreasonable.[32] At the same time however the Court emphasized

---

[29] *Ex parte Chairperson of the Constitutional Assembly: In re Certification of the Constitution of the Republic of South Africa, 1996*, 1996 (4) SA 744 (CC) [hereinafter First Certification case]
[30] *Government of the Republic of South Africa and Others v Grootboom and Others*, 2001 (1) SA 46 (CC) [hereinafter Grootboom].
[31] South African Constitution, 1996, Section 26(2).
[32] Grootboom para 44.

that '[t]he precise contours and content of the measures to be adopted are primarily a matter for the legislature and executive' and stated that the Court 'will not enquire whether other more desirable or favourable measures could have been adopted, or whether public money could have been better spent'.[33]

Applying these arguments to the area of health, and HIV/AIDS in particular, posed a major problem for the Constitutional Court. In the *Treatment Action Campaign*[34] case the Court was asked to require the government to provide a particular treatment — the antiretroviral drug Nevirapine to HIV-positive women in childbirth and their newborn babies — and not merely to have a reasonable policy to address the overwhelming HIV/AIDS pandemic within the confines of the state's resources. The Court's decision to require the provision of Nevirapine marked an important extension of the principle's laid out in *Grootboom* and an extraordinary reversal in the Court's approach to health rights which only a short time earlier in a case involving access to renal dialysis[35] had seemed to be frozen by a combination of medical prerogatives and resource scarcity. Relying on the constitutional guarantee of a right to the progressive realization of access to health care services, the Constitutional Court argued in *TAC* that under the circumstances, in which the cost of Nevirapine and the provision of appropriate testing and counseling to mothers was less burdensome to the state then the failure to provide the drug, the government had a constitutional duty to expand its program beyond the test sites already planned. While a subsequent case in which non-citizen permanent residents challenged the denial of social welfare benefits[36] was decided by the Court through an analysis of intersecting rights that brought together the courts concerns for equality and access to social resources, thus again progressively extending the protection of socio-economic rights, the Court's reliance on a form of reasonableness review in this area continues to draw concern.[37]

[33] Grootboom para. 41.
[34] 2002 (5) SA 721 (CC).
[35] *Soobramoney v Minister of Health* (KwaZulu-Natal) 1998 (1) SA 765 (CC).
[36] *Khosa v Minister of Social development; Mahlaule v Minister of Social development* 2004 (6) SA 505 (CC).
[37] See, Davis, D 'Adjudicating the Socio-Economic Rights in the South African Constitution: Towards "Deference Lite"?' 22 *South African Journal on Human Rights* 301 (2006).

THE OLD FORT, CONSTITUTIONAL PATRIOTISM, AND THE COURT'S LEGITIMACY

Adding to the symbolic stature of the new Constitutional Court has been the project of renovating and transforming the site of a cluster of prisons, known as the 'Old Fort' which is located in the center of Johannesburg. While the Constitutional Court was first housed in a Johannesburg business park, the building of the new Court building in the center of the site of the Old Fort along with the renovation of the Old Fort and related prison buildings into historical monuments to the history of the 'lawful' violation of rights, has placed the Constitutional Court in the midst of a project to build what has been termed in the German context 'constitutional patriotism'. This 'project', pursued more vigorously by some Justices in particular, seems to be aimed at solidifying the historic role of the Court in the building of a new South Africa. Despite the continuing social inequalities and what at times is a blatant disrespect for rights by some government officials, there is a consistent public assertion by government of the notion that South Africa is building a culture of rights based on the new Constitution. As long as the political leadership in all branches of government continue to assert that the Constitution is South Africa's highest achievement in the transition away from Apartheid, then the Court will be able to pursue its public promotion of a culture of rights and constitutional supremacy, both through its decisions and the articulation of a project of constitutional patriotism.

There can be little doubt that the Constitutional Court is one of the most successful institutions to emerge in post-apartheid South Africa. Not only is it the guardian of the political transitions most explicit symbol – the 'final' Constitution – but unlike all other branches of government it began its life as a brand new institution, its personnel largely untainted by apartheid, and its most explicit task is to uphold the promise of rights that embody the hopes and aspirations of those who struggled against apartheid. These attributes do not however guarantee power or authority given the inherent institutional limits of an apex Court. Instead the Court has used its symbolic authority to publically engage in what has been termed a 'post-liberal' or 'transformative constitutionalism'[38] – a rejection of the negative past, a generous interpretation of rights and a commitment to 'inducing large-scale social change through nonviolent political processes grounded in law'.[39] At the same time however the Court has always wielded this

---

[38] See, Klare, K 'Legal Culture and Transformative Constitutionalism', 14 South African Journal on Human Rights 146 (1998).
[39] Id. p. 150.

power with a strategic eye to its own role, in what may be paradoxically viewed as a form of judicial pragmatism rather than the symbolic judicial activism that the Court's rights jurisprudence has led most international observers to applaud.

STRATEGIC ENGAGEMENT OR JUDICIAL PRAGMATISM

Asserting a constitutional patriotism and declaring a culture of rights is all very well, but at the same time the Court has always been concerned about its own role in the new political order. Aware of their unique status within the new constitutional order, the justices of the Constitutional Court have been careful to define its role as upholding the law and have denied claims that they might be substituting their own political decisions in their role as interpreters of the Constitution. The Court has in fact had to manage a number of quite explicit challenges to its role, including the demand in one case that all the justices recuse themselves because they were appointed by President Mandela, but at the same time it has been quite conscious of the different ways in which it is responsible for ensuring the transition to democracy. As a result, the Constitutional Court of South Africa has managed to become a central institution in the management of conflict in post-apartheid South Africa, whether between regions of the country, among branches of government, or between the government and civil society.

CERTIFICATION JUDGMENTS

Thrust into the unique role of arbiter in the second and final phase of the constitution-making process, the Constitutional Court was faced with a number of distinct pressures. First, the democratically-elected Constitutional Assembly represented the pinnacle of the country's new democratic institutions empowered with the task of producing the country's final constitution – the end product of the formal transition. Given a history of Parliamentary sovereignty and the failure of the courts to check the anti-democratic actions of the executive in the dark days of Apartheid and during the States of Emergency, how was a newly appointed Constitutional Court going to stand up against the first truly democratic constitution-making body in South African history?

Second, the credibility of the Constitutional Court was at stake. As the court heard argument on the Certification of the Constitution, numerous sectors, including important elements within the established legal profession, openly speculated whether the Court had sufficient independence to stand up to the Constitutional Assembly, particularly over the key issue of the entrenchment of the Bill of Rights. Failure to refuse certification on at least this ground would in this view have amounted to a failure of the certification function and proof that the Court lacked the necessary independence.

Third, the Constitutional Court's certification powers were not only unique but were to be exercised on the basis of a set of Constitutional Principles negotiated in the pre-election transition. The Principles had, in the dying days of the multi-party negotiations become the focus of unresolved demands leading to the incorporation of a number of contradictory Principles designed more to keep the contending participants within the process than to establish a coherent set of Constitutional Principles by which a future draft Constitution could be judged.

Fourth, many of the grounds upon which the Court declined to certify the text had institutional implications for the Court. For example, the Court's demand to strengthen the procedures and threshold for amendment of the Bill of Rights and its striking down of attempts to insulate the labour clause from judicial review, both indicated a profound concern with securing the role of the Court, as guardian of a constitutional democracy, based on the explicit foundations of constitutional supremacy.

Despite this imperative, refusing to certify the final constitution, even after it's adoption by 86% of the democratically-elected Constitutional Assembly, was on its face a bold assertion of judicial power. At the same time the Constitutional Court was careful to point out in its unanimous, unattributed, opinion, that 'in general and in respect of the overwhelming majority of its provisions', the Constitutional Assembly had met the predetermined requirements of the Constitutional Principles. In effect then, this was a very limited and circumscribed ruling. The Court itself was careful to point out that the Constitutional Assembly had a large degree of latitude in its interpretation of the principles and that the role of the Constitutional Court was a judicial and not a political role. This approach had the effect of limiting the political response to the decision as the major political parties rejected any attempt to use the denial of certification as a tool to reopen constitutional debates and instead the Constitutional Assembly focused solely on the issues raised by the Constitutional Court.[40]

The Court took a similarly robust attitude to its judicial role in its second certification judgment when the Court eventually certified the 'final' Constitution.[41] In this case the Court was faced with attempts by political

---

[40] Madlala, C 'Final fitting for the cloth of nationhood', *Sunday Times*, Oct. 13, 1996, at p.4. col. 2.

[41] *Ex parte Chairperson of the Constitutional Assembly: In re Certification of the Amended Text of the Constitution of the Republic of South Africa, 1996*, 1997 (2) SA 97 (CC) [hereinafter Second

parties and other interested groups to reopen issues which had not been identified as the basis for the Court's refusal to certify in the first round of the certification process. While accepting these challenges the Court noted the 'sound jurisprudential basis for the policy that a court should adhere to its previous decisions unless they are clearly wrong .... [and that] having regard to the need for finality in the certification process and in view of the virtual identical composition of the Court that considered the questions barely three months ago, that policy is all the more desirable here'.[42] As a result the Court made it clear that a party wishing to extend the Court's review beyond those aspects identified in the first certification judgment would have a 'formidable task'. Through this reliance on a classic judicial strategy of deference to past decisions, the Court was able to significantly limit the scope of its role in the final certification judgment. It was this change in posture towards the certification process and the fact that the Constitutional Assembly fully addressed all but one of the Court's concerns that ensured a swift certification on the second round. Significantly, the Court now relied less on the specifics of the Constitutional Principles and instead emphasized the fundamental elements of constitutionalism contained in the text – 'founding values which include human dignity, the achievement of equality, the recognition and advancement of human rights and freedoms, the supremacy of the Constitution and the rule of law'.[43] While the Court still had to recognize that the powers and functions of the provinces - the most contentious issue in the whole constitution-making process - remained in dispute between the parties, the Court held in essence that the removal of the presumption of constitutional validity of bills passed by the NCOP had tipped the balance.[44] Thus despite the recognition that provincial powers and functions in the Amended Text remained less than or inferior to those accorded to the provinces in terms of the Interim Constitution, this was not substantially so and therefore no longer a basis for denying certification.[45]

CONSTITUTIONAL STRUCTURE AND THE PROBLEM OF POWER

The Constitutional Court's assertion of its constitutional powers in rights cases stands in marked contrast to the Court's dramatic shift in approach

---

Certification Judgment].
[42] *Second Certification Judgment* at para. 8.
43 *Second Certification Judgment* at para. 25.
44 *Second Certification Judgment* at paras 153-157.
45 *Second Certification Judgment* at para. 204(e).

to the use of its authority when addressing the allocation of powers, particularly regional or provincial powers. Tensions between the central ANC government and non-ANC controlled provinces soon brought cases to the Constitutional Court in which it was called upon to define the parameters of cooperative government. Although wide-ranging in scope these early cases have addressed three issues central to the question of legislative authority under the 1996 Constitution. First, the Court was called upon to define the constitutional allocation of legislative power in a case in which a Province claimed implied legislative powers to define the structure of its own civil service. Second, the Court was required to determine the scope of residual national legislative power in a case where the national government claimed concurrent authority over the establishment of municipal governments despite the Constitution's simultaneous allocation in this field of specific functions to different institutions and spheres of government. Finally, an attempt by the national government to extensively regulate liquor production, sale and consumption, a field in which the regions were granted at least some exclusive powers under the Constitution, required the Court to define the specific content of the exclusive legislative powers of the provinces.

One of the first such cases involved a challenge to national legislation which sought to define the structure of the public service including all provincial public services. The Western Cape argued that the legislation infringed 'the executive power vested in the provinces by the Constitution and detracts from the legitimate autonomy of the provinces recognised in the Constitution'.[46] The Court however pointed to the fact that not only did the national Constitution provide that the public service is to be structured in accordance with national legislation, but also that the Western Cape Constitution required the Western Cape government to implement legislation in accordance with the provisions of the national constitution.[47]

Describing national framework legislation as a feature of the system of cooperative government provided for by the Constitution, the Court noted that such legislation is especially required to ensure sound fiscal planning, procurement and related matters.[48] While the Court agreed that provincial governments are empowered to 'employ, promote, transfer and dismiss' personnel in the provincial administrations of the public service', it rejected the idea of an implied provincial power depriving the national government of its 'competence to make laws for the structure and functioning of the

---

46   *The Premier of the Province of the Western Cape v The President of the Republic of South Africa and the Minister of Public Service,* CCT 26/98 (1999), 1999 (12) BCLR 1360 (CC) para. 4.
47   *Public Service Case,* Para 8.
48   *Public Service Case,* Para 9 .

civil service as a whole', which is expressly retained in section 197(1) of the Constitution.[49] Turning to the national government's structuring of the public service and whether this encroached on the 'geographical, functional or institutional integrity' of the provincial government, the Court focused on the provisions of Chapter 3 of the Constitution dealing with cooperative government. The Court's interpretation of these provisions emphasized the description of all spheres of government being 'distinctive, inter-dependent and inter-related', yet went on to point out that the 'national legislature is more powerful than other legislatures, having a legislative competence in respect of any matter', and that the 'national government is also given overall responsibility for ensuring that other spheres of government carry out their obligations under the Constitution'.[50]

While the Court accepted that the Constitution prevents one sphere of government from using its power to undermine other spheres of government it concluded that the section 'is concerned with the way power is exercised, not whether or not a power exists'.[51] The relevant question before the Court in this case however was whether the national government had the constitutional power to structure the public service.[52] Finding that indeed the power vests in the national sphere of government, the Court emphasized that the Constitutional Principles 'contemplated that the national government would have powers that transcend provincial boundaries and competences' and that 'legitimate provincial autonomy does not mean that the provinces can ignore [the constitutional] framework or demand to be insulated from the exercise of such power'.[53] The Court did however strike down a clause in the law empowering the national minister to direct a provincial official to transfer particular functions to another department (provincial or national) because such power encroached on the ability of the provinces to carry out the functions entrusted to them by the Constitution.

Although the Court seemed to come down strongly in favor of national legislative authority, at least when it is explicitly granted in the Constitution, the question of the allocation of legislative authority soon arose again, this time in the context of a dispute between the national government and the regional governments of the Western Cape and KwaZulu-Natal.[54] The

---

[49]   *Public Service Case*, Para 11.
[50]   *Public Service Case*, Para 18 and 19.
[51]   *Public Service Case*, Para 23.
[52]   *Public Service Case*, Para 23 and 24.
[53]   *Public Service Case*, Para 25.
[54]   *The Executive Council of the Province of the Western Cape v The Minister for Provincial Affairs and Constitutional Development of the Republic of South Africa; Executive Council of KwaZulu-Natal v the President of the Republic of South Africa and Others*, 1999 (12) BCLR 1360 (CC).

provincial governments in this case challenged provisions of the *Local Government: Municipal Structures Act 117 of 1998* in which the national government claimed residual concurrent powers to determine the structure of local government, despite the provisions of the local government Chapter of the Constitution which set out a comprehensive scheme for the allocation of powers between the national, provincial and local levels of government. Considering this allocation of power, the Court recognized that the Constitution left residual legislative powers to the national sphere. But the Court also determined that section 155 of the Constitution — which controls the establishment of local governments — allocates powers and functions between different spheres of government and the independent demarcation board so that:

(a) the role of the national government is limited to establishing criteria for determining different categories of municipality, establishing criteria and procedures for determining municipal boundaries, defining different types of municipalities that may be established within each category, and making provision for how powers and functions are to be divided between municipalities with shared powers; (b) the power to determine municipal boundaries vests solely in the Demarcation Board; and (c) the role of the provincial government is limited to determining the types of municipalities that may be established within the province, and establishing municipalities 'in a manner consistent with the [national] legislation enacted in terms of subsections (2) and (3).[55]

Applying this scheme to the challenged legislation the court found unconstitutional the attempt in section 13 of the Municipal Structures Act to tell the provinces how they must set about exercising a power in respect of a matter falling outside of the competence of the national government. Despite claims by the national government that the provincial official was only obliged to take the guidelines into account and not to implement them, the Court argued that what mattered was that the national government legislated on a matter falling outside its competence.[56] Thus, despite the Court's earlier recognition of the predominance of the national sphere of government in the scheme of co-operative government, here it drew the line and clarified that there was a constitutional limit to the legislative power of the national government.

---

[55] *Municipal Structures Case*, Para 14.
[56] *Municipal Structures Case*, Para 20 and 21.

Although these early cases seem on the whole to have rejected the autonomy claims of the provincial governments by recognizing the commanding role of the national legislature, the Court was soon given the opportunity to explore the arena of exclusive provincial power after the national parliament passed legislation which sought to regulate the production, distribution and sale of liquor through a nationally defined licensing scheme.[57] Referred to the Constitutional Court by President Mandela, who had refused to sign the Bill on the ground that he had reservations about its constitutionality, the law sought in part to control the manufacture, wholesale distribution and retail sale of liquor, functions which at least with respect to licensing are expressly included as exclusive legislative powers of the provinces in Schedule 5 of the Constitution. Citing a 'history of overt racism in the control of the manufacturing, distribution and sale of liquor', the national government contended that the 'provisions of the Bill constitute a permissible exercise by Parliament of its legislative powers'.[58] The Western Cape complained however that the 'Bill exhaustively regulates the activities of persons involved in the manufacture, wholesale distribution and retail sale of liquor; and that even in the retail sphere the structures the Bill seeks to create reduce the provinces, in an area in which they would (subject to section 44(2)) have exclusive legislative and executive competence, to the role of funders and administrators'.[59]

Responding to the province's claim, the Court argued that cooperative governance includes the duty 'not [to] assume any power or function except those conferred on them in terms of the Constitution' and that the Constitution's 'distribution of legislative power between the various spheres of government' and its itemization of functional areas of concurrent and exclusive legislative competence, must be read in this light.[60] Accepting that the national government enjoys the power to regulate the liquor trade in all respects because of the industry's impact on the 'determination of national economic policies, the promotion of inter-provincial commerce and the protection of the common market in respect of goods, services, capital and labour mobility', the Court went on to conclude that the structure of the Constitution precluded the national government's regulation of liquor licensing.[61] The Court came to this conclusion by carefully defining three distinct objectives of the proposed law and distinguishing those

[57] *Ex Parte the President of the Republic of South Africa, In Re: Constitutionality of the Liquor Bill,* CCT 12/99, 11 November 1999, 2000 (1) BCLR 1 (CC).
[58] *Liquor Licensing Case,* Para 33.
[59] *Liquor Licensing Case,* Para 37.
[60] *Liquor Licensing Case,* Para 41.
[61] *Liquor Licensing Case,* Para 58.

functions which would apply predominantly to intra-provincial regulation as opposed to those aspects of the liquor business requiring national regulation because of their extra-provincial and even international impact.

Having defined an aspect of the Bill which focused primarily on the provincial level, the Court then proceeded to define the primary purpose of granting exclusive competencies to the provinces as implying power over the regulation of activities 'that take place within or can be regulated in a manner that has a direct effect upon the inhabitants of the province alone'. In relation to 'liquor licences', it is obvious, the Court argued, 'that the retail sale of liquor will, except for a probably negligible minority of sales that are effected across provincial borders, occur solely within the province'. Given this fact the Court concluded that the heart of the exclusive competence granted to the regions in the Constitution, must in this arena 'lie in the licensing of retail sale of liquor'.[62] Having failed to justify the necessity of national regulation in 'regard to retail sales of liquor, whether by retailers or by manufacturers, nor for micro-manufacturers whose operations are essentially provincial', the national Parliament did not have the competence, the Court held, to enact the Liquor Bill and the Bill was therefore unconstitutional.[63]

RIGHTS, POLITICS AND THE MARGINS
OF JUDICIAL POWER

While the Constitutional Court has made many important decisions there has been concern that it was yet to address a range of difficult issues affecting the majority of ordinary South Africans and which hold the potential of confronting some of the more ingrained aspects of inequality and conflict which continue to pervade post-apartheid society. Most recently the Court has decided a group of cases which hold profound consequences for the hopes and aspirations of the majority of South Africans. These cases include challenges to the 'customary' laws of succession on grounds of gender discrimination;[64] the KwaZulu-Natal Pound Ordinance on the grounds that it denied cattle owners rights of equality and access to the courts;[65] and the Land Claims Court's decision that a community claiming land under the Restitution of Land Rights Act had failed to prove that their dispossession

---

[62] *Liquor Licensing Case*, Para 71.
[63] *Liquor Licensing Case*, Para 87.
[64] *Bhe et al v Magistrate, Khayelitsha et al*, CCT 49/03, decided 15 October 2004 [hereinafter *Bhe*].
[65] *Xolisile Zondi v Member of the Traditional Council for Traditional and Local Government Affairs et al*, CCT 73/03 [hereinafter *Zondi*].

was the result of discriminatory laws or practices.[66] In each of these cases the decision of the Court would hold important consequences for the relations of power: between men and women living under indigenous law; between land owners (usually white) and landless or land hungry stock owners (usually black); as well as between land owners and land claiming communities whose claims did not self-evidently fall within the terms of the Restitution of Land Rights Act.

In both the *Bhe* and *Richtersveld* cases the majority of the Court acknowledged the constitutional status of indigenous law. In the first instance the Court struck down a rule of customary law which discriminated on the basis of gender while in the second instance the Court held that 'indigenous law is an independent source of norms within the legal system', but like all other 'law is subject to the Constitution and has to be interpreted in light of its values'.[67] The result in *Bhe* was for the Court to directly strike down – at least with respect to intestate succession – the 'customary' rule of primogeniture held by many traditionalists and others to be a key element of the customary legal system. In effect, the Court's decision will profoundly impact the rights of wives and daughters who until now relied upon the system of extended-family obligation historically inherent in indigenous law but long since disrupted by social and economic change. On the other side, the Court's decision in *Richtersveld* recognized indigenous law as a source of land rights thus strengthening the claims of those who have argued that their land rights – including rights to natural resources – were not automatically extinguished by the extension of colonial sovereignty over their territories. Their dispossession, through means other then the direct application of specific, discriminatory, apartheid land laws, will thus also be recognized for the purpose of claiming restitution of their land rights. Even if not as broad in its impact, the symbolic value of this recognition of indigenous land rights makes an important contribution to legitimizing the new constitutional order among ordinary South Africans.

Finally, the Zondi case involved a challenge to a set of legal provisions that formed a central plank of the system of control and dispossession in the rural areas of apartheid South Africa. Under the Pound Ordinance land owners were historically empowered to seize and impound animals trespassing on their land without notice to the livestock owner, unless the owner was a neighboring land owner. Subsequently the livestock would be sold in execution if the owners could not afford the impounding fees and damages claimed by the land owner or could not be readily identified.

---

[66] *Alexkor Ltd et al v The Richtersveld Community and Others, CCT 19/03,* decided on 14 October 2003 [hereinafter *Richtersveld*].

[67] *Richtersveld,* para 51.

Without notice requirements or judicial process the effect was that white landowners used these rules to exert power over rural communities who lived on the land as sharecroppers, labor tenants or wage laborers and held what little wealth or economic security they had in livestock. In effect, these rules, while not racially-based, interacted with the racially-based landownership rules to both structure rural social relations and to perpetuate a continuing process of dispossession as the ownership of livestock continually shifted at below market prices from black to white farmers.

Facially race-neutral the Pound Ordinance survived the dismantling of apartheid laws but nevertheless continues to have a predominantly racial effect because rural land ownership remains, even a decade after apartheid, largely in white hands. On the other side, as Justice Ngcobo noted in his opinion, are people such as 'Mrs Zondi, who belongs to a group of persons historically discriminated against by their government . . . which still affects their ability to protect themselves under the laws of the new order'.[68] With respect to the question of notice, the Court noted that the statute did not even require anyone to tell the livestock owner of the impending sale and Justice Ngcobo pointed out that even a general public notice in government publications or newspapers is likely to be insufficient 'where a large portion of the population . . . is illiterate and otherwise socially disadvantaged. Mrs Zondi is indeed illiterate. The thumbprint mark she affixed to her founding affidavit bears testimony to this'.[69] Furthermore, the statute permitted the landowner to 'bypass the courts and recover damages through an execution process carried out by a private businessperson or an official of a municipality without any court intervention'.[70] Holding the statutory scheme unconstitutional, among other reasons because its effect is to limit the right of access to the court's, Justice Ngcobo noted that the scheme removes 'from the court's scrutiny one of the sharpest and most divisive conflicts of our society. The problem of cattle trespassing on farm land . . is not merely the ordinary agrarian irritation it must be in many societies. It is a constant and bitter reminder of the process of colonial dispossession and exclusion'.[71]

[68] Zondi para 51.
[69] Ibid.
[70] Zondi para 75.
[71] Zondi para 76.

ENFORCING RIGHTS, REMEDIES AND JUDICIAL AUTHORITY

While the Constitutional Court has been held in high regard and the government has repeatedly acknowledged its authority and accepted its decisions,[72] a period of heightening political tensions has seen the law increasingly used as a weapon in internecine conflict among government officials and within political parties. Along with this atmosphere of legal conflict has come increasing tension over the work of the judiciary, individual judges, and the process of judicial appointments itself. While the Ministry of Justice has proposed statutory reforms and constitutional amendments designed to improve the functioning of the courts and the administration of justice, these have raised fears that government is undermining the independence of the judiciary. Even as the government was forced to withdraw some of these proposals, the Judicial Service Commission publically acknowledged that it was unable to attract sufficient numbers of highly qualified individuals, acceptable to the members of the JSC, as candidates for judicial appointment. It is in this context then that the courts, and the Constitutional Court in particular, are having to confront a growing concern at the failure of government officials to effectively implement court orders requiring public officials to resolve systemic problems of public administration and corruption, especially at the local level.

The failure of government to effectively protect the rights: of welfare recipients;[73] property owners;[74] indigenous land-claiming communities;[75] women in the context of intestate succession in indigenous law;[76] or to adequately protect newborns against the mother-to-child transmission of HIV;[77] or to recognize the marital rights of same-sex couples,[78] have all led to extraordinary decisions by the courts and created intense debates about the types of remedies the courts should provide.[79] Although there has been a constant clamoring for bolder judicial action – demands that the courts award mandatory relief and retain supervisory jurisdiction –

---

[72] See, *Minister of Health v Treatment Action Campaign* (No 2), 2002 (5) SA 721 (CC), in which the Court stated that, "The government has always respected and executed orders of this Court. There is no reason to believe that it will not do so in the present case," para 129.
[73] *Khosa v Minister of Social Development* 2004 (6) SA 505 (CC).
[74] *President of the Republic of South Africa v Modderklip Boerdery (Pty) Ltd*, 2005 (5) SA 3 (CC).
[75] *Alexkor Ltd v The Richtersveld Community*, 2004 (5) SA 460 (CC).
[76] *Bhe et al v Magistrate, Khayelitsha et al*, 2005 (1) SA 563 (CC).
[77] *Minister of Health v Treatment Action Campaign* (2), 2002 (5) SA 721 (CC).
[78] *Minister of Home Affairs and Another v Fourie et. al.*, 2006 (1) SA 524 (CC).
[79] See, Roach, K and Budlender, G 'Mandatory Relief and Supervisory Jurisdiction: When is it appropriate, Just and Equitable?' 122 (2) *South African Law Journal* 325.

the Constitutional Court in particular has been very careful to frame its orders in ways that encourage compliance but also attempt to bring the democratic organs of government into the decision-making process. While the Court has asserted its right to provide appropriate relief, including mandatory orders and structural relief, it has also used its ability to suspend declarations of invalidity so as to give the legislature or executive the time and the flexibility to formulate constitutional alternatives.[80] In this way the Court has effectively engaged in a 'dialogue' with the other branches of the government in its attempt to both assert its power but also preserve and protect its own institutional authority against potential popular and political backlashes.

CONCLUSION

The creation and legitimation of a Constitutional Court in South Africa provided a unique institutional site within which the process of mediation between alternative constitutional imaginations could be sustained. It created the possibility that the judiciary in its role as primary interpreter of the Constitution would be able to sustain and civilize the tensions inherent in the repeated referral and contestation of political differences in the post-apartheid era. However, there has been growing concern among non-government organizations and human rights bodies that the social crisis in the country — including the continuing disparities in wealth and its racial character as well as the levels of violence and criminal activity – may put pressure on government to sidestep and hence erode some of the exemplary human rights gains of the democratic transition. In this sense, debates over the funding of the independent constitutional institutions such as the Independent Electoral Commission, the Human Rights Commission and the Commission on Gender Equality – constitutionally mandated bodies designed to protect and further democracy – have focussed on the relationship between their fiscal dependence and a potential threat to their autonomy from the ruling party and government. Those concerned with the autonomy of these institutions have expressed their concerns in terms of both the continuing need to implement the Constitution's human rights guarantees as well as a broader concern about the future of democracy itself. Others, including most notably the ruling ANC, argue that it is the very socio-economic disparities and their continuing racial character that need to be addressed if the future of democracy and human rights are to be secured.

[80]   Id.

While the Constitutional Court has played a distinct role in enabling the democratic transition in South Africa, the conditions of its emergence as well as the strategies of the justices have enabled the institution to play a number of other roles, from promoter and symbol of a transformed justice to the more traditional role of conflict resolution and absorber or deflector of intense inter-regional political conflict. While the initial conditions of its creation and the caliber of its justices enabled the Court to build significant legitimacy among a range of constituencies, from the bar to government officials and the ruling party, the changing conditions of the country have begun to reshape the terrain upon which the Court functions. At first it was the persistence of inequality and the tragic HIV/AIDS pandemic that saw the court increasingly confront the government and more recently it has been the political struggle within the ruling party that has created a political vortex into which an increasing array of constitutional and public institutions, from the Public Protector to the National Prosecuting Authority and its investigative arm, the Directorate of Special Operations (Scorpions) have been sucked. While their dominant motivations in the past may have been to enhance the power and legitimacy of the institution, today the justices of the Constitutional Court are themselves, as a body, defending their own integrity in publically announcing a complaint of interference against a senior Judge of the High Court who is publically aligned with Jacob Zuma, the presumptive future President of South Africa.

While South Africa's experiment in constitutionalism is very young, the conditions which gave rise to the new constitutional order as well as the continuing problems of a post-colonial society, facing the dual challenges of extreme inequality and a devastating HIV/AIDS pandemic, has brought domestic tension as well as global interest to the work of the Constitutional Court. Caught in the cross-hairs of struggles for the realization of the extensive promise of rights entrenched in the Constitution and the limitations of governmental capacity and resources, the Court has thus far treaded a careful path, avoiding the easy declaration of rights yet continuing to question government failings. At the same time, the courts themselves are undergoing transformation and tensions over this process continue to simmer within the courts and between the courts, government and the legal profession.[81] The challenge facing the Court, as its composition changes and it becomes increasingly part of a 'normal society' will be whether it is able to continue to strike a balance between the need to address the legacy of

---

81   See, 'National Judges Symposium,' *The South African Law Journal*, Vol. 120(4) pp. 647-718, 2003. This is a report, including many of the speeches given, to the first plenary meeting of South African judges in seventy years and took place against a background of public controversy between senior judges and politicians.

apartheid, including the historic exclusion of the indigenous legal systems, and continue to uphold the claims of individual freedom and dignity which have become the hallmark of its first decade and a half.

ASIA

Constitutional Courts in East Asia: Understanding Variation

TOM GINSBURG *

After decades of authoritarian rule, East Asia has experienced a wave of democratization since the mid-1980s. Transitions toward more open political structures have been effectuated in South Korea, Taiwan, Thailand, Mongolia and Indonesia, and even the Leninist states of China and Vietnam have experienced tentative moves toward more participatory politics.[1] These political transitions have been accompanied by an important but understudied phenomenon: the emergence of powerful constitutional courts in the region. In at least four countries, Indonesia, Thailand, South Korea and Mongolia, constitutional courts created during the democratic transition have emerged as real constraints on political authority. A fifth court, the Council of Grand Justices in Taiwan, re-awakened after years of relative quiet to play an important role in Taiwan's long political transition to democracy.

Given the cultural and political history of the region, this is a phenomenon that might be seen as surprising. After all, most political systems in the region had until the 1980s were dominated by powerful executives without effective judicial constraint. The political systems of non-Communist Asia involved varying degrees of "authoritarian pluralism," wherein a certain degree of political openness was allowed to the extent it did not challenge authoritarian rule.[2] Thus there was little precedent for active courts protecting rights or interfering with state action.

Furthermore, traditional perspectives on Asian governance, resuscitated by proponents of "Asian values," have tended to view political culture in

* University of Chicago Law School
1 Balme S and Sidel, M (eds) (2007) *Vietnam's New Order*, Palgrave Macmillan.
2 Scalapino, R (1997) 'A Tale of Three Systems' 8(3) *Journal of Democracy* 150.

East Asia as emphasizing responsibilities over rights and social order over individual autonomy.[3] Both Buddhist and Confucian religious traditions emphasize the ideal of concentrating power in a single righteous ruler (the Buddhist *dhammaraja* or the Emperor enjoying the Mandate of Heaven) rather than establishing multiple seats of competing power and authority as a means of effective governance.[4] These traditional images of a single righteous leader have been exploited by rulers in the region, from Ho Chi Minh to Chiang Ching-kuo, usually to justify and perpetuate authoritarian rule.

Although the extent of the new constitutional constraint varies across countries and issue areas, it seems apparent that the phenomenon is real and lasting. It is appropriate, even at this early juncture, to take stock of the phenomenon from a comparative perspective to determine what factors might explain the emergence of and success of constitutional review in East Asia. This paper focuses on four courts: the Constitutional Courts of Thailand, South Korea, Mongolia and the Council of Grand Justices on Taiwan.[5] We briefly describe the emergence of each court. We then analyze institutional design and court performance in comparative perspective. Finally we consider several possible factors that might help explain the emergence of effective constitutional constraint by courts. It is hoped that this exercise, consistently with the purpose of this book, might help contribute to the development of broader comparative theories to understand judicial review and its role in democratization.

THE EMERGENCE OF CONSTITUTIONALISM IN ASIA

Traditional Asian political thought provides few resources for developing an indigenous theory of judicial review of legislation.[6] Most East Asian societies had some influence from the imperial Chinese tradition, in which

3   Jacobsen, M (2000) *Human Rights and Asian Values,* RoutledgeCurzon; Mahbubani, K (2002) *Can Asians Think?* Steerforth Press; Davis, M (1998) 'The Price of Rights: Constitutionalism and East Asian Economic Development' 20 *Human Rights Quarterly* 303; Bell, DA (2000) *East Meets West: Human Rights and Democracy in Asia,* Princeton University Press; Bauer, JR and Bell, DA (eds) (1998) *The East Asian Challenge for Human Rights,* Cambridge University Press.
4   The situation is of course a bit more complicated than this characterization would suggest. In classical Confucianism, particularly as manifested in Korea rather than post-Ming China, advisors to the emperor exercised significant authority and can be seen as a competing power center. See Palais, J (1975) *Politics and Policy in Traditional Korea* Harvard University Press. In classical Buddhist thought, the wheel of power was also to be constrained by the wheel of *dharma,* so the *sangha* might serve as an alternative power center to state authority.
5   Indonesia and Thailand are compared in the article by Harding and Leyland in this issue.
6   Ginsburg, T (2002) 'Confucian Constitutionalism? The Emergence of Judicial Review in Korea and Taiwan' 27(4) *Law and Social Inquiry* 763; Ginsburg, T (2003) *Judicial Review in New Democracies: Constitutional Courts in Asian Cases* Cambridge University Press.

judicial and executive functions were not separated and all power emanated from a single figure at the center of the political system. Even in systems where power and authority were separated, as in Japan, the notion of an *independent* constraint on power was absent in traditional politics.

The strong history of centralized political authority throughout the region has continued in the twentieth century, and many have connected Asian authoritarianism with more general notions of political culture, arguing that there was a strong resonance between classical political traditions and the modern systems of one party, or one-and-a-half party, a form of governance that was remarkably consistent from Japan to Indonesia.[7] In South Korea, a series of military-authoritarian regimes governed, with one brief interlude in 1961, from the end of Japanese colonialism through 1987. In Taiwan, the Kuomintang (KMT) relied on traditional Chinese notions of government as modified by Sun Yat-sen's political thought to legitimize a quasi-Leninist authoritarian party regime. Thailand experienced a cycle of alternating periods of corrupt civilian and military government. Mongolia had a governmental structure parallel to that of the Soviet Union, headed by a classically Leninist party. In all four countries, a meritocratically selected state apparatus provided continuity and exercised much influence, though of course the precise extent of that influence in the capitalist economies is an issue subject to intense controversy.[8]

Judicial review in East Asia was similarly constrained, even though it formally existed in many systems. Only the Philippine Supreme Court can be seen as exercising review with regularity. The Japanese Supreme Court has been constrained by the long rule of the Liberal Democratic Party and has issued only eight decisions on unconstitutionality of legislation.[9] In other countries, including Malaysia, Korea and Taiwan, judicial efforts to constrain the state were met with harsh attacks on the courts.

Beginning in the 1980s and accelerating in the 1990s, a global wave of democratization and political liberalization led to significant changes in East Asia and beyond. In many countries, this was accompanied by a shift away from traditional notions of parliamentary sovereignty toward the idea

[7]   Pye, L (1995) *Asian Power and Politics: the Cultural Dimensions of Authority* Harvard University Press.
[8]   Gownder, JP and Pekkanen, R (1996) 'The End of Political Science? Rational Choice Analyses in Studies of Japanese Politics' 22 *Journal of Japanese Studies* 363; Johnson, C (1982) *MITI and the Japanese Miracle* Stanford University Press; Rosenbluth, F (1989) *Financial Politics in Contemporary Japan* Columbia University Press; Kernell, S (ed.) (1991) *Parallel Politics: Economic Policymaking in Japan and the United States* Brookings Institution.
[9]   Ramseyer, JM and Rasmusen, EB (2003). *Measuring Judicial Independence* University of Chicago Press; Beer, L and Maki J (2000) *The Constitutional Case Law of Japan* University of Washington Press.

of constitutional constraint by expert courts. The causes were complex, and the pressures were global in character. The next section describes the constitutional courts under consideration in more detail.

Taiwan

Taiwan continues to be governed under an amended version of the 1947 Constitution of the Republic of China (ROC) adopted in Nanjing. This Constitution, which nominally governed all of China, was emasculated for many years through the use of so-called "Temporary Provisions" that legitimated one-party government by the KMT. Democratic transition in Taiwan began in earnest only in the mid-1980s, when President Chiang Ching-kuo announced reforms and tolerated the creation of the opposition Democratic Progressive Party (DPP). After Chiang's death, Taiwan-born President Lee Teng-hui presided over a long and complex democratic transition, culminating in the election of DPP leader Chen Shui-bian as President in 2001.

The power of judicial review formally existed throughout this period, to be exercised by the Council of Grand Justices of the Judicial Yuan. Under the 1947 Constitution, the Council was composed of seventeen members who were appointed by the President with approval of the Control Yuan (a separate branch of Government) for renewable nine-year terms.[10] Constitutional amendments have lowered the number of Grand Justices to fifteen, shortened the terms to eight years, transferred approval power to the legislature, and provided for staggered appointments that coincide with the four-year presidential election cycle.[11] These amendments also assigned the power to declare political parties unconstitutional to the Council of Grand Justices, removing regulation of parties from the executive branch. The Council's primary functions are to issue uniform interpretations of law and to interpret the Constitution upon request from litigants or government agencies.[12]

After some early efforts to constrain the exercise of political power by government, the Grand Justices were punished by the legislature in the late 1950s. The legislature raised the voting threshold to issue constitutional

---

[10]   Although Article 81 of the Constitution grants 'judges' life tenure, the Grand Justices are not considered to fall into that category.

[11]   Additional Articles of the Constitution of the Republic of China, Article 5. The Article also provides that the Judicial Yuan's draft budget may not be eliminated or reduced by the Executive Yuan in their submission of the budget to the Legislative Yuan.

[12]   Under the 1947 Constitution there are five branches of government (yuan), three corresponding to the Montesquieuan framework and two drawn from the Chinese imperial tradition, the Control Yuan for audit and the Examination Yuan for entry into the civil service.

interpretations and restricted interpretations to the constitutional text. From then until the recent liberalization, the Justices were cautious. Indeed, in the early era, the Council can be seen as an instrument of the KMT regime. It never accepted a case on the (dubious) constitutionality of the Temporary Provisions, which were the basis of authoritarian rule. The Temporary Provisions suspended the two-term limitation for the presidency and allowed the president to govern through decree powers without legislative approval.[13] The Council declined to hear challenges to these Provisions, and issued a number of decisions that facilitated KMT rule within the confines of at least nominal constitutionalism. Most prominently, it issued a decision suspending elections to the National Assembly during the "national emergency", so that representatives elected on the mainland in 1948 to represent all of China continued to serve in power for several decades.

After the election of Lee Teng-hui in 1987, however, the Council gradually became more active.[14] It began to strike administrative actions that were vague or delegated too much power to the executive branch. In 1990, the Council was called on to rule on the constitutionality of the continued sitting in the National Assembly of members elected on the mainland in 1948. These members had become a major obstacle to reform since the Assembly was the body solely responsible for constitutional amendment. The Assembly thus had an effective veto over efforts to abolish it, as well as to undertake other institutional reforms desired by the reformers.

Council Interpretation No. 261, announced on June 21, 1990, called for new elections and forced the retirement of the decrepit old guard of the KMT. This was undoubtedly the most important case in the history of the Council of Grand Justices and removed the last legal barrier to rapid institutional reform in Taiwan. Without this decision of the Grand Justices, the democratization process would have remained at a standstill, with the possible consequence that then-President Lee Teng-hui would never have cultivated his strong position within the KMT, and reform would have been delayed indefinitely. Following the decision, several stages of constitutional amendments transformed the governmental structure of Taiwan to be more effective, only nominally retaining the fiction of governing all China.

---

[13] 'Temporary Provisions Effective During the Period of Communist Rebellion'. These were adopted in 1948 at the first meeting of the First National Assembly in Nanjing, and came into effect on May 10 of that year. For a discussion of the constitutionality of the Temporary Provisions, see Mendel, FF (1993) 'Judicial Power and Illusion: The Republic of China's Council of Grand Justices and Constitutional Interpretation' *Pacific Rim Law and Policy Journal* 2: 157-89.

[14] See generally Ginsburg (2003), supra note 6, at ch. 5.

After appointment of a new set of Grand Justices in 1994, the Council became more active in striking legislation and constraining executive authority. Many of the new Justices were Taiwan-born and thus more likely to share Lee Teng-hui's vision of an independent Taiwan. They systematically dismantled the quasi-Leninist system of KMT control, for example by ending the ban on rallies advocating secessionism or communism as a violation of free speech; allowing universities to refuse to allow military "counselors," whose presence in dorms had formerly been mandatory; and allowing teachers to form a union outside the "official" union structure.

The Council has also played a major role in introducing international norms of criminal procedure into Taiwan, forcing a complete revision of the Criminal Procedure Code. It struck provisions of an anti-hooligan law that had reduced procedural protections for those designated by police as hooligans, and when the legislature modified the statute in question, the court demanded further revisions. It has also constrained both police and prosecutors in significant ways.

The Council has been involved in political controversies as well. After the election of the DPP's Chen Shui-bian as President in 2001, the Council embarrassed his government by preventing it from halting construction of a major nuclear power plant. It also was thrust in the center of political controversy when President Lee Teng-hui sought to retain Vice-President Lien Chan as "acting prime minister" after the 1997 presidential election. The legislature had protested this as a violation of the Constitution. Although the Constitution does not clearly state that the Vice-President cannot serve as Prime Minister, the Council found that this was not consistent with the spirit of the Constitution. It thus allowed Lien to retain office, though a few months later his government was removed for political reasons.

Constitutional amendments in 1992 provided for the Council of Grand Justices to hear (sitting as a Constitutional Court) challenges against "unconstitutional" political parties, defined as those whose "goals or activities jeopardize the existence of the ROC or a free democratic constitutional order." These clauses were thinly targeted at the Democratic Progressive Party (DPP), particularly its pro-independence factions that would eliminate the ROC and declare a new state of Taiwan which would no longer claim to be the titular government of all of China. The transfer of the power of regulating political parties to the Grand Justices reflects continuing German influence in Taiwan's constitutional law,[15] and was seen

---

[15] Under the German Basic Law, the Constitutional Court also has the power to disband political parties that 'seek to impair or abolish the free democratic basic order'. Basic Law, Article 21. Kommers, D (1997) *The Constitutional Jurisprudence of the Federal Republic of*

as progressive in that it took the determination of party unconstitutionality away from an Executive Yuan "Political Party Screening Committee," which had the previous January agreed to punish the DPP for its pro-independence plank. Giving this power to the Council is an important step in the Taiwan context.

The Council has thus been active in using the power of judicial review to strike legislation and administrative action. It has served as an *instrument* of democratization, both by giving life to the constitutional text and elaborating on the text in accordance with the constitutional spirit and international norms. It has also become involved in major controversies of a political character, though it has thus far avoided any major attacks on its powers. It is an exemplar of the role a constitutional court can play in facilitating democratization.

South Korea

South Korea's last military regime, headed by Chun Doo-hwan, took power in a coup in 1979. In part because of a massacre of hundreds of non-violent protestors at Kwangju in May 1980,[16] the government enjoyed little legitimacy, and opposition politicians demanded that the regime allow direct elections and liberalization. The Korean democratization process began in earnest in 1986, when widespread demonstrations involving the middle class led military dictator Chun Doo-hwan to resign the Presidency. His successor, former general Roh Tae-woo, gave in to opposition demands for a directly elected presidency and oversaw a process of political negotiation that produced the 1987 Constitution.

One of the central features of this Constitution was the design of a new Constitutional Court, roughly along the lines of the German model. The Court is composed of 9 members who serve renewable six-year terms, with 3 members each nominated by the President, National Assembly and Supreme Court. I characterize this appointment method as "representative" because each institution has the ability to pick its nominees unimpeded. The Court has the power to consider the constitutionality of legislation or administrative action at the request of political bodies or a court, can resolve competence disputes among governmental institutions, and can respond to constitutional complaints from citizens if fundamental rights have been abused by government action or omission, or if an ordinary court fails to refer a constitutional question to the Constitutional Court.

Germany (2d ed) Duke University Press, at 223-29.
[16] The precise facts of the incident are hotly disputed, including the number of dead, estimates of which range between the official figure of 191 up to 2000.

Although earlier Korean Republics had formal provisions for judicial review, oscillating between centralized and decentralized models, judicial review in Korea had never effectively served to constrain the state. In the early 1960s, a Supreme Court decision striking a legislative act upset President Park Chung-hee, who shortly afterwards moved to concentrate his authority in the so-called Yushin Constitution of 1972. After these reforms, Park fired all the judges who had voted against his position in the earlier case. Constitutional review power under the Yushin Constitution was centralized in a Constitutional Council that remained dormant. It is thus not surprising that most observers of the 1987 constitutional reforms did not expect the Korean Constitutional Court to play a major role in the society.[17]

However, the Court has surprised these observers by regularly overturning legislation and administrative action.[18] Indeed, in its very first case, it struck as a violation of the equality principle of the Constitution a law providing that held that the State could not be subject to preliminary attachment orders in civil cases. The Court insisted that equality under the law requires treating the state no differently than a private citizen or corporation. In doing so it challenged the philosophical underpinnings of the postwar Korean political economy, wherein the state played a major role in directing private economic activity.

One sign of the Court's boldness has been its willingness to create new rights by reading the text of the constitutional document quite broadly. For example, in 1989 the Court found an implied 'right to know' based on several clauses of the Constitution, echoing Japanese constitutional case law. It subsequently strengthened that provision by referring to the Universal Declaration of Human Rights. In 1991, the Constitutional Court read Article 10 of the Korean Constitution, which grants citizens a right to pursue happiness, to encompass a right to freedom of contract.[19] Again, this is fairly radical in the formerly *dirigiste* Korean context.

The Court has also been involved in sensitive political issues. For example, it was drawn into efforts to achieve retroactive justice for the bloody Kwangju incident of the Chun regime. Many believe that President Kim Young-sam, who in 1992 became the first civilian to assume the Presidency, had agreed not to pursue claims against his predecessors,

---

[17] Ginsburg, supra note 6, at ch. 7.

[18] West, J and Yoon, DK (1992) 'The Constitutional Court of the Republic of Korea: Transforming the Jurisprudence of the Vortex' 40 *American Journal of Comparative Law* 73; Yang, K (1993) 'Judicial Review and Social Change in the Korean Democratizing Process' 41 *American Journal of Comparative Law* 1; Ahn, KW (1998) 'The Influence of American Constitutionalism on South Korea' 27 *Southern Illinois Law Journal* 71.

[19] Ahn, ibid.

the Generals Roh Tae-woo and Chun Doo-hwan, as part of the deal that allowed Kim to take power and democratization to proceed. Early in Kim's term, prosecutors had investigated the two generals and dropped all charges related to treason during the 1979 coup or the deaths in the 1980 incident at Kwangju. Later, however, responding to public pressure and seeking to deflect allegations of corruption, Kim changed his mind. The Constitutional Court was asked to rule on the constitutionality of special legislation, passed at Kim's instigation, to facilitate prosecution even after the normal period of statutory limitations had expired. In a carefully worded decision, the Court found that the legislation had been passed after the expiry of the period of statutory limitations for the 1979 coup, but that prosecutions for the Kwangju incident could proceed. The Court's analysis highlighted Kim Young-sam's failure to take action against Chun and Roh early in his Presidency when the statute of limitations would not have been an issue. Ultimately, both men were found guilty, and subsequently pardoned at the instigation of President-elect Kim Dae-jung in December 1997.

The Court has been especially important in dealing with the legacies of the authoritarian regime, particularly the National Security Act (NSA) and the Anti-Communist Act. These laws were used to suppress independent political organizations by providing draconian sanctions against dissenters and loosely-defined illegal associations. The laws were therefore a target of human rights activists and regime opponents. The statutes operated by carving out exceptions to normal requirements of criminal procedure. For example, Article 19 of the NSA allowed longer pre-trial detention for those accused of particular crimes, and this was struck by the Constitutional Court in 1992 as a violation of the right to a speedy trial. The Court also found that a clause criminalizing anyone who "praises, encourages, or sympathizes with the activities of an anti-state organization or its members, or . . . by any means whatever benefits an anti-state organization" to be vague and overbroad, and to threaten constitutional guarantees of freedom of the press and speech, freedom of academic study, and freedom of conscience. The Court did not strike the NSA, but rather sought to limit and channel its application to constitutional purposes.

Perhaps the greatest political controversy the Court has had to deal with was the impeachment of President Roh Moo-hyun, an activist labor lawyer who took office in 2003 with a reformist agenda.[20] Roh faced a hostile National Assembly, and was soon beset by a split in his party and

---

[20] See generally Lee, YJ (2005) 'Law, Politics, and Impeachment: The Impeachment of Roh Moo-Hyun from a Comparative Constitutional Perspective' 53 *American Journal of Comparative Law* 403.

a corruption scandal related to campaign contributions that erupted in October. Roh staked his future on a mid-term legislative election, but—in violation of South Korean law—appeared to campaign for his own party by urging voters to support it. The majority in the National Assembly responded with a motion for impeachment which passed by the necessary 2/3 vote.

Under Korean law, Roh was suspended from office and the Prime Minister assumed the duties of the President. The case was then sent to the Constitutional Court for confirmation, as required under the Constitution. During the deliberations of the case, however, the mid-term election was held and Roh's party received overwhelming support, winning an absolute majority in the Assembly.

Perhaps responding to the public's preferences, the Constitutional Court rejected the impeachment motion one month later. In addressing the issue, the Court bifurcated the issue into the question of whether there was a "violation of the Constitution or other Acts," the predicate for impeachment, and whether those violations were severe enough to warrant removal. Although the Court found that Roh had violated the election law provisions that public officials remain neutral, along with other provisions of law, it decided that it would not be proportional to remove the President for the violation. Instead, the Court asserted that removal is only appropriate when the "free and democratic basic order" is threatened. Roh's violations were not a premeditated attempt to undermine constitutional democracy. The Court further rejected some of the charges, namely those concerned with campaign contributions that took place before he took office.

In short, the Korean Constitutional Court has been playing a significant role in Korean politics and society. It has become an important site of political contestation, as interest groups have begun seeking to use the Court to achieve social change. The Court frequently strikes legislative action and also regularly overturns prosecutorial decisions, particularly important given the central role of prosecutors in the authoritarian period. At the same time, the Court has trod on careful ground in those cases likely to lead to political backlash, as in the impeachment case and in its handling of the National Security Act. At the time of this writing, the Constitutional Court is the most popular government institution in Korean society.[21]

---

[21] JoongAng Daily, July 3, 2007, available at http://joongangdaily.joins.com/article/view.asp?aid=2877553

Thailand

The Thai Constitutional Court was established with the 1997 Constitution. This emerged as part of a dramatic transition to democracy designed to break the cycle of coups and political corruption that had plagued Thailand's history since the end of the absolute monarchy in 1932. Depending on how one counts, Thailand had experienced between 17 and 19 coups, and had 16 different Constitutions during this period.[22] However, a coup in 1992 had provoked the ire of the middle class when protests were violently suppressed. Pressure grew for the renewal of democracy, accelerating after the King intervened to castigate the coup leaders. Ultimately the citizens' movement prevailed. The result was the so-called "people's constitution," adopted after widespread public input and debate. It was the first ever of Thailand's constitutions to include such input from the public.

Faced with the history of instability, and with an endemic form of electoral corruption that had made civilian rule as ineffective as the military was illegitimate, the drafters of the Thai Constitution focused on limiting governmental power. Academics played an important role in the drafting process, as the drafting commission was led by Chulalongkorn University Law Professor Bovornsak Uwanno. The Constitution emerged as a kind of mega-constitution, with 336 articles covering over 100 pages of text. In part this reflected the desire to specify rights in detail so as to avoid the possibility of mis-interpretation.

The Constitution had a number of radical features designed to increase participation and accountability. First, it tried to decentralize power to the hitherto moribund local governments. Second, it established extensive administrative rights to information, to sue the government and receive reasons for adverse decisions by government. It introduced elections for the upper body of parliament, the Senate, and made it into a non-partisan body. It also created several new institutions to enhance participation and human rights protection. Two powerful new independent bodies were set up to improve the political process, an Election Commission and a National Counter-Corruption Commission (NCCC). The former was designed to minimize the chronic problem of vote-buying; it had the power to monitor elections, ban candidates and political parties, and order a re-run of any election it deemed to have been fraudulent.[23] The NCCC collected reports on assets from politicians and senior bureaucrats to ensure that there were no mysterious increases during the time they were in public service. Those

---

[22] See the article by Harding and Leyland in this issue.
[23] In the first Senate election in 2000, the Election Commission threw out 78 out of 200 election results because of fraud.

who failed to report assets could be barred from office, subject to approval from the new Constitutional Court.

The new Constitutional Court was one of the key institutions designed to enhance legality and check a Parliament traditionally seen as a hotbed of corruption and special interest. It was to be a permanent body with 15 members appointed by the King upon advice of the Senate for nine year non-renewable terms. Members had to be forty years of age. In keeping with the need to secure various kinds of expertise in constitutional interpretation, the body included a variety of qualifications and appointment mechanisms. Cases could be referred to the Constitutional Court by ordinary courts in the course of litigation; the presidents of each house of Parliament; the Prime Minister; and other designated political bodies. As in Fifth Republic France, there was a provision for minority groups of legislators to submit legislation before promulgation by the King, but no power of direct petition from the public.

In addition, the Court exercised a wide array of ancillary powers. Besides the power to confirm findings of and evaluate disclosures submitted to the Election Commission and NCCC described above, the Court could, *inter alia*: review whether any appropriations bill would lead to involvement of an elected official in the expenditure of funds (Section 180); determine whether an Emergency Decree is made in a real emergency (Section 219); determine whether Election Commissioners should be disqualified (Section 142); and decide whether political party regulations violate the Constitution or fundamental principles of Thai governance (Section 47). Because of the overarching concern with corruption that animated the 1997 Constitution, the Court had the power to demand documents or evidence to carry out its duties. In this sense it was a kind of inquisitorial Constitutional Court. The Court's early history was mostly uneventful but it quickly became embroiled in the politics surrounding billionaire populist Thaksin Shinawatra, who became Prime Minister in 2001.

Just before the election won by his Thai Rak Thai Party, Thaksin was found by the NCCC to have filed a false assets report. The Constitutional Court was called on the confirm the finding, and was put in a difficult position. In a divided decision that has been described as confused, the Court found that the false report hadn't been filed deliberately and allowed Thaksin to take the post of Prime Minister. Thus began a long chapter in which Thaksin used his money and influence to dominate Thai politics, undermining many of the guardian institutions that were supposed to protect the constitutional scheme.[24] The Court was tainted in some eyes for allowing Thaksin to take power, but on some occasions did constrain him. For example, it ruled that a couple of appointments, including those of Election Commissioner and the Auditor General, had not followed proper procedure.[25] Still, the general perception was that these offices did not function as they should have. Following widespread allegations of electoral corruption in 2006, the Constitutional Court found that a legal case against him was non-justiciable.[26]

Frustrated with political institutions, opposition forces took to the streets. Thaksin called a snap election for April 2006, but this was boycotted by the opposition, leading to a constitutional crisis when too few members of Parliament could be seated. At this point, on April 26, 2006, the King met with the leaders of the Constitutional, Supreme and Administrative Courts and publicly called for them to resolve the constitutional crisis, suggesting they should void the April election. The Constitutional Court responded by annulling the election, and three election commissioners were jailed, on the grounds that the time allowed for the election campaign had been too brief and that some polling booths had been positioned to allow others to view the ballots as they were cast. Five new election commissioners, who had just been chosen after months of deadlock, would be replaced. Nevertheless, with political institutions at a standstill, the appointment process could hardly operate. The Constitutional Court seemed to have failed to resolve the problem completely. This is a paradigm example of the politicization of the judiciary that is a risk for constitutions placing so much power in the hands of guardians.

Thaksin's domination of politics eventually provoked a reaction from the military and in September 2006, he was replaced in a coup. Pointedly, the Interim Constitution promulgated by the military disbanded the Constitutional Court, even though most of the other guardian institutions were allowed to continue operating. In August 2007, a new constitution was approved by referendum, and a new Constitutional Court established. The new Court is a nine-member body, serving a single nine-year term selected in simpler fashion by a selection committee.[27]

The Thai story is of a court that disappointed many of those who had high hopes in it, yet it is not fully clear exactly what the court could have done to resist the billionaire populist whose reach extended into virtually

---

[24] Leyland, P (2007) 'Thailand's Constitutional Watchdogs: Dobermans, Bloodhounds or Lapdogs?' 2(2) *Journal of Comparative Law* 151.
[25] Leyland, ibid. at 159.
[26] Leyland, ibid. at 168
[27] Constitution of Thailand 2007, sections 200, 202.

every institution in Thailand. If anything, the story cautions against expecting courts to be able to do too much, and to single-handedly save a democratic system from itself.

Mongolia

The world's second communist country, Mongolia was governed for many years as a *de facto* satellite of the Soviet Union. This changed only in 1989 when demonstrations led by intellectuals led the ruling Mongolian People's Revolutionary Party (MPRP) to revise the political system and allow for multi-party elections. After a brief period of transition, these reforms were crystallized in the 1992 Constitution.

The Constitutional Court (called the *Tsets* from the traditional word for a judge in Mongolian wrestling) was designed to supervise the Constitution. Although the drafters of the Constitution briefly considered the institution of American-style decentralized judicial review, the adoption of the Kelsenian centralized model was considered more compatible with Mongolia's civil law tradition. The Court had nine members, three selected by each of the President, the Parliament and the Supreme Court. Cases can be brought by ordinary citizens through constitutional petition, as well as referral by various political institutions.

In its early years, the Court's primary role was in resolving competence disputes between the powerful legislature and the directly elected President. The Court also responded to citizen complaints and issued a number of decisions overturning government actions that violated the constitutional text. However, the Court's own decision that the Constitution did not give it jurisdiction over ordinary court decisions meant that certain areas important for human rights protection, most notably criminal procedure, were outside its purview.[28]

The Court has been somewhat hampered by a peculiar institutional design that allowed the Parliament to reject initial findings of the Court. In the event the Parliament rejected the decision, the Court could hear the case again *en banc* and issue a final, binding decision by a two-thirds vote. This institutional design probably reflected residual socialist notions of parliamentary sovereignty, as well as a similar scheme that existed in the Polish Constitution before amendments in 1997. Although the Mongolian Court's early decisions were accepted by the Parliament, the election of an overwhelming majority of MPRP to the Parliament in 1998 meant that the party had the easy ability to reject Court decisions as a matter of course.

---

[28] Ginsburg, supra note 6, at ch. 6.

This situation was exacerbated by a particular series of poorly considered decisions by the Court on the shape of the political system.[29] Following the first election victory of the opposition coalition in 1996, the Court decided that a constitutional clause that said "members of parliament shall have no other employment" prevented the Government from forming the cabinet out of sitting parliament members. This question went to the core of the nature of the political system: was it a parliamentary system or a presidential one? The case produced a series of institutional conflicts between the parliament and the Court. After the Court rejected legislation passed to allow the government to be formed out of parliament as unconstitutional, the parliament passed a series of constitutional amendments designed to remedy the defect. These amendments were themselves rejected by the Court as unconstitutional. The crisis was only resolved some five years later in 2001, when the Court finally backed down and allowed a second round of constitutional amendments to go forward. The story of the Mongolian Court is thus one of poor decision-making that squandered institutional capital that had been built up in the very first years of the institution.

Summary

These four cases illustrate a range of environments in which constitutional courts operate. They include former communist regimes and former military regimes. They range geographically and culturally. But all four courts are playing an important role in political conflict, and with the somewhat strange exception of Mongolia, have by and large helped to resolve these conflicts effectively. All the courts have played a role in underpinning and facilitating democratization. The next sections consider some comparative questions in light of these brief case studies.

UNDERSTANDING INSTITUTIONAL DESIGN

The four courts under consideration exhibit a range of features. Yet all four reflect the Kelsenian model of a centralized institution, paradigmatically embodied in the German Constitutional Court, rather than the American decentralized model in which any court can make a declaration of unconstitutionality. This choice of the continental model was made despite substantial American influence on the law and politics of Korea and Taiwan, and American advice into the Mongolian constitutional drafting process. In this sense, courts in Asia are reflecting the dominant role of the continental model in all legal systems except those subject directly

---

[29] Ginsburg, T and Ganzorig, G (2001) 'When Courts and Politics Collide: Mongolia's Constitutional Crisis' 14 *Columbia Journal of Asian Law* 309. See also Ginsburg, ibid.

or indirectly to British colonialism. In a global sense, only a very few courts without British or American colonial experience have adopted a decentralized model of judicial review.

The Table One on the next page summarizes several features of institutional design of the four courts.

While the prestige of the German model may explain the decision to centralize review in a single designated body, the details of institutional design are likely to reflect in large part the political configuration during the time of constitutional drafting. Thus the appointment mechanisms are most complex in Thailand, wherein drafters sought to insulate the justices from politics by setting up an intricate array of appointment mechanisms and committees. Although many American states and several countries use mixed committees to appoint ordinary judges, the Thai scheme is particularly byzantine and reflects the importance of various professional factions in the drafting process. In Taiwan, in contrast, the drafting of the constitutional text in 1947 reflected the dominance of Chiang Kai-shek in the KMT. The President plays the major role in appointing the Grand Justices, a desirable feature for a powerful figure certain to win the Presidency.

Mongolia and Korea utilize the Italian model of representative appointments by each of three political branches. This representative model may be desirable when parties are uncertain of their position in government after the constitution is adopted. Whereas Chiang Kai-shek knew he would be able to appoint the Grand Justices and was happy to keep the power centralized in the Presidency, situations of greater political uncertainty are likely to lead drafters to ensure wide representation on the court.[30] When each institution appoints a third of the members, no institution can dominate the court. Mongolia and Korea utilize the Italian model of representative appointments by each of three political branches. This representative model may be desirable when parties are uncertain of their position in government after the constitution is adopted. Whereas Chiang Kai-shek knew he would be able to appoint the Grand Justices and was happy to keep the power centralized in the Presidency, situations of greater political uncertainty are likely to lead drafters to ensure wide representation on the court.[31] When each institution appoints a third of the members, no institution can dominate the court.

---

[30] Ginsburg, (2003), supra note 6.
[31] Ginsburg, ibid.

Table 1 : Features of Institutional Design

	Thailand	Korea	Taiwan	Mongolia
date of establishment	1997-2006	1989	1947; as modified by constitutional amendments	1992
# members	15	9	15	9
How appointed	7 elected by top courts; 8 selected by a mixed commission as qualified in law and political science; confirmed by Senate	3 each from Court, President and National Assembly	By President with approval by the National Assembly	3 each from President, Parliament and Supreme Court
Term length in years	9	6	8	6
Terms renewable?	No	Yes	No	Yes
Constitutional petitions from public?	No	Yes	No	Yes
Abstract/concrete review	Both	Concrete	Abstract but includes referrals from ordinary courts	Both
Review of legislation ex post/ ex ante	Both	Ex post	Ex post	Ex post
Decisions final?	Yes	Yes	Yes	Initial decisions can be rejected by the legislature, but subsequently confirmed by *en banc* sitting of court
Important ancillary powers	Overseeing corruption and electoral commissions	Impeachment, dissolution of political party	Declare political parties unconstitutional	Impeachment, overseeing electoral commission

This dynamic is best illustrated in Korea, where the Constitution was drafted behind closed doors by three factions with roughly equal political support.[32] Situations of such uncertainty mean that each faction believes it is likely to be *out* of power. This may also give the drafters the incentive to include the power of constitutional petition by citizens. Constitutional petition guarantees that political losers will have access to the constitutional court in the event the winners trample their rights.

Another issue in constitutional court design is that of term length. It is usually suggested that longer terms are likely to lead to more independent adjudication. There seems to be a tradeoff in our four cases between short renewable terms (Korea and Mongolia) and longer non-renewable terms (Thailand and Taiwan). While this does not reflect any apparent political pattern, it is interesting that the shift to non-renewable terms in Taiwan only took place after democratization began in earnest; in the one-party period it may have been politically useful for the KMT to wield the threat of non-reappointment over the Grand Justices.

This illustrates that dominant party regimes may be in a better position to hinder strong review power in constitutional design. Strong parties that believe they are likely to control the legislature are likely to want weaker courts. In both Mongolia and Taiwan, strong party regimes built in controls over the court in the design process: in Mongolia through the anomalous institution of parliamentary approval of initial decisions by the court on constitutionality, and in Taiwan, through the centralized appointment mechanism. The more diffuse political environments of Thailand and Korea, wherein multiple political parties were competing for power, may have contributed to more powerful court design.

Other features of institutional design reflected political concerns associated with particular circumstances. Examples include the emphasis on anti-corruption and the mechanism of abstract pre-promulgation review of legislation in the Thai Constitutional Court design. These features both reflect the overarching distrust of partisan politics in Thailand. As the French experience has shown, abstract pre-promulgation review tends to lead to the insertion of the constitutional court into the legislative process.[33]

In short, institutional design of constitutional courts should be understood as reflecting a process of adapting foreign models with local

---

[32] Other institutions of the 1987 Constitution, including the single term Presidency, reflect the uncertainty that any one of these three factions would win the first election. The single term has allowed the presidency to be rotated by the three major political figures involved in the drafting—Roh Tae-woo, Kim Young-sam, and Kim Dae-jung.

[33] Stone, A (1992) *The Birth of Judicial Politics in France* Oxford University Press.

institutional needs. This account suggests that political considerations play an important role in understanding court design in Asia and elsewhere.

UNDERSTANDING COURT PERFORMANCE

What about the performance of these constitutional courts? What roles are they playing? While of course each court presents its own story in a distinct political social and cultural context, several broad themes emerge from the regional snapshots provided above.

First, constitutional courts have been useful in striking, one at a time, elements of the old system. They served as consolidators of democracy, rather than the bodies triggering the process. This function was particularly important in the relatively gradual transitions from authoritarian rule in Taiwan and Korea. In Thailand, the military regime was not systematically entrenched in the society, having been in power only a short time and reflecting the less pervasive character of the Thai state in controlling the ordinary lives of its citizens. The primary threat to democracy was seen to be the corrupt political process itself, and the constitutional text reflected that concern. In Mongolia, the Court played less of a rights-protecting role than in Korea and Taiwan; this may have been appropriate since the complete break with the past marked by the transition from socialism meant that by definition the old regime was less intact.

Second, ancillary powers of constitutional courts are important, though they have received relatively little scholarly attention in Asia and elsewhere. In Thailand, for example, cases involving constitutional review of legislation were not nearly as important as the Court's role in supervising the electoral process.[34] The most prominent case in Korea's constitutional history was an impeachment case—far from the exercise of judicial review as classically defined. Giving the Council of Grand Justices on Taiwan the ability to declare political parties unconstitutional marked a major step in ensuring that such declarations would be conceived of in legal rather than political terms, and reflected a shift toward the rule of law.

Third, all four of the constitutional courts have been involved in issues related to the composition of government. In Thailand, the high profile cases involving Prime Minister Thaksin are the best examples; in Taiwan and Korea the courts adjudicated interim appointments of the Prime Minister by a President in a split executive system, and the Korean impeachment also involved government composition in one sense. The Mongolian Constitutional Court was called on to determine the fundamental character

---

[34] Harding and Leyland's article in this issue.

of the political regime as parliamentary or presidential. In all these cases, the transfer of political struggle from the streets to the courtroom is a significant step. Regardless of the outcome, the fact that political forces have an alternative place to resolve core questions may facilitate democratic consolidation.

These types of disputes, however, place constitutional courts in difficult positions in that they are called on to wield expertise that they may not have, and may have to substitute for more democratic processes. One need only consider the reaction to the United States Supreme Court's system in *Bush v. Gore*[35] to understand the perils associated with these kinds of decisions. Arguably the Korean and Taiwanese courts took the best approach by ducking the issue and letting the political process decide the outcome. In Thailand, the Court could not avoid the issue, but in the end it took a similar approach by deferring to the democratic majority that had elected Thaksin despite reports of his failure to file a complete declaration of assets with the NCCC. In contrast, the Mongolian Court derailed the entire constitutional system by refusing to allow the newly elected majority to form a government of its choosing. This led to a severe conflict with the political branches and the depletion of the court's authority. The lesson then, is one of caution on core issues of the political process for courts in new democracies.

This leaves attention to fundamental rights and constraint of state authority as the real roles the courts can play. Here the Courts of Korea and Taiwan have been active in introducing international norms into new contexts, with both courts forcing significant reforms in criminal procedure. The Mongolian Court also played such a role, at least early in the post-socialist period. Given the less severe character of Thai criminal justice even under the military government, it is perhaps understandable that the court has not yet emerged as a major voice in this area.

This discussion has implicitly assumed that courts are strategic actors. Courts make choices as to what cases to hear and how to handle them. Because judicial behavior and motivation in general is so poorly understood, it is difficult to develop predictive conclusions about how courts will act in particular cases.[36] What we *can* conclude, however, is that variations in performance may also be affected by broader cultural, political and social factors. The next section considers some of these.

---

[35]   531 US 98 (2000).
[36]   Baum, L (1997) *The Puzzle of Judicial Behavior* University of Michigan Press.

EXPLAINING THE EMERGENCE OF
CONSTITUTIONAL REVIEW

What are the implications of this story for broader comparative understanding of the emergence of constitutional review? Because the adoption of constitutional review is intimately bound up in the broader phenomena of global political liberalization and expansion of judicial power, it implicates issues much larger than can be resolved here. However, we will use these four cases to draw some conclusions on factors that might be relevant to the conditions for the successful emergence of constitutional review.

Cultural traditions are sometimes seen to provide important supporting conditions for the exercise of legal authority. From this perspective, judicial review is the ultimate expression of a tradition of autonomous law associated with the modern West. The four environments considered here have no cultural tradition of autonomous law. The robust exercise of judicial power in all settings helps to confirm that cultural factors are not insurmountable obstacles to judicial review. We need not rehash the entire debate over "Asian values" except to note that, too often, those arguing for Asian exceptionalism reason backward from the existence of illiberal regimes to the values that allegedly support those regimes. At a minimum, we can conclude that the existence of non-Western values at one point in history is not an insurmountable barrier to the later emergence of constitutional constraints on politicians.

One factor that might be called cultural concerns the *receptivity* of the society to foreign ideas, a factor particularly important in an era of "globalization". All four examples considered here are drawn from small countries. Three of them have historically been subject to Western influence while a fourth, Mongolia, has recently turned to the West as a counterweight to Chinese and Russian influence. Such small countries may be particularly open to influence from the modern West because of their fear of cultural and political domination by more proximate large states. Judicial review from this point of view is one element of a package of modernizing reforms that are adopted because of their very western-ness, as part of a complex security strategy.

"Westernization" gives the West a stake in the society, and hence may deter the large neighbor from expansionism. Because all four of our case studies share this attribute of smallness, we cannot draw firm conclusions about the relevance of this factor for the adoption and development of judicial review. However, we can say that Western influence did not determine institutional form. For Taiwan and Korea, the United States provided a reference society that influenced institutional and systemic changes during the long authoritarian period. Yet neither country has adopted the decentralized system of judicial review. Institutional design appears to be an issue where local, not international, forces are determinative.

One might also expect that *prior history of judicial review* would provide an important source of support for constitutional judges in new democracies. After all, it is generally hypothesized that democratization has been easier in those countries where authoritarian regimes had displaced prior democracies. History, the argument runs, provides a source of inspiration as well as models of institutional design for new democracies.[37] In the Eastern European context, for example, the inter-war history of democracy in Czechoslovakia and Hungary are thought to support the more rapid democratization of those countries than the ambivalent cases of Rumania and Bulgaria.[38]

Yet prior experience can constrain as well as inspire. In particular, when an institution exists under authoritarianism, it may develop an institutional culture that favors restraint. Further, it is unlikely to be seen as legitimate in the very early years of democratization. In the case of Taiwan, the Grand Justices existed under the authoritarian regime, and this may have hindered rather than supported the emergence of a more activist conception of judicial review. The Council of Grand Justices in Taiwan was quite cautious in building up its power, treading very carefully, in part because its legacy complicated the task of identifying core constituencies. Even its most famous decision, forcing the retirement in 1990 of the legislators who had been elected on the mainland decades earlier , is perhaps best understood as siding with one ascendant faction of the KMT over another, and not truly about the constraint of power. The Korean and Mongolian Constitutional Courts, as new institutions, had a bit more freedom to operate. In Thailand, formal provision for the exercise of judicial review in earlier constitutions lay dormant. This suggests that prior history is neither a necessary nor sufficient condition for the successful functioning of a particular constitutional court.

Some scholars have attempted to tie the exercise of judicial power to the *type of previous regime,* with a peculiar threat posed by military authoritarians.[39] Our cases provide counter-evidence to the assertion that military authoritarian regimes hinder the development of judicial review. The Korean Constitutional Court has developed active judicial review in the shadow of a departing military-authoritarian regime. Thailand's 1997

---

[37] Elster, J, Offe, C and Preuss, UK (1998) *Institutional Design in Post-communist Societies* Cambridge University Press, at 60-61.
[38] Sadurski and Lach's article in this issue.
[39] Ackerman, B (1997) 'The Rise of World Constitutionalism' 83 *Virginia Law Review* 771-97.

Constitution, embodied in the Constitutional Court itself, was designed in part to secure the permanent removal of the military from politics. Taiwan's Council of Grand Justices has also systematically dismantled the military-Leninist system of control of civil society. It may be helpful that the only tool the military has to influence the court is to overturn the entire constitutional order, the political equivalent of a nuclear warhead; civilian political parties and institutions have more subtle ways of engaging with the court to communicate their preferences and to encourage judicial modesty. Paradoxically, this means military regimes may actually be associated with judicial autonomy—after all, both officers and judges see themselves as professionals insulated from the dirty politics of legislatures and parties.

The *pace of transition*, in particular the timing of constitutional reform, may affect the exercise of judicial review. In Korea, as well as Mongolia and Thailand, constitutional reform was accomplished quickly at the outset of the transition process (though other democratic reforms were gradual in Korea). This provided the courts with an identifiable constitutional moment to invoke. Where constitutional reform is a gradual process, as in Taiwan, the court must fear the real possibility of constitutional override of any unpopular decisions and therefore will likely be more cautious. Further research on other countries is necessary to evaluate this hypothesis, but our cases suggest that quick transition can support judicial review.

Ackerman (1997) has suggested that *strong presidencies* are helpful for the exercise of judicial review.[40] In this regard, one might add that the adoption of a French-style split executive creates a need for independent courts to arbitrate institutional disputes. Three of our countries have such split executive systems, while Thailand relies on a traditional parliamentary structure of government. Korea and Taiwan were both more strongly weighted toward presidential power than the weak semi-presidential system in Mongolia.

Probably more important is the type of party system. The party system is the crucial factor that determines how the institutions interact, not the mere fact of presidentialism. If a single dominant party exists and controls the legislature and executive, inter-institutional conflict is likely to be minimal. Where divided government holds, however, institutional conflicts will provide the court with a role to play and more policy space in which to render decisions. Split executive systems often produce divided government, and Korea and Taiwan, the two cases with arguably the most robust exercise of judicial review, both had periods of divided government in the 1990s. In Mongolia, the Court's challenge of an overwhelming

---

[40] Ackerman, B (1997) ibid.

parliamentary majority after 1998 put it into a battle it could not win; ultimately it had to capitulate.

Certain other variables may affect demand for judicial review by creating incentives for plaintiffs to bring cases to courts. In particular, a *vigorous civil society* provides interest groups that may seek to challenge government action in courts.[41] Furthermore, an *unrestricted legal profession* may create incentives for individual lawyers to act as entrepreneurs by pursuing constitutional litigation. These two demand-side variables would support plaintiffs' propensity to bring constitutional cases. Charles Epp has argued that these are necessary underpinnings for a "rights revolution."[42]

On both of these scores, Korea provides counterevidence to the hypothesis. In contrast with Taiwan and Mongolia, associational life has been limited in Korea.[43] While certain types of private associations exist, for the most part these are not focused on public-interest issues of the type that would lead to greater demand for judicial review. If anything, the presence of an increasingly active system of judicial review has encouraged the formation of new interest groups, suggesting that the causal relationship runs in the opposite direction. Similarly, Korea and to a lesser extent Taiwan have historically placed significant restrictions on the practice of law, limiting entry into the profession to a greater extent than Thailand. This should dampen demand for judicial review. But Korea's activist system of judicial review existed and thrived prior to recent efforts to liberalize the profession.

More broadly, however, the emergence of a *middle class*, seen to be so important in the broader process of democratization, may be a necessary condition for constitutional review to thrive. All four countries can be said to have vigorous middle classes that played an important role in demanding democratic reforms.[44] The presence of this broader middle class allows the court to have an alternative means of legitimation—the court can protect itself from attack by political institutions through building up a wellspring of popular support. Of course, such a move requires the court to take a particular strategy in choosing cases of most interest to the middle class and their rights-claims. The Mongolian Court notably declined to do this, and found itself without much public support when it became embroiled in conflicts with the parliament and government. In contrast, Korean and Taiwan societies have seen the development of some interest groups that

[41]   Voigt, S (1998) 'Making Constitutions Work – Conditions for Maintaining the Rule of Law', 18 Cato Journal 191.
[42]   Epp, CR (1998) *The Rights Revolution: Lawyers, Activists and Supreme Courts in Comparative Perspective* University of Chicago Press.
[43]   Koo, H (ed) (1993) *State and Society in Contemporary Korea* Cornell University Press.
[44]   Compton, RW (2000) *East Asian Democratization: Impact of Globalization, Culture and Economy* Praeger.

seek to advance their causes through litigation. Such groups by definition have a stake in the Court's continued independence and vitality.

Table Two summarizes some of the possible explanatory variables discussed here. The obvious conclusion is that constitutional courts can emerge and thrive in a variety of environments. Even the rather odd Mongolian case should not be generalized to other post-socialist contexts, for some such courts have been very effective at building up effective support and constraining their politicians. The Hungarian case is perhaps best known in this regard.

Table 2: Explanatory Variables

	Thailand	Korea	Taiwan	Mongolia
Confucian cultural tradition	No	Yes	Somewhat	No
colonialism	None	Japanese	Japanese	Russian
previous judicial review?	Minimal	Yes	Yes	No
previous democracy?	Yes	Yes	No	No
type of previous regime	Military	Military	Dominant Leninist party	Dominant Leninist party
type of transition	Quick	Quick	Gradual	Quick
governmental structure	Parliamentary	Semi-presidential	Semi-presidential	Semi-presidential
divided government?	No	Yes	Yes	No
middle class?	Yes	Yes	Yes	Yes*
capitalist economy?	Yes	Yes	Yes	No
History of authoritarian pluralism	Yes	Yes	Yes	No

CONCLUSION

In recent decades, judicial review has expanded around the globe from the United States, Western Europe, and Japan to become a regular feature of constitutional design in Africa and Asia. Constitutional courts have exercised review to challenge political authorities when conflicts arise among government institutions or governments impinge on individual rights. Although the formal power to exercise judicial review is now nearly universal in democratic states, courts have varied in the extent to which they are willing to exercise this power in practice.

The four courts described above all emerged as major political actors as part of the democratization process. We draw four main conclusions from this account of the Asian cases. First, these cases highlight the important role of constitutional courts in mediating the political process, sometimes by using powers ancillary to the primary, high-profile function of reviewing legislation for constitutionality. Here the existence of the constitutional court can facilitate institutional dialogues among political actors, encouraging peaceful resolution of political disputes and facilitating consolidation.

Second, the emergence of constitutional review in Asia suggests that supposed cultural barriers to the emergence of constitutional constraint are no longer operative, if they ever were so. Third, although a wide variety of social contexts can support constitutional review, the existence of a middle class appears to be an important factor in creating a bulwark of support for constitutional courts.

Fourth, it seems that political diffusion matters. Dominant parties are less likely to design open and powerful systems of judicial review, and are less likely to tolerate powerful courts exercising independent power once the constitution enters into force. In contrast, constitutional design in a situation of political deadlock is more likely to produce a strong, accessible system of judicial review as politicians seek political insurance. Political diffusion creates more disputes for courts to resolve, and hinders authorities from over-ruling or counter-attacking courts. In this sense, the emergence of powerful constitutional courts in Asia *reflects* democratization, and is not counter-democratic as has been argued in the U.S. context.

The Constitutional Courts of Thailand and Indonesia: Two Case Studies From South East Asia

ANDREW HARDING AND PETER LEYLAND *

INTRODUCTION

This article is a comparative study which considers the role of constitutional courts in two emerging democracies with contrasting systems. Most obviously, Thailand has a constitutional monarchy and a parliamentary system, while Indonesia is a republic with a presidential system. While Thailand adopted a new constitution in 1997 and again in 2007 (both of these introducing a slightly different model of constitutional court), Indonesia extensively modified its 1945 Constitution almost beyond recognition in a series of amendments during the period 1999-2002. However, in each case the framers of the present constitutional arrangements have been concerned to engineer a strong separation of powers, and, to this end, they placed considerable faith in constitutional adjudication. The challenge is not simply to create a counterweight to the abuse of executive power and to the conduct of politicians by placing power in the hands of judges, but to create respected institutions which are to some extent insulated from the political fray. As one well known commentator has argued: 'a deliberative democracy, operating under a good constitution, responds to political disagreements not simply by majority rule but also by attempting to create institutions that will ensure reflection and reason giving'.[1] An important

* Professor of Asia-Pacific Law, University of Victoria, BC, Canada; Professor of Public Law, London Metropolitan University, UK. The authors would like to acknowledge the

focus of this article is to evaluate to what extent these broad objectives have been achieved within these respective constitutional systems through the establishment of a constitutional court. The discussion commences by setting out the legal and political context of first the Thai and then the Indonesian constitutional court. The second part of the article proceeds with comparative analysis by offering a side-by-side discussion of important institutional characteristics, including respective methods of appointment and tenure, rules of standing, and approaches to judicial decision-making. In the final section there is a brief evaluation of the performance of these courts, each set against its own particular constitutional backdrop.

THE ORIGINS OF THAILAND'S CONSTITUTIONAL COURTS

Since the end of absolute monarchy in 1932 Thailand has had an extraordinarily unstable constitutional history. Periods of democratic rule have been punctuated by periods of military rule and on 18 occasions a new or interim constitution has been adopted to mark or facilitate a new beginning. In this article it will become apparent that, although the 1997 Constitution was transcended by yet another military coup in September 2006, this particular Constitution differed greatly from its predecessors.[2] It was distinctive not only because it was drafted after a period of popular consultation, but also because it has left Thailand with an institutional legacy comprising a battery of constitutional bodies which were designed to tackle manifest political abuses and which continue to function in spite of the coup of 2006 and the drafting of a new Constitution in 2007.[3] For the first time the boundaries of this intricate system were patrolled by a constitutional court.[4] The Constitutional Drafting Assembly (CDA) of 1997 placed great faith in a cohort of judges to finally determine many of the most important constitutional questions.[5] Klein emphasizes the significance of the Constitutional Court in the Thai constitutional context:

---

extremely helpful comments of Jörg Fedtke and Tom Ginsburg; and the assistance of Joana Thackeray, Nuthamon Kongcharoen and Manthana Yawila.

[1] Sunstein, C (2001), *Designing Democracy: What Constitutions Do*, Oxford University Press, at 239.

[2] McCargo, D (2002), (ed), *Reforming Thai Politics*, NIAS; Harding, AJ (2001), 'May there be Virtue: "New Asian Constitutionalism" in Thailand', 3 *Australian Journal of Asian Law* 24.

[3] Leyland, P (2007), 'Thailand's Constitutional Watchdogs: Dobermans, Bloodhounds or Lapdogs?' 2:2 *Journal of Comparative Law* 151.

[4] Harding, AJ (2009), 'A Turbulent Innovation: the Constitutional Court of Thailand, 1998-2006' in Harding, AJ and Nicholson, P (ed), *New Courts in the Asia*, Routledge (forthcoming).

[5] Uwanno, B and Burns, W (1998), 'The Thai Constitution of 1997: Sources and Process' 32 *University of British Columbia Law Review* 227.

Thai politicians, the military and senior civilian bureaucrats have always reserved for themselves the power to interpret the meaning of law and the intent of the constitution. The 1997 Constitution seeks to remedy these problems by reversing the course of Thai constitutional law. It establishes the Constitution as the basis for all law, thereby reducing the power of politicians and bureaucrats to subvert constitutional intent.[6]

Indeed, familiar rationales that often motivate constitution-makers in creating a constitutional court were evident in debates concerning the 1997 Constitution. First, it was reasoned that such a court would ensure adherence to the Constitution and its protection against legislative majorities; second, it would provide unity and finality in interpretation, avoiding the possibility of different courts adopting different interpretations of the Constitution; third, the court would stand as a visible symbol of constitutional progress; and fourth, the advent of a constitutional court offered the prospect of reversing a trend of judicial deferentialism, which may have characterized previous regimes of judicial review.[7] Despite strong historical links with France in the field of law and law reform, both public and private,[8] it was in fact the German and Austrian models of the court[9] that influenced the CDA most. In one sense a review of the case law will reveal that Thailand is a laboratory where this particular model of strong constitutional adjudication has been (and continues to be) tested.

Thailand's Constitutional Narrative 1997-2008

The 1997 Constitution which established the first version of the Thai Constitutional Court was adopted as a response to an economic crisis greatly exacerbated by glaring defects in governance and the rule of law. A Constitutional Tribunal appears in some of the 1997 Constitution's forerunners since 1945,[10] although these bodies enjoyed neither a monopoly

---

[6] Klein, JR (2001), 'The Battle for the Rule of Law in Thailand: the Constitutional Court of Thailand', in Raksasataya, A and Klein JR, *Constitutional Court of Thailand: the Provisions and the Working of the Court*, Constitution for the People Society.
[7] Ferreres Comella, V (2004), 'The Consequences of Centralizing Constitutional Review in a Special Court: Some Thoughts on Judicial Activism', 82 *Texas Law Review* 1705.
[8] See e.g. Bhalakula, B (2003), *Pridi and the Administrative Court*, Office of the Administrative Courts, Bangkok (on file with the authors); Harding, AJ (2008), 'King Mongkut, His Successors and the Reformation of Law in Thailand', in Nicholson, P and Biddulph, S (ed), *Examining Practice, Interrogating Theory: Comparative Legal Studies in Asia*, Martinus Nijhoff.
[9] See the articles on France and Germany in this issue.
[10] Setabutr, N (2000), 'The Constitutional Court and Society's Expectations', King Prajadhipok's Institute, Bangkok ('KPI').

on interpretation nor wide powers. The proposal to create a constitutional court proved controversial. The judiciary, particularly the Judges of the Supreme Court, had expressed opposition to it on two grounds of principle: first that the power to interpret the Constitution was a quintessentially judicial power that should be exercised by the ordinary judiciary; and second, that the proposal involved the appointment of political scientists to the proposed court, thus diluting the primacy of legal logic in the task of interpretation. The constitution-makers were, however, of the view that a constitutional court would be more likely to take a broad as opposed to a narrow view of its function based on legal interpretative techniques, and that there was merit in having a flagship institution with responsibilities only in respect of the Constitution. Influential members of the CDA clearly did not think that the judiciary had proved itself equal to the task of interpretation, given the sea-change in Thai constitutionalism that was contemplated. Even so, the CDA conceded something to the judiciary in that seven of the 15 Judges of the Constitutional Court were drawn from the ranks of the ordinary judiciary and only three political scientists would sit on the court.[11]

In common with other constitution-makers interested in democratic, rule-of-law reforms during the 1990s, the CDA decided to create a range of 'watchdog' bodies[12] constituting a complex series of checks and balances to ensure that power would be exercised in the public interest; these were the Election Commission (EC), the National Counter-Corruption Commission (NCCC), the National Audit Commission, the Administrative Courts,[13] the National Human Rights Commission,[14] the Ombudsman,[15] the Special Division of the Supreme Court for Criminal Cases Against Persons Holding Political Office, and the Anti-Money-Laundering Office.[16] This plethora of jurisdictions also opened up the possibility of turf wars between the

---

[11] Constitution of Thailand (herein after TC) 1997, section 255.
[12] Leyland, P (2008), 'Courts and Watchdog Bodies: Appointment Processes Reviewed and Compared', in Harding, AJ and Bureekul, T (ed), *Constitution Reform: Comparative Perspectives*, KPI.
[13] Leyland, P (2006), '*Droit Administratif* Thai Style: a Comparative Analysis of the Administrative Courts in Thailand', 8:2 *Australian Journal of Asian Law* 121; KPI (2003), *Monitoring and Evaluating of Performance of the Administrative Court.*
[14] Harding, A (2006), 'Thailand's Reforms: Human Rights and the National Commission' 1:1 *Journal of Comparative Law* 88; KPI (2004), *Monitoring and Evaluating of Performance of Independent Organizations: the National Human Rights Commission of Thailand.*
[15] Leyland, P (2007), 'The Ombudsman Principle in Thailand', 2:1 *Journal of Comparative Law* 137.
[16] Uwanno, B and Burns, W, supra note 5. The AMLO was set up under statutory provisions, and is not strictly independent of the executive, but may be seen as a significant part of the reform process.

respective bodies.[17] The Constitutional Court under the 1997 Constitution[18] was designated the final arbiter of many such constitutional questions and, as a result, it had a clearly defined function at the core of the entire constitutional system.[19] For example, as a judicial safeguard the findings of certain watchdog bodies required confirmation of the Constitutional Court before the decision had binding effect. Most crucially, the decisions of the Constitutional Court were made explicitly binding on all state institutions and individuals.[20] In order to establish the rule of law it was therefore essential that all the constitutional players fully complied with the judgments laid down by the Court.

The constitutional watchdogs were rapidly recruited and put into operation. The early signs until 2001 were encouraging. The EC and the NCCC in particular prosecuted constitutional abuses with considerable vigour.[21] However, as will be apparent from the discussion of performance of the Court which follows, the failure of the combined strength of the watchdogs and the Court to achieve compliance with constitutional norms by the political leaders, including the Prime Minister, was a major contributory factor which prompted the military coup.

The Constitutional Court ceased functioning after the revocation of the 1997 Constitution and adoption of an Interim Constitution by a Royal Decree of September 2006 following the military coup. The military junta in introducing the Interim Constitution was careful to replace the Constitutional Court with an (interim) Constitutional Tribunal in order to prevent challenges concerning the legitimacy of the coup, and any possible adverse implications under the 1997 Constitution for those responsible for engineering the coup.[22] The Interim Constitution did not repeal ordinary statute law, and the existing courts and 'watchdog' bodies, with the exception of the Constitutional Court, remained in operation under their organic laws. However, all cases pending from the previous Constitutional

---

[17] See e.g., 'Watchdog, Judges in Turf Battle Administrative Court Claims Jurisdiction', *The Nation*, Bangkok, 2 October 2002.

[18] TC 1997, section 255, specifies academic political scientists.

[19] It should be noted that although in constitutional terms the Constitutional Court was at the pinnacle of the system and had the final word, this authority did not apply to general matters of law, where the Supreme Court and the Supreme Administrative Court enjoyed a roughly equivalent status as appellate courts for civil/ criminal and administrative matters, respectively.

[20] TC 1997, section 268.

[21] Leyland, supra note 12, at 167.

[22] Constitution of the Kingdom of Thailand (interim) B.E. 2549 (2006) ('TC 2006'), sections 35,37. See, further, Harding, AJ (2009), 'Emergency Powers with a Moustache: Special Powers, Military Rule and Evolving Constitutionalism in Thailand', in Ramraj, VV and Thiruvengadam, A (ed) *Emergency Powers in Asia*, Cambridge University Press, forthcoming.

Court were transferred under section 35 of the Interim Constitution to the (interim) Constitutional Tribunal consisting of nine judges.[23]

Undoubtedly, the Constitutional Tribunal's most significant judgment, delivered on 30 May 2007, related to the investigations into the alleged misconduct of the main political parties (Thai Rak Thai and the Democrat Party) during the elections of 2 April 2006.[24] The Democrat Party was acquitted but Thai Rak Thai and its most senior officials were unanimously found guilty on charges of bribing small parties to compete in the election, in order to fulfil the 20% minimum turnout requirement. The Tribunal sanctioned the dissolution of Thai Rak Thai and also banned 111 of its senior members, including its leader, former Prime Minister Thaksin Shinawatra, from politics for a period of five years. This outcome was welcomed in some quarters as a reasoned judgment which responded to evidence presented before the court, but given the undemocratic prevailing constitutional circumstances, the generals being still in charge, the result could hardly be regarded as a triumph for the rule of law.

The Constitutional Court under the 2007 Constitution

The military junta cited the subversion of the 1997 Constitution as the main justification for its action when it seized power, and, at the same time, declared its intention to restore democracy and further the reform process. The Interim Constitution set in train a complex constitutional drafting process.[25] However, the Constitution Drafting Assembly was in effect required to take the 1997 Constitution as the basis for the new constitution.[26] The constitution-drafters clearly saw the need to enhance the powers of the Constitutional Court. Indeed, a revamped Constitutional Court is established under the 2007 Constitution, comprising a President and eight judges.[27] A quorum of five judges must preside over any case brought before the Court[28] and the Court may decide matters by majority vote. The

---

[23] The interim court comprised the President of the Supreme Court as President; the President of the Supreme Administrative Court as Vice-President; five other Supreme Court Justices; and two other Supreme Administrative Court Justices.

[24] 'The Constitutional Tribunal disbands Thai Rak Thai' *The Nation*, Bangkok, 30 May 2007; 'Summary of the Decision of the Constitutional Tribunal: Thai Rak Thai', *The Nation*, Bangkok, 6 June 2007.

[25] TC 2006, sections 19ff.

[26] The process laid down by TC 2006 (supra note 22) required the Drafting Committee to justify any deviation from the provisions of TC 1997. Moreover, in the event of the draft not being approved by the prescribed referendum, the government was empowered to bring into effect any previous constitution with appropriate amendments.

[27] TC 2007, section 204.

[28] TC 2007, section 216.

decision of the Court must at least consist of the background or allegation; a summary of facts obtained from hearings; the reasons for the decision on questions of fact and law; and the provisions of the Constitution and the law invoked and resorted to. The 2007 Constitution has also somewhat redefined the powers of the Constitutional Court; in particular the Court now has the power to hear an individual citizen's petition alleging violation of rights. Under both the 1997 and 2007 Constitutions the Constitutional Court is granted final authority over all matters of constitutional interpretation.[29] This jurisdiction arises under many provisions of the respective Constitutions, but principally by reference to the Court from an ordinary civil or criminal court, where a constitutional question arises;[30] or by a reference from the National Assembly or the Prime Minister before an impugned bill became law.[31]

THE ORIGINS OF THE INDONESIAN
MAHKAMAH KONSTITUSI

As with many other examples in Asia and elsewhere, the creation of a Constitutional Court ('the *Mahkamah Konstitusi*', hereafter 'MK'), which, following a constitutional amendment in 2001 and an organic law passed in 2003, opened its doors in August 2003, was due to a combination of general and specific factors. The creation of the MK should be seen as a final but crucial component of reforms effected by a series of amendments to the Constitution of 1945 passed by Indonesia's 'super-legislature', the *Majlis Permusyawaratan Rakyat* (MPR) during 1999-2002, as part of the process of '*reformasi*'[32] that began with the resignation of President Suharto in May 1998. It is interesting to note here that, as we have seen, in Thailand it has been usual in times of fundamental change to draft a new Constitution; in Indonesia, on the other hand, during the axial period of *reformasi*, and following a similar economic collapse to that of Thailand in 1997, reforms arguably even more far-reaching than those in Thailand were effected, not by a new constitution but by a root-and-branch renovation of the Republic's first Constitution. The resulting document is in fact about three times longer than the original version of 1945.

---

[29] TC 1997, section 268; TC 2007, section 154.
[30] TC 1997, section 264; TC 2007, section 211. The Court is given discretion to reject the case if it considers that it would have no bearing on the decision of the ordinary court.
[31] TC 1997, section 262.
[32] The term usually given to the period of reform following the resignation of President Suharto in May 1998, and to date. See, further, Lindsey, T (2008), 'Constitutional Reform in Indonesia: Muddling Towards Democracy', in Lindsey, T (ed), *Indonesia: Law and Society*, 2nd ed, Federation Press.

Preceding the creation of the MK, under the amendments of 2000, was the incorporation of an extensive bill of rights, based on the international bill of rights, into the Constitution, so that effectively for the first time citizens of the Indonesian Republic were able, in the juridical sense at least, to enjoy rights held independently of the state and, with the amendment of 2001 these would now also be enforced by a powerful court. This development indicated a remarkable shift in jurisprudence: the 'integralist' state enshrined in the 1945 Constitution under the influence of Professor Supomo[33] acknowledged no distinction between society, citizens, and state, so that rights as such were held to be unnecessary, or even a contradiction in terms; this position was, following intense debate and struggle during the 1960s, taken to a logical conclusion by the Judiciary Act of 1970, which denied the power of judicial review, bringing the judiciary under the control of the government.[34] The constitutional amendments of 2002 reversed this theory, the creation of the MK being linked decisively with the previous amendments of 1999-2001, which, with accompanying statutory reforms, introduced direct presidential elections; increased the powers of the *Dewan Perwakilan Rakyat* (DPR or parliament) to legislate and call the government to account; ended the system of appointing members to the MPR; removed the political role of the military; reformed the judiciary and established its independence from the executive; decentralized government; and introduced a new assembly of provincial representatives. The MK, as in Thailand, was the keystone of an arch whose pillars were democracy and the rule of law; its task was to enforce the renovated Constitution and thereby entrench the '*negara hukum*' or rule of law state.

Undoubtedly Indonesians were influenced by the advance of 'new Asian constitutionalism' as in the cases of Taiwan, Thailand and South Korea, which impelled close consideration of South Korea's Constitutional Court in particular as a model.[35] Intense debates took place about judicial review, disenchantment was expressed with the judiciary in general, and Indonesian society addressed concertedly the problems of how to advance the reform process.[36] In particular there was an intense debate concerning

---

[33] Supomo, a legal scholar educated in Leiden and with an enthusiasm for *adat* (Indonesian customary law), considered that the law of the new republic should be an expression of the *volksgeist*. Lev, DS (2000) Legal Evolution and Political Authority in Indonesia, Kluwer Law International at 27, 55ff.

[34] Lev, D (1978), 'Judicial Authority and the Struggle for an Indonesian Rechtsstaat', 13 *Law and Society Review* 37; Butt, S (2008), 'Surat Sakti: The Decline of the Authority of Judicial Decisions in Indonesia', in Lindsey supra note 32.

[35] Hendrianto (2009), 'Institutional Choice and the New indonesian Constitutional Court', in Harding and Nicholson, supra note 8.

[36] Lindsey, T and Mas Achmad Santosa (2008), 'The Trajectory of Law Reform in Indonesia: a Short Overview of Legal Systems and Change in Indonesia', in Lindsey supra note 32.

how, following the impeachment of President Abdurrahman Wahid in 2001, to lay down a satisfactory legal as opposed to political process for presidential impeachment. Commentators have indeed stressed the last of these issues as particularly crucial, even though in practice the exercise of constitutional jurisdiction has in the event been directed more towards the enforcement of constitutional rights than towards other, ancillary, powers.[37] Undoubtedly the collapse of Suharto's *orde baru* ('new order') in 1998, together with its oppressive 'integralist state' ideology, had hastened the victory of arguments in favour of judicial control over government that had continued at some level almost since the creation of the Republic in 1945; Butt refers to this factor as 'the fading of [the] barriers to judicial review' – increasingly judicial review proponents found themselves pushing at an opening door.[38] Some voices, as in Thailand, were skeptical about constitutional reform in times of economic hardship, arguing, as popular discourse had it, that 'democracy and the rule of law cannot be eaten'; the prevailing view was, however, as in Thailand, that good governance reforms would provide the basis for stable economic recovery and social justice.

These factors did not of course determine what model of court or judicial review should be adopted. Some preferred an independent constitutional court, some preferred a constitutional chamber of the Supreme Court, and others opposed to judicial review preferred review by the MPR itself.[39] A study tour of MPR legislators to 21 countries, of which only 11 in fact have a constitutional court, seems to have been influential in resolving a deadlocked debate on this issue; ultimately the MK as provided for by the constitutional amendment of 2001 was a compromise position under which there would be an independent court but with circumscribed powers: the court would be able to review primary but not delegated legislation, the power of review over which would remain with the Supreme Court. The significance of this distinction is very great in the Indonesian context, because most parliamentary legislation is highly skeletal, whereas delegated legislation provides most of the flesh. In addition, there is no

[37] See Lindsey, T and Butt, S (2008), 'Economic Reform when the Constitution Matters: Indonesia's Constitutional Court and Article 33', 44:2 *Bulletin of Indonesian Economic Studies* 239.
[38] Butt, S 'Judicial Review in Indonesia: Between Civil Law and Accountability? A Study of Constitutional Court Decisions', University of Melbourne PhD thesis, 2006 (unpublished); Fenwick, S (2008), 'Administrative Law and Judicial Review in Indonesia: the Search for Accountability', in Ginsburg, T and Chen, Albert HY (ed) (2008), *Administrative Law and Governance in Asia*, Routledge.
[39] Hendrianto, supra note 35; and, further, compare the article by Frosini and Pegoraro in this issue. It has also been observed that politicians were in general not fully aware of the implications of voting for the creation of the MK: Fenwick, supra note 38.

power for the ordinary courts to refer issues of constitutional interpretation to the MK.[40]

One reason for political forces opposed to an independent court to compromise on their position was that, during the debate on this issue in 2001, President Abdurrahman Wahid was impeached; fearing a similar and highly politicized impeachment attempt being mounted in future, the new President, Megawati Sukarnoputri, and her PDI-P party decided to support the establishment of the MK because of its proposed powers over presidential impeachment.[41]

The outcome was a court which has most of the powers one associates with constitutional courts, and actually more than the Korean court,[42] although less than the Thai court under the 2007 Constitution: although the ordinary courts cannot refer a constitutional issue to the MK, it can entertain individual petitions based on constitutional violation; conduct impeachment proceedings; dissolve political parties; and resolve electoral disputes and disputes between state agencies. With regard to the selection process (discussed in more detail below), this proved to be less controversial than one would have thought, it being widely accepted that the 'Korean system' under which three judges are chosen by each branch of the state was fair, workable, and a good compromise.[43] Other features of the MK which correspond to the Korean example are the diversion of judicial review of delegated legislation to the Supreme Court, and the process for presidential impeachment. The MK is empowered by Article 24C in very general terms, to make the final decision in 'reviewing laws against the Constitution, determining disputes over the authorities of state institutions whose powers are given by this Constitution, deciding over the dissolution of a political party, and deciding disputes over the results of general elections'.[44] It also has power under Article 7B to investigate charges against the President or Vice-President that he or she has violated the law through an act of treason, corruption, bribery, or other act of a grave criminal nature, or is otherwise guilty of moral turpitude, or no longer meets the qualifications to serve as President or Vice-President.

---

[40] Hendrianto, supra note 35.

[41] This is perhaps a good example of Ginsburg's 'insurance' theory in operation: see Ginsburg, T (2003), *Judicial Review in New Democracies,* Cambridge University Press, at 33.

[42] The Korean court cannot entertain individual petitions or resolve electoral disputes, although it does deal with referrals by ordinary courts.

[43] Cf., for this system of appointment as it operates in Italy, the article by Groppi in this issue.

[44] General elections are those of the members of the DPR (Parliament, whose members are also members of the MPR), the DPD (House of Regional Representatives), the President and Vice-President, and the DPRDs (Regional People's Representative Councils): Constitution of the Republic of Indonesia 1945, Article 22E.

INSTITUTIONAL INDEPENDENCE AND THE
SELECTION PROCESSES COMPARED

This brings us to a comparison of the selection processes. The degree of reliance on a judicial process at the core of the constitution needs to be understood in the constitutional and political context. In marked contrast to politicians and civil servants, Thailand's judges, and the legal system more broadly, has enjoyed a relatively high reputation for professionalism and independence since the modernization programmes of Rama V.[45] This is in marked contrast to Indonesia, where the judiciary has enjoyed an extremely low, although now rapidly increasing, reputation throughout the history of the Republic. The judiciary has been both legally and in fact clearly subservient to the executive, and judicial review of constitutional issues is a concept of very recent origin; on the other hand judicial review of administrative actions has been recognised since at least 1986 when the administrative court system was introduced.[46] The enormous faith placed in the hands of the Thai judiciary to decide crucial issues was identified by some critics as the 'dominant theme' of the 2007 Constitution.[47] Both the 1997 and 2007 Constitutions include numerous provisions to guarantee (in theory at least) the institutional independence of the Court. Not only must the Office of the Constitutional Court have autonomy in its personnel, administration and budget, but it must have its own autonomous secretariat with a Secretary-General responsible to the President of the Court and nominated by the President with the approval of the Court's judges.[48] The judges hold office for nine years from the date of their appointment[49] and may serve only for a single term.[50] Conflicts of interest are expressly forbidden as judges serving on the Constitutional Court are prohibited from having any governmental position, business interests or engagement

---

[45] Terweil, B (2005), *Thailand's Political History: From the fall of Ayutthaya to recent times*, River Books, at 226; Harding, AJ (2008), 'King Mongkut, His Successors, and the Reformatoin of Law in Thailand', in Nicholson, P and Biddulph, S (ed), *Examining Practice, Interrogating Theory: Comparative Legal Studies in Asia*, Martinus Nijhoff.

[46] Bedner, AW (2001), *Administrative Courts in Indonesia: a Socio-Legal Study*, Kluwer Law International.

[47] 'Judicial Role in the Constitution: From People's Charter to Judges Charter' *The Nation*, Bangkok, 30 April 2007.

[48] TC 2007, section 217.

[49] Under section 209 it is provided that in addition to the expiration of the nine year term, the President and judges of the Constitutional Court vacate office upon: death, retirement at 70, resignation, disqualification, Senate's resolution for removal under section 274, prohibitions under section 205 or acts in violation under section 207, if sentenced to a term of imprisonment.

[50] TC 2007, section 208.

in any profession.[51] Furthermore, politicians, judges and members of other independent agencies under the Constitution are specifically excluded from serving on the Court.[52]

Above all, the Thai judicial appointment system, which is the most complex probably of any country discussed in this issue, is clearly of pivotal importance. On the one hand, the selection process under both the 1997 and 2007 Constitutions reflected the requirement that the composition of the court needed to draw upon the existing pool of professionally trained judicial talent, the assumption being that selection to the Court would be on grounds of seniority, experience and merit. Currently, more than half of the nine members of the constitutional bench are chosen from serving judges. The Supreme Administrative Court nominates two judges while the Supreme Court nominates three judges (as compared to 3 and 4 respectively of the 15 judges under the 1997 Constitution). On the other hand, in regard to the appointment of the other four members of the Court with expertise in political science or law, the robustness of the intricate selection process has come under close scrutiny.[53] The revised procedure under the 2007 Constitution also requires a Selection Committee to be formed,[54] but this time it comprises the President of the Supreme Court, the President of the Supreme Administrative Court, the President of the House of Representatives, the Leader of the Opposition in the House of Representatives, and a further representative elected by independent organisations established under the Constitution. Persons selected by this committee who consent are nominated to the President of the Senate, but the selection resolution must be by open vote and must be by a two thirds majority of the existing members of the selection committee.[55] A special sitting of the Senate is then called within 30 days by the President of the Senate to pass an approval resolution by secret ballot of the selected persons. If the nominations are ratified the names will be presented to the King to be appointed. If the nominations are rejected, wholly or partly, the matter is referred to the Selection committee for reselection. At this point, unlike the 1997 procedure, where the Senate had the final say, the Selection Committee can *re-affirm* its original nomination of candidates unanimously, which will result in the names of the selected persons being forwarded by the President of the Senate for appointment by the King. The selection committee dominated by judges and professionals thus has the

[51] TC 2007, section 207.
[52] TC 2007, section 205(3).
[53] 'Two Judges to be Chosen for Constitutional Court' *The Nation*, Bangkok, 24 April 2008
[54] TC 2007, section 206.
[55] For a decision to be valid at least half of the committee must be present.

final say rather than the Senate. If the selection committee does not approve unanimously there must be a reselection process within 30 days. Under the Constitution the three judges elected from the Supreme Court judges select a President of the Court from among their own number.[56] A quorate bench can be formed from any five judges of the panel of nine.

The explanation for the reduced role of the Senate in the selection processes is that the elected Senate under the 1997 Constitution was designed as a politically neutral body which had a key role in many constitutional appointment processes, but in practice it was gradually captured by Thai Rak Thai,[57] the ruling party (2001-2006), and was therefore able to officially approve a number of highly controversial appointments.[58] The composition of the Senate under the 2007 Constitution has changed, so that it is now half elected and half appointed.[59]

The complexity of the selection process has important ramifications. For example, under the 1997 Constitution the delay in replacing the President of the Court, Kramol Tonghamachart, following his mandatory retirement on his 70th birthday, had a number of knock-on effects. It left a situation where there could be an even number of judges and therefore no casting vote. Selection committees for other important constitutional bodies were also invalid as the Constitution required the President of the Constitutional Court to be a member.[60]

The method of appointment of the Indonesian MK was, perhaps surprisingly, less problematical or controversial than in Thailand. Here the Korean 'representative' method was followed on the basis that the Korean Court had proved successful and Korea was, like Indonesia, an Asian country. The representative model of appointment under Article 24C of the Constitution involves each element of the state (executive, legislature, and judiciary) nominating an equal number (here three) of judges (making nine in total);[61] the judges are confirmed in office by the President and elect a Chair and Vice-Chair from their own number, for a period of three years. Each constitutional justice 'must possess integrity and a personality that is not dishonourable, and shall be fair, shall be a statesperson who

---

[56] TC 2007, section 204.
[57] In the sense that rather than being independent a majority Senators displayed covert support for this party even though prohibited from being members of the party under the TC 1997.
[58] Sharp differences arose under the TC 1997 between the Senate and the Supreme Court over the Senate's investigation of the backgrounds and qualifications of proposed justices.
[59] TC 2007, section 111.
[60] 'Lack of Head for Top Court Creating lots of Problems' *The Nation*, Bangkok, 10 November 2005.
[61] For discussion of Korean influence on the design of the MK, see Hendrianto, supra note 35.

has a command of the Constitution and the public institutions, and shall not hold any position as a state official'. Selection is to be 'on the basis of transparency and accountability'.[62] The judges hold office for a maximum of two terms of five years, but have to retire at 65.

The attraction of this method in the eyes of Indonesian legislators was that it would avoid conflict (and indeed it has done so) between the branches of the state, especially between the President and the DPR. Under this system, three judges are appointed by the President, three by the DPR, and three by the Supreme Court. Thus the difficult question of how to compose a selection committee and provide for a (presumably complex and potentially highly controversial) appointment process, has been neatly finessed.

COMPARISON OF GATEWAYS TO THE COURT

Access to a court tends to determine in significant ways the extent of its jurisdiction and the nature and practical incidence of its powers. In determining the extent of access to a constitutional court a balance has to be struck between ensuring that relevant issues that arise falling under its jurisdiction are referred for determination and finding a means of protecting the court from being inundated with frivolous claims.

Under the 1997 Constitution of Thailand individual citizens did not have any right to petition the Court except indirectly. However, under the 2007 Constitution any citizen who considers that his or her rights have been violated by any 'State organ or State agency' is able to make a challenge on grounds of constitutionality before the Constitutional Court. This constitutional provision potentially opens up the system to widespread challenges but this right of referral has been made a remedy of last resort, to the extent that the claimant must have first exhausted all other existing remedies, which might include the right to take a case to the administrative courts.[63] In addition, this Constitution, in common with its predecessor, grants a broad power of referral to the Court for an individual who believes that a person or party has exercised a right or liberty prescribed by the constitution to overthrow the democratic regime of government or to acquire power to rule the country by unconstitutional means. In such a case the Prosecutor General investigates and then submits a motion to the Constitutional Court for determination.[64]

---

[62] Constitution of the Republic of Indonesia 1945, Article 19.

[63] TC 2007, section 212.

[64] TC 2007, section 68 (formerly TC 1997, section 63). If the Constitutional Court finds against the person or party concerned as it did on a number of occasions in 2008 in relation

In regard to determining the validity of legislation prior to its enactment[65] and draft rules of procedure relating to Parliament,[66] at least 10% of the members of either House of Parliament or the Prime Minister must call upon the Court to consider the constitutionality of such provisions. The same threshold applies when requiring the Court to consider violations of the Constitution through the misappropriation of public funds,[67] but a threshold of 20% is set in respect to triggering a challenge of proposed emergency decrees before the Court.[68] In a different context, the Court exercises its role in arbitrating finally where there is a conflict between the powers and duties of public bodies (for example the National Assembly, the Council of Ministers, or other non-judicial state organs) when called upon to do so by the President of the National Assembly, the Prime Minister or by the public body in question.[69]

An unusual[70] but important feature of the 1997 reforms[71] which has been included as part of the 2007 Constitution[72] was that the Ombudsman had been granted a special function to police compliance with the terms of the Constitution.[73]

In Indonesia it was initially proposed that, as was the case in Thailand up until 2007, individual petitions would reach the MK only via the Ombudsman (National Ombudsman Commission). As a result of protest against this limitation on access, and tracking similar debates in Thailand, it was instead provided in the MK Law of 2003,[74] that standing is given to any individual citizen, public and private legal persons, and representatives of traditional communities; but damage to constitutional rights must also be proved. By this means it was expected that the MK would use standing rules to restrict access and thereby prevent a flood of litigation. In fact, the MK has adopted a particularly broad view of standing, allowing what are essentially public interest cases, and has even embarked 'in the public

---

to PMs Samak and Somchai and the PPP Party, it issues a decision ordering the dissolution of the party and disqualifies the person or persons for five years.

[65] TC 2007, section 154.

[66] TC 2007, section 155.

[67] TC 2007, section 168.

[68] TC 2007, section 185.

[69] TC 2007, section 214.

[70] This is not unique. Article 162 of the Spanish Constitution of 1978 allows the Spanish Ombudsman (Defender of the People) to lodge an appeal or an appeal of unconstitutionality before the Constitutional Court.

[71] TC 1997, section 198.

[72] TC 2007, section 245.

[73] See TC 1997, section 198 and the Ombudsman Act 1999, section 17. Under TC 2007 section 280 the Omudsman's role has been extended to include the investigation of the ethical standards of politicians and officials.

[74] Article 51(1).

interest' on review of legislation where the applicant actually lacked standing. With NGOs it has been sufficient to establish standing on the basis that the organization's articles of association encompass the defence of constitutional rights. So far the MK has not sought to impose with any consistency any principled restrictions on standing, although it has denied standing in some cases because of a lack of connection between the applicant and the alleged violation of rights.[75]

COMPARISON OF INTERPRETATIVE TECHNIQUES

Recent work on Constitutional Courts in Asia indicates that the interpretive techniques and the style of the rendering of judgments in the court are critical to establishing the legitimacy of constitutional courts.[76]

The Thai Constitutional Court of 1998-2006 was required to give a decision setting out the allegations, facts, reasons of law and fact, and the legal provisions relied upon;[77] and the decisions of the Court and of each judge were required to be published in the Gazette. Dissenting opinions (an innovation also adopted in Indonesia) were therefore published and were actually quite frequent in practice, an interesting development in a civilian jurisdiction, where dissenting judgments are not usual. In the case of the Thai court, formalistic, French-style judgments were given which avoided elaboration as to the reasoning processes, creating the impression that the decisions were arbitrary and unrelated to each other. This impression needs to be moderated, however, by certain other considerations. First, all justices were obliged to enter individual judgments. Second, dissents were allowed (an innovation also adopted in Indonesia) and became a regular feature of the decisions, which were often split ones in important cases. Third, the Court made some reference to its own previous decisions in an attempt to provide a consistent and rational jurisprudence; it also consistently consolidated cases raising similar issues.[78] Finally, the Constitutional Court can refuse to accept for review a specific provision of law on which it had previously issued a decision.[79]

Turning to Indonesia, a quorum consists of seven justices but cases are often heard by a full panel of nine. The final decision is drafted at a judicial deliberation meeting held in strict confidence, presided over by the Chair

---

[75] Butt, S 'Judicial Review in Indonesia: Between Civil Law and Accountability? A Study of Constitutional Court Decisions', University of Melbourne PhD thesis, 2006 (unpublished).
[76] Butt, ibid.
[77] Section 267.
[78] For example, a large number of cases involving changes in bank interest, brought in 1998-9.
[79] TC 2007, section 215.

or Deputy Chair. The Court is required to adopt principles of deliberation by consensus, but if unanimity is not possible the decision is made by majority, with the Chair having the casting vote. Dissenting judgments are recorded as part of the decision and cases of the MK are reported more fully than in Thailand.[80]

A major study has criticized the MK for failing to implement consistent doctrinal positions through the cases. This criticism can also be made of the Thai Constitutional Court, despite the apparent attempts related above to deal with this issue. The problem here seems not so much a failure of constitutional law expertise as the nature of the approach to judicial reasoning in a civil law context. Judgments tend to be formulistic, having what Butt calls 'an air of inevitability;'[81] they do not engage with the arguments presented or those referred to by other judges or in other cases dealing with similar issues, especially those with which the judge presumably disagrees; they fail in general terms to justify the decisions taken; holdings are binding but not the reasoning. Dissenting judgments are allowed and indeed frequently resorted to (Butt estimates that only 57% of cases are unanimous, and several important cases have been decided by a 5-4 or 6-3 majority), but this has not led to a flow of constitutional discourse through the cases. It is difficult even for lawyers to see beyond the practical effects of the holdings to the reasons behind the decisions, which therefore tend to appear arbitrary. It would appear that this is a major problem for the development of constitutional jurisdiction in Asia.

THE PERFORMANCE OF THE CONSTITUTIONAL COURTS

Thailand

The implementation of the 1997 Constitution of Thailand revealed many problems with Thai constitutionalism. The text itself could hardly have been clearer in its unequivocal adherence to constitutional values: it made extensive provision for human rights,[82] the rule of law, accountability for abuse of power, and for stable, elected, civilian government.[83] The result in

---

[80] See Constitutional Court Regulation No. 06/PMK/2005; Procedures of Judicial Review of Laws, Articles 29-32, 10/PUU-VI/2008. For Thailand, see Regulation on the Procedure and Decision-making of the Constitutional Court of 2007 (*Royal Gazette*, 21 December 2007, Volume 124).

[81] Supra note 75.

[82] Harding, AJ (2006), 'Thailand's Reforms: Human Rights and the National Commission' 1 *Journal of Comparative Law* 88.

[83] Bowornsak, U and Burns, W (1998), 'The Thai Constitution of 1997: Sources and Process' 32 *University of British Columbia Law Review* 227.

practice was much more ambiguous, especially during 2001-6, the period in which Prime Minister Thaksin and the Thai Rak Thai Party were in power. Abuses of power and of human rights, and widespread corruption[84] were stated reasons for the 19 September coup. The members of the National Counter-Corruption Commission (NCCC) resigned in June 2005 after making an unlawful decision in their own interest, and were all replaced. Other acute political controversies gave rise to Constitutional Court decisions which are discussed below.

Arguably, the pivotal decision under the 1997 Constitution was when the Constitutional Court failed to uphold the findings of the NCCC in 2001 after the election of Prime Minister Thaksin Shinawatra. The case was of enormous political importance. It involved an investigation of claims that before becoming Prime Minister he had concealed most of his fortune as part of a dishonest scheme to eliminate conflicts of interest which were outlawed under the Constitution. Vast sums, certainly by Thai standards, were involved comprising 2.4 billion baht (£38.5 million), 1.5 billion baht (£23 million), and 0.6 billion baht (£9.2 million).[85] It was found that the assets had been registered in the names of his housekeeper, chauffeur, driver, security guard and business colleagues. The NCCC duly conducted its investigation and passed a judgment by an 8-1 margin upholding the allegations. If the decision of the NCCC had been allowed to stand unchallenged, the result would have been a 'red card', namely, an automatic suspension from politics for five years operating with immediate effect, thus depriving Thaksin of the premiership. Thaksin refused to accept these findings as part of a legitimate constitutional process. Rather, he maintained that the entire investigation was conducted as a political smear campaign.[86] He contended that the charges were made because the political establishment objected to his personal success and that of Thai Rak Thai. The newly elected Prime Minister in 2001 was seeking to represent an alternative vision (compared to the traditional Thai politics) of modernity and prosperity. The decision of the NCCC was challenged before the Constitutional Court where it was argued that the failure to declare these assets was no more than an honest mistake. Although the argument was not accepted, the Constitutional Court voted narrowly in Thaksin's favour.[87] This decision was indeed a

---

[84] Phongaichit, P and Piriyarangsan, S (1996), *Corruption and Democracy in Thailand,* Silkworm Books.

[85] Thaksin's staff were recorded as among the top 10 holders of shares on the Thai stock exchange.

[86] See Phongpaichit, P and Baker, C (2005), *Thaksin: The Business of Politics in Thailand,* Silkworm Books, at 3.

[87] The 8-7 outcome was reached after two votes. The first rejected Thaksin argument that he was not required to make an asset declaration by a margin of 11-4. The second vote rejected

surprising outcome on the facts, given that in 17 other similar cases decided previously, the Constitutional Court had always endorsed the decision of the NCCC. The failure to act decisively and punish the PM for this manifest breach of the rules severely undermined the credibility of the combined strength of the constitutional watchdogs. In the face of severe political pressure and possibly even interference the Constitutional Court, at the very pinnacle of the Constitution, appeared to cave in. Nevertheless, it should be recognized that quite apart from any illegitimate pressures that may have been placed on them, the judges on the Constitutional Court had an unenviable choice in making their decision. A vote by the Court confirming Thaksin's disqualification by the NCCC, if it had been carried, would have in effect invalidated the result of the election with the prospect of political turmoil, and the ensuing crisis would have placed further strain on the constitutional arrangements with unpredictable effects.

The Constitutional Court is charged with exercising an identical role under the 2007 Constitution of being the final arbiter where there are alleged conficts of interest. For example, in July 2008 the Court ruled in a case referred by 36 Senators that Public Health Minister, Chaiya Samsomsap, was disqualified from holding office for failing to declare some of his wife's assets, in particular the fact that she held more than 5% of stock in a private company in violation of Article 92 of the Constitution. Senator Prasarn Maruekha-pitak stated that: '... the court's ruling demonstrated its role of building trust in the justice system and setting standards for Thai politics.'[88]

In another critical case, the decision of the Election Commission (EC) to allow the general election which was held on 2 April 2006 was challenged before the 1997 Constitutional Court.[89] During the election itself, there were many allegations of widespread vote-buying.[90] The EC failed to uphold objections to the results and the Constitutional Court initially confirmed individual results which had been called into question. Although Thaksin won the election, following street demonstrations he announced that he

---

Thaksin's assertion that the concealment of assets had been an honest mistake by a margin of 7-4. Overall, according to the conventions of the court's unusual voting system, the two votes of 4 were added together to make 8 which is set against the 7 who had voted him guilty on the second ballot. See McCargo D and Pathmanand U (2005), *The Thaksinization of Thailand*, Copenhagen, NIAS Press, at 16.

[88] 'Court Bans Chaiya from Office' *The Nation*, Bangkok, 10 July 2008; 'New Blow for Government as Court finds Chaiya Broke Charter' *Bangkok Post*, Bangkok, 10 July 2008.

[89] An early election was called by the Prime Minister to head off the controversy which had arisen from the Shin Corporation (telecommunications company) deal. The PM's family sold their 49.6% stake in the Corporation of $1.88 billion without any payment of capital gains tax following a change in the law to make this exemption legal.

[90] These led to the Constitutional Tribunal's decisions of 30 May 2007 dissolving the Thai Rak Thai Party: see below.

would only serve as a caretaker Prime Minister until a new government was formed; but after taking short vacation he showed no signs of going. In an unprecedented move the King intervened on 26 April 2006 by addressing the judges of the Constitutional and Administrative Courts directly. He suggested that they should assert their authority under the Constitution to invalidate the election, which had been boycotted by opposition parties.[91] On 5 May 2006 the Constitutional Court held that the April elections were invalid, principally on the grounds that the ballot was not secret due to the manner in which polling booths had been placed, and that the Thai Rak Thai Party had manipulated the attainment of a quorum of votes cast in certain constituencies order to 'validate' the election.[92] The King's personal intervention was a demonstration of the failure of the constitutional mechanisms to function in the manner intended and to uphold democratic principles.

As the final constitutional arbiter on many issues under the 2007 Constitution the Court was soon exposed to intense political controversy. Most notably, it ruled in September 2008 that Prime Minister Samak had violated the conflict of interest provisions[93] by being paid for his appearance on a TV cookery show and therefore had to step down from the premiership.[94] Then, in December 2008 the Court unanimously decided that his successor, Prime Minister Somchai and the ruling coalition, had been guilty of electoral fraud. He too was forced to step down from office and the ruling coalition parties were immediately disbanded by order of the Court. The Court's President declared that this: 'set a political standard and an example ...' [also observing that] 'dishonest political parties undermine Thailand's democratic system'.[95] These decisions were taken against a background of well orchestrated anti-government demonstrations by the opposition People's Alliance for Democracy (PAD), culminating in the closure of Bangkok's international airport with far-reaching economic consequences for the entire nation. The judgment of the Constitutional Court which was in line with the rigorous anti-corruption provisions of the constitution[96] had removed an alleged Thaksin nominee as Prime Minister and was therefore hailed as a victory by the demonstrators. At the same

---

[91] See 'Charter Court to Examine the Legality of Poll' *The Nation*, Bangkok, 1 May 2006.
[92] See 'Thai Court Rules Election Invalid' BBC News, 8 May 2006, http://news.bbc.co.uk/1/hi/world/asia-pacific/4983600.stm (accessed 12 December 2008).
[93] TC 2007, section 267.
[94] Case no. 12-13/2551 (BE). See also 'PM Disqualified for Violating Charter with Cookery Show' *The Nation*, Bangkok, 10 September, 2008.
[95] 'Thailand Prime Minister to Step Down after Court Strips Him of Office' *The Guardian*, London, 2 December 2008.
[96] See e.g. TC 2007, section 68.

time it gave the PAD an excuse to end their action. In the short term the Constitutional Court's decision defused a crisis but many PPP government supporters have, perhaps not surprisingly, accused the court of being partisan and merely doing the bidding of their opponents.[97] These cases also raise a rather different but related issue, namely, whether the Constitutional Court should be placed in a position to summarily disqualify an elected PM and party for relatively minor abuses without any further appeal.

There were other early indications of a greater willingness of politicians to comply with constitutional norms under the 2007 constitution. For example, an important ruling of the Constitutional Court in July 2008 prompted the resignation of Thailand's foreign minister. Noppadon Pattama supported a UNESCO World Heritage bid which would have resulted in the Preah Vear Hindu temple on the Thai-Cambodian border being listed as a World Heritage Site despite its disputed ownership. This decision, affecting Thailand's national interest without reference to Parliament, was held to be in violation of the Constitution,[98] which requires ministers, before concluding treaties or agreements, to publicize relevant information, make arrangements for public hearings, and put the matter before the National Assembly for approval.[99]

Indonesia

One of the fascinating but puzzling aspects of constitutional jurisdiction is what determines the incidence of cases, both in numbers and in subject matter. The case load of Indonesia's MK has been considerable. In only three months following the 2004 general and presidential elections the court received 449 petitions, in itself perhaps a sign of a healthily contentious emergent democracy and confidence in the new mechanisms. Most of the important cases have been ones involving statutory review (104 cases to May 2007 – more than in Thailand, but far fewer than in Korea); but very few cases have involved disputes between state organs.[100] In contrast most of the Thai cases have involved emergency powers, qualification of office-

[97] Wehfritz, G and Seaton, J 'Thailand Slides Toward Civil War' *Newsweek*, Amsterdam, 15 December 2008.
[98] TC 2007, Article 190.
[99] 'Temple Ruling puts Foreign Ministry Lawyers in a Flap' *The Nation*, Bangkok, 10 July 2008. Thailand Foreign Minister Quits, BBC, 10 July 2003; 'Thai Foreign Minister Noppadon Pattama Resigns,' *The News and Observer*, Raleigh NC, 11 July 2008.
[100] An exception is a highly prominent dispute between the Judicial Commission and the Supreme Court, for which see Butt, S (2007), 'The Constitutional Court's Decision in the Dispute Between the Supreme Court and the Judicial Commission: Banishing Judicial Accountability?', in McLeod and MacIntyre (ed), *Indonesia: Democracy and the Promise of Good Governance*, ISEAS.

holders, issues of jurisdiction of state organs, and political party mergers and dissolutions, rather than the major human rights and constitutional interpretation issues that have dominated MK jurisprudence.

One explanation for this (there may well be others) is that although the validity of a conviction or a regulation cannot be directly litigated in the MK, the MK has been astute to allow successful challenges to the law on which such conviction or regulation is based, often therefore indirectly achieving the same result as would probably have been achieved without these limitations on the MK's jurisdiction. It should be noted that, as with Thailand, there are also administrative courts (*Pengadilan Tata Usaha Negara* or PTUN) which are empowered to deal with unconstitutional executive actions. It is presently uncertain whether they must follow the decisions of the MK, and perhaps a constitutional provision making it clear that all state organs, including judicial ones, must abide by MK decisions, would be useful.

The really striking aspect of the MK's performance is that, although its establishment and jurisdiction did not receive multi-lateral or general support, its actual impact has been remarkable. Crucially the MK has used the Constitution rather than political or administrative expediency as its touchstone. It struck down a provision in its own organic law that purported to restrict its jurisdiction over legislation to statutes passed after the reform process began in 1999, arguing that this restriction was not apparent in the Constitution itself – thereby at a stroke opening new order (pre-1999) statutes, including colonial era statutes, to scrutiny.[101] It has thus been able, for example, to strike down a law removing voting rights from members of the Indonesian Communist Party, and an old sedition law prohibiting the voicing of hostility to or hatred of the government.[102] It has, not entirely consistently perhaps, enforced the constitutional prohibition on retrospective laws so as to invalidate the retrospective application of the Anti-Terrorism Law of 2003 but allow prosecutions before the Human Rights Court established to deal with human rights abuses in East Timor.[103] It has compelled the government to comply with a constitutional provision prescribing the education budget. It has, in face of some controversy and causing attempts to circumvent the decisions, struck down privatization laws as contrary to national ownership provisions in the Constitution.[104] It has also made important decisions on constitutional structural issues

---

[101] Butt, supra note 75, at 182.
[102] International Herald Tribune, 17 July 2007, http://www.iht.com/articles/ap/2007/07/17/asia/AS-GEN-Indonesia-Free-Speech.php (accessed 5 January 2009).
[103] Fenwick, supra note 38.
[104] Fenwick, ibid; Butt and Lindsey supra note 37.

such as judicial independence and regional autonomy. In the *West Papua* case the Indonesian government sought to divide that province into three new provinces, a move intended to outflank secessionist tendencies.[105] The establishment of Central Papua was challenged by a petition of the Speaker of the Papua Provincial Parliament when a Presidential Instruction was issued to establish the new province. Being unable to deal with delegated legislation the MK accepted the petition and ruled the law authorizing the Presidential Instruction invalid.

Of particular interest is the case brought by the Supreme Court against the Judicial Commission, which pointed to the potential difficulties - contradictions even - in constitutional jurisprudence in emergent democracies. The Supreme Court (SC), reformed and vastly improved in image and performance in recent years, faced allegations of judicial corruption from the Judicial Commission (JC), and demands to investigate these further. The SC, in a highly publicized argument, refused, claiming it had already answered to the Anti-Corruption Commission on these matters and that the JC had no jurisdiction, basing its argument, in a suit before the MK, on the principle of judicial independence. Unhappily, the principle of judicial independence here contradicts the policy of taking stringent action to root out judicial corruption, which is still prevalent in Indonesia. The MK handled the matter in the following way. Having established to its own satisfaction that JC jurisdiction over 'judges' referred to career judges, not to the MK judges themselves, it proceeded to conclude that SC judges were subject to JC jurisdiction; however it supported judicial independence by striking down the JC's organic law provision allowing supervision of SC judges, because the law allowed the JC to report on judicial decisions and was vague in terms of the standards to be applied in the JC's discharge of its functions under the Law.[106]

Another area of concern is the MK's approach to cases involving economic policy. In several cases the MK has struck down the government's privatization initiatives on the basis that Article 33 of the Constitution requires the state to control important branches of production and natural resources, and that mere regulation as opposed to direct management fails to comply with this provision. This contrasts with the approach of the Thai Court to the emergency economic measures of 1998/9.[107] Understandably the government has attempted to find a way round these decisions via use of delegated legislation, which, as is discussed above, it outside the Court's jurisdiction. While it is true that this jurisdictional lacuna is unfortunate, it is

---

[105] Butt, supra note 75.
[106] Butt , supra note 100.
[107] Harding, supra note 22.

equally unfortunate that in these cases the MK seemed not to appreciate the difficulties involved in courts scrutinizing legislation relating to economic issues.

CONCLUSION

First in regard to Indonesia, most authors assessing the MK and its performance after five years of operation have mixed reactions. There are a number of contradictions. The MK has presented an image of efficiency and independence. It has supported the Indonesian *reformasi* project by insisting on the Constitution as its point of reference and has been courageous where necessary to implement the rule of law. However, as has been seen, some of its most striking decisions have actually in practice impeded important aspects of the same project such as rectifying the abuses of the past, dealing with terrorism, reforming the economy, countering secessionism, and rooting out corruption. Even in the process of supporting judicial independence the MK has appeared to elevate itself above other judges in a self-serving manner. The general law and the legal traditions in a civil law jurisdiction seem to act as a brake on the MK's effectiveness in terms of delivering the kind of judgments which can be regarded as authoritative. The MK is prevented from reviewing decisions and regulations so that the implementation and interpretation of laws are in general beyond its control.

We have also observed that both in Thailand and Indonesia the constitutional court has been established as a specialist court designed to determine issues such as the validity of legislation which can be directly referred to it for resolution. Indeed, the existence of such a court has technical advantages, for example, the potential of avoiding the legal uncertainty of conflicting interpretations by ordinary courts.[108] However, the main concern which emerges from the discussion of Thailand is the degree of reliance on the Constitutional Court under the 2007 Constitution as the final arbiter for many controversial political as well as legal questions, to the extent that it becomes one of the keys to constitutional success. In order to perform their role effectively any Constitutional Court requires a cohort of judges that are insulated from direct influence. In the Thai case, the appointment process has been refined to this end and it largely draws upon experienced judges and political scientists. The problem is not only that enormous pressure is placed on a small judicial panel (sometimes a quorum of five) to decide key

---

[108] Romeau, F (2006), 'The Establishment of Constitutional Courts: A Study of 128 Democratic Constitutions' *Review of Law and Economics*, 2:1, 103, at 109.

constitutional appointments but that the Constitutional Court may become the main locus for determining political issues. Even the most worthy and able judges may ultimately be unable to resolve highly controversial issues satisfactorily.[109] They simply have recourse to various alternative theories to justify whatever decision they finally reach. One view might hold that the solution is for the situation to be turned on its head: 'Doing away with [constitutional] review would have one clear effect. It would return all constitutional decision-making to the people acting politically. It would make populist constitutional law the only constitutional law there is'.[110]

On the other hand, where there is a torrid constitutional climate final recourse to a constitutional court has obvious advantages. The court may have the power positively to protect individual and minority rights and to support other constitutional watchdog bodies, but even where called upon to resolve exposed political questions a respected court has the potential to provide a more carefully reflected response, and also to operate as a force for restraint at times of crisis. This position remains a hope rather than an actuality in South East Asia, as we have seen, but we have also seen that there are reasons for thinking that this hope might be fulfilled if the dangers and problems outlined can be avoided.

---

[109] See Waldron, J (2006) 'The Core of the Case Against Judicial Review' 115 *The Yale Law Journal* 1346, at 1379.
[110] Tushnet, M (1999), *Taking the Constitution away from the Courts*, Princeton University Press, 1999, at 155.

SOUTH AMERICA

Constitutional Courts in Latin America: A Testing Ground for New Parameters of Classification?

JUSTIN O. FROSINI AND LUCIO PEGORARO*

Attempting to classify the constitutional adjudication systems in Latin America is by no means an easy task given the 'creativity' that has been used in developing them. Very rich and diverse approaches have been taken and one would commit a gross generalisation if one were to talk of a 'Latin American model of constitutional justice'. In many respects the object of this research poses a challenge that comparatists are typically faced with: on one hand, the need to avoid oversimplified classifications as these would not meet the aim of providing a precise picture of the legal institutions that are the object of study, on the other, the necessity of also avoiding classifications that are too detailed as these would risk thwarting the very aim of classifying i.e. to group together on the basis of similarities taking into account the differences the components of a certain group might bear to one another.[1]

* Justin O. Frosini is Lecturer of Public Law, Bocconi University, Milan, and Director of the Center for Constitutional Studies and Democratic Development, Bologna, Italy. Lucio Pegoraro is Full Professor of Comparative Public Law, University of Bologna, Italy. This article is the result of the combined efforts of both authors, however, the first two paragraphs (i.e. "Object of Analysis" and "Models of Constitutional adjudication and the Parameters of Classification") were written by Lucio Pegoraro while the others (starting with "Latin America and Conventional Models of Constitutional Review: A Historical Overview") were written by Justin O. Frosini. The premise and the concluding remarks are by both.
The authors would like to thank Francesco Biagi for his help in research of data and Andrew Harding, Antonio Hernández and Peter Leyland for their useful comments and constructive observations.

OBJECT OF ANALYSIS

To begin we must ask ourselves what exactly is the object of our study? In other words what do we imply by 'Latin America' and what meaning do we intend to give to this expression herein? These questions would appear banal, but in actual fact they are anything but that because without a clear geographical delimitation this research would inevitably lose value.

From a random survey of research done on Latin America in the most diverse of fields – from psychoanalysis[2] to biogeochemistry[3] – one discovers that there is no standard or universally accepted, geopolitical definition of Latin America. Some authors consider it to be that part of the Western Hemisphere south of the United States where Spanish, Portuguese and French are the official languages. Others consider Latin America to be a geographic and cultural region comprised of the eighteen Spanish-speaking countries plus Brazil or generally the areas that Spain and Portugal colonised in the Americas. For reasons of brevity we cannot go into the etymology of the term herein – related to the French expression *Amérique latine* coined by Napoléon III – but what we should emphasise is that we shall give the expression 'Latin America' the same meaning as the term 'Ibero America', where the prefix 'Ibero' obviously refers to the Iberian peninsula which includes Spain and Portugal (but also Andorra and Gibraltar).

More precisely our study shall take into consideration all the American members of the Organization of Ibero-American States (*Organización de Estados Iberoamericanos, Organização dos Estados Ibero-americanos*) formally known as the Organization of Ibero-American States for Education, Science and Culture. We have therefore considered neither the European members (Spain, Portugal and Andorra) nor the African member (Equatorial Guinea). Furthermore, two of the American members have also be excluded i.e. Cuba and Puerto Rico. The former has been left out because it is a Socialist State,[4] while the latter is not taken into consideration given its unusual

---

[1] For the difficulties related to the methodology of classification see Pegoraro, L and Rinella, A (2007), *Diritto pubblico comparato. Profili metodologici* Cedam at 15.

[2] Maria, A et al (2005) 'Yes, we have bananas!' (86) *The International Journal of Psychoanalysis* 86, 993–1009.

[3] Martinelli, LA et al (2006) 'Sources of reactive nitrogen affecting ecosystems in Latin America and the Caribbean: current trends and future perspectives' (79) *Biogeochemistry* 3-24.

[4] According to Art. 75 of the Cuban Constitution of 1976 'The National Assembly of People's Power is invested with the following powers [...] c) deciding on the constitutionality of laws, decree-laws, decrees and all other general provisions'. This provision is coherent with the principle of unity of state power that is at the basis of Socialist Republics and is the very reason for their adversion towards constitutional adjudication, see Pegoraro, L (2007) *Giustizia costituzionale comparata* Giappichelli at 64 to 66, Pegoraro, L (2004) *La Justicia*

status as a semi-autonomous Commonwealth of the United States. As a result eighteen countries are examined in this article: Argentina, Bolivia, Brazil, Colombia, Costa Rica, Chile, the Dominican Republic, Ecuador, El Salvador, Guatemala, Honduras, Mexico, Nicaragua, Panama, Paraguay, Peru, Uruguay and Venezuela.

One final observation from a methodological standpoint: given the number of countries that are the object of this study we have made ample use of tables so as to graphically illustrate some of the classifications that we have made.

MODELS OF CONSTITUTIONAL ADJUDICATION AND THE PARAMETERS OF CLASSIFICATION

Before examining the role and functions of Constitutional Courts in Latin America, we must set forth a theoretical-reconstructive premise concerning models of constitutional adjudication so as to create a framework that we can then use to examine the evolution of constitutional review in the countries under scrutiny. As we shall underline during the course of this article it is our belief that in order for a classification of constitutional adjudication in Latin America to make any sense one must go beyond the conventional models.[5]

The Conventional Dichotomy

The models of constitutional adjudication have been amply addressed in the Introduction to this book so it suffices to recall them very briefly herein. It is common knowledge, that one of the first writers to make a classification of models of constitutional adjudication was Mauro Cappelletti. The founder of the Florence Institute of Comparative Law made two main distinctions: first of all between 'political review' and 'judicial review' and then, with regard to the latter, between 'decentralised' and 'centralised' systems.[6] As

---

Constitutucional. Una perspectiva comparada Dykinson at 86.

[5] There is a vast literature concerning constitutional adjudication that, for reasons of brevity, cannot be exhaustively cited herein. Allow us therefore to refer to Pegoraro, L Giustizia costituzionale comparata supra note 4 at 1 to 3, notes 1, 2 and 3 and Pegoraro, L La Justicia Constitucional. Una perspectiva comparada supra note 4 at 13 to 15 notes 1, 2 and 3. Among the many books concerning constitutional justice in Latin America the following deserve a special mention: García Belaunde, D and Fernández Segado, F (eds) (1997), La jurisdicción constitucional en Iberoamérica, Ediciones Juridicas and Fernández Segado, F (2009), La justicia constitucional una vision de derecho comparado. Tomo III La justicia constitucional en América latina y España Dykinson..

[6] See Cappelletti, M (1968) Il controllo giudiziario di costituzionalità delle leggi nel diritto comparato Giuffré, Id (1971) Judicial Review in the Contemporary World, The Bobbs-Merill

an example of a body that carried out political review Cappelletti took the *Comité constitutionnel* introduced with the 1946 Constitution of the French IV Republic,[7] but at the same time he also considered the Soviet Union to be another prototype of political control of constitutionality.

As an example of a decentralised model of judicial review[8] Cappelletti took the United States based on the famous *Marbury vs. Madison* case of 1803 and the doctrine of Chief Justice John Marshall.[9]

The prototype of the centralised model of constitutional review is of course the system introduced in Austria with the Constitution of 1920 (i.e. the system that existed before the constitutional amendments of 1929 and 1975).[10] It should, however, be noted that a form of centralised constitutional review existed some decades earlier in Latin America (Venezuela 1858) although unlike the Austrian model it did not develop into a prototype.

In recent years this dichotomy has been much debated and some commentators now talk of a so-called 'tertium genus' i.e. a hybrid model that combines elements of both the US and Austrian models, also known as the 'incidental model' of constitutional review (examples being Italy, Spain and Germany).[11]

Given the object of this book it is important to point out that there is a certain debate among constitutional scholars as to what countries should

---

Company.

[7] In truth Cappelletti also considered the *Conseil Constitutionnel* of the Fifth Republic to be an example of a body that exercised political review. On the evolution of constitutional adjudication in France again see Pegoraro, L *Giustizia costituzionale comparata* supra note 4 at 19.

[8] Sometimes defined as 'diffused' or 'dispersed' review, see Mavčič, A (1995) *Slovenian Constitutional Review. Its position in the World and its role in the transition to a new democratic system*, Založba Nova revija at 19.

[9] As illustrated in the Introduction the US model of judicial review is repressive (or *a posteriori*) i.e. the law is reviewed after it has come into force. Second, judicial review is concrete because it is anchored to an actual controversy among real adversaries. Third, judicial review is decentralised (or diffused) because it can be carried out by all ordinary courts and not just by the Supreme Court.

[10] The Austrian Model – illustrated in detail in Anna Gamper and Francesco Palermo's article – is whereunder constitutional review is centralised because it is carried out by an ad hoc Constitutional Court and not by the ordinary courts and whereby review is abstract because it is not linked to an actual controversy, but is the result of a so-called special or principaliter proceeding. The system introduced in Austria in 1920 is what is known as the *Versfassungsgerichtsbarkeit* and it is a heuristic model based on the ideas of the Prague-born jurist Hans Kelsen.

[11] Pegoraro, L *Giustizia costituzionale comparata* supra note 6 at 35. The salient features of the Constitutional Courts of Italy, Germany and Spain are dealt with in more detail in the articles by Tania Groppi, Russell Miller and Victor Ferreres Comella respectively. In a recent book French scholar Guillaume Tusseau argues that comparative constitutional justice cannot be studied on the basis of the traditional dichotomy see Tusseau, G (2009) *Modelli di giustizia costituzionale. Saggio di critica metodologica – Contre les «modèles» de justice constitutionelle. Essai de critique méthodologique* Bononia University Press.

be included in the centralised and decentralised models and which systems are to be considered "hybrid". Taking Italy as an example, some scholars consider it to have a hybrid rather than a centralised system of constitutional review because unlike the 1920 Austrian prototype petitions can be filed in the Constitutional Court not just by constitutional bodies and by sub-state entities, but also by a regular judge during an ordinary court case (what is known as incidental recourse or incidenter proceedings). Due to the fact that the judge has a certain discretion in remitting the issue to the Constitutional Court (in fact, if he thinks that the question that has been raised is clearly unfounded he will not suspend the case) many think that this renders the system hybrid because regular court judges carry out preliminary review, something typical of decentralised systems. Other commentators refute this theory claiming that these are minor variants to the Austrian prototype and that what is determinant in defining the model as centralised is the fact that constitutional review is concentrated in the Constitutional Court. Another element that is sometimes taken to define a system as hybrid rather than centralised is the object of review. Again Italy is a good example because constitutional review on the part of the Constitutional Court is strictly limited to primary legislation i.e. statute law and acts having force of law such as legislative decrees and law decrees. Secondary sources of law such as government regulations and administrative acts, on the contrary, come under the scrutiny of the administrative courts in a decentralised manner. Again not all commentators agree that this suffices to define a system as hybrid rather than centralised.[12]

One last observation with regard to the issue of hybridity: as will be illustrated in the following paragraphs all the Latin American countries are hybrid to some degree or another because even those systems where there is only a Supreme Court and no Constitutional Court (Argentina for example) individuals have the possibility of filing petitions directly in the Supreme Court without having to go through the lower courts something that differentiates them from the US decentralised model of constitutional review: this is the very reason why, in the context of this book, we will also deal with Latin American countries that do not actually have a Constitutional Court.

---

[12] Again see Tania Groppi's contribution for a further explanation of this concept.

The Evolution of Constitutional Adjudication and the Need for New Parameters of Classification

Constitutional adjudication has evolved significantly over the last few decades and even the original US and Austrian models have undergone important modifications. On one hand, the US Supreme Court no longer acts automatically as an Appeal Court,[13] thus becoming evermore like a Constitutional Court stricto sensu (although judicial review can still be carried out by all the courts) and, as anticipated above, the Austrian Constitution was amended in 1929, thus introducing diffused elements to the centralised model of constitutional review.

Alongside the 'tertium genus' mentioned earlier some scholars now talk of a 'quartum genus' i.e. hybrid systems of constitutional adjudication,[14] which are the result of the transition to democracy of those Central and Eastern European countries[15] that once belonged to the Soviet bloc and, of course, the evolution of the authoritarian-populist regimes of Latin America, which are the object of this study.[16]

With the global spread of constitutional adjudication the question is whether one should maintain the classic dichotomy illustrated above or whether other elements should be taken into consideration in order to classify systems of constitutional review. With regard to Latin America we believe the latter to be a necessity.

An alternative could be to consider the territorial organisation of the state and the role that is played by Constitutional Courts in resolving jurisdictional disputes between the State (central government, federal government) and the sub-state entities. In our opinion this element is useful, but in itself not sufficient to construct a model of constitutional adjudication. Still with regard to territorial organisation one could also consider the existence of State Constitutional Courts alongside Federal Constitutional Courts.[17]

Other factors that one could take into account are the parameters and object of review. It is common knowledge that in France the 1971 decision

---

[13] With just the writ of certiorari the Court chooses its docket allowing it to concentrate on the more important cases having a 'constitutional tone'.

[14] On the basis of which, on one hand, the ordinary judges can decide not to apply a statute law if they believe it to be unconstitutional and, on the other there is ad hoc Constitutional Court.

[15] See the article by Kasia Lach and Wojciech Sadurski.

[16] One could also include Portugal, Greece, Russia and various countries in Northern Europe in this category, see Pegoraro, L *Giustizia costituzionale comparata* supra note 6 at 52.

[17] This parameter was used in an interesting study concerning Mexico, see Astudillo Reyes, CI (2004) *Ensayos de justicia constitucional en cuatro ordenamientos de México: Veracruz, Coahuila, Tlaxcala y Chiapas*, Unam.

of the *Conseil constitutionnel* to incorporate the Preamble of the 1958 Constitution (and therefore the Declaration of the Rights of Man and the Citizen of 1789 and the social and economic rights of the 1946 Constitutional Preamble), radically transformed the role of the Constitutional Council turning it into a true and proper Constitutional Court albeit limited to preventative review.[18] This is a demonstration of the importance that the parameter assumes in the context of constitutional review. Many countries (including some in Latin America, as we will see in the following paragraphs) have elevated international treaties and international customary law to constitutional level, thus changing the very concept of the Constitution as the 'higher law'. This can often have rather paradoxical affects given the fact that international treaties are usually incorporated in the domestic legal system through sub-constitutional sources of law (often Acts of Parliament).

Moreover, in many countries constitutional amendment laws may be first the object and then the parameter of constitutional review. If one accepts that the Constitutional Court has the jurisdiction to review amendments to the Constitution then the very idea of constitutional review changes: the Court is no longer a guardian against abuses of power that undermine the supremacy of the Constitution, but it becomes the 'controller' *tout court* of constituent and constituted power (we will address this issue in more detail in the penultimate paragraph of this article).

Furthermore, could one classify systems of constitutional adjudication on the basis of the number of entities or individuals that have locus standi to lodge a claim with the Supreme or Constitutional Court? Again France with its *saisine parlementaire* – i.e. the possibility for a group of members of Parliament to file a constitutional petition introduced in 1974 – demonstrates how important this element is. One could also consider the incidental recourse that exists in Italy and Germany or the locus standi that, in some countries, is given to municipalities and other local government authorities. In addition, one cannot forget the direct petitions that can be filed by single individuals (such as the *Verfassungsbeschwerde* in Germany or the *recurso de amparo* in Spain and, as we shall see, Latin America).

Finally, another element could be taken into consideration to classify Supreme and Constitutional Courts and that is the limit to their jurisdiction. In other words, alongside constitutional review stricto sensu, do Constitutional Courts exercise other powers? The answer is, of course, affirmative because most Constitutional Courts are plurifunctional.

Latin America is a perfect testing ground for these 'new parameters of classification' given the fact that, as we shall explain, nearly all the countries

---

[18]   See the article by Marie-Claire Ponthoreau contained in this book.

examined would have to be termed as 'hybrid systems' if we were to limit our analysis to the conventional models of constitutional adjudication outlined above (and in the Introduction to this book).

LATIN AMERICA AND CONVENTIONAL MODELS OF CONSTITUTIONAL REVIEW: A HISTORICAL OVERVIEW

Before examining existing systems of constitutional adjudication in Latin America a brief diachronic analysis is required. With reference to Cappelletti's preliminary distinction between political and judicial review, it should be underlined that historically the first model of constitutional adjudication to be transplanted in Latin America was political review. The reason for this was the fact that Latin American countries were influenced by the Continental European tradition and, as a result, they all belonged to the civil law system. On the contrary, the common law system was exported by the English to the Anglophone parts of America including of course the United States. As many writers have underlined it is not until the mid 19th Century that Latin American countries were actually influenced by the United States' model of judicial review. Furthermore, the way the US model was actually imported differed significantly from country to country.

The first country to introduce the model of political review carried out by the Senate as outlined in the French Constitution of 1799 (year VIII in the French Republican calendar) was Bolivia.[19] Other countries that introduced political review were Brazil,[20] Ecuador,[21] Chile and Peru. As some writers have pointed out there are still remnants of political review in some contemporary Constitutions such as Art. 102.2 of the Peruvian Constitution of 1993, which assigns Congress with the task of protecting the Constitution.

By the mid 19th Century, however, it was clear that the US model of decentralised judicial review had influenced most of the countries in Latin America, which adopted this system in one form or another (Dominican

---

[19] See Fernández Segado, F (2006) 'La jurisdicción constitucional en América latina. Evolución y problematica desde la indipendencia hasta 1979' in Ferrer Mac-Gregor, E (ed.) (2006) *Derecho procesal constitucional* (5th ed.) Porrúa 149 at 154 and Fernández Segado, F *La justicia constitucional una vision de derecho comparado. Tomo III La justicia constitucional en América latina y España* supra note 5, 455-538.

[20] Brazil which was not only influenced by the French model, but also by the ideas of Benjamin Constant who argued that judges should not be given the power to verify the constitutionality of statutes laws. This Constitution was then amended in 1834 so as to introduce a form of preventive political review see Mezzetti, L (2007) 'La Giustizia costituzionale: storia, modelli, teoria' in Mezzetti L. et al (2007) *La Giustizia Costituzionale*, Cedam 1 at 79.

[21] With the introduction of a State Council.

Republic 1844, Colombia 1850, Mexico 1857, Venezuela 1858, Argentina 1860, Brazil 1890). More precisely some countries began exclusively with a decentralised system of constitutional review and then later integrated it with a centralised system (this is the case of Mexico and Brazil), while others from the very beginning adopted a hybrid or mixed system (examples being Venezuela, Colombia, Guatemala and Peru). Argentina is the only country in Latin America that has always had and still has a system of judicial review similar to that of the United States. Let us take this country, together with Brazil and Mexico, as an example of this evolution.

The 1860 Constitution of Argentina, using terminology similar to that of the 1787 Constitution of the United States, underlines the supremacy of the Constitution, but just like the US Constitution it does not expressly confer the power of judicial review on the Supreme Court or any other courts. It is indeed curious to note that – again exactly as occurred in the United States – judicial review is 'judge made' i.e. it is the result of a decision taken by the Argentinian Supreme Court. What is even more startling is the fact that the decision taken in the *Sojo Case* 1887 consisted of the striking down of a law that aimed at extending the jurisdiction of the Supreme Court: in other words *Sojo* is very much Argentina's *Marbury vs. Madison*.

Rather like Argentina, originally Brazil's system of constitutional adjudication was also very similar to the US model. Unlike the United States and Argentina, however, the 1891 Constitution expressly gave the Federal Supreme Court the power, in last instance, to decide on judgments delivered by other Courts or judges. The Federal Supreme Court could do this in three cases: first, when the decision taken by the lower court was in contrast with a provision of the Constitution, a federal law or a treaty; second, when the lower court declared a treaty or a federal law unconstitutional; third, when a law or another act of a local government authority was in contrast with the Constitution or a federal law.[22] These constitutional provisions thus established a decentralised system of constitutional review on the part of all the Courts as well as the power of the Federal Supreme Court to intervene in any proceeding that concerned the pursuance of a law with the Constitution.

Finally, Mexico was also strongly influenced by the United States in terms of its system of constitutional adjudication. In fact the 1847 Constitution introduced a decentralised system of judicial review by establishing that it was the duty of all the federal courts to protect the rights and freedoms provided for in the Constitution against unconstitutional action taken by the executive bodies of the States or the Federation. The system then

[22] See Art. 102, III of the Constitution.

acquired its own peculiar characteristics with the Constitution of 1857 by introducing a second legal instrument for challenging the constitutionality of a law: so-called *juicio de amparo* (this will be examined in more detail later). This is now regulated in Mexico's present Constitution.

CONVENTIONAL MODELS OF CONSTITUTIONAL REVIEW AND LATIN AMERICA TODAY

Constitutional Courts or Supreme Courts?

After this brief historical overview let us now examine how constitutional adjudication operates today in Latin America. In order to do this one must first be acquainted with the court system.

Countries with a Constitutional Court	Countries with a "Sala Constitucional" within the Supreme Court	Countries with a Supreme Court
Bolivia *(Tribunal Constitucional)*	Costa Rica *(Sala Constitucional de la Corte Suprema de Justicia)*	Argentina *(Corte Suprema de Justicia)*
Chile *(Tribunal Constitucional)*	El Salvador *(Sala de lo Constitucional de la Corte Suprema de Justicia)*	Brazil *(Supremo Tribunal Federal)*
Colombia *(Corte Constitucional)*	Honduras *(Sala de lo Constitucional de la Corte Suprema de Justicia)*	Dominican Republic *(Suprema Corte de Justicia)*
Ecuador *(Corte Constitucional)*	Nicaragua *(Sala de lo Constitucional de la Corte Suprema de Justicia)*	Mexico *(Suprema Corte de Justicia)*
Guatemala *(Corte de Constitucionalidad)*	Paraguay *(Sala constitucional de la Corte Suprema de Justicia)*	Uruguay *(Suprema Corte de Justicia)*
Peru *(Tribunal Constitucional)*	Venezuela *(Sala Constitucional del Tribunal Supremo de Justicia)*	Panama *(Corte Suprema de Justicia)*

Table 1: Court Structure

As summarised in Table 1 the eighteen Latin American countries that are the object of this study can be divided into three categories: first, countries having an ad hoc Constitutional Court; second, countries with a '*Sala*

Constitucional' within the Supreme Court (i.e. a Constitutional Chamber of the Supreme Court) and, third, countries which only have a Supreme Court. If our analysis were strictly based on the *nomen iuris* of the Courts then in theory the only countries that one ought to take into consideration would be those belonging to the first category i.e. Bolivia, Chile, Colombia, Ecuador, Guatemala and Peru, but as we will see functions typical of Constitutional Courts are carried out by the Constitutional Chambers of Supreme Courts or by Supreme Courts as a whole (especially through direct petitions) thus providing a further demonstration of the hybrid character of constitutional adjudication in Latin America that we have underlined several times during the course of this article.

Selection Procedure

Still with reference to the structure of the Courts, let us also briefly examine how judges are appointed.

Apointed by the Legislative	Appointed by the Executive and Legislative	Appointed through a Mixed System
Bolivia *(2/3 of Congress)*	Argentina *(President with Senate approval)*	Chile *(3 by the President, 4 by Congress, 3 by the Supreme Court)*
Costa Rica *(2/3 of Legislative Assembly)*	Brazil *(President with Senate approval)*	Colombia *(Senate from a list of three presented by the President, Supreme Court, Council of State)*
El Salvador *(2/3 of Legislative Assembly)*	Mexico *(President with Senate approval)*	Dominican Republic *(National Magistrates' Council)*
Honduras *(2/3 of Congress from a list presented by a Nomination Board)*	Nicaragua *(Elected by the majority of the National Assembly are chosen from lists presented by the President and by the Deputies)*	Ecuador *(Committee composed of members appointed by the Legislative, the Executive and the Transparency and Social Control Body)*
Peru *(2/3 of Congress)*	Panama *(Cabinet with Legislative approval)*	Guatemala *(Supreme Court, Congress, President, University Council, Bar Council)*

Uruguay *(2/3 of General Assembly)*		Paraguay *(Senate with President's approval, from a list presented by the Magistrates' Council)*
Venezuela *(2/3 of National Assembly)*		

Table 2: Selection of Judges to Constitutional or Supreme Courts (note that on the basis of Table 1 the selection system refers to the Constitutional Court for those countries that have both Constitutional and Supreme Courts).

As one can see from Table 2 there is no uniform procedure for selection and appointment of judges to Constitutional or Supreme Courts in Latin America. A strong influence of the United States clearly emerges in Argentina, Brazil and Mexico where judges are chosen by the President with the approval of the Senate. In other countries, such as Peru and Venezuela, the legislative branch plays a central role. Furthermore, in all seven countries where the judges are chosen by the legislative body a qualified majority (2/3) is required, thus preventing the political majority from being able to appoint judges to the Court without coming to an agreement with the opposition. It should be pointed out, however, that despite these entrenched procedures the appointments system in some Latin American countries has not always prevented the judges from being politically influenced. An eloquent case is Peru where, according to many commentators, the short term in office of constitutional court judges has rendered them less independent.

Finally, with regard to the countries with a Constitutional Court (see Table 1), it is interesting to note that in three cases out of six (Chile, Colombia and Guatemala) the Supreme Court plays a role in the selection of the constitutional justices, thus reaffirming conventional doctrine according to which ad hoc Constitutional Courts are not to be considered part of the judiciary stricto sensu.

How Centralised and Decentralised Review operate in Latin America

As we know, according to Hans Kelsen's heuristic model, centralised constitutional review should be carried out by an ad hoc court-like body that is separate from the rest of the judiciary, but as we have just seen only six countries in Latin America actually have a Constitutional Court, therefore with regard to centralised review diverse solutions have been adopted.

In some countries concentrated review is carried out by a Supreme Court, which is at the top of the judiciary system. This is the case in Costa Rica, Mexico and Venezuela while in other countries the ad hoc Constitutional Court has sole competence for carrying out concentrated constitutional review. Countries that have opted for this solution include Bolivia, Chile, Colombia, Ecuador, Guatemala and Peru all of which, as we saw in Table 1, have a Constitutional Court.

The way centralised review is carried out in most countries in Latin America is therefore sui generis with respect to the conventional Austrian model. As we know, again according to Kelsen, it was necessary to build a system in which constitutional review, entrusted to a single court, constituted not a third parallel power but one above the others that was charged with monitoring the three essential functions of the state (executive, legislative and judicial) to ensure they were exercised within the limits of the Constitution. Latin America as a case study, however, demonstrates the fact that centralised constitutional review can be carried out without the Constitutional Court necessarily having to be outside the traditional categories of state power.[23]

More precisely, we can divide countries into two groups according to the body that actually performs centralised constitutional review: first, there are countries where centralised review is carried out exclusively by a Supreme Court or by the Constitutional Chamber of the latter and second, countries where centralised review is carried out by a Supreme Court or by a Constitutional Court in the context of a hybrid system of constitutional adjudication.

What about the US model of judicial review? Most countries in Latin America also have a system of decentralised review, although none of these countries have carried out an 'adoptión servil'[24], there is no doubt that there are similarities with the US model. Nevertheless, again, as with centralised review, Latin America represents a sui generis case with regard to the decentralised model and the reason for this is the fact that all the countries examined belong to a differ family of law with respect to the prototype of

---

[23]   See Brewer-Carías, AR (1997) 'La jurisdiccion constitucional en America Latina' in García Belaunde, D and Fernández Segado, F (eds) (1997) *La Jurisdiccion constitucional en Iberoamerica* Dykinson 117 at 135. When we say that the Courts are *separate* from the judiciary we imply that they have functions that cannot be exercised by other courts, but at the same time they do not exercise the judicial powers of the ordinary judiciary. Furthermore, their separation can also be seen in the way that the judges are appointed and the salary they receive, which are both different to the rest of the judiciary.

[24]   ...a 'servile adoption'. This effective expression is used by one of Latin America's most illustrious constitutionalists Domingo García Belaunde see García Belaunde, D (2006) *La Constitución y su Dinámica* (2nd ed.) Palestra Editores at 35.

decentralised judicial review, the United States. In fact while the latter is a common law country, the former all have civil law systems.

Now, if we read the works of Mauro Cappelletti and his distinction between decentralised and centralised models of judicial review, this difference is highly significant given the fact that the Italian comparatist was convinced that decentralised judicial review could only exist in common law countries. In fact Cappelletti argued that decentralised judicial review in the United States was capable of upholding and protecting the Constitution because of the existence of binding and persuasive precedents and the principle of stare decisis.[25] As we know in *Marbury vs. Madison* the US Supreme Court declared that courts can adjudicate disputes arising under the Constitution in a way that is binding to the parties (inter partes), but it did not specify whether those interpretations of the Constitution were meant to be authoritative or binding erga omnes. Supreme Court decisions have been treated as generally binding on everyone, although there have been recurring challenges to this notion.[26] The question we therefore have to ask ourselves with regard to decentralised judicial review in Latin America is do these civil law countries ensure a uniform interpretation of the Constitution in the absence of rules on binding precedent that exist in the case of common law adjudication? The answer in many respects is quite simple: each country has adopted specific measures to try and overcome this problem.

Let us begin with Mexico. Art. 107, Section XIII, para. 1 of the Constitution states that 'The law shall specify the terms and cases in which the precedents of the courts of the federal judicial branch are binding, as well as the requirements for their modification' and this is exactly what the *Ley de Amparo* has done. According to the Law on Constitutional Petitions, the Supreme Court decisions on *amparo* cases will have inter partes effect unless there are at least five decisions that resolve the issue in the same way.[27] This rather awkward constitutional provision has been the target of criticism and is the source of problems in Mexico.

---

[25] The issue is actually rather more complicated given the fact that, as we underlined earlier, the Supreme Court no longer acts as an Appeal Court. With just the writ of certiorari it chooses its docket and therefore it will not necessarily hear all cases coming from lower courts.

[26] See Rosenfeld, M (2005) 'Constitutional adjudication in Europe and the United States: paradoxes and contrasts' in Nolte, G (ed.) (2005) *European and US Constitutionalism* Cambridge Univeristy Press 197 at 202.

[27] In other words a decision by the Supreme Court will only apply to that particular case and not to others unless there have been five decisions concerning that topic after which one will have binding case law that can be applied in all other subsequent cases.

In Argentina and Brazil, two countries, which have followed the US model quite closely, there is a legal instrument known as the *recurso extraordinario de inconstitucionalidad* (extraordinary claim of unconstitutionality) which can be filed in the Supreme Court against last instance judgments in which a federal law has been declared unconstitutional and therefore inapplicable in the specific case. The decision of the Supreme Court has an in casu and inter partes effect, but because it has been delivered by the highest court in the country the lower courts are obliged to comply with it, therefore the decision de facto has an erga omnes effect.

Another solution is the one adopted in Venezuela. Here Art. 321 of the Civil Procedure Code states that 'judges shall apply the jurisprudence of the Cassation Chamber in analogous cases so as to protect the integrity of the legislation and the uniformity of the case law': in other words the binding effect of Supreme Court decisions is codified.

In other countries in Latin America, this problem is resolved by the very fact that the system of constitutional adjudication is hybrid. This is the case in Bolivia, Colombia, Guatemala and Peru, but also in Venezuela and Mexico as an addition to the solutions illustrated above. In these countries the Supreme Court or the Constitutional Court can intervene in order to formally declare invalid laws that are not in pursuance of the Constitution: these decisions have an erga omnes effect. In other words, on one hand, any court may simply declare a law unconstitutional and not apply it in a concrete case or controversy (i.e. inter partes effect), on the other, the Surpreme or Constitutional Court may definitely strike down a law that has been challenged (i.e. erga omnes effect).[28]

As the Venezuelan constitutionalist Brewer-Carías has underlined, Latin America is proof of the fact that Cappelletti's theory according to which decentralised constitutional review may only exist in common law countries is disputable. In fact, while common law countries have developed the doctrine of stare decisis in order to resolve the problem of legal uncertainty and the possible conflict between different courts with regard to judicial review, countries belonging to the Roman law family of legal systems have adopted other legal mechanisms in order to overcome the problems that arise from court decisions that only have an inter partes effect. In other words, as Latin America demonstrates, there is no necessary connection between the way constitutional review is carried out (e.g. decentralised or centralised) and the common law or civil law tradition of the country.

---

[28] This means that the law that has not be applied in a certain case will remain part of the system of legal sources until a decision is taken by the Constitutional or Supreme Court.

As anticipated at the beginning of this article if we take into account solely the conventional distinction between decentralised and centralised constitutional review nearly all the countries in Latin America have a hybrid system. Furthermore, with regard to territorial organisation that we referred to earlier, one should note fact that in the federal systems in Latin America (or pseudo-federal, as is the case in Venezuela) rather like the United States the judicial system is actually made up of two different court systems: the federal court system and the state (or provincial) court systems. While each court system is responsible for hearing certain types of cases, neither is completely independent of the other, and the systems often interact. Mexico is of particular interest in this regard given the fact that the single states have introduced Constitutional Courts.[29]

This said, on the basis of our theoretical-reconstructive premise let us now broaden our analysis and take into consideration other elements in order to classify the systems of constitutional justice in this region.

FUNCTIONS OF CONSTITUTIONAL AND SUPREME COURTS IN LATIN AMERICA

Let us begin with the last element considered in the premise i.e. whether alongside constitutional review stricto sensu, Constitutional or Supreme Courts in Latin America exercise other powers.

As we can see from Table 3 the answer is affirmative. First, in all eighteen countries examined herein, either the Constitutional or Supreme Court (and sometimes both) carry out constitutional review as amply illustrated above (and that, in certain respects, is self-evident).

	Constitutional review	Resolution of jurisdictional disputes	Impeachment	Power to declare political parties unconstitutional	Legislative initiative	Power of appointment
Argentina	Yes	Yes	No	No	No	No
Bolivia	Yes	Yes	No	No	No	No

---

[29] Astudillo Reyes, CI (2004) *Ensayos de justicia constitucional en cuatro ordenamientos de México: Veracruz, Coahuila, Tlaxcala y Chiapas* supra note 16.

Brazil	Yes	Yes	Yes	No	No	No
Chile	Yes	Yes	No	Yes	No	No
Colombia	Yes	No	No	No	No	No
Costa Rica	Yes	Yes	No	No	No	No
Dominican Republic	Yes	No	Yes	No	No	Yes
Ecuador	Yes	Yes	No	No	No	No
El Salvador	Yes	Yes	No	No	No	Yes
Guatemala	Yes	Yes	No	No	No	No
Honduras	Yes	Yes	No	No	No	Yes
Mexico	Yes	Yes	No	No	No	No
Nicaragua	Yes	Yes	No	No	No	Yes
Panama	Yes	No	No	No	No	No
Paraguay	Yes	Yes	No	No	No	No
Peru	Yes	Yes	No	No	Yes	No
Uruguay	Yes	Yes	No	No	No	Yes
Venezuela	Yes	Yes	Yes	No	No	No

Table 3: Functions of Constitutional and Supreme Courts in Latin America. Note that in countries where there is a Constitutional Court separated from the Supreme Court, we mention only the functions of the former and not the latter (see Table 1). Furthermore, we have not included in this chart decisions on constitutionality when these are limited to errors of procedure and not the substantive content.

As Table 3 clearly illustrates, with the exception of Colombia, the Dominican Republic and Panama, all the Latin American Constitutional or Supreme Courts also have the power to resolve jurisdictional disputes (we will further examine this function below, see Table 8).

As regards other functions assigned to the Courts, some have impeachment powers. In particular, the Federal Supreme Court in Brazil judges the ordinary crimes of the President, Vice-President, Members of the Congress and Ministers. It also decides on the high crimes of the Ministers, while the Supreme Court of Justice in the Dominican Republic judges – in single instance – crimes committed by the President, Vice-President,

Deputies, Senators, Secretary of State. Finally, in Venezuela, the Supreme Court of Justice judges the impeachment of the President.

In a certain number of countries the Constitutional or Supreme Courts also have powers of appointment. The Supreme Courts of the Dominican Republic and Uruguay have the power to appoint officials and other employees whose responsibilities come under the judiciary power (in Uruguay the Supreme Court also appoints the public defenders), while in El Salvador it has the power to appoint first instance judges, appeal judges, justices of the peace and coroners.

Finally there are two functions that are each exercised only by one Constitutional Court: that of Chile has the power to declare political parties unconstitutional, while that of Peru has the power of legislative initiative (i.e. the power to present legislative proposals to Congress).

On the basis of this analysis we can therefore affirm that the two main functions exercised by Constitutional and Supreme Courts in Latin America are constitutional review and resolution of jurisdictional disputes. At this point, in line with our theoretical-reconstructive premise, we need to examine these two functions in more detail. In particular, with regard to constitutional review one must pose the question of what acts may come under scrutiny and the extension of the parameters that are used,[30] while as concerns the resolution of jurisdictional disputes we need to determine what types of conflicts come under the jurisdiction of the Courts.

The Object of Constitutional Review

As is clearly illustrated in Table 4, in all eighteen countries statute laws (i.e. acts of Parliament or Congress) may come under constitutional review, but with regard to other acts and sources of law there are considerable differences between the countries that were examined.

	Statute Laws	De-crees	Regu-la-tions	Ordi-nances	Charters of Asso-ciations or Trade Unions	Interna-tional treaties
Argentina	Yes	Yes	No	Yes	No	Yes

---

[30] i.e. what the French would call *bloc de constiutionnalité* (see the article by Ponthoreau, this book), or what in Spanish is known as the *bloque de constitucionalidad*.

Bolivia	Yes	Yes	No	No	No	Yes
Brazil	Yes	Yes	Yes	No	No	No
Chile	Yes	Yes	No	No	No	Yes
Colombia	Yes	Yes	No	No	No	Yes
Costa Rica	Yes	Yes	Yes	No	Yes	Yes
Dominican Republic	Yes	Yes	Yes	No	No	No
Ecuador	Yes	Yes	Yes	Yes	No	Yes
El Salvador	Yes	Yes	Yes	No	No	No
Guatemala	Yes	No	Yes	No	No	Yes
Honduras	Yes	No	No	No	No	No
Mexico	Yes	No	No	No	No	Yes
Nicaragua	Yes	Yes	Yes	No	No	No
Panama	Yes	Yes	No	No	No	Yes
Paraguay	Yes	Yes	Yes	Yes	No	No
Perù	Yes	Yes	Yes	Yes	No	Yes
Uruguay	Yes	Yes	No	No	No	No
Venezuela	Yes	Yes	Yes	Yes	No	Yes

Table 4: Object of Constitutional Review

In some Latin American countries, such as Argentina, Costa Rica and Peru, the object of constitutional review is quite extended (for example in Costa Rica even charters of associations, trade unions and cooperatives may come under scrutiny), in others there is a numerus clausus (for example, in Honduras only statute laws may be the object of review).

In this context, Colombia is of particular interest because the 1991 Constitution establishes that the decrees with which the President and his government declares a 'state of exception' (see Art. 213) must be sent to the Constitutional Court the day after promulgation so that the latter can verify their constitutionality (Art. 214.6) Significantly in fact, given the present situation in Colombia, the Constitution (Art. 214.2) states that during a state of exception 'Neither human rights nor fundamental freedoms may be suspended. In all cases, the rules of international humanitarian law will be observed.'

If, on one hand, up until now by referring to the conventional models of constitutional review (decentralised and centralised) or to the number of functions of the Constitutional and Supreme Courts we have been unable to clearly distinguish between the different constitutional justice systems in Latin America, employing the object of review as a parameter for classification permits us, for the first time, to differentiate between the eighteen countries we have examined.[31]

As we can see in Table 5, one can categorise them into three groups: broad, medium and restricted review.

Broad	Medium	Restricted
Argentina	Bolivia	Honduras
Costa Rica	Brazil	Mexico
Ecuador	Chile	Uruguay
Paraguay	Colombia	
Perù	Dominican Republic	
Venezuela	El Salvador	
	Guatemala	
	Nicaragua	
	Panama	

Table 6: Classification of Latin American countries on the basis of the extension of the object of constitutional review.

Parameters for Constitutional Review

Let us now turn to another element that allows us to distinguish between the various countries in Latin America i.e. the parameters that can be used in constitutional review.[32]

---

[31] It should be noted that, as we will illustrate below, another possible object of review are constitutional amendment laws. These have not been included in Table 4 because there is much dispute among legal scholars, legislators and Constitutional Courts as to whether such laws should come under scrutiny of the latter. As we will see, this issue is of the utmost importance because it is determinant in answering the question of who is the true holder of constituent power (i.e. what German scholars define as the *Verfassungsgeber.*

[32] A clear definition of the *bloque de constitucionalidad* can be found in a decision taken by

In many of these countries the *bloque de constitucionalidad* is in part determined by provisions of the Constitution and in part by the case law of the Constitutional and Supreme Courts themselves. Furthermore, it should be underlined that, as occurs in a great number of other countries, defining the parameters of constitutional review often gives rise to significant scholarly disputes.

First of all, as illustrated in Table 7, we have not included the Constitution itself as it is self-evident that in all eighteen countries the Constitutional or Supreme Court uses it as a parameter for constitutional review.[33]

	International Human Rights Law	Constitutional Practice	Case Law	Other Parameters
Argentina	Yes	No	No	No
Brazil	Yes	No	No	No
Bolivia	Yes	No	No	No
Chile	Yes	No	No	No
Colombia	Yes	No	No	No
Costa Rica	Yes	Yes	No	Yes*
Dominican Republic	Yes	No	Yes*	No
Ecuador	Yes	No	No	No
El Salvador	No	No	No	No
Guatemala	Yes	No	No	No
Honduras	Yes	No	No	No
Mexico	No	No	No	No
Nicaragua	Yes	No	No	No

the Colombian Constitutional Court in 1995: 'it refers to all those norms and principles that, although not contained in the provisions of the Constitution are used as parameters for constitutional review because, through different ways, they have become an integral part of the Constitution', see Decision C-225-95.

[33] For reasons of brevity we shall not address the issue of whether the preamble to the Constitution is to be considered part of the *bloque de constitucionalidad* or not. On this topic see Torres del Moral, A, Tajadura Tejada, J (eds) (2003) *Los preámbulos constitucionales en Iberoamérica* Centro de Estudios Políticos y Constitucionales.

Panama	Yes*	Yes	Yes*	Yes*
Paraguay	Yes	No	No	No
Peru	Yes	No	No	No
Uruguay	Yes	No	No	No
Venezuela	Yes	No	No	No

Table 7: Parameters for constitutional review. *See text for more details.

The Constitutional and Supreme Courts of all the countries under scrutiny, with the exception of Mexico and El Salvador, use International Human Rights Law as a parameter for constitutional review. Just to take one example, Art. 93 of the Colombian Constitution of 1991 clearly states that 'International treaties and agreements ratified by the Congress that recognise human rights and that prohibit their limitation in states of emergency have priority domestically.' That same constitutional provision goes on to affirm that 'The rights and duties mentioned in this Charter will be interpreted in accordance with international treaties on human rights ratified by Colombia'. In other words, not only can international treaties on human rights be used as a parameter in constitutional review, but they can also be used to interpret the human rights that are laid down in the Constitution itself. It is interesting to note that a much more restrictive stance is taken in Panama where international law cannot be used as a parameter in constitutional review *unless* it establishes fundamental rights that are essential for the Democratic State.

Mexico is the only Latin American country that uses solely the Constitution as a parameter for review, while Costa Rica and Panama are the two countries that have the most extended *bloque de constitucionalidad*. More precisely, in both countries parliamentary standing orders may be used as a parameter in constitutional review of legislative procedure and, most interestingly, the Costa Rican Constitution of 1871 (which is no longer in effect) can still be used to carry out constitutional review of statute laws that were approved when that Constitution was in force. In fact if these statute laws infringe provisions of the 1871 Constitution they can be struck down. The 1946 Constitution of Panama, which too is no longer in force, can be used in much a similar manner. Again with reference to Panama, the constitutional case law of its Supreme Court may also be employed as a parameter in constitutional review. This is also the case in the Dominican Republic where the *bloque de constitucionalidad* also includes the resolutions of the Inter-American Court of Human Rights.

Disputes that come under the jurisdiction of the Constitutional and Supreme Courts

As we have seen, the other significant function of the Constitutional and Supreme Courts in Latin America is the resolution of jurisdictional disputes. But precisely what conflicts come under the jurisdiction of the Courts? As illustrated in Table 8, we have established six types of dispute.

	Conflicts between branches of Government	Conflicts between States	Conflicts between the Union and a State	Conflicts between courts	Conflicts between munici-palities
Argentina	No	Yes	Yes	Yes	No
Bolivia	Yes	No	No	No	Yes
Brazil	No	Yes	Yes	Yes	No
Chile	No	No	No	No	No
Colombia	No	No	No	No	No
Costa Rica	Yes	No	No	No	Yes
Dominican Republic	No	No	No	No	No
Ecuador	Yes	No	No	No	Yes
El Salvador	Yes	No	No	Yes	No
Guatemala	No	No	No	No	No
Honduras	Yes	No	No	No	No
Mexico	Yes	Yes	Yes	No	Yes
Nicaragua	Yes	No	No	No	Yes
Panama	No	No	No	No	No
Paraguay	No	No	No	No	No
Peru	Yes	No	No	No	Yes
Uruguay	No	No	No	No	No
Venezuela	Yes	Yes	Yes	Yes	Yes

Table 8: Types of dispute resolved by Constitutional or Supreme Courts

367

It should come as no surprise that disputes between States and between the Union (Federal Government) and the States come under the jurisdiction of the Supreme Courts of Argentina, Brazil, Mexico and Venezuela i.e. the four federal states in Latin America.

In just over half the countries examined the Constitutional or Supreme Courts resolve disputes between branches of government.

In all these cases, the Constitutional or Supreme Courts not only act as guardians of the Constitution, but also as super partes arbiters.[34]

THE WRITS OF AMPARO, HABEAS CORPUS AND HABEAS DATA

Earlier in this article, we stressed the fact that if one uses the conventional models of constitutional adjudication devised by Cappelletti most of the countries in Latin America have a hybrid system that combines concentrated and diffused review. However, as we anticipated, the hybridity of constitutional justice in Latin America is not solely due to the fact that both the Constitutional or Supreme Courts and ordinary judges can carry out constitutional review, but also because, alongside the conventional gateways for invoking the jurisdiction of the Courts, many Latin American countries establish specific action for the protection of human rights. Although the terms used in the single countries may differ slightly, these petitions generally include the writs of *amparo*, habeas corpus and habeas data (as illustrated in Table 9).

	Writ of Amparo	Writ of Habeas corpus	Writ of Habeas data
Argentina	Yes	Yes	Yes
Bolivia	Yes	Yes	Yes
Brazil	Yes (but known as *mandado de securança*)	Yes	Yes
Chile	Yes (but know as *recurso de protección*)	Yes (but known as *recurso de amparo*)	No
Colombia	Yes	Yes	Yes
Costa Rica	Yes	Yes	No

---

[34] On the role of Constitutional Courts as arbiters see D'Orlando, E (2006) *La funzione arbitrale della Corte costituzionale tra Stato centrale e governi periferici* Clueb.

Dominican Republic	Yes	Yes	No
Ecuador	Yes (but known as *acción de protección*)	Yes	Yes
El Salvador	Yes	Yes	No
Guatemala	Yes	Yes	Yes
Honduras	Yes	Yes	Yes
Mexico	Yes	No	Yes
Nicaragua	Yes	Yes	Yes
Panama	Yes	Yes	Yes
Paraguay	Yes	Yes	Yes
Perù	Yes	Yes	Yes
Uruguay	Yes	Yes	No
Venezuela	Yes	Yes	Yes

Table 9: Writs of Amparo, Habeas Corpus and Habeas Data

The writs of *amparo*, habeas corpus and habeas data undoubtedly represent one of the distinguishing features of Latin American constitutional justice, established as an extraordinary judicial remedy specifically conceived for the protection of fundamental rights against possible violations on the part of public authorities or individuals. In particular, the writ of amparo was first introduced in the Federal Constitution of Mexico in 1857 (although its origins go back to the Constitution of Yucatan, 1841). Over time, in Mexico this type of action has evolved into the unique *juicio de amparo*, where it is used not only to protect individuals against public authorities, but also as a way of evoking constitutional review of legislation. In all other Latin American countries the writ of amparo is an extraordinary judicial petition established exclusively for the protection of constitutional rights.

Given that, for reasons of brevity, we cannot illustrate the procedural rules of all eighteen countries for presenting these three types of writ it suffices to say that their aim is to protect fundamental rights and freedoms (writ of *amparo*), personal freedom (writ of habeas corpus) and freedom of information (writ of habeas data[35]).

---

[35] The literal translation from Latin of Habeas Data is "[we command] you have the data"

Thus if we refer to locus standi as a possible parameter for classifying different types of constitutional adjudication, as we mentioned in our theoretical-reconstructive premise, then we can say that all the countries in Latin America have 'open' systems where there are numerous gateways for invoking the jurisdiction of the Courts in contrast to what we might define as 'closed' systems, such as Italy, where citizens cannot directly lodge a claim in the Constitutional or Supreme Court.

THE COURTS IN ACTION

Before drawing our conclusions let us briefly examine how the Constitutional and Supreme Courts have performed in practice since the beginning of the 1990s (i.e. after the completion of what Samuel P. Huntington defined as 'Democracy's Third Wave', [36] that involved all the countries in Latin America). Laying no claim to being exhaustive, this overview has the objective of briefly contextualising this research and dissipating the risk of providing a sterile theoretical analysis of constitutional adjudication in Latin America.

From an examination of the case law, one can note that the evolution of Latin American constitutional justice (or *Derecho Procesal Constitucional* as most Latin American scholars prefer to define this subject[37]) is characterised by issues that are related to both substantive law and procedural law.

With regard to some issues the experience of the American subcontinent is not dissimilar to that of the rest of the world. As elsewhere, the Constitutional Courts are called upon to address controversies concerning basic rights and freedoms, in particular those related to personal freedom and freedom of information (for which specific writs are available as illustrated in the previous paragraph), but more recently also those regarding environmental law, protection of minorities and bioethics. Again as occurs in other countries around the globe, Constitutional Courts have the task of balancing opposing interests such as, for example, the right to

---

and is a constitutional right granted in several countries in Latin-America. In general, it is designed to protect, by means of an individual complaint file in the Constitutional or Supreme Court, the image, privacy, honour, information, self-determination and freedom of information of a person.

[36] Huntington, SP (1991) 'Democracy's Third Wave' (2) *Journal of Democracy* 12 at 13. Also see Id (1991) *The Third Wave: Democratization in the Late Twentieth Century* University of Oklahoma.

[37] ...literally 'Constitutional Procedural Law' see García Belaunde, D (2000) *De la Jurisdicción Constitucional al Derecho Procesal Constitucional* (2nd ed) Grijley; Palomino Manchego, JF (ed.) (2005) *El Derecho Procesal Constitucional Peruano. Estudios en Homenaje a Domingo García Belaunde* I-II, Grijley; Ferrer Mac-Gregor, E *Derecho Procesal Constitucional* supra note 19.

work and the right to a clean and healthy environment, the right of defence and the right to an efficient judicial system and so forth.

Let us just briefly mention some decisions delivered by Constitutional or Supreme Courts as examples.

With regard to habeas corpus rights two judgments that are strictly related to the transition to democracy should be cited. In Argentina an important decision was undoubtedly the *Simón Case* of 2005,[38] with which the Argentinian Federal Supreme Court struck down the amnesty laws i.e. legislation that forbade the prosecution of military officers suspected of atrocities during the so-called 'Dirty War' the campaign waged against left-wing opponents by Argentina's ruling military junta.[39] Another landmark decision is the one taken by the Constitutional Court of Peru in 2003 when it ruled that some of the country's anti-terrorism laws were unconstitutional, paving the way for appeals by hundreds of imprisoned left-wing rebels. The measures were passed under the former president, Alberto Fujimori, to help quash left-wing guerrilla movements in the 1990s.[40]

Turning to Brazil and the issue of social rights, an interesting decision was taken in 1999 by the Federal Supreme Court when it ruled that a law approved by Congress that raised civil servants' pension contributions was unconstitutional. The judgment proved to be a serious blow to the government's attempts to reach strict budget targets agreed with the International Monetary Fund.

Concerning ethical issues four judgments deserve a special mention: first, in Chile in 2008 the Constitutional Court declared healthcare legislation permitting the use of the morning after pill to be unconstitutional[41] because it was considered an equivalent of abortion and therefore an infringement of the right to life. Second, in Colombia in May 2006 the Constitutional Court took the historic decision to legalise abortion in cases where the pregnancy endangers the life or health of the mother, or results from rape or incest, or if the foetus is unlikely to survive.[42] The third case again by the Colombian Constitutional Court concerned freedom of sexual orientation. In 2007 the Court established that homosexual couples should have the same property

---

[38]   *Fallos* 2005-328-2056.
[39]   The campaign ended with the country's return to civilian rule in 1983.
[40]   Exp No. 010-2002-AI/TC.
[41]   Rol 740 18/4/2008 see http://www.tribunalconstitucional.cl/index.php/sentencias/download/pdf/914.
[42]   It should be underlined that a few months later the Constitutional Court, in line with its May decision, allowed an 11-year old girl, who became pregnant after being raped by her stepfather, to obtain an abortion. As a result, the Colombian Catholic Church controversially excommunicated all judges, politicians and legislators involved in the decision, as well as the doctors, nurses and the girl's parents.

371

rights as their heterosexual counterparts. In fact, the constitutional justices said a provision of a 1990 law giving property rights to de-facto couples was unconstitutional because it provided that these couples had to be composed of a man and a woman with the discriminatory exclusion of same-sex couples.[43] Finally, another interesting decision was that of the Brazilian Federal Supreme Court in 2008 which judged legislation that allows research on embryonic stem cells to be in conformity with the Constitution.

There are other issues, however, where Latin America presents far more peculiarities with respect to other parts of the world.

First what appears to currently distinguish Latin America from other continents is the power exercised by many Constitutional Courts in reviewing constitutional amendments. This has undoubtedly been a central theme over the last few years.

Many of the new leaders in Latin America have sought to pursue populist politics and have used constitutional reform as a way of implementing their social-oriented policies. As a result, conflicts have arisen between the power to amend the Constitution and the power to review constitutional amendments. Often what lies behind this dispute is the anxious desire of certain leaders to amend the Constitution in an illegitimate way (the case of Venezuela[44]) or to deny that the Constitution is truly the fundamental law because at the time, it was adopted in an illegitimate manner (the case of post-Fujimori Peru).[45]

Again Latin America is proving to be an interesting testing ground with regard to an issue that has provoked an ongoing and fundamental scholarly debate i.e. the question of whether constitutional amendments can ever be considered unconstitutional.

An example of a judgment of this sort can be found in Argentina with regard to the constitutional reform of 1994 mentioned earlier. In 1999 the

---

[43]   C-075/07.
[44]   In particular see the paper presented at the Ninth Argentinian National Congress of Constitutional by Haro García, JV (2008) 'Derecho y democracia en Latinoamérica: el caso de Venezuela y los reciente intentos de reforma constituticional o de cómo se está tratando de establecer una dictadura socialista con apariencia de legalidad' in *Ponencias desarrolladas IX Congresso Nacional de Derecho Constitucional* Editorial Adrus 735 – 756. It is worth underlining that the author aptly begins by citing Simón Bolívar, *El Libertador*, one of Latin America's heroes of the Wars of Independence: '*Nada es tan peligroso come dejar permanecer largo tiempo a un mismo ciudadano en el poder. El pueblo se acostumbra a obedecerle y él se acostumbra; de donde se origina la usurpación y la tiranía*'. These words are almost prophetic given the present situation in Venezuela under Chávez and they are also reminiscent of Lord Acton's famous affirmation 'Power tends to corrupt, and absolute power corrupts absolutely'.
[45]   See Sagües, NP (2008) 'Notas sobre el poder constituyente irregular' in *Ponencias desarrolladas IX Congresso Nacional de Derecho Constitucional* supra note 34, 869 – 881.

Federal Supreme Court – in the so-called *Fayt Case* – declared an article of the 1994 reform unconstitutional because it was ultra vires the powers of the Constitutional Convention established with Law no. 24.309).[46]

On the contrary in 2005 the Colombian Constitutional Court declared *Acto Legislativo* No. 2 (December 27, 2004) approved by the Colombian Congress to be in pursuance of the Constitution. This law amended the provision of the 1991 Colombian Constitution, which banned the re-election of the President thus paving the way for a second term in office for incumbent Álvaro Uribe Vélez.[47]

Still with regard to the re-election of the President (an 'obsession' for many leaders in Latin America) and review of constitutional amendments, another interesting case is constituted by Costa Rica where first the Constitutional Chamber of the Supreme Court threw out a petition challenging a provision of the constitutional reform of 1969 introducing a ban on re-election of the President (see Art. 132, Costa Rican Constitution), then in 2003 it overturned its previous decision and declared the prohibition to be unconstitutional. As a result, the law reverted back to the 1949 Constitution, which permitted former presidents to run for re-election after they had been out of office for two presidential terms, or eight years, thus allowing Óscar Arias, President from 1986 to 1990 and Nobel Peace Prize winner in 1987, to be re-elected Chief Executive in 2006.

Finally let us turn to Venezuela. In November 2007 the Constitutional Chamber of the Supreme Court delivered a series of judgments that threw out several petitions demanding that the Court declare unconstitutional the wide-ranging and controversial constitutional amendments purported by President Chávez. More precisely, the Supreme Court announced it would not rule on the constitutionality of the proposal to reform more than sixty articles of Venezuela's Constitution until after the upcoming constitutional referendum scheduled for 2nd December 2007. In fact, the Court explained that the constitutionality of the proposal could not be ruled on unless it

---

[46] This decision by the Supreme Court was severely criticised by many scholars see Hernández, A.M., (2001) 'El caso Fayt y sus implicancias constitucionales' (5) *Anuario Iberoamericano de Justicia constitucional* 453 ff.

[47] See C-1040/05. At present Art. 197 of the Colombian Constitution states that the President of the Republic can remain in office for no more than two mandates. If we might hazard a critical comment one must say that the reasoning of the Court was not particularly convincing, especially when it stated that the re-election of the President did not concern the 'exercise of the power of constitutional amendment, but rather a choice to be made by the electorate...'! It is interesting to note that just a few months ago more than five million supporters of President Uribe signed a petition with which they requested a further amendment to the Constitution to allow him to run for a third term in 2010. If the Colombian Congress does approve this amendment then it is highly likely that the Constitutional Court will one again be called upon to decide whether it is in pursuance of the Constitution.

was approved in the national referendum and took legal effect. In other words, the Supreme Court did not deny its power to review constitutional amendments, but it clearly underlined that it had the power only to carry out repressive, *a posteriori* review and not preventative, a priori review (see paragraphs above). It is common knowledge that Chávez's controversial reform proposals were then defeated in the December referendum by a razor thin margin of 51%, thus there was no need to return to Supreme Court for constitutional review.[48]

Finally, still with reference to Venezuela, but going beyond the issue of judicial review of constitutional amendments, it is worth remembering that the Constitutional Chamber of the Supreme Court also played an important role in the recall referendum that was held on 15th August 2004.[49]

After the National Electoral Committee had twice judged the majority of the signatures collected under Arts 72 and 233 of the Venezuelan Constitution to be invalid the petitioners appealed to the Electoral Chamber of the Venezuelan Supreme Court, which decided that nearly 1 million disputed signatures were on the contrary to be considered valid thus bringing the total to well above the number needed to authorise the referendum. Chávez, however, appealed to the Constitutional Chamber of the Supreme Court, which overturned the Electoral Chamber's decision alleging that the latter did not have jurisdiction for that ruling, thereby considering it to be unconstitutional. Though important, this decision did not prove to be decisive because the needed number of signatures was collected again and this time considered valid. The referendum was finally held in August 2004 and won by Hugo Chávez.

In addressing the issues mentioned above one cannot ignore the relationship between the Courts and the legislative and executive branches of government and, more in general, the guarantees of independence. The solutions adopted in Europe (appointment of judges by various branches of government, prohibition of re-election, long term of office) or in the United States (life tenure) are not always respected in Latin America. As

---

[48] As this book goes to print it should be underlined that the referendum lifting the term limits for elected official was repeated on 15th February 2009 and this time 54% of the voters were in favour of the constitutional amendment. This means that in three years time Hugo Chávez will be able to run for President for a third term.

[49] It should be noted that the date of this recall referendum was of the utmost importance: had it been held just four days later Chávez would have been into the last two years of his term in office and therefore, in the event of an unfavourable result, his vice president José Vicente Rangel would have become President. On the contrary, the vote was held before this deadline and therefore had Chávez lost there would have been fresh Presidential elections after thirty days. Chávez had already made it clear that he would have once again stood for the presidency, although members of the opposition and many academics claimed that he would have been disqualified.

underlined previously, in Peru judges remain in office only for five years and are often influenced politically. Furthermore, in those countries that have an ad hoc Constitutional Court there is strong antagonism between the latter and the ordinary judiciary to an extent that in academic writings and conferences in Latin America there is evermore frequent talk of a 'war between courts' with regard to the strong reluctance of the ordinary judiciary in handing over powers to the new Constitutional Courts. In a comparative perspective, it is interesting to observe that this phenomenon occurred in the past in Germany and Italy and is still taking place in Spain.

CONCLUSIONS

This overview of the systems of constitutional adjudication in Latin America has, by no means, the aim of being complete and exhaustive. Furthermore, we are well aware of the fact that our research does not overcome the '*sollensein* dilemma'. Using the diachronic and synchronic methodology we have undoubtedly given more weight to the provisions on constitutional adjudication contained in the Constitutions and in specific procedural laws with respect to the actual performance of the Supreme and Constitutional Courts. The reason for this is that the jury is still out with regard to the effectiveness, independence and ability to interpret the constitution of these Courts and their capacity to emerge as referees in constitutional matters.

In truth, as illustrated in the previous paragraph, we cannot ignore the fact that between 1974 and 1990 nearly all the countries that have been examined herein were involved in Huntington's 'Democracy's Third Wave'.[50] In fact in 1975 only two countries in South America were led by elected Chief Executives, while all the countries in Central America, with the exception of Costa Rica were under a dictatorship. Only 'the open and competitive presidential elections that Brazil and Chile held in 1989 marked the first time that all the Ibero-American nations, except Cuba, enjoyed the benefits of elected constitutional governments at the same moment'.[51] Having said this one should bear in mind the distinction that Larry Diamond makes between 'electoral democracy' and 'liberal-democracy'[52] and thus remember that – in spite of what the supporters of 'exporting democracy' might claim – elections in themselves are not the panacea of all the evils of authoritarianism as the present situation that we have seen in Venezuela under Hugo Chávez clearly demonstrates.

---

[50] Supra note 32.
[51] Valenzuela, A (1993) 'Latin America: Presidentialism in Crisis' (4) *Journal of Democracy* 3 at 3.
[52] Diamond, L (1996) 'Is the Third Wave Over?' (4) *Journal of Democracy* 3 at 3.

On the whole the Latin American judiciary system has always been quite weak and highly dependent on the politics of the moment, but what we can certainly affirm is the fact that the development of constitutional adjudication has been a factor of democratic consolidation in the area. Of course a constitution may well prescribe an optimal balance of independence and constitutional adjudication powers, but regime instability and a powerful presence of undemocratic practices and forces will stop them from effectively being exercised.

Having said this constitutional adjudication may certainly be used as a 'litmus test' of democratic consolidation, therefore any judgment on the third wave of democratisation in Latin America should inevitably be based not only on fair and free elections, but also on a system of constitutional adjudication not just 'in the books' but also 'in action'.

Constitutional Courts Index

INDEX

Constitutional courts

age and development of 25

ambivalence towards role 55

analytic framework 6

comparatist's dilemma 2-3

comparative perspective 1-27

effectiveness 23-25

  constitutionalism; and 24

  criteria 23

  state avoidance of decisions 25

  essential feature 3-4

  executive acts and decisions, and 8

finality of interpretation 9-10

forms 1-27

frame

  analysis 8-9

functions 1-27, 6-10

  centrality 7-8

gateways to 19-21

historical and contemporary experience 2

interpretation 21-23

legal transplantation; and 5

legitimacy 26

meaning 3

means of access 19-21

modes of access to 9

motivation for 4-5

performances 21-26

"political matters", and 14-15

political tensions, and 5

practice 1-27

Rechstaat, and 27

supra-national influences 10

symbolic value 14

Constitutional jurisdiction

comparative models 14

consolidated democracies, and 14

democratization, and 12

distrust of judiciary, and 11-12, 13

meaning 6-10

rationales for introduction 11-15

Constitutional review 4

Costa Rica *see* Latin America

Dominican Republic *see* Latin America

East Asia 291-316

"Asian values" 291-292

centralised political authority 293

constitutional courts as political actors 316

cultural traditions 311

democratization 291

emergence of constitutionalism 292-305

explaining emergence of constitutional review 311-315

explanatory variables 315

globalization 311

institutional design 305-309

middle class 314

pace of transition 313

prior history of judicial review 312

strong presidencies 313

type of party system 313-314

type of previous regime 312—313